Irish Women Artists

From the Eighteenth Century to the Present Day

Irish Women Artists

From the
Eighteenth Century
to the
Present Day

The National Gallery of Ireland
The Douglas Hyde Gallery
1987

Published on the occasion of an exhibition organised by
The National Gallery of Ireland and the Douglas Hyde Gallery,
Trinity College, Dublin and shown in July-August 1987 at:

The National Gallery of Ireland
The Douglas Hyde Gallery, Trinity College, Dublin
The Hugh Lane Municipal Gallery of Modern Art, Dublin

In publishing the Catalogue, The National Gallery of Ireland and
the Douglas Hyde Gallery acknowledge the generous support of
GPA Group Limited.
Catalogue co-ordinated by: Wanda Ryan-Smolin, Jenni Rogers and Patrick T. Murphy.
Exhibition co-ordinated by: Kim-Mai Mooney, Wanda Ryan-Smolin,
Jenni Rogers and Patrick T. Murphy.

British Library Cataloguing in Publication Data
Irish women artists: from the eighteenth
    century to the present day.
    1. Women painters — Ireland — Exhibitions
    2. Painting, Irish — Exhibitions
    3. Painting, Modern — Ireland — Exhibitions
    I. National Gallery of Ireland   II. Douglas
    Hyde Gallery
    759.2'915   ND485

    ISBN 0-903162-40-7
    ISBN 0-907660-22-3

Edited by Wanda Ryan-Smolin, Elizabeth Mayes & Jenni Rogers.
Photography by Michael Olohan & John Kellett.
Design origination and print production by Printset and Design Ltd., Dublin
Printed in Ireland by The Ormond Printing Co. Ltd.

Front cover: detail of *Winter* by Harriet Hockley Townshend (cat. no. 61).
Back cover: detail of *Garden in Autumn* by Cecily Brennan.

Contents

Preface

Tony Ryan
Chairman and Chief Executive, GPA Group Limited

GPA Group Limited is delighted to be associated with the National Gallery of Ireland and the Douglas Hyde Gallery in presenting an exhibition of the work of Irish Women Artists from the eighteenth century to the present day. It continues our tradition of supporting the arts in Ireland by encouraging and assisting the endeavours of those professionally engaged in music and the visual arts.

The Exhibition is an important one and the Catalogue documents for the first time many artists whose work, over the centuries, has been forgotten. In the case of more recent artists it assesses them in a new context and offers a retrospective of the main developments in Irish art over the last half century or so.

By supporting the production of the Catalogue we hope it will be possible for it to reach a wider audience as we believe it makes a significant contribution to the history of Irish art.

Foreword

Patrick T. Murphy & Homan Potterton

The Exhibition, *Irish Women Artists from the Eighteenth Century to the Present Day* and this Catalogue which accompanies it, surveys a wide territory and presents to the public, in many cases for the first time, the work of a great number of artists who worked in Ireland over the past two and a half centuries. What they all have in common is the fact that they were women.

While, of course, we would make no claim that the paintings and sculptures in the Exhibition are in any way different to those produced by men (apart obviously from differences of artistic style), the circumstances under which women artists worked, certainly in centuries earlier than our own, were different; and often very different. The strictly amateur status accorded to lady artists in the eighteenth century and indeed throughout most of the nineteenth century, their lack of opportunity for training and the vicissitudes they faced in attempting to exhibit their work, is described in the essays by Anne Crookshank, Jeanne Sheehy and Shirley Armstrong Duffy. Yet the pictures in the Exhibition prove that these artists had indisputable talent. By the closing decades of the nineteenth century, women artists were allowed to travel and train and even sell their work, and at this time a number of Irish women, like their contemporaries from other European countries and America, gravitated towards France. At home in Ireland many talented women, in attempting to shake off the shackles of domesticity, became involved in encouraging the artistic talent of women through arts and crafts workshops and co-operatives; and by the nineteen forties at the latest, women were fully accepted as artists in their own right. As far as Ireland is concerned it is worth emphasising that the introduction of the Modern Movement in art into this country was due in large part to the efforts of women, Mainie Jellett, Evie Hone, Norah McGuinness and others. In the case of contemporary art there are in fact a remarkable number of women artists at work in Ireland today.

The brief for the Exhibition and Catalogue was that up to 1943 we should attempt to be as comprehensive as possible, and after that date, because of the great range of artists, it should be selective. Inevitably some artists will have been overlooked where we have attempted to be comprehensive; and when we have been selective, we recognise that there may not be universal agreement with our selection. Our aspiration for the Exhibition is that it will act as a catalyst for further investigations and explorations. We also hope, that in the case of women artists of an earlier age, it will lead to new artists being discovered and their talent being recognised.

The exhibition is the first occasion that the National Gallery of Ireland and the Douglas Hyde Gallery have collaborated to present an entire survey of Irish art and we are pleased that a section of the Exhibition is to be shown in the Hugh Lane Municipal Gallery. The collaboration has been a happy one and we hope that the fruits of our endeavours will be welcomed. The co-ordination of the Catalogue, to which so many scholars and critics have generously contributed, has been very complex. This unenviable task has been undertaken in the National Gallery by Wanda Ryan-Smolin and Kim-Mai Mooney and in the Douglas Hyde Gallery by Jenni Rogers. Their brief, not least because of the schedule involved, was a difficult one; and on account of that we willingly take responsibility for any omissions or inadequacies there may be, while at the same time applaud them for their contribution to what we believe will be a very important Exhibition.

Contributors to the Catalogue

AOC	Anne O Crookshank
ALH	Adrian Le Harivel
BA	Bruce Arnold
BM	Barbara McGowan
COC	Cynthia O'Connor
CM	Christopher Moore
EB	Eileen Black
ECN	E. Charles Nelson
FG	Frances Gillespie
HP	Hilary Pyle
JC	Julian Campbell
JGC	J. George Cruickshank
JOG	John O'Grady
JS	Jeanne Sheehy
KMM	Kim-Mai Mooney
KOG	The Knight of Glin
MA	Martyn Anglesea
MW	Michael Wynne
NA	Nicole Arnould
NGB	Nicola Gordon Bowe
NS	Nell Spillane
PL	Peter Lamb
RR	Rebecca Rowe
SAD	Shirley Armstrong Duffy
WR	Wanda Ryan-Smolin

Explanation of the Catalogue

The National Gallery of Ireland and the Douglas Hyde Gallery, Trinity College, Dublin have co-operated in the arrangement of the Exhibition and the preparation of the Catalogue. The National Gallery has arranged the section dealing with artists from the eighteenth century to 1943, (a watershed year when the first Irish Living Art Exhibition was held); and the Douglas Hyde Gallery has co-ordinated and prepared the section from 1943 to the present day. Because of the nature of the work described and exhibited, the approach to each section is slightly different: for example, all the works of art exhibited in the earlier section are fully described and illustrated in the catalogue, but this format has not been followed in the later section.

In preparing the Exhibition the first decision to be made was the nature of the work which would be shown. It was obvious that the Exhibition should include paintings (in all media) and sculptures; but throughout the centuries, and not least in the present time, Irish women have created objects which might easily be categorised as either art or crafts; and in this area some difficult decisions had to be made as to what would be included. As a general rule only paintings and sculptures are included (although there are, for example, some designs for stained glass and some prints); but the essays in the Catalogue do describe the contribution made by Irish women to crafts when that contribution is significant in a wider context.

In the preparation of the section of the Exhibition up to 1943, a number of new painters have been discovered. In the case of many of them their work is not exhibited either because we have been unable to locate an example or because it is not of sufficiently high quality, although their biography is given in the *Dictionary* at the end of the Catalogue. For artists before 1943 the *Dictionary* is intended to be comprehensive; but after that date, because of the considerable number of women artists working in Ireland today, it has not been possible to be as comprehensive as one would wish.

The essays which describe the activities of women artists in Ireland in the eighteenth, nineteenth and early twentieth centuries chart new territory and highlight particular areas of activity. From the forties to the present day five critics were commissioned to review separate periods, namely the nineteen-forties, the nineteen-fifties, the sixties to mid-seventies, and the mid-seventies to the present. Because of the range of possibility in art-making over the past twelve years and thus the range of critical response, two critics were asked to examine that period. In this section an attempt has been made to identify trends, select specific artists for discussion and to isolate and recognise the specific contribution made to art in Ireland by artists who are women. Due to limitations of space the Exhibitions in the Douglas Hyde Gallery and the Hugh Lane Municipal Gallery have been further refined to give the essence of the periods covered.

Abbreviations

AIB	Allied Irish Banks
ANCAD	Associate of the National College of Art and Design
ARHA	Associate of the Royal Hibernian Academy
CAN	Cork Art Now
CEMA	Council for the Encouragement of Music and the Arts
DAAD	Deutsche Akademischer Austauschdienst (German Academic Exchange Service)
EVA	Emerging Visual Artists
GPA	Guinness Peat Aviation
HRHA	Honorary Royal Hibernian Academician
ICA	Institute of Contemporary Art
LCC	London County Council
NCEA	National Council for Educational Awards
NCAD	National College of Art and Design
NIHE	National Institute of Higher Education
RHA	Royal Hibernian Academy
RSA	Royal Scottish Academy
SADE	Sculpture and Drawing Exhibition
TSWA	Television South West Arts

Acknowledgements

This Exhibition and the Catalogue would not have been possible without the assistance and co-operation of a great number of people and the National Gallery of Ireland and the Douglas Hyde Gallery gratefully acknowledge this assistance. Our first debt is to the contributors to the Catalogue who are listed under 'Contributors to the Catalogue'; and, additionally, to those scholars and critics who have written essays for the Catalogue. We would particularly like to thank Anne Crookshank and the Knight of Glin for allowing free access to their archive of photographs of Irish art; and Nicola Gordon Bowe whose particularly diligent research has enhanced the Catalogue in a significant way. On reading the proofs Brian de Breffny made a number of valuable suggestions. We also acknowledge the assistance of the following: Pauline Boaden, Mary Boydell, David Caron, Lord Dunluce, Daniel Gilman, Patrick Kelly, Brian Kennedy, Elizabeth Kerr, Henry McDowell, John Meagher, David Pym, Susannah Pym, Audrey Scales, Edith Synge; The Paul Mellon Centre for Studies in British Art, London for photographs of catalogue numbers 4 and 5; Mairead Byrne of GPA Group Limited. Within the National Gallery the following assisted greatly in the production of the Catalogue: Sergio Benedetti, Susan Dillon, Nuala Fenton, Paula Hicks, Adrian Le Harivel, Maighread McParland, Elizabeth Mayes, Veronika Montag, Andrew O'Connor and Michael Olohan.

The idea of the Exhibition was first suggested by Ann Reihill on behalf of the Committee of the Third International Interdisciplinary Congress on Women which takes place in Dublin at the time of the Exhibition opening. The Douglas Hyde Gallery acknowledges its funding by The Arts Council/An Chomhairle Ealaíon and Trinity College, Dublin. For allowing a section of the Exhibition to be shown in the Hugh Lane Municipal Gallery acknowledgement is made to the Curator, the Art Advisory Committee and Dublin Corporation. Finally, the Exhibition would not have been possible without the generosity of those artists and collectors who have made available works of art from their collections; and the Catalogue could not have been realised without the generous support of GPA Group Limited.

List of Colour Illustrations

Plate 1.   Susanna Drury, *The East Prospect of the Giant's Causeway,* (cat. no. 3).

Plate 2.   Elish Lamont, *Miss O'Hara,* (cat. no. 22).

Plate 3.   Helen Mabel Trevor, *The fisherman's mother,* (cat. no. 32).

Plate 4.   Sarah Purser, *Summer flowers*, (cat. no. 39).

Plate 5.   Edith Œnone Somerville, *Retrospect,* (cat. no. 41).

Plate 6.   Rose Barton, *Going to the Levée at Dublin Castle,* (cat. no. 45).

Plate 7.   Mildred Anne Butler, *A preliminary investigation*, (cat. no. 48).

Plate 8.   Jane Service Workman, *Ombre et Lumière,* (cat. no. 52).

Plate 9.   Kathleen Fox, *The Fortune Teller*, (cat. no. 71).

Plate 10.   Estella F. Solomons, *A gay day in Donegal,* (cat. no. 76).

Plate 11.   Kathleen Isobel Mackie, *The Market,* (cat. no. 77).

Plate 12.   Eileen Murray, *'This or Emigration'*, (cat. no. 86).

Plate 13.   Grace Henry, *The Red House at Mougins,* (cat. no. 93).

Plate 14.   Lilian Lucy Davidson, *Night in Claddagh,* (cat. no. 94).

Plate 15.   Letitia Hamilton, *Snow in Co. Down,* (cat. no. 99).

Plate 16.   Margaret Clarke, *Ann with cat,* (cat. no. 102).

Plate 17.   Moyra Barry, *Self-Portrait in the artist's studio*, (cat. no. 103).

Plate 18.   Kathleen Bridle, *Lough Erne from Rossfad,* (cat. no. 110).

Plate 19.   Beatrice Glenavy, *The Intruder,* (cat. no. 112).

Plate 20.   Evie Hone, *A landscape with a tree,* (cat. no. 122).

Plate 21.   May Guinness, *Still-life with Tulips,* (cat. no. 126).

Plate 22.   Hilda Roberts, *Portrait of George Russell (Æ)*, (cat. no. 128).

Plate 23.   Mary Swanzy, *Young woman with flowers*, (cat. no. 133).

Plate 24.   Mary Swanzy, *Samoan scene,* (cat. no. 135).

Plate 25.   Norah McGuinness, *The Thames, 1932-34*. Private collection.

Plate 26.   Nano Reid, *A Wild Day, 1959.* Private collection.

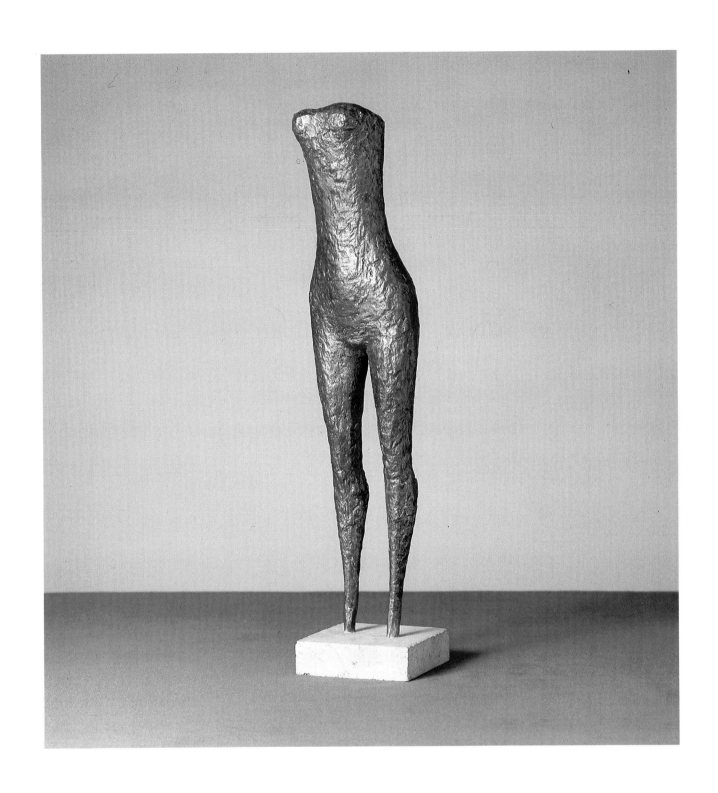

Plate 27.   Melanie Le Brocquy, *Female Figure, 1964.* Collection of the artist.

Plate 28.   Camille Souter, *Washing by the Canal c.1964.* Limerick Municipal Art Gallery.

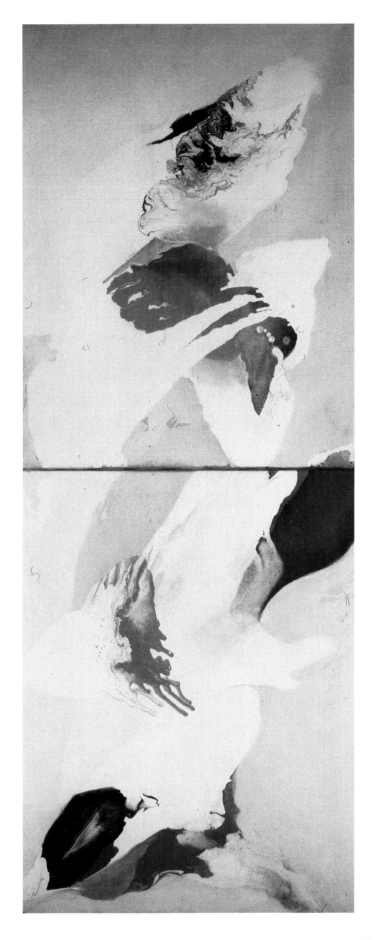

Plate 29.   Anne Madden, *Diptych, 1967*. Allied Irish Banks Collection.

Plate 30.   Kathy Prendergast, *Untitled, 1982-83*. Collection of Noeleen and Vincent Ferguson.

Plate 31.   Maggie Magee, *Discontinent, 1985, Still from a Video Mural.* Collection of the artist.

Plate 32.   Eithne Jordan, *Study of three heads, 1986*. Collection of the artist.

Introduction

Anne O. Crookshank

Due to the unsettled state of Ireland during the late medieval and early modern periods, little enough is known about the arts in this country during the sixteenth and first half of the seventeenth centuries. There is therefore a great gap between the justly famous early Christian and medieval periods and the art which developed from the 1660's onwards. What was created during that intermediate period was largely destroyed by the seventeenth century wars which were hugely destructive of buildings and their contents. It can thus be argued with some truth that, because only a mere handful of male artists can be identified before 1700, it is not surprising no women are known in the arts before that date.

Native Irish culture had not concentrated on urban development, the few existing towns in the seventeenth century being of Viking and Norman origins. Thus the conditions under which most ordinary Irish women lived, in isolated, rural areas, must have prevented them from developing any artistic talents except possibly in the area of textiles. The visual arts were too by tradition connected, as in many societies, with religious institutions and the aristocracy. Different but equally circumscribing conditions existed for the new settlers. In many cases they were established in entirely new towns and villages where they must have endured much the same difficulties in life as the American settlers in the same period. Some literally saw their houses being built and, given the recurrent wars and rebellions, in many instances they saw this happen more than once. All their goods destroyed, they had to reassemble furniture, linen, cooking equipment etc. with painful difficulty to fill the second and even sometimes their third home.[1] Under those conditions even the bravest could hardly have been interested in the arts.

The only women, (and they were not free from the recurring and disastrous effects of war), who had the time and the money to take an interest in art were members of the aristocracy. Maire Ruadh (Red Mary) O'Brien, a descendant of an ancient Irish family, wears superb lace and a magnificent Italian renaissance brooch in her naive and unflattering portrait (Fig. 1). Presumably her house, Lemeneagh, Co. Clare, was equally well furnished.

But the woman who is best known to us for her artistic achievements in creating truly magnificent interior decorations in her houses, was Lady Elizabeth Preston, the daughter and heiress of the Earl of Desmond and his wife, the only daughter of Black Tom, Earl of Ormond. Elizabeth Preston inherited in her own right a large part of the Butler estates, including Kilkenny Castle and Dunmore House and made what turned out to be a happy and successful dynastic marriage in 1629 with her cousin James Butler, later first Duke of Ormond. Due to the law suits between the two branches of the Butler family which occurred prior to their marriage, Kilkenny Castle was stripped of most of its furniture by the time they went to live in it first in 1632 and Elizabeth spent many years refurbishing the Castle and rebuilding and redecorating Dunmore. However the Cromwellian wars intervened and she had to leave for France in 1648 even before her husband who was finally forced to leave Ireland in 1650.

However in 1653 she obtained permission from the Cromwellian government to return, though not to Kilkenny Castle. She was allowed to retain Dunmore House and £2000 per annum from the estates she had inherited from her parents.[2] She set about the rebuilding of Dunmore during the Cromwellian period on the grandest scale and even began importing pictures from France[3] though the majority of the collection must have been made after the restoration in 1660. Though she travelled much between England and Ireland, the rehabilitation of Kilkenny which she and her husband returned to in 1662, and of Dunmore remained very important to her. In February 1671, she wrote from London to her husband's half brother, George Matthews concerning these houses, after she had interviewed 'Trotter the painter' saying that he 'has received my instructions what is further to be done by him in both places' and she goes on to discuss how all is to be paid for out of her money.[4] From inventories of the two houses, it is clear that they were filled with pictures, family portraits, landscapes, Italian allegorical pieces, a few religious pictures, watercolours but above all else with many, many Dutch pictures, still lifes, flower pieces etc.

A visitor to Kilkenny in 1698, John Dunton described the castle

Fig. 1   Early 17th century, *Maire Ruadh*. Private collection.

Fig. 2   *The Print Room, Castletown House.* Photograph courtesy of the Castletown Foundation.

Fig. 3   *Embroidered stomacher of Mrs. Delany's court dress.* Photograph courtesy of the Courtauld Institute.

and its splendours in the most glowing terms. He noted 'gilded leather' on the walls, much silver, 'gilded chairs and the curious pictures that adorn it'. He felt it had 'no equal in the three kingdoms and perhaps not in Europe'.[5] However absurd that last phrase seems, Elizabeth had revivified her homes in a truly magnificent way.

Her taste and interest was uncommon. There is much evidence that even the houses of the rich in the eighteenth century were often bleak and ill-kempt, closer to Maria Edgeworth's description of Castle Rackrent than their magnificent exteriors would make one think. This aspect of art, interior decorating, has only recently become a 'profession' but undoubtedly in the past it was the nearest many women came to having a professional career in the arts.

Lady Louisa Conolly, a daughter of the second Duke of Richmond, is the finest example of this in the eighteenth century. She lived in Ireland after the death of her parents when she was eight, living with her sister the Duchess of Leinster, in Carton and in 1758 she married, now all of 15, Tom Conolly of Castletown House, Co. Kildare. It is her decoration of that greatest of all Irish houses that we see to-day. Happily, unlike Elizabeth, Duchess of Ormond's work, Lady Louisa's survives. She started work on the house almost at once. It had been left unfinished by its builder Speaker Conolly who died in 1729, and though his widow survived him by 23 years, she did little to the house. Even the main staircase was not built and Louisa started on this immediately for she writes about the stuccadore Francini in 1759 who worked on the staircase hall.[6] It was Louisa who employed Sir William Chambers to reconstruct and redecorate several rooms;

she who started to collect prints for her print room as early as 1762 and probably designed it herself (Fig. 2); she who ordered the chandeliers for the Long Gallery from Venice and wrote that 'they are the wrong blue for the room' (as they still are) and supervised its decoration in the 'Pompeian' manner. By 1778 when Lady Louisa was a mere 35, the job was done and it was described by Lady Caroline Dawson as both 'delightful' and in 'very good taste'. It still is, and is a monument to Louisa's remarkable and precocious talents.

Fig. 4 *Japanned Cabinet,* Castletown House. Photograph courtesy of the Castletown Foundation.

Fig. 5 *Cut paper work silhouette with a chinoiserie landscape* by a lady of the McDonnell family. Photograph courtesy of The Viscount Dunluce.

On a much smaller scale Mrs. Delany, wife of the Dean of Down, made with a modest income a relatively small house, Delville, a home which must have been truly enchanting. Her own talents lay in the applied arts. She collected the shells and did the shell decorations in the house, and of course her incomparable embroidery, a little of which survives, must have made her clothes as pretty as any rococo picture (Fig. 3). The very high competence of ladies in the applied arts was widespread. Even old Mrs. Conolly may well have painted the landscapes in a Japanned cabinet (Fig. 4) still in Castletown house and even done the Japanning following instructions in a book published in the late seventeenth century.[7] How ladies were taught to paint remains a total mystery though Mrs. Delany does give a hint in that she regularly records borrowing pictures to copy and lending prints for others to do the same. On 11 January 1745/46 she says; 'I lent her [Letty Bushe] some prints of Claude Lorraine that she has copied to great perfection' and a little later in the same month, 25 January, she says Letty 'is now drg. some beautiful landscapes in the Indian book Mrs. Mead gave me...' and in a later letter, 8 February 1745/46, she indicates that drawing other than copying was strange to her. She says that Letty Bushe 'is so good as to draw almost every day for me, and has inspired me with landscape drawing out of my own pate; I have invented three which the Dean is very fond of'. Copying continued as the principal method by which many talented amateurs learnt, clearly

well into the nineteenth century, when we find that in the early watercolour exhibitions copies predominated: indeed in the third exhibition held in Carlow by the Irish Amateur Drawing Society in 1872 out of 121 exhibits, 78 were copies.[9] Women in the country must sometimes have been forced into taking up the arts out of the sheer boredom of their lives led in isolated houses imprisoned by bad weather. An exquisite cut paper work silhouette with a chinoiserie landscape in Glenarm Castle, Co. Antrim done by a lady of the McDonnell family has a sad inscription on the back recording that the artist had created it one bad winter 'done having nothing better to do in the dull days in the Country at Glenarm 1770' (Fig. 5).

While amateurs often reached very high standards, the education of the few professional women remains a problem. Susanna Drury came of a family of artists who presumably taught her and she treated her work seriously. Mrs. Delany records, 8 October 1758,[11] that she 'lived three months near the place and went almost every day' when she was making her superb gouaches of the Giant's Causeway. It is interesting how intrepid women were. Miss Drury's drawings are the first accurate delineations of the Causeway which could only be reached by a wretched steep, narrow path. Letty Bushe (Fig. 6), who for all her gentility, can only be described as professional, made the drawing for the first print of the Lakes of Killarney as well as drawing Lough Neagh for engraving. The engraving of Killarney is very poor and Mrs. Delany records, 17 February 1751, that 'the engraver hath not done justice to the delicacy of her pencil'. Miss Bushe seems to have been 'a companion' staying for months at a time with friends and no doubt she taught her hostesses and their children. Another artist whose competence was at professional level was Caroline Hamilton who was lucky enough to have the ex-art master from Harrow, John Inigo Spilsbury, engaged as her tutor, but she had recourse also to prints and books as well for she found Hogarth and Le Brun better tutors when she wished to express the Passions.[12]

A great deal of work, because it was by amateurs, has unfortunately been completely lost. Mrs. Delany, who made a very fair judgement of Letty Bushe, reserves her highest praise

recently the only book on that artist in English. Despite its defects it is an extraordinary feat for a woman completely without formal education. Anna Jameson, whose career was less meteoric but whose art history was more sustained, came from a more promising background. Her father, a miniature painter, was taught at the Dublin Society Schools by John Robert West whose knowledge of art history was renowned in his day. No doubt Anna's interest was initially aroused by her father and later stimulated by a number of successful jobs as governess in aristocratic houses which included one which took her as a bear-leader of a young lady to France and Italy. Her unsuccessful marriage must have given her some financial backing and she turned to writing for her career, travelling in Germany and Italy making many friends. She was practical in her beginnings, writing a guide book *Companion to the Public Picture Galleries of London* in 1842 and writing articles for magazines. Her book entitled *Early Italian Art* was remarkable for its date — 1845 — in its interest in early Italian artists, and her four volume *Sacred and Legendary Art* which she had not finished at her death was considered good enough to be finished by Lady Eastlake.

An interest in art history seems to have been quite widespread in educated Dublin circles. A doctor like William Stokes, when he went on holidays on the continent in 1836, was familiar with and eager to see Flemish primitives.[14] His interests outside medicine were in Irish archaeology and he was the friend and

for one Dorothy Forth (Letty's cousin) who married a son of the Earl of Abercorn. On the 25 November 1731 she describes her paintings[13] of flowers and insects as 'unrivalled'. It is a pity none are now known. The association of women artists with flower painting continued till quite recently as it was connected with their other acceptable social activities, gardening and of course, flower arranging for the house. The higher the social status of the artist the less chance had she to develop as an artist. Grace Osborne, if she had not married the Duke of St. Albans and been an heiress, might well have been able to study and use her undoubted talent to more advantage. It was easier to be a writer. Maria Edgeworth who, of course like all ladies, drew with great freedom and wit, though without much skill, was fully accepted as a professional writer while Caroline Hamilton could not have achieved the same position if she had tried as a painter. Caroline's contemporary, Maria Spilsbury (Mrs. Taylor) did work as a professional portrait painter and teacher but she came from a middle class background.

Strangely enough, Ireland produced three remarkable art historians in the nineteenth century, Sydney Owenson, Lady Morgan (c.1783-1859), Anna Brownell Murphy, Mrs. Jameson (1794-1860) and Margaret Stokes (1832-1900). Sydney Owenson was the daughter of an actor and no doubt her upbringing in the Irish theatrical world helped to develop her remarkable and flamboyant character which survived being a governess, and took her into the ducal world of the Abercorns at Baronscourt and into a world more interested in the arts than any she had met before. Most of her writing was about her travels, or patriotic Irish works but suddenly in 1823 she produced a book on Salvator Rosa, until

FIG. 44.—CROSS OF CONG.

Fig. 7 Margaret Stokes, *The Cross of Cong*. Illustration from *Early Christian Art in Ireland* (1887).

Fig. 8 Mary Swanzy, *The Drawing Room, Mespil House* painted for Sarah Purser. Private Collection.

Fig. 9 *The Dun Emer Press* (precursor of the Cuala Press), *1903* with (from left to right) Ester Ryan, Beatrice Cassidy and Lollie Yeats. Photograph courtesy of Michael B. Yeats.

biographer of George Petrie whose work on early Irish art was renowned and it is not surprising that his daughter Margaret Stokes should become one of Ireland's early 'learned ladies', an Honorary Member of both Royal Irish Academy (RIA) and of the Royal Society of Antiquaries of Ireland (RSAI). She learnt through travelling with her father, and meeting his friends who included Petrie, Burton, O'Donovan, Dunraven and Wilde and other artists and archaeologists. She had no education (other presumably than that provided by a governess) and as the unmarried daughter in a busy doctor's house, she had little enough time to develop her marked artistic talents, let alone her scholarship. She said herself that 'she came out at 50'[15] no doubt implying that till her father's death freed her of domestic responsibilities, she could not settle down to work. Her writings on early Irish art remain some of the most intelligent and carefully considered of her era (Fig. 7). It is indeed a tragedy that such brains and talent should only have had a chance to flourish towards the end of her life.

Art History as a university subject also owes its origins in Ireland to a woman, Sarah Purser, an artist and collector of note in the first half of the twentieth century (Fig. 8). In 1934 she persuaded her cousin Sir John Purser Griffiths to join with her in making money available for a scholarship and prize to be given in alternate years by Trinity College, Dublin and University College, Dublin

to the best candidates in an examination in the History of European Painting. As a result Françoise Henry started a course of tuition in University College, Dublin for this scholarship. Eventually, in the 1960's, both universities founded Art History departments under women, Françoise Henry and myself.

Women as professional artists were still very rare by the end of the nineteenth century. They were by now being trained; they were running societies; they were exhibiting; but they still remained at home unless they were poor enough to be governesses when of course they could not develop their talents fully. To some extent Sarah Purser broke this stalemate. She came of a family with both learning and business acumen though it was a financial crisis that decided her to earn a living as a portrait painter and to get herself trained in France. She had the social position to assist her talent and she said that she 'went through the British aristocracy like the measles',[16] painting their portraits, and making a great deal of money. But Sarah's most important characteristic was that she approved of making money, even of women making money and of art making money. The commercial success of the stained glass studios she founded, called An Túr Gloine (The Tower of Glass), which employed so many fine women artists through its long history — Catherine O'Brien, Wilhelmina Geddes and Evie Hone to name only three — must

5

have made women feel inches taller. The Yeats sisters' Cuala Press (Fig. 9), after all, was a home industry but Sarah Purser's was not. It was closely analagous to a factory and required very physical work as well. Her amazing strength of character was undoubtedly the turning point for women in art. They were not so much equal as sometimes frankly superior, getting commissions which twenty-five years earlier would not have been considered even remotely appropriate for women. Wilhelmina Geddes was employed after the 1914-18 war on numerous windows of which the Memorial Window at Ypres in Belgium was perhaps the most important. After the 1939-45 war, Evie Hone obtained one of the most exciting commissions of the period in these islands for the huge East Window in Eton College Chapel. She was now working independently from An Túr Gloine but it and Sarah Purser had been her jumping-off point in this aspect of her career. The window, superb in form and colour and majestic in size, is truly a memorial to the talents not just of Evie Hone but of all Irish women. It is a triumphant milestone in their battle for equality.

Sarah Purser links in too with her seventeenth-century predecessors as she was also a great collector of pictures and an important patron of the arts, famous for her hospitality and her wit. Her forceful personality helped in the acceptance of modern movements in this country. Here she was ably assisted by Mainie Jellett the artist, who, with Evie Hone, brought Cubism to Ireland in the early 1920's. Mainie, with her own art and writing, her lecturing and her teaching, held the torch for progress and adventure in art. It was the women, not the mainly very conservative male artists[17] of the twenties and thirties who brought Ireland into the 20th century. Always free of the shackles which men had made for themselves in their academies and in their attitudes to life, women — now that they could go out and earn a living — were able to experiment with excitement and verve. Their minds had never been imprisoned, as had their bodies, by domesticity and now at last the world was theirs. One has only to look at the ratio of women to men in exhibitions in Ireland to-day to see that they have not neglected their opportunities.

1. Elizabeth Freke's diary gives some idea of what they went through, she wrote on Nov. 12, 1692: 'I found my House quit Burntt downe ... And this was the Fifth Time I came to Bare Walls & a Naked House since I were married'. Admittedly some of her disasters were due to family troubles. *Journal of the Cork Historical and Archaeological Society,* 2nd series, vol. 17-18, 1911-1912, p.48. I am indebted to the Knight of Glin for this reference.
2. HMC *Ormonde* mss. new series, vol. 2, 1903, pp.373-75.
3. I must thank Jane Fenlon for bringing this inventory (National Library of Ireland, Ormond Papers, mss. 2552, pp.21-24) and other information on the Ormond Collections to my attention.
4. National Library of Ireland mss. 2503.
5. John Dunton, quoted by E. P. Shirley and the Rev. James Graves in the *Journal of the Kilkenny and S. E. of Ireland Archaeological Society,* new series, vol. IV, 1862-3, (Dublin 1864), pp.14-15.
6. Lady Louisa's work in Castletown is well described and illustrated in Desmond Guinness and William Ryan, *Irish Houses and Castles,* (London 1971), pp.202-07.
7. Stalker (John) M.A. and Parker (George) of Oxford, *A Treatise of Japanning and Varnishing, being a complete discovery of those arts ... with ... patterns for Japan-work ...* (Oxford 1688).
8. Lady Llanover (ed.), *Autobiography and Correspondence of Mary Granville, Mrs. Delany,* (6 vols.) (London 1861-62). These three quotations are on pp.412, 415, 422 respectively. This book is referred to later as *Mrs. Delany.*
9. Shirley Armstrong-Duffy, *Late Nineteenth century sketching clubs in Ireland,* unpublished B.A. thesis, T.C.D., 1984, p.27.
10. Information kindly supplied by the Hon. Hector McDonnell.
11. *Mrs. Delany,* vol. 3, p.521.
12. Marianne C. Hamilton, *A Short History of the Hamiltons of Hamwood and their Antecedents,* (1851).
13. *Mrs. Delany,* vol. 1, p.319.
14. Sir William Stokes, *William Stokes,* (London 1898), pp.55-56.
15. Caesar Litton Falkiner, article in *Dictionary of National Biography,* vol. 22, Supplement, (Oxford 1921-22), pp.1234-35.
16. Elizabeth Coxhead, *Daughters of Erin,* (London 1965), p.131.
17. Jack B. Yeats was an obvious exception.

The training and professional life of Irish women artists before the twentieth century

Jeanne Sheehy

As a topic, *Irish Women Artists* presents several difficulties of definition. In the first place, who is to be considered as Irish? I have decided to settle for those to whose background and training Ireland had made a contribution, and also for those born outside Ireland who had made a substantial contribution to the artistic life of the country. The definition of 'artist' is more difficult. Until well into this century few women made it into the upper reaches of fine art, as they were mostly barred from the kind of training which would enable them to paint figure subjects in oils, considered since the Renaissance as the apex of artistic achievement in painting. Those women who established reputations in the arts did so, on the whole, in the less elevated genres such as miniature portraits or landscape, and in humble media such as water-colour or crayon. They were most successful in the applied arts, generally considered by the academies as inferior to 'pure' art. If we are to do any justice to women as artists before the twentieth century, we must admit as artists practitioners of the lesser genres and media, as well as embroidresses, decorators of porcelain, makers of flower arrangements in wax, and so on. Even the word 'woman' presents problems of social status. Proficiency in the arts, whether 'fine' or 'applied' was part of the accomplishment expected of a 'lady' or 'gentlewoman', but however skilled they were, these women were usually regarded as amateurs. Lower down the social scale, however, women could, and often did, practise trades such as printmaking.

Institutional life for the arts in Ireland began with the establishment of the Dublin Society in 1731. In 1739, in order to encourage the fine arts, the society began to award premiums for painting and sculpture. That these were open to women as well as men is borne out by the fact that, in 1740, Susanna Drury was awarded a premium of £25 for her water colour of the Giants' Causeway, and that Mary Anne Hunter was awarded prizes in 1769, 1770, and 1772.[1] In 1746 the Society offered premiums 'to the boy or girl, under fifteen years old, who should produce the best drawings, performed by him or her in 1745' and 'to such boys and girls, under fifteen years old, who shall produce the best patterns made by them in 1745, for damask or printed linens ...' The premium of £5 for the best drawing went to 'Miss Jenny

Tudor, for her drawings in black and white after Raphael and Titian, which were very well done'. Some distinction was made between girls and boys, however, as the boys who were awarded premiums were invited to attend, and draw the outline of a head, and the girls were not. In 1749 twenty eight boys competed for the 'best drawing' prize. Girls are again mentioned, however, among the five who produced patterns for damask, printed and stained linens 'which far exceeded any of the like kind produced before, in the beauty of the pattern, right colouring and shading, which are of so much use in many kinds of manufactures'. From then on girls seem to have been confined to the applied art portion of the competition. In 1761 there were twelve prizewinners, including two girls. In 1762 there were twenty boys and four girls.[2] So we see that, though girls in Ireland were initially fortunate in being given the same opportunities as boys, this situation did not last. When the Society set up formal drawing classes in the 1740's the pupils were all boys. This lack of opportunity for formal training was one of the major problems met with by women who wished to become artists. At least until the middle of the nineteenth century women who made any professional mark were generally from families of artists, as this was the only way in which they could get a professional training.[3]

Susannah Drury was sister of the miniature painter Franklin Drury. Miss Forster, the miniature painter, was the sister of the landscape painter John Forster, though she was taught by Thomas Boulger. Mary Anne Hunter was the daughter of the portrait painter Robert Hunter, married a portrait painter, John Trotter, and had two daughters who were painters. The sculptor Eliza Kirk was sister of two sculptors, and daughter of another. She assisted her father, Thomas Kirk RHA, in his studio. Pasquin mentions several women artists, all of them the relations of male artists, and though Strickland lists twenty eight women in their own right, he mentions at least fourteen more in the entries on their male relatives.[4] The Claytons, a dynasty of engravers, produced two distinguished women. Caroline Clayton, better known by her married name of Millard, had a considerable reputation as an engraver in the mid nineteenth century, her best known work is the engraving for the frontispiece of *The Spirit of the Nation* after Burton's design. Her niece, Eleanor Creathorne Clayton, did some illustrations and designs for such things as Christmas cards, but, like Anna Jameson and Edith Somerville, soon turned to writing as a means of earning her living. Her book, *English Female Artists*, was published in 1876. Given the fact that she came of a long line of artists, and was one herself, her opinions, quoted below, carry some weight:

'As we pass down the fair ranks of the earlier Female Artists, we shall find that they almost invariably follow in the footsteps of a brother or a father. In the case of Englishwomen there is scarcely an instance to the contrary. The reason being, in all likelihood, the impossibility of studying under other instruction.'[5]

The only other training open to women was in the private drawing schools which flourished in Dublin in the eighteenth and nineteenth centuries. Though women were not formally admitted to the schools of the Dublin Society, masters such as James Mannin seem to have taken females as private pupils, and reputable masters like as James Ballard and Henry Brooke took female pupils.[6]

Once trained, artists needed to make a reputation and find patrons. One way of doing this was by public exhibitions. There were several attempts, from 1765 onwards, to establish annual exhibitions in Dublin, and women as well as men were admitted to these.[7] Women were very much in the minority, however. In the exhibitions held by the Society of Artists in Ireland between 1765 and 1780 there were only twenty one, out of a total of one hundred and eighty five. Of the twenty one, twelve were listed as 'Honorary Exhibitors' and six, presumably children, as 'pupils to Mr Boulger'. The remaining three, listed among the ordinary exhibitors, were wives or sisters of exhibiting artists.[8] The Royal Hibernian Academy held its inaugural exhibition in 1826, and women were admitted from the beginning. There is scarcely an Irish woman artist of any distinction in the nineteenth century who did not exhibit with the RHA.[9]

There were limited possibilities for women to earn a living in the arts. If they came of families of artists they followed the same line as their male relations, often on the borders between 'trade' and 'fine art'. Caroline Clayton, for example, became an engraver, like her father and grandfather. Clementina Robertson was a miniature painter, taught by her father the miniature painter Charles Robertson. Left a widow, she continued to earn a living as a miniature painter. One of the principal ways in which women artists earned a living was by teaching. The five daughters of Solomon Williams were 'teachers of drawing' at 23 Holles Street, Dublin. In an address to the Royal Dublin Society in 1844 Stewart Blacker praised them, along with Mrs Anne Gonne and Miss Marshall of Belfast, as 'able instructors'.[10]

There were certain kinds of subject matter that were considered particularly feminine, what Blacker in 1844 called 'the graceful and feminine department of fruit and flowers'. In the earliest exhibitions such subjects appear frequently.[11] Landscape and topography were also popular with women artists, and this also was very much related to the kind of accomplishment expected of educated women. Another area considered suitable for women was applied art, and it was here that they often attracted the most extravagant praise, like the eulogy of Mrs Caulfield in Dr Campbell's *Philosophical Survey of the South of Ireland*:

'This lady, from the mere resources of her own genius, has not only arrived at such a pitch of excellence in needlework, drawing of all sorts, painting in oil and watercolours ... as procured her the admiration of everybody ...; but she has moreover struck out a new species of art. With a manly and happy boldness ... she has reached the summit of perfection in colouring by a peculiar combination of such mean materials as Taylor's Shapings. She began with fruit and flowers, which she soon executed to the temptation of both taste and skill ... she has at last advanced to human figures, and has animated her spirited designs with such warm tints of smiling innocence and rosy health as would strike a blush into the cheek of Rubens could he now see himself so far outdone!!.'[12]

In the early exhibitions women often exhibited work in media which were more associated with craft than with fine art. Mrs Braddock of Dorset Street exhibited *A Peacock* and *A Group of Flowers*, both worked in straw, at the Society of Artists in Ireland in 1766.[13]

Design for industry was not as important in Ireland as in England, but where it did occur women seem to have been very much involved. We have seen how girls who succeeded in getting premiums from the Dublin Society in the early years were making designs for printed and linen damask. Women also designed decorations for porcelain.[14] Annie Langley Nairn, through her marriage to Robert Armstrong, an architect who was one of the founders of the company, found an outlet for her talent in the design of porcelain for Belleek. The characteristic early porcelain produced by the company, decorated with seaweed, seashells, coral and rockwork, is attributed to her.[15] It is a commentary, however, on the lesser role played by women, that it was her husband, and not she, who was Art Director.

At the top end of the social scale a woman was encouraged to be 'accomplished' in the arts. This operated on two levels. In the first place she was expected to bring taste to bear on her dress and on the the furnishing of her house, and in the second, she was expected to have a civilising effect on society.[16] Mrs Watson was praised by Pasquin for her services to the females of Ireland, as 'an improver of their taste in the articles of personal adornment'.[17] Mrs Delany was admired for her artistic talent in work which we would consider as craft, she made decorations in cut out coloured paper, and her shell work and embroidery were much praised.[18] Many other women did shellwork, or made settings for the display of engravings. They did bead work and made braid. Maria Edgeworth wrote to Mrs Charles Kendal Bushe in 1832:

'A bag if you please of your own braidwork my dear Mrs Bushe — Louisa Beaufort ... tells me that your braidwork is so beautiful that I do covet this souvenir from you. The least *Forget me not* or *Heartsease* will fulfill my wishes ...'[19]

Ladies were also expected to have enough skill to paint a landscape or a portrait in water colours. Beyond that women were not expected to develop their talent. Charles Kendal Bushe wrote to his wife in 1810:

'Mrs Edgeworth is uncommonly agreeable ... She is a perfect Scholar, and at the same time a good Mother and housewife. She is an excellent painter, like yourself, and like you has been oblig'd by producing Originals to give up Copying.'[20]

Mrs Bushe, née Nancy Crampton:

'had a rare and enchanting gift as an artist, which, even in those days, when young ladies of quality were immured in the padded cell of the amateur, could scarce have failed to make its mark ... In her time there were few women who gave even a moment's thought to the possibilities of individual life as an artist, however aware they might be — must have been — of the gifts they possessed.'[21]

There is further evidence that, in Ireland in particular, there was considerable social pressure on women 'of good family' not to become artists. Few Irishwomen, Eleanor Clayton noted in *English Female Artists*, had distinguished themselves as artists, and she quoted 'an Irishwoman' of her acquaintance on the subject:

'In Ireland a lady may seek notoriety as a rider, a huntress, or a flirt in the ball-room or promenade, without committing any flagrant breach of propriety. She may attract every eye by the style and extravagance of her dress, provided always she be duly chaperoned. And she may share the manly triumph of the hunting field, and be in at the death ... But woe be to her if Nature has been unkind enough to weight her with any extra portion of artistic talent, and with it the fatal desire to cultivate the same beyond that point which has been determined as the extreme limit of feminine indulgence, or ladylike development. The moment she dares to cross that Rubicon which separates so widely the professional artist from the fashionable amateur, she forgets ... her social position, and is henceforth barely tolerated.'[22]

This, Eleanor Clayton thinks, is why it is difficult to find any artists of note among the ladies of Ireland. She lists only one artist in her book whom she considers Irish, Wilhelmina Walker, though she mentions two more Irish-born women, Katharine King, an animal painter, and herself 'born some thirty odd years ago in Gloucester Terrace, Dublin'.

Opportunities for women in the arts in Ireland took a new turn when the schools of the Royal Dublin Society came under the South Kensington system as one of the 'Government Schools of Design' in 1849. The Schools had been set up to provide proper training in design for manufacture. It was accepted that women had an aptitude for design, and that it would be a suitable occupation for women who needed to earn a living. Apart from that, women were regarded as an important part of the workforce.[23]

So the Schools of the Royal Dublin Society were at least opened to women, though not, it appears, with great enthusiasm. There are frequent references, in the early speeches and annual reports, to their 'admirable demeanour', to the 'taste displayed in the arrangement and composition of ... groups of flowers', and to the 'domestic character of the female mind'.[24]

Female recruitment to the schools was very rapid. In the first two years, out of an average daily attendance of three hundred and fifty-five, one hundred and thirty-three were women. In 1851 there were one hundred and seventy female pupils, and they won eighteen of the forty-two premiums awarded. In 1852 also, the women took a large share of the prizes. Their most conspicuous success was in competing for medals in the scientific subjects, botany, chemistry, optics, anatomy and zoology. Women won all of the medals except the one for anatomy 'and it is to be observed that from that course of lectures the female pupils have been excluded'. This may not be as severe a judgement on the quality of male art students as it appears. It seems likely that the women had a better general education than the men, that many of them were middle-class women in search of 'accomplishment' or a genteel occupation. In 1851 sixty-nine planned to be teachers, five to be artists and ten designers, with a large number of undetermined. The men, on the other hand, had more practical aims. Twenty planned to be architects, ten civil engineers, five carvers and gilders, six teachers and twelve prospective artists.[25] Until the early twentieth century there seems to have been a tension in the school between men who were artisans, and mostly attended night classes, and middle class women. The men considered themselves to be there for serious professional purposes, and regarded the women as privileged amateurs. In the first years of their admission women were also discriminated against when it came to official recognition of their achievements. Traditionally the schools of the Royal Dublin Society had a ceremonial annual prizegiving, attended, with great pomp, by the Lord Lieutenant. This practice was continued after 1849, but, though the women bore off a large proportion of the prizes 'it has not been thought advisable to invite them to take part in this public display' on the grounds that it would be 'inconvenient and disagreeable' to them.[26]

Though there seem to have been numbers of private academies, the Government Schools of Design in Dublin, Belfast, Cork and elsewhere provided the only means by which women could obtain any formal education in the arts. Men intending to be fine artists went to the School of Design in Dublin, but it was generally only preparatory to going on to the schools of the Royal Hibernian Academy or abroad. Until 1893 women were not admitted to the schools of the RHA, so those women who intended to become serious artists achieved this in areas associated with arts and crafts, or went abroad for their training. Sarah Purser, for example, spent a couple of years at the Metropolitan School of Art (as the Schools became in 1877) before going abroad. Edith Somerville, having relations in London with whom she could stay, attended classes at South Kensington, before going to Düsseldorf and Paris. Her experience is an interesting example of the kind of difficulty a woman had to face if she decided to become an artist. Though her family did not oppose the notion of her being a painter, and seems even to have encouraged her early training, it was a different matter when she decided to study in Paris.

'Paris!'. They all said this at the tops of their voices ... They said that Paris was the Scarlet Woman embodied; they also said, 'The IDEA of letting a GIRL go to PARIS!'. This they said incessantly in capital letters ... and my mother was frightened. So a compromise was effected, and I went to Paris with a bodyguard consisting of my mother, my eldest brother, a female cousin, and with us another girl ...'[27]

This is an extreme example, but it does demonstrate not only the social, but also the economic pressures that beset a woman artist — not every family could afford such a retinue of chaperones, or would be willing to spend so much on the education of a daughter. Access to the right kind of models was another difficulty for women. 'High art' in Europe since the Renaissance had been based on a study of the human figure. For many years, as we have seen, women were not admitted to the schools where such studies could take place. When they were, women were either barred from the life class, or the model was decorously draped. At the Royal Dublin Society's School they were even excluded from the classes in anatomy. One of the attractions of Paris for women from England and Ireland was that some of the private studios offered life classes to women.

Women were eventually admitted to the schools of the Royal Hibernian Academy in 1893, mainly, it seems, because the Academy was having difficulty in recruiting men. According to Catterson-Smith, the secretary, there was an immediate dropping off of attendance by men because they would not work with the women.[28] In 1905 an average of twenty-three students attended classes in drawing and painting from life, and seventeen of these were women. There seems to have been a general feeling that women art students were the daughters of the Dublin bourgeoisie in search of accomplishment, and were not to be taken seriously. Harry Clarke, describing the situation at the Metropolitan School of Art said:

'Serious students of this period would joke about the daughters of wealthy Dubliners who would come in during the day to amuse themselves and dabble in arty-crafty pursuits, while the worthy but improverished night students would slave away in the hope of winning scholarships. A favourite trick was to pile up the chairs at night so that the ladies would have nowhere to sit. Certainly the contemporary fashion for arts and crafts contributed to this female influx.'[29]

George Russell shared the same view.

'I am quite sure that Mr Hughes and Mr Orpen would make it very uncomfortable for young ladies, who come there because they have nothing else to do.'

he told the 1906 Commission.[30] It is interesting to note, however, that neither John Hughes not William Orpen seems to have treated his female pupils in this patronising way.

The idea of applied art as a suitable occupation for women was still current at the end of the nineteenth century. The Queen's Institute for the Training and Employment of Educated Women was founded in 1861. Its main aim was 'to assist Gentlewomen of limited means, by training them to the pursuit of suitable professions and occupations'. Though these classes included subjects like 'Foreign Correspondence' and 'Law Writing' a large proportion of classes were in the applied arts, including lithography, wood engraving, illuminated painting, painting photographs and painting porcelain. In terms of subject matter, the painting of flowers, fruit and landscape are conspicuous on the curriculum.[31] Such emphasis on applied art as suitable to the talents of 'gentlemen' is one we have already encountered in the eighteenth century. What is different at the end of the nineteenth century is the status of craft in relation to fine art, it has become a much more acceptable pursuit. This is probably due to the influence of William Morris and the arts and crafts movement. In the last years of the nineteenth century, and well into the twentieth, many women distinguished themselves, on an equal footing with men, in the applied arts. The system set up when the Schools of the Royal Dublin Society came under South Kensington in 1849 no doubt laid the foundation for this, but it received tremendous impetus in 1900, when the school came under the authority of the Department of Agriculture and Technical Instruction for Ireland. Practical, as well as design, classes were set up, with notable success in the case of stained glass, enamelling and mosaic. One of the new teachers was a woman, Eleanor Hollwey, who had been employed in the team of lady mosaicists working on the new Cathedral at Westminster. Among the women trained in the Metropolitan School of Art who distinguished themselves in the applied arts were the stained glass artist Catherine O'Brien and the mosaicist Ethel Rhind.[32]

As far as the public showing of artists' work was concerned, the RHA annual exhibitions continued to be the main event. Women exhibited there increasingly as the nineteenth century wore on. The Watercolour Society of Ireland was formed in 1870 as The Amateur Drawing Society. This was one of the rare institutions in which women had an executive, as well as a passive, role. For example, the committee in 1877 consisted of five women and two men. In 1892 the committee of twelve included seven women. Among them were the distinguished water-colourists Fanny Currey, Rose Barton and Mildred Butler.[33] The Dublin Art Club was founded in 1886, a very active club with annual exhibitions. Membership was divided between working members (limited to fifty), non-working members (limited to twenty), corresponding members (limited to ten) and, last of all, lady members (limited to ten), which gives one a fair notion of the status accorded to women artists.[34] In the late nineteenth century, women artists were still, on the whole, treated as amateurs, with little regard for the quality of their work. They often confined themselves to media such as watercolour, and subject matter such as landscape, which were considered suitable for women and amateurs. Many prolific and talented women artists, like Rose Barton and Mildred Butler, came of well-off professional or landed families, and did not need to sell their work. This probably contributed to the perception of their painting as mere accomplishment.

In spite of the improvement in the prospects of women artists by the end of the nineteenth century, they still suffered considerable disabilities compared with men. As far as the institutions were concerned, they certainly occupied an inferior position. When Sir William Abney reported on the arts in Ireland in 1901 he suggested that, since 'some of the best artists in Ireland are ladies' it would strengthen the RHA to elect them as associates.[35] In spite of this, even so distinguished a painter as Sarah Purser had to wait until 1923 for associateship and 1925 for full membership, and, to this very day no officer of the RHA has been a female. This may be one reason why women have played so active a role in the *avant garde* in the twentieth century.

1.   When not otherwise credited, biographical information comes from W.G. Strickland, *A Biographical Dictionary of Irish Artists,* (Dublin 1913).
2.   *Notices of the Proceedings of the 'Dublin Society' in Reference to their Drawing Schools, 1746-1750 and 1761-1764 Extracted from Faulkner's Dublin Journal by W. Vicars Griffith, Esq.,* (Dublin 1852).
3.   This was not a situation peculiar to Ireland, and it has frequently been discussed by writers on women artists. There is now a substantial body of writing on the subject, of which a selection is given below.

> Ellen C. Clayton, *English Female Artists,* 2 vols, (London 1876).
> Charlotte Yeldham, *Women Artists in Nineteenth Century France and England,* (New York and London 1984).
> Norma Broude and Mary D. Garrard (eds), *Feminism and Art History,* (New York 1982).
> Germaine Greer, *The Obstacle Race,* (London 1979).
> Elaine Hedges and Ingrid Wendt (eds), *In Her Own Image,* (New York 1980).
> Thomas B. Hess and Elizabeth C. Baker (eds), *Art and Sexual Politics,* (New York and London 1973).

Rozsika Parker and Griselda Pollock, *Old Mistresses, Women, Art and Ideology,* (London 1981).
4.   Anthony Pasquin, *An Authentic History of the Professors of Painting, Sculpture and Architecture who have Practised in Ireland,* (London nd.).
5.   Clayton, *op. cit.* p.7.
6.   George Breeze, *Society of Artists in Ireland, Index of Exhibitors 1765-80.* (Dublin 1985), *passim.*
7.   Strickland, *op. cit.* pp.604-05.
8.   Breeze, *op. cit.*
9.   Ann M. Stewart, *Royal Hibernian Academy of Arts, Index of Exhibitors 1826-1979,* 2 vols., (Dublin 1986). The final volume has still to appear, and I am grateful to Ann Stewart for allowing me access to her notes.
10.   Royal Dublin Society, Public Distribution of Premiums, 1844, p.22.
11.   Breeze, *op. cit.,* and Stewart, *op. cit.*
12.   Quoted in *Strickland, op. cit.,* vol 2, p.163.
13.   Breeze, *op. cit.*
14.   6th and 9th Annual Reports of the Queen's Institute, 1868 and 1871. I am grateful to Shirley Armstrong Duffy for this material.
15.   S. McCrum, *The Belleek Pottery,* Ulster Museum, (Belfast, nd, 1970s?).
16.   For a thorough discussion of this topic, see Yeldham, *op. cit.*
17.   Pasquin, *op. cit.,* p.42.
18.   Clayton, *op. cit.,* pp.96ff.
19.   Edith Somerville and Martin Ross, *Irish Memories,* 4th ed. (London 1918), p.56. I am grateful to Gifford Charles Edwards for this reference.
20.   Somerville and Ross, *op. cit.,* p.47.
21.   *ibid.,* p.52.
22.   Clayton, *op. cit.,* p.152.
23.   Discussed in Yeldham, *op. cit.*
24.   Royal Dublin Society, Distribution of Premiums, 1844-1854.
25.   See John Turpin, *The Royal Dublin Society and its School of Art, 1849-1877,* and *The South Kensington System and the Metropolitan School of Art, 1877-1900,* Dublin Historical Record, vol. 36, 1 and 2, (December 1982 and March 1983).
26.   Royal Dublin Society, Distribution of Premiums, 1844-1854.
27.   Somerville and Ross, *op. cit.,* pp.110-11.
28.   *Report of the Committee of Enquiry into the Work Carried on by the Royal Hibernian Academy and the Metropolitan School of Art.* (H.M.S.O. 1906).
29.   Quoted by John Turpin, 'The Metropolitan School of Art (1900-1923)' *Dublin Historical Record,* vol. 37, no. 2, pp.59-78, (March 1984).
30.   1906 Report, *op. cit.,* p.63, para. 1273.
31.   Queen's Institute reports, *op. cit.*
32.   *Dublin Institutions of Science and Art, Annual Reports 1901-1928,* H.M.S.O.
33.   Catalogues of the exhibitions of the Irish Fine Art Society, the Irish Amateur Drawing Society and the Water Colour Society of Ireland, 1870 onwards. I am grateful to Shirley Armstrong Duffy for this material.
34.   The Dublin Art Club Winter Exhibitions 1886-92.
35.   1906 Report, *op. cit.,* Appendix A.

Acknowledgements. I should like to thank Shirley Armstrong Duffy for her research, which contributed greatly to this essay. I should also like to thank Kim Mai Mooney, Wanda Ryan Smolin and Ann Stewart for their help.

The role of women in Irish sketching clubs in the late nineteenth century

Shirley Armstrong Duffy

The last three decades of the nineteenth century were the heyday of sketching clubs in Ireland and women must be given the credit for being the instigators. The earliest group formed is recorded by Strickland[1] as a local drawing society founded in 1870 in Lismore, County Waterford, by six ladies which included Baroness Pauline Prochazka and Miss Fanny Currey. Their object was the 'mutual improvement in painting and drawing and the cultivation of a taste for art'.

This group held two exhibitions in 1871 and the third in 1872 in Carlow, under the name of the Irish Amateur Drawing Society. The catalogue of this exhibition of drawings, watercolours and oils lists some forty-five exhibitors; it is interesting to note that of one hundred and twenty-one watercolours, seventy-eight of these were copies. Another feature of these early shows was the number of categories; in 1877 for example, there were seventeen. The Society continued to hold exhibitions in different centres round the country until 1891 and one in Dublin annually from 1877.

As early as 1884 the need was felt for a society specifically to represent the watercolourists, '... Ireland should have such a society and the Irish Fine Art Society [which the I.A.D.S. had become in 1878], many of whose members compete for and gain places in the London and Paris Galleries, seems ... the nucleus on which to form it ...'[2] The name Watercolour Society of Ireland was officially adopted for their Belfast exhibition of 1887/88.

Each year the proposition of watercolours to oils increased as artists could show oils with the Royal Hibernian Academy, but unless watercolours were outstanding enough to be shown in the front room, they were relegated to a back room with bad lighting.

This wish for a chance to display watercolours in a more favourable setting than that offered by the R.H.A. seems to have been one of the reasons behind the formation of the first sketching club in Dublin. In 1872 Miss Deane (possibly a relation of Thomas Deane, R.H.A.) 'and a few ladies started the Ladies' Sketching Club. At that time the R.H.A. was the only public exhibition held in Dublin and the need for a smaller exhibition where Amateurs and Tyros in Art could exhibit their work, was felt as a growing necessity with the rapidly increasing taste amongst all classes for Drawing and Painting.'[3]

The following year gentlemen were admitted to membership, but the management remained in the hands of the ladies. This club also changed its name; it now became the Dublin Amateur and Artists' Society.

In 1874 Miss Deane resigned her secretaryship in favour of Miss M. K. Benson. The Society appears to have become known as 'Miss Benson's Society', in much the same way as the Watercolour Society and its forerunners had become known as 'Miss Currey's'.

Another feature which the W.C.S.I. and the Dublin Amateurs shared was a strongly competitive element. The 1872 Carlow exhibition of the Irish Amateur Drawing Society awarded prizes in over a dozen categories. The judges' report reads as follows:

'We spent Thursday, the 9th of May, in examining and judging the pictures of the Irish Amateur Drawing Society and are glad to express ourselves as much gratified by the number and class of pictures exhibited. We trust that original pictures may continue to be contributed in increasing numbers and that copies, particularly from chrome-lithography may decrease in a corresponding degree.

(Signed) John F. Crampton, Bart.
W. Primrose, Colonel,
Charles Grey, R.H.A.[4]

The 1885 exhibition of the Dublin Amateur and Artists' Society was very fully reported by the *Daily Express*.[5] The judges in this case were Thomas A. Jones, P.R.H.A., B. Colles Watkins, R.H.A. and Bingham McGuinness, R.H.A., who commented that the best work was contributed by former prize-winners. Apparently former winners were not eligible to compete again — an admirable attempt at sharing, but also something of an inbuilt obsolescence. Mildred Butler was one of the dozen artists who were awarded certificates the others being Miss G. Fry, Pamella K. Symes, Miss S.A. Black, Mrs. G.H. Orpen, Charles A. Lodder, Mrs. Close, Capt. Kiddle, Johnson Inglis, Celia P. Culverwell, Miss R. Apjohn and Mrs. Altamont Smythe.

In 1888 'Miss Benson, the Committee and Members, feeling it has done its work (namely that of encouraging Amateur Artists and through them cultivating the taste for art amongst the upper classes), thought it expedient to amalgamate with the [Dublin] Sketching Club, who had recently admitted ladies as members under very similar conditions to those already existing in the older society, and the members of the Society joined the Club as Corresponding Members.'[6]

Unfortunately, another thing shared by these two pioneering societies is the absence of records which must have been meticulously kept by their hard-working secretaries. In the case of the Dublin Amateurs, we do not have even a catalogue and all our information comes from press reports and from the Report of their activities made at the time of their amalgamation with the Dublin Sketching Club.

The women, having shown how successful societies for amateurs could be, had their idea taken up with enthusiasm by the men. Here we are fortunate to have the records of the Dublin Sketching Club which were most conscientiously kept by the painter Alexander Williams. These records are supplemented by the personal scrapbook of press-cuttings kept by Williams which has been treasured by the Club for a hundred years.

To quote Williams on the formation of the Club: 'A number of gentlemen were interested in Art matters in Dublin and expressed their regret that there was no society where artists and people of artistic temperament could meet socially in the evenings for discussion and improvement. Some attempts had been made by gentlemen inviting some artists to their houses where music and art were indulged in, but it remained for one very enthusiastic Dublin dentist Mr. William Booth Pearsall to organise a special meeting at his place in Westland Row to form a society where good artistic work might be done on a special evening of the week ...'[7]

Mr. Pearsall invited the following artists to his house on the evening of October 20th 1874: J. Todhunter, M.D., John Woodhouse, A.R.H.A., Edmund Purdon, Jnr., Chichester Alex Bell, Thomas Urrey Young, Charles Edward Fitzgerald, M.D., John Leech, William Stokes, M.D., G. Pim, Jnr., Bram Stoker, Alexander Williams and Alfred Grey, '... for the purpose of forming a sketching club on the plan of the London Artists Clubs.' The ladies are given no credit for being first in the field in Dublin, but then the approach was very different.

Two evenings later the new club met; '... a long table down the centre of the room was prepared for sketching purposes round which the members sat and for two hours worked to illustrate the two subjects chosen .. "Sunset" and "Reflection".' Time was called at ten-fifteen and each member placed his work on a screen where it was criticised by those present.

'A light supper of cheese and bread washed down with ale followed'. They decided to rent premises and chose no. 212 Gt. Brunswick Street. (Gt. Brunswick St. is now Pearse St. , and no. 212 was then a Riding Stables; it became Mackenzies and is now the Department of Social Welfare.) From the beginning they held Conversaziones and Smoking Concerts when their work was exhibited. Apparently their success was so pronounced that most of the active members of the R.H.A. became members.

The D.S.C.'s first public exhibition was held in the Leinster Hall, Molesworth Street, in 1876. The show's catalogue states that the Club's purpose is to bring together '... artists, amateurs and gentlemen interested in Art, in friendly and social intercourse promoting a taste for the fine arts in Dublin and aiding, by the sale of the sketches done during the weekly meetings, ... the funds of the Artists' General Benevolent Institution.'

The main part of the Exhibition was devoted to the two-hour sketches which appear to have fascinated both the press and the public. Immediately the fun of a Victorian parlour game was suggested. The sketches could be admired for their ingenuity and the circumstances under which they were produced, even if they were not all works of art. The Irish Amateur Drawing Society had had a set subject in Carlow in 1972 — 'Solitude'; it would be interesting to know if this was where the D.S.C. got the idea.

Annual Exhibitions were usually opened by the Lord Lieutenant with '.. a large and fashionable attendance' and musical evenings were organised during the exhibitions. One under Professor Glover, assisted by Messrs. Williams, O'Rorke, Jones, Oldham and Alfred Manning, '... included a glee, 'Spring's Delights', 'M'apari', 'Solo profugo', 'When I beheld the anchor weighed', etc. A most agreeable evening was spent and the specimens of art hung around the hall afforded the visitors an ample theme for interesting conversation ...'[8]

This was the pattern the Club followed for the next twenty years and society flocked to their Exhibitions and Entertainments; unlike the ladies' societies, entertainment was a major part of their raison d'être.

In 1883 the Club offered members classes in the Art of Modelling in Clay at the Institute of Porcelain Painting in no. 27 Molesworth Street. Two years later when they moved premises in Merrion Row, they introduced sessions with a 'Draped Model'. It was at this time that Corresponding Members — 'who may be LADY ARTISTS'[9] were introduced. These ladies were to have the privilege of sending work to the annual exhibitions, but have no voice in the management of the Club. Actually, women had been exhibiting at all their exhibitions and Sarah Purser had been an Honorary Member for several years.

The ladies now joined the fortnightly summer sketching expeditions. Perhaps the reports of these suggest that the work of the women was not taken too seriously, but they do suggest enjoyment, for example: 'Excursion to Balrothery by 2 p.m. steam tram from Terenure ... The day was brilliant sunshiny east windery hot coolery kind of day ... The beauty of the fair members being only equalled by the landscapes submitted for their efforts.' The Daily Express of July 18th, 1888 recorded that on an excursion by steam tramway to Blessington, special stops were made along the way for them to admire the scenery. Another expedition to Dalkey of two men and six women, '... one of the best days the Club has experienced this season resulted in very few sketches.'[10]

By the time the Club had taken premises in Leinster Street they had acquired plaster casts for drawing from the antique and were holding monthly Club dinners, the food being supplied by the Misses Gardener '... in the best possible style considering the reasonable figure charged ...' and '... a gallon of whiskey to be kept for Club Dinners and a Piano hired ...'[11]

In 1886 the President and twelve members of the D.S.C. resigned. The records become very discreet at this point and no hint of the cause is given, but the Hon. Secretary, Alexander Williams and the Hon. Treasurer, Eldred Oldham held the Club together; in fact it seems to have gone from strength to strength.

The splinter group formed themselves into the Dublin Art Club. In their Preliminary Circular they propose that their constitution should be based upon that of the Arts Club, Hanover Square, London.

An Exhibition was immediately organised to take place in the Leinster Hall and was opened with an At Home. The guest list was headed by Their Serene Highnesses Prince and Princess Edward of Saxe-Weimar and included a distinguished section of Dublin society with representatives of the medical and legal professions, Dublin University and many well-known artists.

An undated press report in the D.S.C. Scrapbook reads: 'The fears which some friends of Art had not hesitated to express that the frequency with which exhibitions of paintings have of late been held in Dublin would militate against their success were ... very pleasantly dispelled ... The Gallery has been draped and festooned in a manner familiar to those who visit the smaller exhibitions in Bond Street ... it is quite impossible that an exhibition like this should be thrown open without the public taste being educated ...' This exhibition included a loan section with works by Burne Jones, Alfred Parsons, H.S. Marks, Edwin Hayes and Ernest Waterton, R.W.S., as well as a number of Irish Academicians.

Loan exhibitions had also been a feature with the Dublin Sketching Club, who in 1884 had held a Whistler loan exhibition which claimed to be the largest and most representative collection to be seen outside London. There were about a dozen pictures including the portraits of Thomas Carlyle, Lady Meux and the *Portrait of My Mother* which had won a medal in the Paris Salon of 1883. Julian Story, John Sargent and Ralph Curtis were also represented.

In the year the Art Club was formed, the Sketching Club also had another loan section at their exhibition. The Langham Sketching Club of London sent fifty pictures, with almost as many from the Bewick Club, Newcastle-on-Tyne and the Atheneum Graphic Club of Manchester.

Several smaller clubs amalgamated with the more successful, probably it was largely a question of premises. The Dublin Sketching Club, as well as absorbing the Dublin Amateur and Artists' Society in 1888, had already taken in the Dublin Amateur Photographic Club. The Dublin Art Club absorbed the Instrumental Club in 1893, since when it has been known as the Dublin Arts Club.

In Belfast, the Ramblers' Sketching Club existed from about 1879 as a semi-private society of unsettled location. The principal rule of this group seems to have been 'That this club be called the Belfast Ramblers' Sketching Club; the sole object being to encourage sketching from nature and Original Compositions'. The Club acquired premises in 1885, and in 1891 changed its name to the Belfast Art Society having developed from '... a dozen desultory sketchers to the position of the first Art Society in the city, with a large and ever increasing membership ..'[12]

There were also a number of small sketching clubs around the country, but where there were no premises, the records seem to be lost. For instance, Percy French and Mary Swanzy belonged to a small sketching group in the early 1890's. Beatrice Gubbins of Dunkathel House was Hon. Secretary of the Queenstown Sketching Club at the turn of the century and there must have been many others.

Full credit must be given to the women amateur painters who banded together in their various groups for their own encouragement and to show their work. Perhaps it is only to be expected that their attitude should have been on the solemn and serious side, for they were being quite innovative. It was much easier for the men to take up the idea and plan their activities like a Gentleman's Club. The women's groups were not totally independent, they included men on their selection and judging committees from the beginning. The men, on the other hand, could seize a good idea and get straight down to enjoying it. Another factor in the men's favour was finance. A group of professional men were in a much better position with regard to commitments that required financial backing. It is much easier to encourage regular meetings and social occasions when permanent premises are available.

The committees and the majority of the members of the Dublin Sketching Club and the Dublin Art Club were based in Dublin which made it easy to organise regular meetings. Besides the pottery classes and the sessions with a 'Draped Model', the Sketching Club arranged a series of classes for their members with Monsieur Rod Christian when he was in Dublin in 1892. These classes were held in Miss May Manning's Studio, no. 17 Gt. Brunswick Street where M. Christian had given lessons the previous year. Once again a woman had been the first organiser in the field.

Women painters contributed substantially to the position of amateur artists in general in late nineteenth century Ireland. By their initiative in banding together and organising public exhibitions of their own work, they started off many amateurs and watercolourists on the path to recognition.

1. W.G. Strickland, *A Dictionary of Irish Artists,* (1913).
2. Scrapbook of the Dublin Sketching Club.
3. Booklet of the Dublin Sketching Club, (November 1898).
4. Oliver Snoddy, 'An Unpublished Item of Carlow Printing', *Carloviana*, (1969).
5. Scrapbook of the Dublin Sketching Club.
6. Booklet of the Dublin Sketching Club.
7. Minute Book of the Dublin Sketching Club.
8. Scrapbook of the Dublin Sketching Club.
9. Minutes of A.G.M. of the Dublin Sketching Club (1885).
10. Minutes of the Dublin Sketching Club (1888).
11. Minutes of the Dublin Sketching Club (January 1891).
12. Catalogues of the Belfast Art Society.

The author is extremely grateful to the Dublin Sketching Club and to the various Societies mentioned for access to unpublished material.

Women and Dublin's municipal collection

Liz Sheridan

It is not widely appreciated that the Hugh Lane Municipal Gallery of Modern Art in Dublin might not exist to-day if it were not for the efforts of women.

Hugh Lane was born in Cork in 1875. His mother Adelaide Persse was the sister of Lady Gregory, one of the central figures in the new Irish Theatre Movement. In 1899 she was a founder figure of the Irish Literary Theatre, later to become known as the Abbey. At eighteen Lane went to work for the Colnaghi Gallery in London and before he was thirty he was reputed to be one of the leading art dealers in Europe. He visited Lady Gregory's house at Coole in 1900 and met for the first time W. B. Yeats, Douglas Hyde, Edward Martyn and Sarah Purser. During a trip to Dublin he visited an exhibition that Sarah Purser had organised for two members of the Royal Hibernian Academy, John B. Yeats and Nathaniel Hone. The show was on view in John B. Yeats' studio in St. Stephen's Green and Lane was very impressed by the paintings. He bought some of Hone's work and commissioned Yeats to do a series of portraits, with the idea that one day they would form part of a collection of modern art for Dublin. He returned to London determined that he could use his talent to do something for Ireland![1]

In 1902 Lane toured Ireland to organise a Loan Exhibition of Old Masters to help the Royal Hibernian Academy, which was in financial straits. Although there were no women members in the R.H.A. (women were not admitted as members until the 1920's) it was women who saw to it that large parties of paying visitors attended the exhibition, and the unprecedented attendance figures ensured that the exhibition was a brilliant success.

In January 1903 the President of the Royal Hibernian Academy, spurred on by the success of the exhibition, wrote a letter to the papers in which he stated 'Art is in the air in Dublin just now'[2] and he went on to say that he advocated support for Hugh Lane's suggestion for a permanent Gallery of Modern Art in Dublin.

In 1904 Lane met the executors for the estate of J. Staats Forbes who were then arranging to sell the Forbes collection of continental art. He made a selection of one hundred and sixty works from those on sale from the collection and arranged that they would be sent to Dublin in the hope that they would be purchased for

the Gallery. The Forbes collection was exhibited in November 1904. The exhibition was titled 'An Exhibition of Pictures presented to the city of Dublin to form the nucleus of a Gallery of Modern Art, also pictures lent by the executors of the late Mr. J. Staats Forbes and others.' Part of Lane's preface to the catalogue read: 'The Corporation of Dublin has in every way shown its sympathy with the scheme; and it is greatly to be hoped that they will now help it in a practical manner by granting a small annual sum, which will enable us to have the collection open free to the public by day and in the evening. On this also will depend many of the most valuable gifts ... the small collection that I have formed myself will only be presented on the condition that certain steps are taken to place the "Gallery" on a sound basis.'[3]

Artists such as Sarah Purser, Sarah Cecilia Harrison, Constance Gore-Booth (Countess Markievicz), Clara Christian, Mrs. Ambrose McEvoy, Rose Barton, Estella Solomons, Mrs. Murray Robertson and Mildred Butler, were all involved. They donated their paintings as well as organising subscription groups to buy works for Dublin from the Forbes collection. Countess Markievicz set up the Ladies' Committee.[4] They were responsible for the mammoth task of co-ordinating all the various activities connected with the collection of subscriptions to purchase works. Lady Gregory gave the benefit of her tremendous organisational ability to this and every other venture connected with the Gallery. Lady Gregory by her enthusiasm and belief was one of the key factors sustaining Hugh Lane, to the very end, in his dream to establish a Gallery of Modern Art in Dublin.

In 1907 Dublin Corporation arranged for the acquisition of Clonmell House, Harcourt Street (now numbers 16 and 17) as a temporary location for the Gallery. After much renovation the first exhibition of Dublin's Collection of Modern Art opened on Monday 20th January 1908. The catalogue, the only illustrated catalogue of the collection ever printed, was compiled by the artist Sarah C. Harrison and sold for the sum of one shilling a copy. The exhibition of three hundred works, which included the contentious thirty-nine masterpieces that now travel between the National Gallery in London and the Hugh Lane Municipal Gallery, contained fifty works that were there solely through the efforts of women. These were either donations of their own work, or works they had raised the money to buy.

In 1913, when Hugh Lane was appointed Director of the National Gallery of Ireland, he retained his Directorship of the Municipal and appointed a woman, Ellen Duncan, as the first curator of the Modern Art Gallery.

Problems about the location of a permanent site for the Gallery caused Lane much heartache. His preferred sites on St. Stephen's Green and across the Liffey at the Halfpenny bridge (both sides with plans for the Gallery building designed by Lutyens) were rejected. Lane's disenchantment with the situation led him to remove the thirty-nine works that are still in dispute and these were loaned to the National Gallery in London. Later Lane made a will in London's favour, but after some consideration, he attempted to change this will by a codicil in which he wrote:

> 'This is a codicil to my last will to the effect that the group of pictures now at the London National Gallery, which I bequeathed to that institution, I now bequeath to the city of Dublin, providing that a suitable building is provided for them within five years of my death. The group of pictures I have lent to Belfast I give to the Municipal Gallery in Harcourt Street. If a building is provided within five years, the whole collection will be housed together. The sole trustee in this question is to be my aunt, Lady Gregory. She is to appoint any trustees she may think fit. I also wish that the pictures now on loan at this (National Gallery of Ireland) Gallery remain as my gift. HUGH LANE.'[5]

After his death, because his signature had not been witnessed, the codicil was not honoured, and no final arrangement has yet been reached regarding these works.

The problem of finding a permanent location for the Gallery continued until 1924, when the first meeting of the Friends of the National Collection of Ireland was held. This group, which has been responsible for the donation of numerous works to both the National Gallery and the Hugh Lane Municipal Gallery, was founded under the leadership of Sarah Purser. At their annual meeting in 1927, it was unanimously agreed that the Friends of the National Collection of Ireland would put their efforts into the final push needed to settle the question of a permanent location

for the Gallery. It was the efforts of Sarah Purser and Sarah Cecilia Harrison in particular that resulted in a public inquiry being held in Dublin on 20th June 1928 into 'the desirability or otherwise of erecting in Dublin a Gallery capable of housing the Dublin Municipal Collection of Modern Art and the pictures which Sir Hugh Lane bequeathed to Dublin by the inoperative codicil to his Will of the 3rd February 1915.'[6]

The findings were positive, and shortly afterwards it was Sarah Purser who suggested that the Georgian mansion, Charlemont House, in Parnell Square, which had recently been vacated by the Government, could be used as a Gallery of Modern Art. Her appeals to President Cosgrave were successful and in February 1929 her plan was adopted by the Government. At a special meeting in September 1929, President Cosgrave handed the keys of Charlemont House to Mr. Seamus Murphy, the Chairman of the Civic Commissioners, on a ninety-nine year lease to the city from the Government. The Collection had found its permanent home at last.

Lady Gregory, who made such a great contribution to the Arts in Ireland, both in literature and theatre, worked tirelessly from Hugh Lane's death until the end of her own life, trying to fulfil his last wish. The codicil has never been honoured, but the paintings are regularly loaned to Dublin by the London National Gallery. The present agreement will be renegotiated in 1993.

The present curator of the Gallery is a woman, Miss Eithne Waldron, and it is of special interest during this exhibition to note that of the five hundred and forty artists represented in the Municipal Modern Art Collection, one hundred and seventeen are women.

Dublin Corporation has continued to maintain and support the growth of the Gallery which is now officially named after its founder.

1. Lady Gregory, *Hugh Lane's Life and Achievement*, (1921).
2. Thomas Bodkin, *Hugh Lane and His Pictures*, (1956), p.7.
3. *Ibid.* p.12.
4. *The Municipal Gallery of Modern Art, Illustrated Catalogue* (1908).
5. Lady Gregory, *Case for the Return of Sir Hugh Lane's Pictures to Dublin*, (1926), pp.34-36.
6. Thomas Bodkin, *op. cit.*, p.65.

Art students and lady travellers

Irish women artists in France, 1870-1930

Julian Campbell

While a large percentage of the major Irish artists of the late nineteenth and early twentieth centuries (including Hone, Osborne and O'Conor), studied in Paris or Antwerp, others such as John and Jack B. Yeats, and William Orpen, received their training in Dublin and London. It could be argued, however, that nearly all of the important women artists of this period, particularly in the twentieth century, were students in Paris at some stage in their careers.[1] Some, such as Sarah Purser, went to Paris to learn a profession, portrait painting, while others, such as Beatrice Elvery and fellow students paid summer visits to the tolerant French studios; Helen Trevor settled in Paris in middle age and Eileen Gray went to Paris as a student and remained there for most of her long life. Others, such as Beatrice Gubbins, did not study in Paris, but were regular travellers on the Continent. A writer in *Studio* magazine in 1903 observed the increasing numbers of women students arriving in Paris to study, many attracted to the Académie Julian and Colarossi's, both of which had studios for women:

'That the life they lead there differs from that led by their male companions, both as regards its freedom and its strenuousness, goes without saying; but it is sufficiently Bohemian for the most enterprising feminine searcher after novelty ....'[2]

Yet the existence of girl students in Paris was nothing new; women had been present in the ateliers for the previous thirty years or so. Already in the 1860's Chaplin had opened an atelier for women. (In the same period in America William Morris Hunt had opened up his studio to forty women pupils). In the 1870's Couture took women students, while the rapidly-expanding Académie Julian opened an 'atelier des dames' in the Passage des Panoramas, A. S. Hartrick wrote of Julian's in 1880:

'During the autumn and winter months there were usually several hundred students of all ages, nationalities and conditions gathered there, the whole going to make such a very free republic that it remained constantly on the borders of anarchy.'[3]

He continues:

'Paris certainly was the centre of the art world in those days, and the best students from all nations tended to gravitate there, for it contained the men with the most vital ideas about art.'[4]

By the 1870's Paris was full of students from all over the world; from Britain and America, Scandinavia and Russia. Some Feminist writers[5] have suggested that women students were discriminated against, with over-crowded studios, the likelihood of being able to draw only and not to paint, infrequent visits by teachers, and so on, yet these were also inconveniences suffered by male students. And there were advantages shared by both men and women: the openness of Parisian ateliers to foreign students, the availability of models; access to eminent French painters, and subsequently to the Salon. Yet in one way was the position of women students on the Continent different from that of men: the Académie in Antwerp was only open to men, whereas Paris took both male and female students.

Hartrick studied with other male students, but he must have been aware that there was also a studio for women 'of all ages and nationalities'. It was here that Sarah Purser, aged thirty, arrived in 1878, the year of the Universal Exhibition in Paris. Her family had experienced financial difficulties, and she resolved to earn her living as a portrait-painter. In the 'atelier des dames' were girls of all nationalities, French, Scandinavian, Greek and Russian, included the Swiss girl Louise Breslau (with whom Sarah shared lodgings), and Russian princess Marie Bashkirtseff whose famous Journals give a lively picture of student life. Elizabeth Coxhead remarks that:

'At thirty she (Sarah) was the oldest and most serious of the band, with no time to waste on cerebral love affairs, and agonies of the soul, nor the raging jealousy that Marie felt for superior talent.'[6]

The professor Robert Fleury visited the studio only once a week. Marie complained of favouritism among the teachers, and resented the words used to describe the girls' work: 'charming', 'exquisite', 'delightful', and so on.[7] Yet Purser's *Le Petit Dejeuner,* painted in Paris in 1885, shows that she had already become a sensitive portraitist, had absorbed the French atmosphere, and the modern influences of Degas and others. One is struck by the spiritedness with which Sarah Purser went to Paris alone aged thirty and on £50 passed 'the hardest six months of her life'.[8] It is this independence and determination which was common to many Irish women students in Paris. It is significant perhaps that their dedication to their work precluded romantic attachments, and the majority of them remained unmarried.

Purser was by no means the oldest, nor indeed the first, Irish woman to study in Paris. Harriet Osborne O'Hagan was almost forty when, encouraged by George Sharp, her teacher in Dublin, she went to Paris in 1869. She studied with Cogniet, Fleury and Couture, probably attending his summer courses for women in the 1870's. (It is said that Harriet opened the first studio for women artists in Paris, but as seen above, this is unlikely.) Helen Mabel Trevor from County Down, a year younger than O'Hagan, also began to start to study art seriously in her forties, first at the Royal Academy in the late seventies, then in Paris c.1880, with Henner, Merson and Carolus-Duran. Mary Kate Benson studied with Lazare, and the watercolourists Mildred Anne Butler and Rose Barton with Henri Gervex. May Manning and perhaps Maria Webb were also students in Paris, and Sarah Purser re-visited the city during the eighties. (Later these three artists were important in encouraging younger girls to study in Paris.) Edith Somerville from Castletownshend studied in London and Düsseldorf (1882) before following her cousin Egerton Coghill to Paris 1884. Her family, alarmed at the thought of her living alone in Paris, at first provided her with a chaperone (her mother, brother, cousin and a friend). In fact Edith's life, in common with that of other Irish students in Paris, was hard-working rather than 'bohemian'; in the studio from 8.00 a.m. until evening. She was at Colarossi's 'ladylike studio'[9] near the Étoile in Spring 1885, then moved to La Grande Chaumière. Quickly, she put her illustrational skills into practice, making sketches at Dr. Pasteur's clinic, and later of studio life, and 'copyists' in the Louvre. In March 1887 she attended Delacluse's studio. Louisa MacCann from Belfast, a student of Robert Fleury, had a watercolour portrait accepted at the Salon.

A girl at the Académie Julian noted the practice among women students to head for Brittany and Normandy in Summer, to 'paint from nature'.[10] In this women were no different from male students who escaped the crowded, noisy ateliers for a season in the open air. The most popular artists' colonies were in Brittany (at Pont-Aven and Concarneau) and the Forest of Fontainbleau (at Barbizon and Grez-sur-Loing). Brittany was furthest from Paris, but its verdant, rolling landscape and dramatic coastline, its pretty villages and picturesque inhabitants in traditional costume, its own language and traditions, its religious festivals, made it all the more exotic. Studies of Breton peasants in traditional headdress, aprons and clogs appeared in innumerable canvases of artist from all over Europe and America. Helen Trevor and her sister Rose left Paris for Normany and Brittany in c.1881-82. They preferred Brittany to Normandy:

'We consider the Bretons a far more gracious race.'[11]

They stayed in Pont Aven (shortly after Thaddeus's visit, and before Osborne's arrival) and joined in with the younger girls at the student hotels:

'There are many artists here, and we have a grand night-class in the large Salon of the Hotel des Voyageurs next door, to which we go three times a week, and have models. Each one carries his or her easel and candle, and then we draw for places. I make pen-and-ink sketches, mostly of the people around me. I find them on the whole better fun than the models.'[12]

Among the other students at the Hotel du Voyageurs were Elizabeth Armstrong (later to marry Stanhope Forbes), and a group of talented Finnish women. Michael Jacobs writes (with some irony):

'It is unlikely that any of them were noticed at the time for their artistic abilities. Most of the growing population of women artists in Pont-Aven, when not engaged in making buttonholes, seem to have been regarded merely for their marriage material. They were mainly amateurs, people who sat down in front of the town's 'ready-made motifs', and started calmly and mechanically to reproduce them in watercolour.'[13]

The Finnish students visited Concarneau in 1883, as also did Trevor. The widely-admired French Realist Bastien-Lepage was also in Concarneau that year, but it is not known if their paths crossed. Her early Breton paintings of school-children and urchins are somewhat sentimental.

Maria Webb was in Brittany in the early 1880's. Her Breton landscapes and market scenes were shown at the Paris Salon in 1883, and at the Royal Hibernian Academy. Mary Benson and her sister Charlotte were painting in Belgium c.1890, then followed the well-worn route south to Brittany, staying at Quimperlé, representing Breton interiors and street scences. A number of Irish artists, including O'Meara, Barry and Coghill, were attracted to the artist's colony at Étaples in the Pas-de-Calais. Coghill's cousin Edith Somerville was here in 1889 and Sarah Cecilia Harrison in 1890. The latter moved west to Brittany; her studies of Breton girls and boys 'en plein air' have an unsentimental realism. Having spent six years in Italy 1883-89, studying the Old Masters and painting outdoor subjects, Helen Trevor and her sister returned to Paris, and re-entered Carolus Duran's atelier. Duran praised her work, but warned her against 'impressionistic' influences.[14] She and Rose re-visited Brittany in the early nineties, and spent the winter of 1894-95 in Concarneau. A considerable change had occurred since her first visit to Brittany: notably, the development of the Pont-Aven School under Gauguin. Trevor's studies of Breton widows in interiors are hardly 'impressionistic' when compared with Roderic O'Conor's experimental studies of Breton peasants at the same period. Nevertheless, her work has a new realism, and of all Irish artists in Brittany she was interested in the lives of the Bretons and in 'Celtic' traditions. In the twentieth century, Irish women continued to visit Brittany, for example May Guinness in 1910-11.

The Forest of Fontainbleau was only forty or so miles south of Paris, and Irish artists such as Nathaniel Hone had been in the artist's colonies of Barbizon and Marlotte since the 1850's. In the 1880's there was a large influx of Scandinavian women at Grez-sur-Loing (as at Pont-Aven). Michael Jacobs remarks of the Swedish women:

'They were all talented artists ... but they were never able fully to develop their talents, perhaps largely as a result of marrying the members of the colony.'[15]

Comparatively few Irish women were at Fontainebleau (Fig. 10). Only Katherine MacCausland became a long-term resident

Fig. 10 *Caroline Benedicks working at Grez,* 1880s. Photograph courtesy of Michael Jacobs.

at Grez, c.1890-1930, buying a house there and becoming friendly with other expatriate artists, American Frank Chadwick and his Swedish wife Emma Löwstadt (Fig. 11). By the twentieth century the great days of the colony were over, but foreigners continued to live there, including composer Frederick Delius from 1897-1934. County Cork artist Beatrice Gubbins was a visitor to Barbizon in 1902.

The turn of the century saw a further influx of Irish girl students in Paris. Helen Trevor had various studios in Montparnasse in the 1890's (Fig. 12), and was a regular exhibitor at the Paris Salon 1889-99. She died at her studio at Rue du Cherche Midi in 1900. In his autobiography *An Irish Portrait*, Paul Henry remembered 'the attractive Miss Gore-Booth'[16] at the Académie Julian off the Rue de Rennes (Constance Gore-Booth studied under Laurens in c.1897), and a chance meeting with Somerville and Ross in Montparnasse in c.1899 (Somerville had returned to Delacluse's for four months). Henry enrolled at Whistler's newly-opened Académie Carmen in c.1898, possibly contemporary with a group of girls from the Slade School, including Gwen John. 1900 was the year of the World Fair in Paris with colourful pavilions of

Fig. 11 *Frank Chadwick and Emma Löwstadt picnicking in the forest of Fontainebleau,* early 1890s. Photograph courtesy of Michael Jacobs.

art, design and industry along the Seine. Henry's future wife Grace Mitchell arrived from Brussels and studied with Delacluse. Also in Paris that year were two German students, Paula Modersohn-Becker and Clara Westhoff. (Paula, one of the most original artists of the period, died in childbirth aged only thirty one.) In 1902 the young Eileen Gray arrived in Paris, and soon established herself as a designer of furniture and rugs. She settled in Paris for the rest of her long life. Dorothy and Beatrice Elvery, Estella Solomons and Frances Beckett, students from the Metropolitan School of Art in Dublin arrived in Paris in Summer 1903, staying at a 'grim'[15] hotel in the Boulevard Montparnasse. They spent the mornings drawing from life at Colarossi's, and the afternoons exploring the city and visiting the Louvre and Luxembourg. Modersohn-Becker, a fellow-student at Colarossi's, complained:

'At the academy one paints almost without colour. The alpha and the omega are the "valeurs", everything else is secondary.'[17]

Fig. 12 *Helen Mabel Trevor in her Studio.* Photograph from H.M. Trevor, *Ramblings of an Artist,* courtesy of the National Library of Ireland.

19

Fig. 13 *Mary Swanzy, c.1918.* Photograph courtesy of Miss M. Tullow.

Beatrice Elvery called on sculptor John Hughes who was in Paris working on the Victoria monument, and he encouraged her to cut stone in Rodin's studio. (Rodin was assisted by a number of eminent girl students, notably Clara Westhoff, the beautiful but doomed Camille Claudel, and Gwen John [who remained in Paris for the rest of her life]). Mary Swanzy and May Guinness were summer visitors to Paris c.1905-07. Swanzy (Fig. 13), encouraged by May Manning and Hughes, studied with Delacluse, then at Colarossi's, and la Grande Chaumière where models were provided but there were no teachers. A possible spell in Matisse's atelier, and the sight of Picasso canvases in Gertrude Stein's house, opened her eyes to the Fauves and Cubists.

During the First World War, May Guinness served as a nurse in the French army (and was awarded the Croix de Guerre), and Eileen Gray worked as an ambulance driver. After the War Swanzy did relief work in Czechoslovakia, then travelled to the South Seas and America. Beatrice Gubbins nursed in England, and travelled extensively in Europe and North Africa in the 1920's. The ending of war meant a new generation of Irish women flocked to Paris. So many Irish girls studied with Cubist André Lhote: Evie Hone, Mainie Jellett, Grace Henry and May Guinness in the 1920's, Norah McGuinness and Harriet Kirkwood in the thirties, (up to Barbara Warren and Margaret Irwin in the fifties), that they were jokingly referred to in Dublin as 'Lhote's daughters'. Hone and Jellett had studied with Sickert in London and, encouraged by Meninsky, moved to Paris. They studied with Lhote in 1921, and then asked Gleizes if they could be his pupils, studying with him regularly 1922-31. Hone's Cubism is interesting in its Christian inspiration, and she and Jellett were important in their introduction of Cubism into Ireland (although Lhote's and Gleizes' Cubism was somewhat theoretical and schematic). Encouraged by Jellett, Norah McGuinness studied with Lhote, c.1930 with students of all nationalities, particularly Americans. As she recalled:

'Lhote taught one what to leave out.'[18]

He took McGuinness and other students on a summer course in Valence. She then returned to Paris for another couple of years.

Lhote's Irish students remembered him as a great teacher, with a considerable knowledge of art history. May Guinness also studied with Aglada and Van Dongen, while Nano Reid attended la Grand Chaumière, with its cosmopolitan atmosphere. During the 1920's Eileen Gray opened three work-shops and a gallery in Paris. The simplicity and modernity of her designs gained her an international reputation. She remained in Paris for seventy four years, until her death in 1976. Her death, and that of Mary Swanzy two years later, (both artists in their nineties) marked the end of an era, which had begun a hundred years before, when Sarah Purser went to Paris to study for six months.

In 1923, in an article entitled 'Women Artists in Ireland', Thomas McGreevy complained that women artists did not have the right to put the letters R.H.A. or A.R.H.A. after their names:

'But the Royal Hibernian Academy can apparently only titter at the idea of a woman artist .... Yet we have several women artists of account, Mrs. Paul Henry, Mrs. Harry Clarke, Mary Swanzy, Willhemina Geddes, Beatrice Elvery ... No less a person than the great Sarah Purser ... has been heard to say in answer to a compliment: "I wish I could paint like Miss Swanzy."'[19]

McGreevy concludes provocatively:

'The dissenting members of the board of the Royal Hibernian Academy might consider what the world will think if they persist in excluding women. It will think that it is because the women are better artists than themselves.'

In the late nineteenth century most women students were on the Continent as individuals. It was not really until the 1920's with Lhote's students that there was an identifiable 'school' of Irish women in France. In retrospect, it is clear that women artists, the majority of whom (such as Purser and Swanzy, Evie Hone and Jellett), were decisively influenced by modern French painting, have played a vital part in twentieth century Irish art.

1. For further information on Irish Women Artists in France, see Julian Campbell, *The Irish Impressionists,* exhibition catalogue, (1984); and Julian Campbell, *Irish Artists in France and Belgium 1850-1914,* (Ph.D. thesis, Trinity College, Dublin, 1980).
2. Clive Holland, *Studio,* vol. 30, (December 1903).
3. A. S. Hartrick, *A Painter's Pilgrimage through Fifty Years,* (London 1939), p.17.
4. *Ibid.,* p.144.
5. e.g. Germaine Greer, *The Obstacle Race,* (London 1979) chapter 16, 'The Nineteenth Century'.
6. Elizabeth Coxhead, *Daughters of Erin,* (London 1965). 1968 edition, p.89.
7. Quoted by Greer, *op. cit.,* pp. 313-4.
8. Coxhead, *op. cit.,* p.88.
9. Violet Powell, *The Irish Cousins,* (London 1970).
10. Isobel Field, *This Life I've Loved,* (London 1937).
11. Helen Mabel Trevor, *Ramblings of an Artist,* (London 1901) (selections from the letters of Helen Mabel Trevor to E. Halse), p.82.
12. *Ibid.,* p.96.
13. Michael Jacobs, *The Good and Simple Life;* (London 1985), p.71.

14. Trevor, *op. cit.*, p.109. Helen showed a sketch of light effects to Henner, who remarked: 'Maintenant, vous êtes dans la voie de ces imbeciles' (referring to the Impressionists).

15. Jacobs, *op. cit.*, p.35.

16. Paul Henry, *An Irish Portrait,* (London 1951), p.11.

17. Gillian Perry, *Paula Modersohn-Becker,* (London 1979), quoting letter from Paula to her husband-to-be Otto Modersohn, 29 Jan. 1900.

18. *Norah McGuinness retrospective exhibition.* Trinity College, Dublin, 1968. Introduction by Anne Crookshank.

19. Thomas McGreevy, 'Women Artists in Ireland', *Irish Independent,* 1923.

Women and the Arts and Crafts Revival in Ireland, c.1886-1930

Nicola Gordon Bowe

'I shall not talk of Art the elusive mistress of our dreams but of the friendly companion who ministers to us all our lives'.[1]

The words of Evelyn Gleeson, artist, suffragist and Gaelic Leaguer, were echoed by *The Studio* magazine[2] in its criticism of the fastidious dilettantism weakening the talents of many a good artist and craftsman. It cited improved teaching, the value of Home Art and Industries associations and the enterprise of provincial art school headmasters as hopeful signs. In Ireland, hopes were pinned on the activities of 'a few enthusiastic pioneers' who 'encourage one to hope that the reign of indifference and inertia is nearly over'.[3]

Ireland was not alone in Europe or America in witnessing an unprecedented increase in the number of women involved in the applied arts during the latter half of the nineteenth century and the early years of this. The importance of their rôle and function in the revival of design and craftsmanship during this period has only recently begun to be assessed.[4]

By the time the Arts and Crafts Society of Ireland held its first exhibition in 1895, the year after its foundation, a broad cross-section of the female population had become actively engaged in some aspect of artistic expression. This included lace-making, spinning and weaving, rug-making, embroidery and needlework. Through the auspices of the Irish Industries Association, The Congested Districts Board, the Irish branch of The Royal School of Art Needlework, a number of convents and zealously philanthropic ladies who instigated local industries with Arts and Crafts philosophies, a large number of hitherto uneducated girls and women all over the country found gainful relief from monotonously grinding poverty and bleak winters. From London, Constance Smedley wrote in 1907: 'Of all the ways in which women's activity has been demonstrated of late years, no more noble work has been accomplished than that which the Irish ladies have set out to do ... To give a list of those women of all stations who have done good work in the last twenty years would be to compile a dictionary of names'.[5]

By the turn of the century, bodies like Sir Horace Plunkett's Irish Agricultural Organization Society, Lady Aberdeen's Irish Industries Associations, Mrs. Hart's Donegal Industrial Fund, The Gaelic League and the Government Department of Agriculture and Technical Instruction at the Metropolitan School of Art in Dublin, as well as privately run classes like Mrs. Vere O'Brien's in Co. Clare, were attracting more affluent young women. Until William Orpen joined the staff of the Metropolitan School as a visiting lecturer in 1906, young ladies were as likely to attend the Royal Hibernian Academy Schools to study painting, if they did not go abroad to London or Paris. Thereafter, the School attracted those who wanted the best available fine art training in drawing and painting (Orpen), modelling (Oliver Sheppard), metalwork and enamelling (Oswald Reeves), stained glass (A.E. Child) and design (Alice Jacob). They could also train to become teachers. What is interesting is how many of them worked proficiently in a variety of media.

By 1900 the School had been removed from the control of South Kensington[6] and placed under the enlightened administration of T.P. Gill, the Secretary, and Horace Plunkett, the Vice President of the Department of Agriculture and Technical Instruction and the experienced directorship of James Brenan. There was a strong Morris-inspired Arts and Crafts legacy from South Kensington School of Design through Walter Crane (its Principal from 1898) and W.R. Lethaby, its Professor of Design from 1900. This resulted in a commitment to 'elevate the public taste and cultivate the faculty of appreciating beautiful work; to train teachers who will maintain a high standard in the schools in other cities and towns; and to produce designers in many branches of applied art and manufacturers in which artistic skill may find scope'.[7] At the same time it was to be a national School of Art, expressing specifically Irish preoccupations and traditions in design and craftsmanship. The Department continued the School's tradition of funding talented students who could not enter the School without scholarships. A pattern emerged whereby the day students were predominantly young women whose parents could afford the fees; most of the others were on scholarships, whereas more than half the students were part time with a large proportion of these male, attending at night after a day's work (Fig. 14).

Fig. 14 *Students at the Metropolitan School of Art, Dublin, c.1908.*
Back row (left to right): Michael Healy, Albert Power, Kathleen Fox, Dora K. Allen; Middle row: G. Scott, M. Ross, Norah Kelly, Jennie Fitzmorris; Front row: Francis Bowe, U. Duncan and Margaret Crilley. Photograph courtesy of Susanna Pym.

By 1916 the School could offer a tempting array of subjects: painting, sculpture, architecture, engraving, lithography, poster designing, writing and illuminating, book illustration, decorative painting, stained glass designing and painting, metalwork and enamelling, wood carving, embroidery, lace and crochet work, leatherwork.[8] Where necessary, the best possible teachers had been invited over from England to establish a new generation of native craftsmen and women. Thus, A.E. Child arrived in 1901 recommended by Christopher Whall, the father of the Arts and Crafts stained glass revival.[9] In 1903 Oswald Reeves arrived from the studio of Alexander Fisher, the hugely influential Arts and Crafts enamellist. It was in these two areas, apart from lace and needlework, that the (mostly female) students were to excel, soon competing favourably against schools in Britain in the annual Board of Education Competition held in London and judged by the stars of the English Arts and Crafts movement, and in the many exhibitions which abounded in Europe before the First World War, culminating in the 1914 Exposition des Arts Décoratifs de Grande Bretagne et d'Irlande, held in the Louvre.[10] Indeed, the years from 1901-23 became the golden years of the School, recapturing some of the eminence it had known in the eighteenth century. First there was Alice Jacob, a brilliant former student of the School at the end of the nineteenth century, whose designs for textiles were always exemplary and who became the influential Head of Design until her death in 1921, and Phoebe Traquair, of the same generation, illuminator, embroideress and enamellist, who became a key figure in the Edinburgh Arts and Crafts movement, but still exhibited in her native Dublin.[11] Then, came the eminently versatile sculptress, designer and later painter, her niece Beatrice Elvery, the enamellist and painter Kathleen Fox, the enamellists, Dora Allen (who married Oswald Reeves), Norah O'Kelly, Eleanor Kelly and Daisy O'Keefe among others, and in stained glass, Ethel Rhind (also mosaic), Kathleen Quigly (also enamels) and Catherine O'Brien.

There is ample evidence that the proportion of women working in these areas soon outweighed the men. Through the popularization of William Morris's idealistic Socialist principles, it had become acceptable, even fashionable for women to seek artistic fulfilment. In Ireland the surge of nationalism (which culminated in the founding of the Free State) was even stronger than the suffragism which prevailed elsewhere.[12]

Evelyn Gleeson, a cousin of T.P. Gill, returned to Dublin from London in 1902, imbued with the spirit of nationalism through her membership of the Gaelic League and Yeats' Irish Literary Club, and suffragism through the Pioneer Club. Her Morris-inspired ideologies ('A wish to find work for Irish hands in the making of beautiful things' which 'of course means materials honest and true and the application to them of deftness of hand, brightness of colour and cleverness of design'[13]) were supported by Elizabeth and Lily Yeats, whose brother, W.B., had fuelled

23

them with a heady mixture of Ruskin, Morris, Nietzsche, Marx and his own literary genius.[14] Evelyn Gleeson set up a craft industry with lady friends and relations as well as a dozen deliberately untrained girls in Dundrum, Co. Dublin, in a house called Runnymede, which she renamed Dun Emer after the wife of Cuchulain 'famed for her skills in embroidery and all house-wifery arts'.[15] Throughout the Arts and Crafts movement in Ireland, there was a continual attempt to revive those industries for which often legendary Celtic forebears had been renowned. There they learned Irish, traditional music, weaving and rug-making, and later bookbinding and enamelling (Fig. 15). From Lily Yeats, who had spent six unhappy years embroidering for May Morris in Hammersmith, they learnt embroidery and with Elizabeth Yeats they studied painting, which she had taught in London and on which she had published three books. In 1903, encouraged by Emery Walker, Elizabeth took a course at the Women's Printing Association in London and set up a printing press, first producing books by her brother and his friends and *Broadsheets* illustrated by her other brother Jack and Pamela Colman-Smith under the Dun Emer imprint; then, after the schism with Evelyn Gleeson, and the establishment of the Cuala Industries by the two sisters in 1908, under the Cuala imprint she produced Jack Yeats' monthly *Broadsides* and many bookplates, posters and

Fig. 15 *Evelyn Gleeson playing the harp at Dun Emer c.1905.*
Photograph courtesy of the National College of Art and Design.

ephemera, some designed by his wife Mary Cottenham Yeats.[16] In 1909 Elizabeth Yeats designed Health and Wealth stamps for the Women's National Health Association of Ireland, one of Lady Aberdeen's many organizations aimed at stamping out tuberculosis in Ireland.[17]

Women of all classes were encouraged and lured into activity during Lady Aberdeen's two terms of office as Vicereine (1886 and 1905-15). She, more than anyone, was indefatigable in her attempts to improve the health, wealth and happiness of the Irish race. In 1886 she had set up the Irish Industries Association in Dublin after the success of the Irish exhibit at the Edinburgh Exhibition of 1886. In 1887 she took over the Irish Lace Depot and started radically improving sales facilities through non-profit making concerns. She had soon galvanized distressed gentlewomen, uneducated young girls, committed suffragists, country women and art students. Next, she set up a Depot specializing in lace in London, after the success of the 1888 Women's Art and Industries section of The Irish Exhibition at Olympia. She reached her apogee with the Irish Village at the 1893 World Columbian Exhibition in Chicago, where she selected forty girls to sell and demonstrate lace making and netted £50,000.

Encouraged by such success, Lord Mayo and a group of colleagues set up the Arts and Crafts Society of Ireland the following year. Its objectives were clear and firmly based on those of its English predecessor (founded seven years earlier):

'To promote and improve the practice of the Artistic Handicrafts in Ireland — and of all the work of an ornamental and decorative character. The Society hopes to be able to develop much natural talent which is now unused or misdirected — and in various ways to aid Irish Craftsmen in regaining for their work the high repute it once possessed for excellence of workmanship and artistic taste'.[18]

Its first exhibition was preceded by a course of lectures 'descriptive of the various examples of art and handicraftsmanship in the Science and Art Museum' (opposite the School of Art) to encourage the collection to be 'more interesting and useful to Dublin handicraftsmen'. It opened in the Royal University Buildings (a legacy of the 1865 International Exhibition) and was divided into three sections: contemporary Irish, retrospective Irish craftsmanship and an exemplary English Arts and Crafts loan section. It was hoped the quality of the very best eighteenth century Irish and contemporary English would inspire a new race of Irish craftworkers. Notable among Irish women exhibiting were Alice Jacob, Edith Somerville, Lily Yeats, Phoebe Traquair, as well as Mrs. Vere O'Brien and her Lace School and Clare Embroidery, Mrs. Hart and her Donegal House Industries and the girls of the Royal School of Art Needlework. Even at this early stage the dual pitfalls of pictorial rather than decorative ornamentation, and a 'slavish reversion to ancient forms'[19] and the inevitable sentimental regard for Celtic interlaced pattern were forecast by George Coffey's lecture on *The Use and Abuse of Celtic Ornament.*

The second exhibition in 1899 followed lectures, pamphlets,

museum tours and practical demonstrations, Lady Lieutenant Cadogan's 1897 Textile Exhibition and a representation to the Inaugural Exhibition at the Glasgow People's Palace in 1898. Apart from an increase in lace, embroidery, needlework and crochet exhibits, new contributors included Alice Shaw's impressive Terenure Carving Class, Lady Castlerosse's Killarney School of Arts and Crafts and Kathleen Scott's woodcarving industry in Bray. By the time the third exhibition was held in 1904, the Society had sent work to the 1901 Glasgow International Exhibition, the 1902 Cork International Exhibition and the 1904 World's Fair at St. Louis.

It now had the added support of the Department of Agriculture and Technical Instruction and the reconstituted Metropolitan School of Art, as well as the annual Art Industries exhibitions at the Royal Dublin Society. A.E. Child and Oswald Reeves were installed and, equally important, in 1903 Sarah Purser had, with the advice of Christopher Whall and Edward Martyn, set up her stained glass cooperative workshop, An Túr Gloine (The Tower of Glass) in Dublin to revive the most demoralized art form in Ireland.[20] This was to be the most successful and long-lasting venture of the Irish Arts and Crafts movement. She shared the ideals of Evelyn Gleeson's Dun Emer Guild, set up the previous year: 'Each window is the work of one artist who makes the sketch and cartoon and selects and paints every morsel of glass him or herself'.[21] She arranged with T.P. Gill that A.E. Child should be the manager and they would select native artists trained by him in the School of Art. The active shareholders in this enlightened enterprise were to be devoted to enhancing the nature of the glass and the strength of their designs by the use of leading and to try and combine the former Celtic glories of metalwork, illumination, jewellery and sculpture. Although she did little designing for the studio, she was 'its principal commercial traveller, never lost an opportunity of pushing her artists, and on a railway journey would choose a carriage already occupied by a minister of religion, produce her pamphlets, and urge upon him the desirability of having artist-designed Irish stained glass in his church'.[22]

Beatrice Elvery, her first female recruit (in 1904), exhibited sculpture at the Arts and Crafts exhibition. Other new female exhibitors included Gwendolen Herbert of the Irish Art Companions (whose plaster models emulated eighteen century plasterwork), Mrs. Montgomery's Fivemiletown Metal Industry from Co. Tyrone and Sophia St. John Whitty and Kathleen Scott's accomplished Bray Art Furniture Industry. The show was much smaller, purposefully selective and predominantly Irish. The Committee called for 'more life and individuality in design' and 'the application of original thought to the vital element of design', reminding craftworkers, 'You do not live in the times of Brian Boru, but of Mr Edison. Recollect that the decorative artist has primarily to decorate objects of utility'.[23]

Back in Ireland by 1907, Lady Aberdeen boosted the lace industry with her Viceregal Lace Ball and there was an applied artwork sub-section in the Home Industries Section of the enormous Irish International Exhibition held in Herbert Park that

THE LITTLE MAN HAD BECOME TRANSFORMED INTO A VERY BEAUTIFUL AND GIGANTIC FIGURE

Fig. 16 Illustration by Beatrice Elvery from Violet Russell's *Heroes of The Dawn* (1913).

year. The most important new craftswomen were Catherine O'Brien and Ethel Rhind who joined An Túr Gloine in 1906 and 1908 respectively, Kathleen Fox and Dora Allen from the Dublin School of Art. By now the School was the pride and joy of the Department, so it was felt the fourth exhibition in 1910 could be still more selective, that the most skilled workers should become members of the newly formed Guild of Irish Art Workers and the exhibition should travel to Cork and Belfast. Distinctive artistic personalities were emerging (Fig. 16), rather than collective industries with beneficent patronesses. Nan Holland and Frances Burroughs joined the ranks of praise-worthy lady enamellists; Rosamond Praeger and Wilhelmina Geddes exhibited from Belfast, hitherto represented by Eva McKee and Edith McDermott of The Irish Decorative Art Association; Mia Cranwill, trained in Manchester, began showing skilled metalwork and enamels.

Oswald Reeves reviewed the fifth exhibition in 1917 and noted the independent character of the Irish movement where 'the call has not come from creative masters' but the artists here have had to 'observe the principles of true craftsmanship and ... find their own expression'.[24] Thomas Bodkin thought the sixth exhibition in 1921 was 'the best the Society has ever organized'.[25] The

THE ARTS AND CRAFTS SOCIETY OF IRELAND
SIXTH EXHIBITION
CATALOGUE PRICE ONE SHILLING

Fig. 17 *Cover of the sixth Exhibition of the Irish Arts and Crafts Society, 1921*
by Wilhelmina Geddes. Reproduction courtesy of the Irish Society of Design
and Craftwork.

cover of the catalogue featured a linocut by Wilhelmina Geddes,
who had by now emerged as the most powerful artist and designer
of the period (Fig. 17). Stephen Gwynn wrote how she, 'like so
many women artists, matured quickly, and even her early work
has in its details the strong expressive drawing, the power of
simplifying without loss of meaning'.[26] A newspaper article [27]
at this time pointed out how little acclaim women artists in Ireland
were given yet, despite enlightened attitudes in some political and
academic circles — 'Yet we have several women artists of account'.
Among these, Grace Henry, Margaret Clarke, Mary Swanzy, Sarah
Purser and Wilhelmina Geddes 'who is producing the finest, the
most sincerely, passionately religious stained glass of our time ...
Miss Elvery, whose pictures and windows everyone knows, and
whose sculptured work is quite remarkable ... Miss Rhind, Miss
O'Brien and Miss Quigly in stained glass all of whom have to
work with the knowledge that a man, no matter how inferior
to theirs his work may be, stands a better chance of recognition
(and of the increased orders that recognition brings) merely because
he is a man'.

Although she continued to produce superlative work until her
death thirty later, Geddes' departure to England in 1925 marks
the swan song of the movement and the last exhibition of the
Society's true Arts and Crafts generation of craftsmen and women.
The great Aonach Tailteann fairs of 1922 and 1924,[28] reviving
the ancient festivities honouring Queen Tailte of the Firbolgs in
celebration of the new Free State, had substantial Arts and Crafts
exhibitions. By the 1932 fair, a number of the older craftswomen
were teaching, had joined The United Irishwomen or established
small craft workshops. A new generation was surfacing and the
early zeal had evaporated. The vocation which the painter Evie
Hone was to find in stained glass a few years later is beyond the
scope of this essay.

1. Unpublished, undated manuscript, Gleeson papers, private collection.
2. *The Studio,* introduction to General Index, vols. 1-42, 1893-1908, (London 1909).
3. *The Studio,* vol. 23, (1901), p.122.
4. See Elizabeth Coxhead, *Daughters of Erin,* (London 1962); Ada Longfield, *Guide to the Collection of Lace,* National Museum of Ireland, Dublin (1970); Liam Miller, *The Dun Emer Press, later the Cuala Press,* (Dublin 1973); William Murphy, *Prodigal Father,* (New York 1978); Anthea Callen, *Angel in the Studio: Women in the Arts and Crafts Movement 1870-1914,* (London 1979); Jeanne Sheehy, *The Celtic Revival: The Rediscovery of Ireland's Past,* (London 1980); Nicola Gordon Bowe, *Irish Stained Glass,* The Arts Council, (Dublin 1983); Brian de Breffny (ed.), *A Cultural Cyclopaedia of Ireland,* (London 1983); Sheila Pim, 'Dun Emer — An Unrecorded Chapter in the Life of Augustine Henry, *Moorea,* vol. 3, (1984); Paul Larmor, 'The Dun Emer Guild', *Irish Arts Review,* vol. I, no. 4, (1984); John Turpin, 'The Metropolitan School of Art', *Dublin Historical Record,* vol. 37, no. 2, (March 1984); vol. 38, no. 2, (March 1985); Nellie Ó Cleirigh, *Carrickmacross Lace,* (Mountrath and London 1985); Jane Houston-Almquist, *Mountmellick Work,* (Mountrath and London 1985); Nicola Gordon Bowe, 'The Arts and Crafts Society of Ireland (1894-1925) with particular reference to Harry Clarke' in *Aspects of British Design 1870-1930,* The Journal of The Decorative Arts Society, no. 9, (1985); Nicola Gordon Bowe, *The Dublin Arts and Crafts Movement 1885-1930,* exhibition catalogue, (Edinburgh 1985); Peter Cormack, *Women Stained Glass Artists of the Arts and Crafts Movement,* William Morris Gallery, London (1986).
5. 'What Women have Done For Ireland' in 'The Work of the Women's World' (ed. Constance Smedley), *The World's Work,* vol. 19, no. 54, (1907), pp.635-43.
6. See 'Educational Policy, The Department of Agriculture and Technical Instruction' and 'Art Instruction in Ireland', *Ireland Industrial and Agricultural,* (Dublin 1902), pp.146-43, pp.289-93.
7. Headmaster's Report, Dublin Metropolitan School of Art, 1902.
8. *The Studio,* vol. 68, (1916), pp.126-28.
9. See Peter Cormack, *Christopher Whall: Arts and Crafts Stained Glass Worker,* William Morris Gallery, London, (1980).
10. See Nicola Gordon Bowe, *The Life and Work of Harry Clarke 1889-1931,* Ph.D. thesis, Dublin University (1982), chapter I.
11. See Elizabeth S. Cumming, *Arts and Crafts in Edinburgh 1880-1930,* exhibition catalogue, Edinburgh (1985); unpublished Ph.D. thesis, Edinburgh University (1986).
12. See James O. Hannay, 'The Wonderful Growth of the Gaelic League', *The World's Work, op. cit.,* pp.604-08.
13. Prospectus for The Dun Emer Guild (1903).
14. W.B. Yeats had written in 1901 on 'Ireland and the Arts' in *The United Irishman:* 'I would have Ireland recreate the ancient arts ... as they were understood when they moved a whole people, not a few people who have grown up in a leisured class and made this understanding their business'.
15. Sheila Pim, *op. cit.,* p.37.
16. See Hilary Pyle, *Jack B. Yeats,* (London 1970), William Murphy, *op. cit.* and Liam Miller, *op. cit.*
17. See Lady Aberdeen's short-lived Journal, *Sláinte,* vols. 1-3, 1909-11.
18. First Journal and Proceedings of the Arts and Crafts Society of Ireland, (Dublin 1896).

19. Sir John O'Connell in his Foreword to the catalogue of the Society's fifth exhibition, (1917).
20. See Robert Elliott, *Art and Ireland*, (Dublin 1906), chapters 1 and 9.
21. Quoted in the 25th Anniversary booklet of An Túr Gloine, (1928).
22. Elizabeth Coxhead, *op. cit.*, p.142.
23. Quoted in the fourth and final Report, Journal and Proceedings of the Society, (Dublin 1906), pp.258-60 and pp.278-87.
24. P.O. Reeves, Irish Arts and Crafts, *The Studio*, vol. 72, (1917), pp.15-22; *The Studio* had commented in 1908 on the unique "reserve and dignity" and restrained subordination of detail in the Irish enamels.
25. *The Studio*, vol. 82, (1921), p.258.
26. Stephen Gwynn, 'The Art of Miss W.M. Geddes', *The Studio*, vol. 82, (1921), pp.257-61.
27. *The Irish Independent*, December 4, 1922.
28. See T.H. Nally, *The Origin, History and Ancient Associations of Aonach Tailteann*, (Dublin 1922).

Irish women artists as natural history illustrators

E. Charles Nelson

The illustration of animals and plants for scientific purposes requires great skill, and thus the best botanical and zoological art is among the finest of any genre. It involves not just the craft of composition, an unerring choice of colours and superb technique, but also the most precise observation of the subject. 'Artistic licence' has no place in scientific illustration because the purpose is to record faithfully the living world.

The most accomplished botanical paintings — as for example those of the Irish-born illustrator William Kilburn — and the best zoological art cannot be excelled, even by modern colour photography, because of the immense amount of detail, both life-

Fig. 18 Ellen Hutchins, *Polysiphonia*. Photograph courtesy of the Sheffield City Museum.

size and magnified, that can be incorporated into each painting. Information of particular importance can be subtly highlighted without falsifying the subject; indeed more can be accomplished within an accurately coloured drawing than in long paragraphs of prose accompanied by colour photographs.

These remarks may seem to over-state the importance of natural history illustration but that is not so. For centuries natural historians have relied heavily on paintings and drawings in their work of cataloguing and classifying plants and animals.

Irish women artists have contributed quietly to the corpus of natural history artwork; most of their work has never been exhibited and the majority has not been published.

In the eighteenth century only a few artists worked within this field, yet Susanna Drury's record of the Giant's Causeway in County Antrim was among the most significant natural history illustrations published, until William Kilburn's botanical work in the 1780's. Undoubtedly many ladies painted birds, butterflies and flowers — just to pass time — but such paintings rarely had a truly scientific purpose. Even Mary Delany's exquisite 'paper mosaicks' were done for fun.

At the beginning of the nineteenth century, natural history was developing rapidly and an immense amount of time and energy was spent in cataloguing and naming creatures. When organisms were difficult to preserve, drawings were made as substitutes. Ellen Hutchins drew and painted the seaweeds of Bantry Bay with such skill that her work (Fig. 18) was published in a number of contemporary botanical books. She was perhaps the first Irish woman to contribute illustrations to scientific textbooks, although the Fitton sisters were active at the same time and probably prepared the plates that were published in their botanical book. In the mid-1800's Mrs Mary Ward, a skilful microscopist, produced her own detailed drawings and published these in a series of natural history books. Frequently brothers and sisters co-operated in scientific work, writing, collecting and drawing; for example Anne and Mary Ball worked with their brother Robert.

At this period many Irish emigrants had become established in new homes overseas, and some of the women undertook the task of recording the flora and fauna of these distant lands. Often their paintings complemented preserved specimens of plants and animals. Marianne Fannin in Natal and Martha King in New Zealand were among the first, and their artwork was used by scientists to assist in the classification and naming of new plants and animals; coloured paintings were still one of the best methods for recording at that time before colour photograph was invented.

While many ladies continued to fill their idle moments by painting, the latter decades of the nineteenth century saw the arrival of the professional woman artist, employed specifically to paint plants and animals. The Botanic Gardens in Dublin engaged and paid three women artists between 1880 and 1920, and wealthy private gardeners also commissioned artists. The work of, for example, Miss Travers and Miss Tisdall which was published in horticultural periodicals during the 1880's and 1890's was done at the behest of W.E. Gumbleton of Cobh, Alice Jacob produced drawings for a gardening manual, Gertrude Hartland painted daffodils for her uncle's bulb catalogues, and early this century Rosamond Praeger prepared several hundred pen-and-ink drawings for her brother's books on botany.

It would be wrong to dismiss the women who painted for leisure as not contributing to the art of natural history. The Plunkett sisters, Lydia Shackleton, Lady Blake and Lady Cuffe all had opportunities to travel and they set out to depict plants and animals accurately — their watercolours are scientific records of the fauna and flora of the lands that they visited. But cameras soon replaced the paintbrushes as essential equipment for the travelling naturalist.

The skill of the scientific illustrator is much in demand today, and the techniques of the craft have not changed — very careful observation is the basic essential. As the paintings of modern natural history artists demonstrate, theirs is still the finest art.

Mainie Jellett and Modernism

Bruce Arnold

Mainie Jellett was the single greatest force for change in art in Ireland between the two world wars. She bestrode those decades as a giant figure. She defined an aesthetic of abstraction and evolved its association with Christian art. She explained tirelessly the importance of art in the home, the factory, the office. She entered the minds of those who listened to her with a penetration that was exhausting and stimulating at the same time. And she was relentlessly intrusive. She never gave up her apostacy. Lectures, radio talks, letters to the papers, introductions to exhibitions, public meetings to promote art, teaching at every age level, and an endless round of discussions with friends, pupils, acquaintances, critics, enemies, colleagues, were the hallmark of her daily life.

She undoubtedly gained authority for this influence on others from her familiarity with what was then the centre of the art world, Paris. Pupil of two of its leading modernists, she moved in their circle, and exhibited with them and their peers on a regular basis during the 1920's and beyond. To this documentary evidence of her significance may be added the visible evidence, in her early works, of her stature and range. A ceaseless process went on in her art through more than two decades, with the extension of ideas always contained within an overall integrity.

The influence of this, both on men and women painters, was remarkable; and it stretched from those who worked in the same Cubist mode, to realists like Gerard Dillon and, in his early years, Louis le Brocquy.

She evolved her own art through a number of different phases. The most obvious of these were the earliest. From childhood drawings and paintings she passed on to various Dublin teachers, including Miss Manning, and culminating in a brief period of study under William Orpen at the Metropolitan School of Art. She then went to London, to the Westminster School, where her teachers included Walter Sickert and Walter Bayes.

In 1921 she went to Paris and became a pupil of André Lhote, her first taste of Cubism. And then, in 1922, she became Albert Gleizes' pupil, together with her friend, Evie Hone, and moved into the realm of pure abstract painting.

All of this she recounted herself in published documents about her work, talking of three 'major revolutions' in her art.[1]

These revolutions, or phases, are obvious to anyone familiar with Mainie Jellett's art. Her exquisite, Sickert-period oils, watercolours and drawings draw from those people who are unsympathetic with abstract art sighs of regret. Why did she not stick with such eloquence of statement, such brilliance of colour, such an impeccably sure touch with pencil, they ask. And the question has been echoed by later generations whose basic attitude to abstract is quite different — being essentially sympathetic — but who fail to see the profundity or greatness contained in what Mainie Jellett did.

Part of the responsibility for this lies with the artist herself. Busy and persistent as she was in making known her ideas to pupils and friends, she ran up against a number of different and conflicting problems. She faced indifference and hostility from the early twenties on. Those who sided with her were few enough. Those who both sided with her, and understood and worked out her theories and practices as a painter, far fewer still. Indeed, it is my considered judgement that not even her closest friend, Evie Hone, fully understood the principles of abstract painting learned from Gleizes and developed and refined in Dublin during the period 1922-32, and her bewilderment — together with her dependence on Mainie to elucidate difficulties — is expressed in some of her letters. Mainie herself left only rudimentary published ideas.

She has been the victim also of the judgments of art history, on Cubism, and these have been unsympathetic to its purest manifestations. The kind of rigour which, in the mid-twenties, conformed with the hungering after new ideas, and the pushing forward of frontiers of understanding, has been replaced by a conveniently foreshortened interpretation of the period, and a reduction of its chief protagonists to a very short list of major names.

For these reasons the major part of this essay is in the nature of a challenge about current interpretations of Cubism, with some attempt to define its origins and its subsequent development, as applied to Mainie Jellett and her generation. She was fighting for new principles in art on two fronts. The first of these was international, in solidarity with Gleizes and others of his followers. The second was domestic, where she wanted to give an artistic ruthlessness to the new Independent Ireland of which she could have been regarded as an uncomfortable part, since she came from the Protestant, Ascendancy, Unionist tradition. She did not feel that way. Unlike her parents, she was a child of the new Ireland, but antagonistic towards any puerile creation of neo-Celtic idiom, believing that Ireland should reach out towards France and other European countries where art was involved with politics and society.

The passion with which she felt these responsibilities, coupled with the authority deriving from her intellect and artistic experiences, made her the natural leader of a whole group of artists active between the two world wars, who were in the process of rejecting traditional attitudes which derived from Edwardian, and essentially British, teaching.

As I have said, Mainie Jellett went to Paris in 1921 to continue her study of art in what she was later to describe as the second and third 'revolutions' in her work, style and ideas. She had left Walter Sickert's Art School in London. She was heading for André Lhote's Studio in Paris. Sickert, 'in the direct line of French impressionist painting was an excellent stepping stone' to her first encounter with modern French art. And, like students from all over Europe and America, she was responding to the irresistible magnetism of the Cubists.

She arrived there at the beginning of February, and enrolled with André Lhote, who was then living at 30 bis Rue Boulard, Paris, where he ran a teaching academy. She took rooms at 56 Rue Vavin, in the Sixième Arrondissement.

The first sketch book of the Paris period is dated February 1921, and contains a series of male and female nude studies, a number of them squared up for paintings which she completed during the summer of that year.

In Mainie Jellett's own words, 'Lhote's Academy at that time was the most advanced of the public academies and, I would say, far the best'. His class and his teaching followed traditional art academy practice. Lhote would himself pose the model on Monday morning of each week, and the class lasted from nine o'clock until noon. A pencil study was the work for the first day, and this was then 'worked on during the afternoon at home with the idea of making it into a composition', suggested by the pose 'or by the geometric rhythmic lines derived from the main directions of movement in the nude model'. These rhythmic lines dominate the drawings in her first sketch book.

On Tuesday the squared-up drawing was transferred to canvas, and work continued on this until Friday, 'when Lhote came for the 'correction', which lasted the whole morning. Usually, the whole class stopped work and listened to the 'correction' of the work of each student, in this way learning by the faults of others, as well as by their own.'

Lhote would himself work on student paintings, moderate success being indicated by slight touches to the canvas here and there. He would also do his own work. He was teaching Cubism. And Cubism was very much in vogue. Art students were travelling to Paris from everywhere, in order to join the Modern Movement, and Lhote had a strong Scandinavian following, as well as Russian and American pupils, though few from France.

Mainie Jellett's view was that his teaching stood halfway between 'the extreme Cubism of Gleizes and official academic teaching and impressionist ideals'. The student started from the model. But the requirement was for the simplification of the figure into cubes, cylinders and cones, and then its integration into a composition which drew its geometric pattern from the main rhythmic movements of the model. Landscape was 'build on', and Lhote sent his pupils to the Louvre and elsewhere to study the Old Masters, learning from them how this problem of integration was solved.

'Lhote's interpretation of the work of the Old Masters was a revelation to us; he opened up vast vistas and made one understand and appreciate their work with a fresh eye ...'

In her sketch books the influence of Lhote is clearly apparent; angular, cross-hatched drawings of a precise and aggressive kind reveal a deliberate liberation from the softer and more conventional work she had been doing in Ireland and then in England in preparation for this new departure.

The sketch books contain diagrams about composition, listings of colours and colour relationships, and occasional names of artists. These include both Old Masters, such as Sassetta and Signorelli, Poussin and El Greco, as well as Renoir, one of whose 'Baigneuses' is the subject of several pencil studies, as are works by Cezanne. 'The student was made to work with a very strong three-dimensional sense. The different sections of the model's body were simplified into cylinders and cubes highly modelled and moving according to contrasting rhythms. A continual contrast of straight lines to curved lines and hot colours to cold colours, light to dark, was insisted upon throughout the whole work. Simple colour harmonies were used and the colour composition and organisation were stressed in conjunction with the formal construction. Lhote made his pupils base their work on natural forms, but these forms were used as a basis for further development and not as an end in themselves.'

In that summer she returned to Dublin, and then travelled with her parents and sisters on holiday to Scotland. She worked a great deal there, her watercolours revealing a sharp development in style, with the same aggressive, angular quality applied to trees, haystacks and cattle, as is to be seen in the Lhote sketch book studies, and in the paintings in oil which derived from that first period of study under André Lhote. They are less 'attractive'; the faithful realism which one associates with Sickert and his pupils, and which had an appealing softness in many works by Mainie Jellett at this time, is replaced with an attack which is aggressively concerned with the means of communications rather than with their end.

In the autumn she returned. She was later to refer to her own decision 'to go further into the extreme abstraction of Cubism', in part because she believed Lhote's ideas were 'a compromise'. But she did not make the move immediately. Throughout 1921 and 1922 she followed, at least some of the time, the rhythmic, realistic Cubism and André Lhote, and she undoubtedly had great respect for him. 'He opened our minds to the vast realm of research and riches in the Old Masters and showed us clearly how his teaching and ideals followed logically the living tradition based on permanent truths which are the heritage of all great art, but which seek re-expression in each new cycle of art movement.'

Mainie remained loyal to Lhote throughout her life, the words above being part of a lecture entitled 'André Lhote', given in Dublin in 1940. She was one of a number of Irish artists who studied at his academy in the 1920's, the majority of whom remained in the Lhote mode. But for Mainie herself, Cubism, the excitement and challenge of which pervaded Paris during the early twenties, attracting vast numbers of students, was already exercising a more austere influence than was represented by the teaching methods of André Lhote. At the beginning of December she went to Albert Gleizes for her first lessons from 'the leader of the most severe type of abstract work without any realistic basis.'

On a single page at the back of her small address book she recorded the payments made for lessons from Gleizes during December 1921 and January and February 1922. She was to study under Gleizes with Evie Hone, with whom she was already studying at Lhote's Academy. And the two of them made regular, and increasingly frequent visits to his various places of work.

Albert Gleizes gives an account of his first meeting with the 'two young Irish girls' which is both lively and moving. He was terrified at their firm demand for lessons. He tried to refuse. He used his own friendship with André Lhote as an excuse: he could not possibly take pupils from a fellow Cubist painter. 'But we are quite free to choose any master we like,' they said. He interviewed them at length, and eventually agreed to let them work under his guidance. He rejected the idea of 'lessons', and chose 'rather the process of bringing forth what was in myself, of violently obliging myself to become aware of what I had up to this been doing empirically which does not, all the same, mean to say unconsciously.'[2]

'Before me,' Gleizes later wrote, 'I had two young students who were wanting me to show them the substantial, rational, explainable method of building up a picture without having recourse to representation, as I did myself, as I had demonstrated in several exhibitions. I had, therefore, to analyse step by step the course of my own act of painting, to follow myself and at the same time to record my movements theoretically ... In my plastic activity I distinguished two characteristics which allowed the surface of the picture to be subdivided without organically changing the nature of it. I called them TRANSLATION and ROTATION.'[3]

Mainie Jellett was twenty-four years old. It was the great watershed in her life, already then more than half over. Gleizes, to her, was the Cubist artist who had produced 'the purest and most austere form of non-representational work'. 'I went right back to the beginning with him, and was put to the severest type of exercise in pure form and colour, evolved on a certain system of composition. I now felt I had come to essentials, and though the type of work I had embarked upon would mean years of misunderstanding and walls of prejudice to break through, yet I felt I was on the right track.'

It is a common error, both in considering Gleizes for himself, and also in analysing his impact as a technician upon his two Irish

pupils, to emphasise the mechanical attributes of Translation and Rotation without investigating the spiritual and intellectual force behind them. Gleizes had spiritual and social commitments of an intense kind. He expressed them forcefully. And he regarded both Mainie Jellett and Evie Hone increasingly as close disciples.

The word is important. There is a strong religious grammar underlying Gleizes' life, as much as it did with both Evie Hone and Mainie Jellett. They were all engaged in a mission, and there were messianic forces at work in art generally.

Between Gleizes and his pupils there was reciprocation. 'I began to understand the benefit I myself had derived from the effort which my determined young Irish girls had exacted of me. And as in that gift of self which is teaching one has first of all to know oneself, it was this knowledge which I had just acquired.' What they drew out of him were 'ideas of a more general order than those concerned directly with the craft of painting'.

Gleizes even then, in the early twenties, was working towards a set of artistic beliefs of a radical kind. He was spending time in the Ardèche, 'far from the restlessness of art circles in the capital, painting, thinking, writing, every day more and more convinced of the disintegration of our world and of the increasing necessity to help to bring about the new one which sooner or later would replace it, more convinced also that man as an integral whole should not be divorced from the craftsman who reflects him body and soul.'

Since her life's work, from that decision about coming to 'essentials', until her death from cancer in a Dublin nursing home early in 1944, hangs upon the judgements she then made, it is important to consider a central argument about Cubism raised by such a starting point. It is generally held that Cubism belongs within clearly defined dates. It was 'discovered' by Braque and Picasso, developed by Leger, Metzinger, Gris, adapted, confronted and then dropped by artists such as Duchamp, Picabia and Delaunay, and rendered theoretical and academic, notably by Albert Gleizes and Andre Lhote. It was 'over' by 1921. Douglas Cooper, in two major Cubist exhibitions, in 1970-71 and 1983, both of which have produced important publications on the subject, has given clear dates, 1907-1921, and even used a phrase, 'The Cubist Epoch' as his title, establishing a termination point for the particular art form.

Cooper's approach is didactic. He distinguishes between 'true' Cubism, the work of Picasso, Braque, Gris, and, somewhat grudgingly, Leger, who 'came near to being a 'true' Cubist for a while, but he does not finally qualify as such because his pictorial purposes were too different from those of the creators.'! He then goes on to categorise dependants of Cubism, those who 'cubified' as a mannerism, those who made a scientific method out of Cubism, and those who transformed it for other pictorial ends. He rejects the categories into which Cubism has traditionally been divided, and instead chooses an approach within which the exclusive idea of an 'epoch' based on 'true' Cubism is central, and he adopts the terms applied to Renaissance art: 'early', 'high' and 'late'. Then there was 'an Aftermath of Cubism', lasting from 1914-21. And there is a termination point: it is therefore not unjustified to take Picasso's masterpiece, 'Three Musicians', painted in the summer of 1921, in which both synthetic cubist and naturalistic currents meet, as marking the end of the Cubist Epoch, which had been initiated by that revolutionary painting now known as 'Les Demoiselles d'Avignon'.

Such a view is entirely consistent with a study of Cubism which gives to Picasso and Braque the lions' share of responsibility. It is also consistent with the view that Cubism's major impact during and immediately after the Great War was on other movements and developments. It was the great revolution, releasing the energies and exploration of Futurism, the Dadaists and Surrealists, the Vorticists, and eventually wide and varied forms of abstract art.

The approach is open to question, however, when it assumes that the departure of the main artists from Cubist ideas and attitudes at the end of the second decade of the century spells the end of Cubism as such, or at best reduces it to an academic and sterile examination of theory and design.

Cubism itself went on. It did so with difficulty precisely because of its own revolutionary impact. It created its own rivals. And in certain lines from Guillaume Apollinaire's *Les Peintres Cubistes*, the optional nature of the future development of its ideals is indicated:

'The secret aim of the young painters of the extremist schools is to produce pure painting. Theirs is an entirely new plastic art. It is still in its beginnings, and is not yet as abstract as it would like to be. Most of the new painters depend on good deal on mathematics, without knowing it; but they have not yet abandoned nature, which they still question patiently, hoping to learn the right answers to the questions raised by life ...

This art of pure painting, if it succeeds in freeing itself from the art of the past, will not necessarily cause the latter to disappear; the development of music has not brought in its train the abandonment of the various genres of literature, nor has the acridity of tobacco replaced the savoriness of food.'

Apollinaire died in 1918. His 'meditations esthetique' do not provide us with any updating of the prophecies about the key painters made five years earlier. But he did then express the dilemma of modernism, between pure painting, becoming more abstract, and the art of the past, reasserting itself.

Apollinaire no more than hints at the spiritual needs which lie within the searches made by artists for understanding linked with expression of themselves. Gleizes, with his two pupils, sought much more than the austere continuation of 'painting without subject', involving the rules which are so clearly at odds with the supposedly intuitive approach adopted by Picasso and Braque. They looked for a redemptive purpose as well. And Gleizes went on to perfect his ideas on this objective, just as Mainie Jellett did in Ireland during the period between the First and Second World Wars.

André Lhote and Albert Gleizes, quite different as painters, and unequal in talent, the latter being of far greater stature, are the

victims of Cubism's evolution, and of this essential dilemma of modernism. By sustaining Cubism they challenged those who moved on. In their work they raise questions about the nature and definition of purity in art. But they do so from a position which ironically becomes 'traditionalist' and academic. Inevitably they have suffered as a result.

In Robert Rosenblum's book, *Cubism and Twentieth Century Art,* they are each relegated to a few paragraphs at the end of the chapter entitled 'The Parisian Satellites' as 'certain little masters' who have obtained a somewhat greater prominence than other of their Cubist contemporaries. The didactic, theoretical nature of Gleizes's writing is detected also in his art, which in general, according to Rosenblum, 'ran the risk of sterile codification'. As early as 1914 'Cubism has almost become a formula to be learned and applied to any subject ... After the First World War, Gleizes's numerous treaties and paintings provided a telling demonstration of the extinction of a marked talent under the academic weight of an all-too-rational doctrine; as a result, his work began to look less like paintings than like geometric diagrams of paintings.'

André Lhote is dealt with even more severely. In a single paragraph which refers to 'an even greater aridity', and which attributes to him the self-appointed role as 'the official academician of Cubism', Rosenblum writes of works 'whose obvious lucidity of structure and colour were eminently suitable to the expansion of their style into the realm of decorative arts.'

A similar approach is to be detected in the bulk of Cubist literature, which adopts a safe, cautious and narrow line on who is 'in', who 'out'.

Yet Gleizes and Lhote are the artists who shaped the maturing mind of Mainie Jellett. And the contribution stands or falls on one's acceptance of the durability and relevance of their kind of Cubism. They set her upon a cycle of work and ideas which was to prove monumentally significant for Ireland, and for succeeding generations of Irish artists.

With Apollinaire, I attribute to Gleizes that 'majesty' which arouses and provokes the imagination, and which, like some precious flickering torch, he handed on to his pupil, Mainie Jellett.

He gave her, as she knew only too well, and said so frequently, a combative role. It was made even more so by the isolation and conservative prejudice about the arts in Ireland. The years of misunderstanding and the walls of prejudice were only too real. They outlasted her, so that her early and very painful death was made more painful by the unfinished business of purifying and revitalising the art of her own time in her own country.

1. Mainie Jellett, 'My Voyage of Discovery' in Eileen MacCarvill (ed.), *The Artist's Vision,* (1958) pp.47-51.
2. Albert Gleizes, 'Hommage A Mainie Jellett' in Eileen MacCarvill (ed.), *The Artist's Vision,* (1958), p.40.
3. Gleizes, *op. cit.*, p.41.

Women artists and the Modern Movement, 1943-49

Brian Kennedy

Modernism in Ireland: a background history

The Modern Movement in Irish art is often regarded as beginning with the first Irish Exhibition of Living Art held in 1943. This is correct only so far as the art of the recent past is concerned; historically the Modern Movement in Ireland can be traced back to the late nineteenth century and, significantly, women have always played a notable role in stimulating public awareness of it.

The first truly avant-garde paintings to be exhibited publicly in Ireland were those by James McNeill Whistler shown at the Dublin Sketching Club's exhibition in 1884.[1] This exhibition excited much press and public debate both about modern art in general and on the issue of whether it was proper in such shows to include works by non-Irish artists. Some critics argued that non-Irish artists should be excluded while others, including George Russell (AE), said that the best way to stimulate the development of art in Ireland was to increase an awareness of trends elsewhere. Thus, in 1889 Russell, Walter Osborne and Sarah Purser arranged the Loan Exhibition of Modern Paintings, shown at the Leinster Hall, Dublin, which included works by some of the better known French Impressionists and the public and press delighted in them. This exhibition demonstrated the aridity of the local scene which was dominated by the Royal Hibernian Academy (RHA). Like most academies, it was conservative in outlook and ignored completely the revolution in painting which began with the Impressionists. The Academy, too, had for long disdained the work of Nathaniel Hone and John Butler Yeats, two of its more forward looking members, and this scorn prompted Sarah Purser to arrange the joint exhibition of their paintings which was held at number six St. Stephen's Green in 1901.[2] This exhibition was a turning point in the history of the Modern Movement in Ireland; it demonstrated the existence of native talent of a progressive kind; it transformed the impecunious Yeats' career by bringing him into contact with the American collector John Quinn and hence regular patronage; it introduced Hugh Lane to Irish art for the first time and began his life-long campaign on behalf of modern painting.[3] Other notable shows in these years were the exhibition of Modern Paintings, held in Belfast in 1906 and two exhibitions of avant-garde painting arranged for the United Arts Club, Dublin, by

Ellen Duncan — who later became the first curator of the Dublin Municipal Gallery — in January 1911 and March 1912. The first of these exhibitions included works by Cézanne, Derain, Gauguin, Van Gogh, Matisse and Picasso and the second included works by, amongst others, Picasso, Gris and Marchand and was the first occasion when Cubist paintings were seen in Ireland. Finally, the exhibition of Modern Paintings arranged by Paul Henry and Arthur Power and shown in Dublin in 1922 again included avant-garde French pictures as well as similar works by British painters of whom the best known were Gilman, Ginner, Gore and Paul Nash.

Following these exhibitions the role of sponsoring the Modern Movement in Ireland was tacitly assumed by the Society of Dublin Painters who performed that function until early Living Art exhibitions of the nineteen forties.

The Society of Dublin Painters 1920-49

By the early nineteen twenties a new generation of painters, many of whom had studied art in Paris and elsewhere and who were thus familiar with the latest trends in art, settled in Dublin and determined to circumvent the exclusiveness of the Royal Hibernian Academy. A characteristic of this generation was the preponderance of women, who included May Guinness, Grace Henry, Eva and Letitia Hamilton, Harriet Kirkwood, Mary Swanzy, Evie Hone and Mainie Jellett and they all became members of the Dublin Painters' Society which was formed principally by Paul and Grace Henry in 1920 as an alternative venue to the Academy for young artists to show their work. Each member of the Society[4] was entitled to hold an annual one-man exhibition, and group shows were held in spring and autumn. From the beginning, women dominated the membership of the Dublin Painters' Society. In its early group shows the Henrys were strongly Post-Impressionist in stance and Swanzy and O'Rorke Dickey showed a familiarity with the more formal approach of Cézanne, while the less avant-garde members such as Jack B. Yeats and Letitia Hamilton emphasized colour rather than academic principles. However, the membership soon changed although it was still dominated by women. Mary Swanzy went abroad in 1922 and Clare Marsh died in 1923; Yeats, O'Rorke Dickey and Paul Henry all left in the mid-twenties; but new members in these years included Hilda Roberts, Joan Jameson, Harry Kernoff and Maurice MacGonigal. In the thirties Beatrice Glenavy, Nano Reid, Lilian Davidson, Norah McGuinness, Jack Hanlon, Margaret Clarke, Frances Kelly and May Guinness all joined; and in the following decade Ralph Cusack, Patrick Hennessy, Patricia Griffith, Gerard Dillon, Thurloe Connolly, Anne Yeats, Eugene Judge and Elizabeth Rivers became members. By the mid-thirties women so dominated the Society that the *Irish Times* commented that its spring show in 1935 was 'the first time that there has been a women artists' exhibition, as this show virtually may be taken to be.'[5] In 1942 Stephen Rynne thought the Dublin Painters were 'the liveliest of the living painters, the explorers and experimentalists,'[6] a view with which James White concurred a year later.[7] But this praise coincided with the beginnings of the Society's decline for too many of its members, with the notable exceptions of Jellett, Reid, May Guinness, Norah McGuinness, Cusack, Dillon and Connolly, became complacent and their work lost its earlier rigour, so that by 1943, when the first Living Art exhibition was held, the Dublin Painters in effect relinquished to the new movement the job of stimulating avant-garde painting in Ireland. By the early forties, too, May Guinness, Mary Swanzy and Grace Henry were elderly and their work developed little; Mainie Jellett died in January 1944 and Evie Hone had concentrated on making stained glass since 1933. Thus, by this time, most of the important female members of the Society, who still exhibited regularly, were of a younger generation than its founders and included principally Norah McGuinness, Nano Reid and Frances Kelly, with Moyra Barry, Patricia Griffith, Hilda Roberts, Lilian Davidson, Dorothy Blackham, Sylvia Cooke-Collis, Stella Frost and Joan Jameson as more minor figures. These were the painters who shaped the Society throughout the forties and later.

By 1943 May Guinness, the eldest member of the Society, was aged eighty. Understandably, from the mid-twenties her work had changed hardly at all. Some of her late works show a mildly Cubist influence in the simplification of forms, but others such as *Mardi Gras* have a delightfully lyrical quality reminiscent of the work of the French painter Marie Laurencin. Grace Henry, sadly, spent much of her career in the shadow of her husband, Paul; with the passage of time she is seen to be a more experimental painter and her reputation is deservedly increasing. By 1943 she was in her seventies and so only her late works can interest us here. She rarely, if ever, dated her paintings so that it is difficult to determine her development, but her later works tended to be expressionistic in manner and she spent much of the thirties painting on the Continent where the warm sunshine of the South of France inspired some of her best works such as *The Red House at Mougins,* 1930s, characterized by the use of strong, vibrant colours. In these years, yachts and harbour scenes bathed in sunshine, as in *Venetian Scene,* 1930s, were also a favourite subject-matter with her. Grace Henry died in Dublin on 11 August 1953.

Eva Hamilton was born in 1876, two years before her sister, Letitia, whose work is perhaps better known. They both studied under Orpen and Eva became best know as a portrait painter.

Fig. 19 May Guinness, *Still-Life, c.1935.* Representative Body of the Church of Ireland.

She held solo exhibitions at the Dublin Painters' gallery in 1925, 1927 and 1929. Letitia Hamilton was a founder member of the Dublin Painters' Society and exhibited there regularly for most of her career. Scenes from country fairs and markets in the Midlands of Ireland, rendered with great economy of means and a limited palette, were a favourite subject-matter with her but she frequently travelled abroad with her sister and in the twenties and late thirties especially painted around the northern Italian lakes. Her pictures of the time are full of sunshine and are characterized by bold, vigorous brushwork, often combined with the use of a palette knife to give a heavy impasto, with an emphasis on atmospheric perspective. Her later pictures, however, were more fussy, her range of colours was extended and her composition became less rigorous. In 1948 she was awarded a bronze medal in the Sport in Art section of the Olympic Games for her composition *Meath Hunt Point-to-Point.*

Harriet Kirkwood (née Jameson) was born in Sutton, Co. Dublin, in 1880. She first studied drawing in Dublin with Miss May Manning before going to the Slade School, London, and finally spending a time in Paris with André Lhote, but he had little lasting influence on her. She joined the Dublin Painters' Society in 1922, became its secretary in 1930 and president in 1936, a position which she held until 1948 when she was succeeded in office by Eva Hamilton. Harriet Kirkwood is best known for her still-lifes and flower studies which are often filled with light and atmosphere as in *Still Life with Fruit and Flowers,* painted in about 1940, now in the National Gallery of Ireland. Other of her works

Fig. 20   Grace Henry, *The Red House at Mougins, 1930's.* Private collection.

such as *House Near Clondalkin,* c.1936, and *Still-life,* c.1939, often have a strong emphasis on formal structures which reveals the influence from Cézanne whom she greatly admired. She abhorred nationalism in art and felt that if Irish artists wished to establish a distinctive school of painting they should strive for quality in their work instead of painting, as so many did, mere symbols of nationality.[8]

Mary Swanzy's career has been documented in detail elsewhere[9] so we need not repeat it here. After a long spell away from Ireland she exhibited at the Dublin Painters' gallery in 1943 and this, with the exception of two paintings shown at the RHA in 1945, was her last exhibition here for twenty-five years. In the late thirties, having previously been influenced by Fauvism and Cubism, she adopted a more representational manner strongly laden with symbolism which reflected her concern at the growing prospect of war, a theme which was reflected in several works shown in her 1943 exhibition. However, due to her long periods of absence from Ireland she had little influence on the development of the Modern Movement here. Mainie Jellett and Evie Hone, too, were early members of the Dublin Painters' Society and, more than anyone else, they strove to introduce a knowledge of Cubism in Ireland. In 1923 at the Dublin Painters' autumn show Jellett

first showed Cubist paintings, possibly including her *Abstract,* 1922; and the following year she and Evie Hone held a joint exhibition of such paintings at the same venue. At that time their work was

Fig. 21   Letitia Marian Hamilton, *Venice, c.1924,.* Private collection.

Fig. 22 Mary Swanzy, *Red House, c.1935*. Hugh Lane Municipal Gallery.

almost indistinguishable one from the other, although reviewing the exhibition, the *Irish Statesman* perceptively thought Jellett possessed the 'surer brush, the firmer version' while Hone, it said, was the 'purer artist.'[10] They continued to exhibit Cubist paintings, often in the face of derision from the critics, at the Dublin Painters' gallery throughout the twenties and thirties, although from 1933 Hone concentrated her energies on making stained glass. Some of her later paintings, however, are delightfully lyrical and free from the constraints of Cubism to which she was never as committed as Jellett. In the thirties, however, the critics began to give Jellett guarded recognition for her pioneering work and in these years she produced a number of paintings including *The Assumption*, 1937, *The Ninth Hour*, 1939, which, along with *I Have Trodden the Winepress Alone*, 1943 and *Madonna of Eire*, 1943, are amongst her best works and pathetically evoke the spirit of the times. Sadly, however, Mainie Jellett died in February 1944 and thus had little influence on the period which we are chiefly discussing.

Of the younger generation of women artists who guided the Dublin Painters' Society in the nineteen forties, Norah McGuinness and Nano Reid were the most important but as they made an even more vital contribution to the early Living Art exhibitions we shall discuss their careers later. Thus it is to Frances Kelly, Moyra Barry, Patricia Griffith, Hilda Roberts and Lilian Davidson that we must now turn our attention, for, next to McGuinness and Reid, they were the influential younger female painters of their time. They were all conservative in approach although none of them could be regarded as being an academic painter.

Frances (Judy) Kelly studied art at the Metropolitan School of Art, Dublin. In 1932 she won the Royal Dublin Society's Henry Higgins Travelling Scholarship and visited Paris where she studied for a time under the Cubist painter Leopold Survage, although she was little influenced by Cubism. She joined the Dublin Painters in 1937 and thereafter exhibited frequently in the Society's group exhibitions. She was well known for her portraits of which those of *George Furlong*, probably painted in the late 1930s and *Seán T.*

Fig. 23   Mainie Jellett, *Abstract, 1922*. Ulster Museum.

Fig. 24 Frances Kelly, *Looking into the Garden, c.1938*. Ulster Museum.

O'Kelly, c.1947-48, are amongst her best. A sense of harmony brought about by brisk brushwork and a strong feeling of light, air and space is the prevailing quality of all her work and even in her portraits the likeness of the sitter is subordinated to it.

In her still-lifes, such as *Looking into the Garden,* c.1938, she would often set bright reds, violets and other colours against a grey background so that the whole becomes vibrant with light and atmosphere. At times her work, as Edward Sheehy once noted,[11] is reminiscent of that of the French painter Marie Laurencin. Moyra Barry was born in Dublin in 1886. She studied art at the RHA Schools and at the Slade School, London. She lived briefly in South America before settling in Dublin in the early thirties. She occasionally painted portraits, such as her *Self-portrait,* 1920, (National Gallery of Ireland), but became best known for her flower paintings of which *Rhododendrons,* c.1934, and *Lilac,* 1941, are good examples and demonstrate her technique of focusing closely on the flowers and foliage thus omitting all reference to the surroundings. Speaking at an exhibition of her work in the Waddington Galleries, Dublin, in 1941, Dermod O'Brien, then president of the Academy, rather patronisingly suggested that she was 'the finest painter of flowers alive',[12] and in 1949 the *Limerick Chronicle* commented that no other Irish painter could compete with her at painting flowers.[13] However, despite such rhetoric, her work was often dull and repetitive and contributed little to the development of modern painting. Patricia Griffith (née Wallace) was born in Dublin in 1913. She studied at the RHA

Schools from 1932-35 and, briefly, at the Slade School along with her friend Bea Orpen, after which she returned to Dublin. In the late thirties, with Lilian Davidson, she produced sets and costume designs for the Torch Theatre in Dublin. Her style was loosely Impressionist in manner as is evident in *Wexford Street,* early 1940s, but occasionally she produced works like *Through the Window at Delphi Lodge,* early 1940s, which were influenced by English painters such as Paul Nash, John Piper and Edward Wadsworth, although Evie Hone also greatly influenced her. In the early forties she occasionally exhibited in Dublin with the White Stag Group and, reviewing one of those exhibitions in 1941, the *Irish Press* noted that for the first time she was showing Cubist paintings,[14] but such works were unusual for her. However, from the mid-forties, due to domestic commitments, she stopped painting. She died in 1972. Hilda Roberts is remembered best as a portrait painter. Born in Dublin in 1901 she studied art at the Metropolitan School under Patrick Tuohy before moving to the London Polytechnic. On her return to Dublin she studied sculpture for a time with Oliver Sheppard and won the Taylor Scholarship for sculpture in both 1924 and 1925.[15] After a year spent in Paris she returned to Dublin determined to become a portrait painter and her portrait of *George Russell (AE),* 1929, (Ulster Museum), is one of her best works. Her style, however, was conservative and she contributed little to the development of the Modern Movement in Ireland. Hilda Roberts died in 1982.

Lilian Davidson, too, was well known as a portrait painter although she also produced many genre scenes and landscapes. Educated at the Metropolitan School, she travelled widely on the Continent. Her best known portrait is probably that of *Jack B. Yeats,* (National Gallery of Ireland), which captures the personality of the sitter but is quite traditional in concept. Probably her best known genre work is *Low Tide, Wicklow,* c.1934, (Ulster Museum), which is handled in a loosely Impressionist manner. Some of her landscapes, such as *Landscape,* c.1940, were in the tradition of Paul Henry and J.H. Craig while others, like *The Way Down,* early 1940s, recall the work of Harry Kernoff. Beatrice Esher (Bea) Orpen, while not a member of the Dublin Painters' Society, was a close friend of Lilian Davidson and Patricia Griffith and was prominent amongst those women painters who influenced the art scene in the forties. Born in 1913, a niece of the artist Sir William Orpen, she studied art at the Metropolitan School before going to the RHA Schools and finally to the Slade and the Central School of Arts and Crafts in London. During the thirties in London she produced many designs for book jackets and other commercial products but once back in Ireland she turned to landscape painting, working almost entirely in gouache, although often the influence of commercial design is evident in her work as in *Siesta,* 1943, which is delightfully economical both in style and range of colour, while her *Countryside,* c.1939-40, exhibits many of the same qualities but is much freer in treatment and is reminiscent of the work of her friend Patricia Griffith.

By and large, the other women associated with the Dublin Painters' Society in the forties were unadventurous in manner and contributed little to the development of Modernism in Ireland.

Fig. 25 Bea Orpen, *Siesta, 1943*. Private collection.

They, along with their male colleagues, typified the conservatism of the Society in the early forties which ultimately led to its decline. The best known of these painters were Sylvia Cooke-Collis, Stella Frost, Joan Jameson and Dorothy Blackham; while others, namely Beatrice Glenavy, Brigid Ganly and Margaret Clarke, were also members of the RHA and thus were essentially academic painters. In the forties, however, Anne Yeats and Phyllis Hayward joined the Society and brought some new zest to it by then, of course, the lead in promoting the Modern Movement had passed to the Irish Exhibition of Living art.

The White Stag Group 1940-45

The outbreak of war in 1939 compelled several of the more progressive Irish artists to return home from abroad. The best known of these artists were Louis Le Brocquy, Ralph Cusack and Norah McGuinness and their presence highlighted the conservatism of the local art scene. Also, at the same time a number of strangers from England and France arrived and, exhibiting under the name of the White Stag Group, introduced the most innovative painting yet seen in Ireland. The White Stag Group centred around Basil Rakoczi and Kenneth Hall, but their associates included Stephen Gilbert and his Canadian-born wife Jocelyn Chewett, Nick Nicholls, Georgette Rondel and Phyllis Hayward. The best known Irish painters to exhibit with them were Patrick Scott, Ralph Cusack and Doreen Vanston and they were joined from time to time by Evie Hone, Mainie Jellett, Nano Reid and Patricia Griffith.

Phyllis Hayward (also known by her married name, 'Teale') was born in England in 1903. She studied at Portsmouth College of Art and at the Central School, London, where in the thirties she met Rakoczi and other White Stag artists. She came to Ireland

in 1940, joined the White Stags in 1941 and the Dublin Painters' Society in 1948. She remained in Dublin until about 1950 when she returned to England. She died in 1985. Although she occasionally painted portraits, flowers and still-life were Phyllis Hayward's favourite subject-matter. She handled these with great bravura, as can be seen in her *Flowers in a Pot*, often employing mixed media such as watercolours, gouache and wax, but always with a strong linear emphasis. Occasionally, too, she worked in monotype. But in the late forties her style became more formal and Cézanne-like as in *Still Life with Fruit*, c.1950. Doreen Vanston was one of the most avant-garde Irish painters of the thirties and forties. Born in Dublin in 1903, her mother was a sculptor and had been a founder member of the Gaelic League with Dr. Douglas Hyde. She studied art at the Académie Ranson, Paris, in about 1920-21 and in 1926, while still in Paris, married a Costa Rican law student and took the name Vanston de Padilla. She and her husband moved to Costa Rica in the late twenties but she returned to Paris in the thirties to work briefly under André Lhote. In about 1940 she returned to Dublin and shortly after joined the White Stags, being associated with the Group throughout the war-years. She exhibited in the first Irish Exhibition of Living Art in 1943 and again thereat regularly from 1948. Her principal subject-matter included figurative compositions and landscapes with figures and animals. Until the mid-forties she had a strongly Cubist manner influenced by Picasso and Lhote, but in the later forties her style became freer and she began to paint landscapes in watercolour based on sketches made earlier in south America. Georgette (Zette) Rondel, a Parisian, came to Dublin with her husband, René Buhler, in about September 1939 and for a time they lived a *ménage à trois* with Nick Nicholls until Buhler and Rondel returned to England in about 1942. Rondel studied art in Paris before working there as a designer of window displays at the Galeries Lafayette. Later she worked as a commercial artist in London and, during her brief stay in Ireland, did the same work in Dublin where she also produced some theatrical designs. She was a fine draughtsman with a bold, authoritative line; and her painting, which had a decorative element as in *Still-life with Fish*, 1940-42, was in the French tradition of Braque and his followers. Georgette Rondel died in England in about 1942. Jocelyn Chewett

Fig. 26 Doreen Vanston, *Composition, 1940*. Private collection.

was, perhaps, the most avant-garde sculptor working in Ireland during the forties. A Canadian by birth, she settled in England with her family in 1913. She studied art at the Slade School before going to Paris where she worked with the sculptors Brancusi and Zadkine for two years, after which she returned to London where she married the painter Stephen Gilbert. The Gilberts came to Ireland in 1940 and remained there until late 1945 before returning to England and, eventually, to Paris where they settled. Jocelyn Chewett died in 1979. Her main interest in sculpture was to explore and elucidate the intrinsic nature of the materials to hand and consequently her forms were strongly stylized and at times abstract. Unfortunately she had little influence on the development of sculpture in Ireland. With the end of the war in 1945 most of the White Stag artists returned to where they had been before the outbreak of hostilities and so their influence which, sadly, always had been minimal, was short lived. Nevertheless, they did help to prepare the setting from which sprang the first Living Art exhibition in 1943.

The Irish Exhibition of Living Art 1943-49

The first Irish Exhibition of Living Art was held at the National College of Art, Dublin in 1943. It was in effect, although not by intent, a *salon des refusés* and resulted from the intransigence of the Royal Hibernian Academy in countenancing any but the most strictly academic art. Women, both artists and non-artists, played an important role in creating the first Living Art exhibition. Sybil Le Brocquy suggested the exhibition in the first place and her son, Louis Le Brocquy, along with Mainie Jellett, Norah McGuinness, Evie Hone, Ralph Cusack, Elizabeth Curran (secretary), Margaret Clarke, Laurence Campbell and the Rev. Jack Hanlon formed the organizing committee, with Jellett as its first chairman. After her untimely death in 1944, however, she was succeeded in office by Norah McGuinness who, with her committee, directed the exhibitions and established their character until the early seventies. The Living Art exhibitions represented the most avant-garde art produced in Ireland until the late fifties by which time the social and economic changes characteristic of the post-war era had begun to alter the art scene. Norah McGuinness was born in Londonderry in 1903. She studied at the Metropolitan School of Art under Patrick Tuohy, Oswald Reeves and Harry Clarke, the latter having a strong influence on her early work as an illustrator.[16] However, in the late twenties she determined to become a painter and, although she supplemented her income with commercial work throughout her career, thereafter painting was her main occupation. On the advice of Mainie Jellett, she went to Paris in 1929 to study under Lhote but, being by that time already set in her ways, was little influenced by his Cubist theories. Throughout the thirties her work was

Fig. 27 Norah McGuinness, *The Thames, 1932-34.* Private collection.

Fig. 28   Nano Reid, *Patrick Hennessy*. National Gallery of Ireland.

characterized by the use of gouache handled in a broadly Fauvist-derived manner with brisk, spontaneous brushwork.

In the early thirties, while living in a flat overlooking the river at Hammersmith, she produced a number of works, including *The Thames,* 1932-34, which are among her best ever paintings. In these her early reliance on line, an influence of Harry Clarke, has given way to an emphasis on tonal relationships which remained a feature of her work for some time. Also there is little attempt to suggest recession and, while the imagery is treated in a representational manner, she emphasizes the flatness of the picture-plane — an influence, no doubt, from her Cubist studies with Lhote. The composition, too, has a decorative quality — this was a constant feature of her work — doubtless an influence retained from Harry Clarke.

During the thirties she exhibited at the Wertheim Gallery, London, as did Basil Rakoczi and Kenneth Hall of the White Stag Group and others who subsequently came to prominence in England. In 1936 she joined the Dublin Painters' Society and that year held her first solo exhibition in Dublin, the critic for the *Irish Independent* praising the fresh vision which she brought to her painting of the Irish landscape.[17] After a brief period in the United States during the late thirties she settled permanently in Ireland in 1939.

Thereafter her subject-matter was principally landscape and still-life and throughout the forties she painted in a loosely Fauvist manner, increasingly lightening her palette and turning from gouache to oil paint which she used as she had hitherto used gouache, always producing delightfully lyrical images as in *Mount Street Bridge* and *Village by the Sea*. Later, in the fifties and early sixties, she turned to a more Cubist form of composition, but these works are outside our scope here.

In 1950, with Nano Reid, Norah McGuinness represented Ireland at the Venice Biennale; in 1957 she was elected an honorary member of the Royal Hibernian Academy; in 1968 a retrospective exhibition of her work was held at Trinity College, Dublin, and Trinity awarded her an honorary D.Litt. degree in 1973. Norah McGuinness died in November 1980. Her contribution to the Modern Movement in Ireland lay not only in her work, but also in her openness towards and encouragement of other, usually younger, painters.

Along with Norah McGuinness, Nano Reid was the most important women painter associated with the early Living Art exhibitions. Born in Drogheda, County Louth, in 1905, she studied at the Metropolitan School of Art, and in Paris where, in about 1927, she attended the Académie de la Grande Chaumière and, occasionally, Colarossi's school.

Later she studied at the Central School of Art, London, under Bernard Meninsky and at the Chelsea Polytechnic. In about 1930 she settled in Ireland. Her painting of a *Galway Peasant*, 1929, shows the bold simplicity of her early style and is reminiscent of similar subjects by Paul Henry done twenty years earlier. She was elected to the Dublin Painters' Society in about 1934 and held her first solo exhibition there that year.

In the mid-thirties she was influenced by the Belgian painter Marie Howet (b. 1897), whose work she saw exhibited in Dublin, and adopted a more expressionist manner and gestural technique of handling paint. Her drawing of the art critic *Edward Sheehy*, c.1944, shows the force of her new style which had a strongly linear emphasis.

However, in later works such as *Friday Fare*, 1945, or *The Hanging Gate*, c.1945, her style was much more lyrical and the adoption of a bird's eye view of things characterized her work thereafter. During the late forties she became even more expressionistic, varying in manner from the Germanic-like *West Cork Mountains* of c.1945 to the Matisse-like *Girl with a Scarf*, of 1947. Landscapes, often of the Boyne valley near Drogheda, occupied her from the late forties and frequently she imbued these works with a strong sense of mysticism, especially when her subject-matter was an ancient monastic or archaeological site. In these years she painted some portraits which are notable for their forceful expression of character, a result of her direct approach and simplicity of style. In 1950 she represented Ireland at the Venice Biennale.

During the following decade she exhibited frequently in solo and mixed exhibitions and was accorded a retrospective exhibition held in both Dublin and Belfast in 1974-75. Nano Reid died in 1981. There is a resemblance between Nano Reid and Norah McGuinness in that, while each was interested in the Modern Movement, neither was a pioneer in any sense. Both were essentially representational painters, but the former had in her work an element of the energy of the post-1945 action painters.

Two other women artists who came to prominence with the early Living Art exhibitions were the painter Anne Yeats and the sculptor Hilary Heron.

Anne Yeats studied drawing and painting at the RHA Schools under Dermod O'Brien and Maurice MacGonigal during the thirties. She spent the early years of her career as a stage designer working mainly at the Abbey Theatre, Dublin, before beginning to paint seriously in the early forties. She exhibited at the first Living Art exhibition in 1943 and became a member of the organizing committee in 1947, the year in which she paid a brief visit to France to see recent French painting. She held solo exhibitions in Dublin in 1946 and 1948, the latter being her last such show until the sixties. *Woman Watching*, 1948, is characteristic of her early work in which she used mainly a

Fig. 29 Anne Yeats, *Caught and Captured*. Collection of the artist.

Fig. 30 Hilary Heron, *Fish, c.1950*. Private collection.

combination of watercolour and wax in a manner which at times recalls the work of the painter William Conor. From the late forties she turned more to oils but her technique here was broadly similar to that of her early watercolours, as is evident in *One Room* and other contemporary works. Hilary Heron was one of the more avant-garde sculptors who contributed to the Living Art exhibitions before the fifties. Born in Dublin in 1923, she studied at the National College of Art from where she won the Royal Dublin Society's Taylor Art Scholarship three times. In 1948 she was awarded the Mainie Jellett Travelling Scholarship which enabled her to visit France and Italy where she greatly admired Romanesque carvings. Later she travelled extensively in Europe, the U.S.A., the U.S.S.R. and China. She held several solo exhibitions in the Waddington Galleries, Dublin, during the fifties and, with Louis Le Brocquy, represented Ireland at the Venice Biennale in 1956. In later life she was a member of the R.T.E. Authority and took an active interest in community services. She died in 1977.

As a student, Hilary Heron was influenced by the work of Henry Moore, Barbara Hepworth and Sumerian, Egyptian and Negro sculpture,[18] although some of her early portraits, such as that of *James Connolly*, 1946, are somewhat academic in both concept and execution. However, those early influences are evident in other works such as *The Flight into Egypt*, 1950, which has a strongly organic quality. In both of these pieces, however, the intrinsic characteristic of her material is given full expression, a feature which became notable in her work from the nineteen fifties onwards when she began to use metal, which she often combined formally with found objects such as pieces of stone.

As we have seen, women played a major role in the development of the Modern Movement in Ireland during this century. With the exceptions of Mainie Jellett and Evie Hone, none of them was a pioneer but the most notable part of their contribution was the fact that they regularly demonstrated that there was an alternative to the stuffiness of the Academy, and thus they helped to prepare the way for the changes which evolved in art in Ireland — as elsewhere — in the years after 1950.

1. For a discussion of Whistler's participation in this exhibition, with a note on press reactions to his works, see Ronald Anderson, 'Whistler in Dublin, 1884', *Irish Arts Review,* vol. 3, (Autumn 1986), pp.45-51. The works by Whistler here exhibited included his *Portrait of the Painter's Mother* (1871), now in the Louvre; *Portrait of Thomas Carlyle* (1872-73), Glasgow; and *Portrait of Lady Meux* (1881-82), Frick Collection, New York.

2. For a detailed note on the background to this exhibition see William M. Murphy, *Prodigal Father: The Life of John Butler Yeats (1839-1922),* (Ithaca & London 1978), pp.225-34.

3. Lane's growing interest at this time in modern art — hitherto he had been interested only in old master paintings — his endeavours to define a distinctively Irish school of painting and his efforts to establish the Dublin Municipal Gallery of Modern Art (now the Hugh Lane Municipal Gallery of Modern Art) are well known and all stemmed from this exhibition. Indeed the establishment of the Municipal Gallery remained the dominant issue in the matter of Irish art and Modernism until the mid-twenties. Lane's association with all of these matters is set out in detail in Thomas Bodkin, *Hugh Lane and His Pictures,* (Dublin 1932) and later editions.

4. The membership was at first limited to ten persons. Later this was increased to twelve, then eighteen and finally twenty.

5. *Irish Times,* 5 February 1935, p.5.

6. Stephen Rynne, *The Leader,* 21 February 1942, p.88.

7. James White, 'Independent Painters', *Irish Art Handbook,* (Dublin 1943), p.40.

8. Harriet Kirkwood, quoted in 'Influence of Nationalism in Art', *Sunday Independent,* 18 February 1940.

9. See especially Julian Campbell in the exhibition catalogue, *Mary Swanzy HRHA (1882-1978),* Pyms Gallery, London, (1986).

10. *Irish Statesman,* 28 June 1924, p.495.

11. Edward Sheehy, 'Art Notes', *Dublin Magazine,* (July-September 1945), p.46.

12. Reported in the *Sunday Independent,* 25 May 1941.

13. Review of her exhibition at the Goodwin Gallery, Limerick, *Limerick Chronicle,* 23 April 1949.

14. *Irish Press,* 13 February 1941.

15. For a biographical note on Hilda Roberts, see Hilary Pyle in the exhibition catalogue, *Irish Art 1900-1950,* Rosc, Crawford Municipal Gallery, Cork, (1975).

16. A detailed biographical note of Norah McGuinness's career is given in Anne Crookshank, introduction to the catalogue of the retrospective exhibition *Norah McGuinness,* Trinity College, Dublin, (1968), pp.5-7. This catalogue, as well as listing the principal exhibitions of her work till that date, also gives details of her designs for the theatre and of books illustrated by her. For reproductions of some of her earliest illustrations, see Thomas Bodkin, 'The Art of Miss Norah McGuinness,' *The Studio,* (September 1925), pp.168-71. Marianne Hartigan in 'The Commercial Design Career of Norah McGuinness,' *Irish Arts Review,* vol. 3, (Autumn 1986), pp.23-25, also reproduces some of her illustrations and designs.

17. *Irish Independent,* 26 March 1936.

18. Hilary Pyle, *op. cit.,* p.76.

Irish women artists in the nineteen-fifties

Brian Fallon

The nineteen-fifties were largely a period of transition — a blanket-term which could apply to so many fields and activities, and so often sounds merely evasive. Arguably, all periods are in transition. Yet this one was particularly so, because it witnessed the waning of the Old Order and the loss of its official status, in favour of Modernism which in the 1940's was still very much a minority culture in Ireland.

When the Living Art Exhibition was founded, Modernism was followed by relatively few people and the Royal Hibernian Academy was still a prestigious and powerful body. But most of the battles had already been fought and won, even if not many people yet realised or accepted this; and once the shift in public taste began, it accelerated very rapidly. The acquisition by Maynooth of Rouault's *Christ and the Soldier*, the furious controversy over Henry Moore's *Reclining Figure*, were signposts to the changing times. By the end of the 1950's the RHA was left with little to hang on to except official portrait painting, and it was even forced to accept the presence of Modernists in its exhibitions (it goes without saying that academicians were not hung in the Living Art shows).

This was in line with postwar trends everywhere, though as usual in Ireland it came a decade late; Modernism was now official, not a revolutionary or subversive cult. But it is necessary to ask what, in an Irish context, Modernism meant. In France it meant the School of Paris, in England it meant Moore, Nicholson, Hepworth, and some rather more 'native' figures such as Ivon Hitchens or even Stanley Spencer. American Modernism meant Georgia O'Keeffe, Edward Hopper, and perhaps the dregs of Thirties regionalist painting — Pollock and his generation were as yet little known. In Ireland it meant a number of things: the Hone-Jellett brand of Irish Cubism, the post-Picasso art of Louis Le Brocquy, which caused such a stir in the immediate postwar years; the 'third period' of Jack Yeats, and the imported, rather nondescript styles of the White Stag group. The latter was vaguely identified with a kind of 'liberated' bohemian culture, the equivalent of the Catacombs and Donleavy's *The Ginger Man* in literature; it melted away very rapidly when the 1940's ended.

The semi-official version of Irish Modernism gives virtually the entire credit to Hone and Jellett, in line with the generally accepted view that European Modernism begins with Cubism. But perhaps this has been applied too automatically to Irish art, and it is my own belief that Hone and Jellett, influential though they were, began only one strain of Irish Modernism and perhaps not the most important one either. Their legacy is plain enough in Norah McGuinness, Father Jack Hanlon, perhaps George Campbell in one phase of his career (though Campbell also went to Picasso and Gris at first hand), but is very inadequate when it comes to explaining the work of the more powerful and original Living Art figures such as Patrick Collins, Nano Reid, or Colin Middleton. The taking-off point of these painters was really Jack Yeats, as I shall discuss later in this essay.

Meanwhile, Hone and Jellett are only a background to the period I am writing about here, and even Norah McGuinness — who developed very little as a painter after the late nineteen-forties, and if anything became more conventional and conservative — counts more in an official capacity than a creative one. Nano Reid is quite different, since she never stood still and some of her most original work was done in late middle age.

The women artists who emerged in the late Fifties and early Sixties were Camille Souter in painting and Gerda Frömel in sculpture — neither of them big producers and neither of them seen much in one-woman exhibitions. Hilary Heron, by far the best-known woman sculptor of the older Living Art generation, has faded out surprisingly; Melanie Le Brocquy, by contrast, stands higher now than she ever did, but again she was an infrequent exhibitor in her earlier days (Fig. 31). (It must be remembered, of course, that sculpture exhibitions were few in Dublin, as sculpture was notably hard to sell, and gallery-owners would rarely run the risk of holding one).

It is easy enough to understand why Hone and Jellett responded to the academic Cubism of André Lhote and Albert Gleizes, since they were both at heart traditional painters. Their Modernism was to a large extent acquired, rather than innate and instinctive, and the 'daemonic' element in the Cubist paintings of Picasso and Gris lay well outside their grasp. At the same time, both were courageous and independent-minded people, gifted with energy,

Fig. 31 Melanie Le Brocquy, *Female Figure, 1964*. Collection of the artist.

Fig. 32 Norah McGuinness, *Garden Green, 1962*. Hugh Lane Municipal Gallery, Dublin.

a talent for organising and teaching, and with strong personalities which opened up paths for them and helped to get things done. The Living Art Exhibition was basically 'their' show, and it remained so even when they were no longer there.

Norah McGuinness was a Northerner, born in Derry, and a masterful, 'managing', energetic woman whose socio-political role in the Irish art world of the time was very central indeed. She was elected Chairwoman of the Living Art exhibition in 1944. She did her best and most typical work in early and middle age; by the 1950's she had stylised herself into a kind of green and brown, bog and water stereotype which she more or less has repeated to the end, though she never corsened her limpid and French-formed technique. (Fig. 32)

Nano Reid was very much an 'instinctive' artist, and I doubt very much if she could have analysed what she did or could even have given a very coherent account of how she did it. Technically she sometimes appears to be 'muddling through', and the occasional turgid, clotted look of the paint surface would seem to bear this out. Yet, she was no 'primitive' or naive painter; she had lived in Paris and London, read a good deal, and was intellectually much more sophisticated and cultured than her slightly countrified outer shell might suggest. Arty and literary Dublin at that time was sharp, cynical and intellectually hard-boiled — in many ways, quite the opposite to what people today believe it to have been like. I remember going around the Living Art exhibition with her about twenty years ago, and her comments were biting and quite uninhibited, but not at all reactionary.

Of course, she was not only French-oriented; as I have said, she belonged to the generation of Irish artists which had digested Jack Yeats. The influence of Yeats has not been studied in depth, in fact it has hardly been studied at all, and recently the tendency has been to assume that Irish Modernism was to a large extent a turning away from most of what Yeats stood for. He was a 'Romantic', and Paris values were self-consciously classical or neo-classical; he ignored developments such as Cubism and abstraction, etc. though it does not follow at all that because he ignored them, he was not aware of them. Yeats — the fact, in my opinion, cannot be stressed too strongly — grew into a thoroughly modern, 'progressive' painter, not a provincial 'original' or outsider with a streak of genius. That can be seen from his very late work, with its obvious affinities with Abstract Expressionism, though Yeats very probably had never so much as heard of Pollock or de Kooning, much less studied their pictures. So to write about a period for much of which he was still alive, and to act as if he was not an active part in it, would be the critical equivalent of colour-blindness.

It seems to me, in fact, that the whole generation of Nano Reid, Patrick Collins, Tony O'Malley, Colin Middleton *et al.* is to a large extent post-Yeatsian, just as the Irish poets of the same generation are post-Yeatsian in a different sense. That their work rarely resembles his does not disprove the thesis — after all, these painters were all individualists and (with the exception of Middleton, who was essentially a talented eccentric) originals. After Yeats, Irish painting had changed, and its sensibility was altered.

It should be remembered, too, that rather few Irish artists of the time travelled often on the continent, apart from the ritual visit to Paris or Rome, and that in the war years they could not and did not travel abroad at all. Many of them had seen rather few modern paintings outside art-book reproductions, and even most of these were in black and white; so their ideas of what a Picasso looked like often did not correspond closely to the paint-and-canvas reality.

This may sound exaggereated, but it is not. Oisin Kelly, probably the best sculptor of the Living Art period, once told me that his favourite twentieth-century sculptor was Barlach, but he had never seen a Barlach in the original — he only knew him from a book of photographs. Similarly, the conception of Picasso which was current at the time was conditioned to some extent also by his second-hand reflection in painters like Jankel Adler (now almost forgotten, but a potent influence in the 1940's, as can be seen also from the work of the Scottish artists Colquhoun and McBryde). But Yeats lived and painted in Dublin and he could be seen or even encountered bodily in Grafton Street or Stephen's Green; his pictures could be seen in Victor Waddington's, or in the homes of collectors and it was the Waddington Gallery, which was the nursery of many Irish artists in the postwar decade.

So Nano Reid was very definitely post-Yeatsian as well as post-Hone. In London, she studied under Bernard Meninsky (no bad painter in his own right); she had been praised quite early in her career by Thomas McGreevy; she represented Ireland twice at the Venice Biennale (the first time, in 1950, with Norah McGuinness); she had exhibitions abroad. So her stay-at-home life in a provincial town (Drogheda) was presumably more a matter of choice than of lack of opportunity.

For financial reasons, she had to paint a number of portraits, a field in which she was not particularly at her ease. I do not think, on the whole, that Nano Reid had a very strong interest in people, outside her immediate family and a very few artist friends, of whom Gerard Dillon was certainly the closest. There was something shy, untamed and slightly feral about her, which suggested that she was only really herself at her easel in her little painting shed, or out in the fields.

Perhaps her watercolours are her most personal and typical achievement, and in them she certainly showed that when she wanted to do so, she could be as transparent and lucid in her handling as Norah McGuinness. But there is something swirling, dark and almost daemonic in her oils, something which seemed to be a direct emanation from the Irish landscape and from the mythic-historic past (Fig. 33). Her imagery seems to emerge out of the paint, spontaneously and organically rather than as conscious

Fig. 33   Nano Reid, *A Wild Day, 1959*. Private collection.

'subject matter'; and in that, she came close to Abstract Expressionism. Nano Reid's late work, in fact, is surprisingly close in brushwork and style to that of certain New York painters, such as Philip Guston (whom, I am reasonably certain, she had never seen).

Nano Reid's work, or the best of it, looks better with time; but some of her generation are fading into little more than historical footnotes. That seems to be happening with the sculptor Hilary Heron, who was once regarded as the leading Irish artist in her field. This is, perhaps, not very high praise, since Oisin Kelly stood almost alone in his generation and F.E. McWilliam identified himself more with British art (though he was always considered himself essentially Irish).

Hilary Heron had enormous energy, and she had a craftswoman's feeling for materials whether they were wood, metal or stone; what she lacked was an original vision. Too often, her work stayed on the arts-and-crafts side of things, rather than crossing over to that territory where, as in Gabo and the truly great, you are not conscious of the materials because they are subsumed into the vision. Probably her metalwork is her most individual contribution, and she was versatile and, on a certain level, inventive. But the inventiveness is often purely a technical and material affair, and while she was always capable of turning out individual good works, there is a lack of consistency or coherence about her output as a whole. She was influenced by primitive art, by Picasso (she was one of the rare people who recognised at the time that he was a great sculptor as well as a great painter), by other influences of the era. It is hard to construct a single unified personality out of all this, though I would be very glad if a well-chosen exhibition of her work proved me wrong, or at least one-sided.

By contract, Gerda Frömel possessed a core of personality — admittedly it was a delicate, veiled, reticent one, both in her art and in her life — which quietly irradiates almost everything she did. I say 'almost' because, at the time of her tragic death from drowning at the age of 44, she had been working on large metal abstract pieces for various public sites and buildings. These were 'designed' rather than created and were in a slightly featureless international style which seemed to derive from one of the last Bauhaus masters, the Swiss sculptor-painter Max Bill. As 'public' pieces they were quite presentable, but Gerda Frömel was essentially a private sculptor as well as a private person.

She was not an innovator, and it is not hard to track down the influences of Lehmbruck, Giacometti and Brancusi. Less obvious, perhaps, is the influence of late Gothic German sculpture, one of the richest chapters in European art — she greatly disliked the over-emphatic, heavy-handed side of Germanic art represented by Barlach, one of her *bêtes-noires*. But you do not admire Gerda Frömel for her originality, but for her refinement, sensitivity and poetic intimacy. Her voice is low, but it is always musical and always audible and it is also very much her own.

As a technician she was not only versatile, but polished to the point of perfectionism. She worked in bronze, stone and most media except, I think, wood; and it is hard to say which material

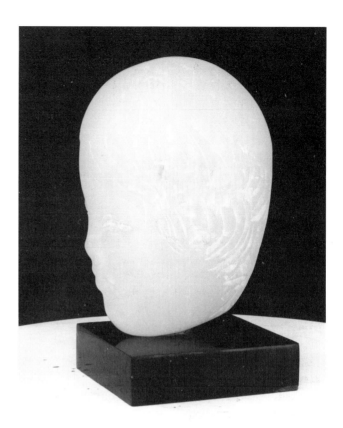

Fig. 34   Gerda Frömel, *Alabaster Head, c.1960*. Private collection.

represented her best, since she brought something individual to them all. In general, her work is rather small in scale and full-length figures are rare, apart from the very beautiful *Eve* which she showed in the old Dawson Gallery. She produced impressive, slightly Giacometti-influenced animals and some 'nature' pieces in bronze, which have a power beyond their modest size. But perhaps her finest pieces are the heads — of women and children, for the most part — which she did in bronze, alabaster and other materials. These again show some debt to Brancusi and Lehmbruck, but Gerda Frömel was one of those highly intelligent artists who can assimilate the work of others and make it their own (Fig. 34).

These heads are usually modelled or carved in low relief and stress the ovoid form, not the features as in the Rodin school. They show that she had a keen eye for the fall of light and shadow, and the effect is delicate, understated and quietly emotional in the manner of such German artists as Riemenschneider and Lehmbruck, not overtly emotional, dramatic or tense as in the Expressionists. To what extent, then, was Gerda Frömel an Irish sculptor rather than a German one? Her German-ness is obvious enough, though it belongs to the Austro-Bavarian South rather than to the more austere, formalistic North; but she identified deeply with Ireland, its landscape and its intellectual world. So both countries can claim her, and certainly Ireland should be glad of the privilege.

If she was the outstanding sculptor of the second (or third, more accurately) Living Art generation, Camille Souter has been its finest

Fig. 35 Camille Souter, *The West, 1964*. Bank of Ireland collection.

painter. The two have a good deal in common, including the fact that neither was Irish-born, that both exhibited rather rarely (at least, in one-woman shows) and that both were 'collector's artists' rather than public ones. If there had been even another three or four artists of the same generation of comparable calibre, the Living Art might have been spared its rapid decline throughout the 1960's. But as the Old Guard died, dropped out, or lost influence, the exhibition was increasingly taken over by careerist mediocrities, who seemed to have little in view except to echo every overseas fashion and to compete for any available art prize. The long-term and short-term results could easily be foreseen, and by the seventies the IELA hardly counted.

It should be remembered that neither of the two identified closely with the Living Art; they were both among the exhibitors in the early Independent Artists exhibitions, which were not directed against the IELA but were a much-needed pointer to the fact that it was in danger of becoming an exclusive clique. Neither, in fact, identified herself with any group or clique and they belonged neither with the conservatives nor the radicals. Both were married, with children (Camille Souter, who is English-born, was married twice and has kept the name of her first husband, an actor; she was born Betty Pamela Holmes in 1929, two years before Gerda

Frömel). Both also made their niche as artists by delicacy and suggestiveness, rather than by scale or rhetoric (Fig. 35).

Camille Souter, oddly enough, started as a sculptor and it is piquant to think of her as a possible rival to Frömel in her own field, but she turned to painting while on a visit to Italy. She went through an abstract phase, like most of the painters of the time — in Dublin in the late 1950's and early 1960's, it was common for people to 'go abstract', either temporarily or permanently. Camille Souter was even a kind of Action Painter in calligraphic, rather hectic style very far removed from her present quasi-impressionist. But she differed from the abstractionists of the time in her generally small scale, and to this day her pictures have remained rather small. She has never been a startling colourist, and those small, vivid areas of red she knows how to place so well, usually make their effect because they sing out from a rather muted 'tonal' background.

Her greatest strength lies in her ability to 'abstract' an image, which may be something very ordinary — a fish on a plate, a flower in a vase, a mini-landscape framed in the window of a railway carriage. To achieve this, she eliminates all 'props' and all formalism, so that she is in effect a kind of minimalist, though not in the fashionable sense. Today's Minimalists offer you

Fig. 36 Dairine Vanston, *Figure on a couch, 1944.* Private collection.

something very bare and banal, with the intention of making you believe that there's a lot more to it than meets the eye — even when they deny 'content'. By contrast, Camille Souter has pared down her subject to the bare essence, but you are aware (as with Patrick Collins) that there is a weight of sheer visual sensation and feeling behind it, and that this is still implicit in the final image.

She has also been a fine landscape painter, and for some years now has developed a passion for painting aeroplanes. The 1980 retrospective exhibition in the Douglas Hyde Gallery was criticised by some people as not being fully representative, and the artist herself felt that the period of the late sixties was inadequately represented, when she painted many canal scenes and landscapes through windows. But at least it set the official seal on her reputation, and since she so rarely has exhibitions, it gave a rare opportunity to see her work in something like bulk.

Two artists who are often overlooked, though they were both exhibitors in the IELA, are Anne Yeats and Dairine Vanston (Fig. 36). Anne Yeats, who seems to have given up showing her work altogether in recent years, was of course a prominent committee woman with the Living Art in its better years. But I have never seen a one-woman exhibition by her, her work is not easily found, and it is extremely difficult to place her as a painter. The pictures I remember from group exhibitions were usually accomplished, but they tended to fluctuate a good deal in style. Since the Dawson Gallery vanished, her pictures are hard to come by.

Dairine Vanston, by contrast, has seen her reputation revive in the 1980's, after at least two decades in which she had seemed almost forgotten. She, again, is one of the generation who took their cue from Paris; there is no Yeatsian element in her style, and somebody coming across it for the first time, and knowing little about either it or her, might easily say: this is the work of a good French painter of the inter-war period, who perhaps admires Chagall. Dairine Vanston did in fact live in Paris for some-time, but she also lived in South America, which accounts for the exotic, high-keyed colour of some of her paintings, and also for their almost Gauginesque subject matter. Like Norah McGuinness,

Fig. 37 Estella Solomons, *Co. Kerry Landscape, 1945*. Private collection.

Fig. 38 Elizabeth Rivers, *Woman by the Fire, Aran*. Private collection.

Jellett and the rest, she absorbed the aerated palette of the School of Paris, its flair for using the primary colours, and its special penchant for clear, luminous greens and blues. It is hard to find anything specifically Irish in it, and in fact she is of Dutch ancestry.

The Independent Artists, again, gave her a forum to show her pictures when she was in need of one, and more recently she has been seen regularly in the Figurative Image shows. A retrospective — or at least a mini-retrospective, since her paintings are hard to track down — should prove very interesting indeed.

In writing this article, I have dealt with a rather special milieu: the postwar years, when Dublin was a smaller, tighter but also more accessible city than it is now. But there were other artists too, most of them well worth revival today. There is, for instance, Caroline Scally, who showed regularly with the group who called themselves the Dublin Painters and was also seen in the Independents on occasion. (I remember hearing her say to the late Seán Keating at some exhibition opening, probably of the Royal Hibernian Academy: 'John, you and I are now the last surviving pupils of Orpen'); Beatrice Glenavy, a variable quantity but creator of some fine works, often with a noticeably Surrealist slant; Estella Solomons, bravely exhibiting with the RHA into her eighties, and one of the best Irish painters, male or female, of her generation (Fig. 37); the formidable Mary Swanzy, a real original and something of a dragon, who did her best work relatively late in life; Barbara Warren, who now shows in the Taylor Galleries and is an artist of quiet quality; Elizabeth Rivers, whose best work was probably her wood engravings (Fig. 38) and Hilda van Stockum, Dutch-born but Irish-trained, who exhibits regularly with the RHA and upholds the Dutch still-life tradition so solidly.

Irish women artists, 1960-1975

Dorothy Walker

Immense changes took place in art and in Irish society in the period 1960-75. For the first time since the Irish State came into being in 1922, economic prosperity became a reality, and boom conditions obtained for a few years. The general optimistic spirit of the sixties throughout the world was prevalent in Ireland. Art flourished; collectors and institutions began buying contemporary art by Irish artists and the number of commercial galleries doubled, trebled, and quadrupled within the decade. The National College of Art and Design was established in 1970 after student agitation had succeeded in having the structures of the old school fundamentally changed. The Arts Council was set up under a full-time professional Director for the first time, with increased staff and with a greatly enlarged policy of activity. Women were active in all areas: Eithne Waldron was appointed Curator of the Municipal Gallery of Modern Art; Professor Anne Crookshank inaugurated the Department of Art History in Trinity College, Dublin, as a sister institution to the Art History Department of University College, Dublin which had existed for many years under the famous woman scholar, Professor Françoise Henry.

Other contributors to this catalogue have mentioned the leading role which women artists played in the development of twentieth century Irish art. Sarah Purser, Evie Hone, Mainie Jellett, and latterly Norah McGuinness were leaders of the art community, art activitists as well as dedicated painters. Norah McGuinness and Nano Reid were the first Irish artists sent by the Irish Government to the Venice Biennale in 1950, and Hilary Heron was the next artist, with Louis le Brocquy, in 1956.

While the 1950's were Norah McGuinness's prime time when her bold, easy, romantic painting coincided with the mood of the local audience, in the 1960's she was still extremely active both as a painter and even more as a vocal and courageous President of the Irish Exhibition of Living Art. Although the work of the young artists coming up in the sixties differed radically from her own, she championed their causes with as much vigour and conviction as in the early days of Living Art in the nineteen forties. A particular rhythm and shape of form emerged in all her painting, whether the subject was the curve of a channel left in the tide in her many paintings of Dublin Bay, the shape of large pebbles, or rounded rectangles slightly pulled to one corner, whether a field, a table top, or a patch of sand. After 1970, her whole *oeuvre* picked up in spirit with the introduction of a new white, locked against demanding areas of brilliant orange, after a period of extremely sombre colours in the late sixties.

Nano Reid is also generally thought of as a painter of the fifties, but in fact her best paintings were made in the sixties. Her very personal style had nothing to do with the many successive schools of the sixties, but pictures like *Tinkers at Slieve Breagh* show how her work speaks directly out of the paint. Before one has seen what the picture is about, it has an abstract expression of its own, conveyed by the colour of the paint, the thickness of the paint, the movement of the paint, absolutely direct from brush to viewer, with no intrusion or curtain of illustrative ideas.

Flowing out of this initial impression, one perceives, as a bonus, a subject which is conceived entirely in terms of paint and two dimensions, and which therefore has a direct power, and toughness, which is missing in more preconceived paintings. (Fig. 39)

The early sixties saw a continuation of the local confidence developed in the fifties, sustained and re-fired by the general sense of energy and optimism of the sixties. The early sixties were also the high point of women's involvement in the visual arts. It is paradoxical that there were twenty-eight artists in the Living Art exhibition of 1961 while within two years of the Brave New Living Art in 1972 with its new young all-male committee, and at a time when the Women's Movement was at its height in Ireland, there were *three*.

Since the Living Art Exhibition continued to be the main public forum for advanced art right through the sixties and since it was a movement which had strong support for and from women artists, I propose to digress forward and give a brief outline of its activities during the period. The Committee had inaugurated a plan to invite artists from different countries each year; thus in 1960 there was a group of English artists from which I can still remember a particularly beautiful pale painting by Ben Nicholson; in 1961, there were French artists, with a large, amazing black painting by Dimitrienko; in 1962 Italians, including a relief 'plank' work

Fig. 39 Nano Reid, *Devotee, 1973*. Private collection.

by Burri, and in 1963 the exhibition included all the great Americans of the time: Motherwell, de Kooning, Gottlieb, Rothko, Tobey, Sam Francis, Rauschenberg, Jasper Johns, and earlier painters like Stuart Davis, Georgia O'Keeffe and Morris Graves. This most interesting practice was discontinued from 1964, when the Carroll's Prizes were substituted. P.J. Carroll & Co., the cigarette manufacturers, were the first industrial concern to take art sponsorship seriously.

To this day they sponsor the Living Art Exhibition. The prizes throughout the sixties, many of which were won by women artists whom I will mention in due course, were of great importance not only as monetary support for the individual artists, but in bringing their work to public notice. Initially the Committee appointed an external assessor to make the awards, and this was the far better system; when the new young committee came in 1972, they decided to make the awards themselves which resulted in a gradual decline of interest and quality.

It is interesting that the Living Art Exhibition was founded by a woman, Sybil le Brocquy, its first President was a woman artist, Mainie Jellett; its next President for the following twenty-eight years was another woman, Norah McGuinness, and that its attackers over the years have always been male critics and male

artists. Of the various groupings which have succeeded it, these have also tended to be all-male, the Project Arts Centre, the Independent Artists. The only woman artist associated with non-Living Art groups has been the print-maker Alice Hanratty. The older annual exhibitions such as the Royal Hibernian Academy, and the Oireachtas, have never had a woman artist as President.

At the beginning of the sixties, the first Living Art generation were still much in their prime: Norah McGuinness, Nano Reid, Hilary Heron, Anne Yeats, Elizabeth Rivers and Dairine Vanston who was the only Irish woman member of the White Stag group.

Hilary Heron was one of the most innovative artists of this group; a retrospective exhibition of her work is long overdue. Her most radical work was done in the fifties; in the sixties she had relaxed into a humorous mode which tended towards the whimsical.

Nevertheless her humour was always visual and her inventiveness as a sculptor extended into new areas: while most of her early work was in carved wood, she now used a combination of stone and metal in the *Lithodendron* flower series, and of welded steel in such literary images as Crazy Jane taken from Yeats' series of poems (Fig. 40). While there were very many women painters, some of the strongest women artists were sculptors and this

Fig. 40 Hilary Heron, *Crazy Jane, c.1960.* Jury's Hotel, Dublin.

Fig. 41 Gerda Frömel, *Mobile.* Carroll's factory, Dundalk.

characteristic of women's art has continued to the present day.

One of the finest artists working in Ireland throughout the sixties until her untimely death in 1975 was the Czech artist Gerda Frömel. She and her husband Werner Schurmann came to Ireland in 1955. He also was a sculptor and bronze-caster, and did much casting for other artists, notably Oisin Kelly with whom they both became very friendly. Schurmann's brother, who was an architect, designed an unusual house and studio for them, very near Oisin Kelly's house, at the foot of the Dublin mountains, and one of those fruitful artistic friendships developed. When Schurmann, who had a fine bass voice, finally abandoned sculpture for operatic singing and left Ireland for his native Germany, Frömel stayed behind with their three sons, and developed her own career as a sculptor with great dedication and success. Her early work was in bronze, in a romantic Impressionist style, having much in common with the Italian sculptor Medardo Rosso, involving tree forms and the heads of small children. While close to a potentially dangerous area of sentimentality, the delicacy and tenderness of her touch avoided the pitfall, and her work developed in time to a totally abstract form where her essential gentleness of character was sustained with immense strength by the materials she used, marble and alabaster particularly, but also stainless steel.

The young sculptor Michael Warren has written of 'a wonderful

sense of psychic well-being and wholesomeness' in her work, but it is also interesting, in formal terms, that her Central European background and her training as a student in Munich which led her to develop the romantic tendencies of her nature, as in her bronze *Girl* and her tiny monumental *Castle*, should have evolved, in Ireland, to an abstract mode echoing not only cup-mark carvings on pre-historic stone monuments in the Irish countryside, but Celtic ornamentation of positive/negative, inner/outer forms, embodied in large scale, free-standing and often mobile sculpture. She captured light and movement in her work first by means of the materials she used such as translucent alabaster and polished stainless steel, but also by a hard-earned simplicity won from the forms, 'embodying enjoyment of the spiritual through the material' to quote James Johnston Sweeney. The poetic quality of her sculpture is easily grasped in her small pieces, whether abstract or figurative, but it is even more remarkably evident in the very large sculpture at Carroll's Factory in Dundalk (Fig. 41): the polished stainless steel has fitting technological overtones suitable to the industrial factory building, which is an extremely fine work of architecture, but the poetic idea of the three tall 'sails' turning in the wind and reflecting in the water of the pool in which they stand, reaffirms the harmony of architecture and sculpture.

Artists from the North of Ireland contributed significantly to the vibrancy of the art scene in the sixties, again particularly in the area of sculpture. Deborah Brown had started as a painter but

Fig. 42 Deborah Brown, *Glassfibre Form, 1974*. Bank of Ireland Collection.

from 1965 her work began to incorporate relief elements. These took the form of abstract fibreglass shapes mounted on a monochrome painted background. Occasionally she introduced colour into the fibreglass, quickening the pace of development of the work. Light, however, was the most important element. Indeed these fibreglass works depended elementally on the play of light in, around, and through them for their qualities to come alive (Fig. 42). At a later stage, the reliefs came off the wall and became fully three-dimensional free-standing sculpture, while the artist pushed the fibreglass to the limits of its own tensile strength so that its became a lacy translucent structure with the fibres showing clearly as in a Japanese paper. The translucence also gave further play to the extra dimension of light which explored the rock-ice formations of caves and inner corridors, and the complexities of convex and concave form.

In 1965, a most interesting Polish artist, Alexandra Wejchert, came to live in Ireland; her young brother, the architect Andrei Wejchert had won the international competition for the layout of the new University College campus at Belfield, and the whole family moved to Dublin from Poland. Alexandra Wejchert had also trained as an architect and had had some success in showing her painting and sculpture in Rome and Paris before she came

to Dublin. Her work, which initially was concerned with abstract reliefs of painted wooden pegs fixed into a painted background, was quite new to the Irish public. She quickly became successful, winning the Carroll's Prize at the Living Art Exhibition in 1968, when the assessor was the well-known Jesuit critic, Cyril Barrett.

Like Deborah Brown, Alexandra Wejchert's work quickly developed from wall reliefs into free-standing sculpture in which she made the most imaginative use of an unlikely industrial material, sheet perspex. She exploited the malleability of the material and the characteristic it has when cut, i.e. that the edge of the sheet appears as a different colour to the sheet itself. Nevertheless she retained the sheet character of the perspex while introducing movement, flight, pattern, interplay of surface and space, complexities of perspective through a pattern of circular holes, not unrelated to her earlier work with wooden pegs.

In the seventies, she went on to develop clear perspex tubing fastened with stainless steel clips in free linear sculptures which were very exciting. Her abstract sculpture and wall-reliefs were popular with architects, and numerous examples of her work may be found in new buildings, such as the Bank of Ireland Headquarters in Dublin, the Arts Building in UCD, and the Irish Life Building in Abbey Street.

Imogen Stuart, a German artist who was married to the sculptor Ian Stuart, tended to specialise in religious sculpture, an area which has remained to some extent hampered by the lack of aesthetic sense of the Catholic Church in Ireland. Not only statuary but church furniture, church publications like Mass-cards, and in particular church music, have suffered from a particular form of genteel vulgarity which is extremely distressing to many of the devout.

But the noble art of Evie Hone had lifted the medium of stained glass to an even higher spiritual level than the renowned Harry Clarke, and after her death in 1955 several women artists carried on working in the medium in spite of gradual decline in demand. Frances Biggs completed the windows in Gonzaga College, Dublin, and Helen Moloney and Phyllis Burke carried on the abstract tradition of older artists like Catherine O'Brien who had worked with Evie Hone.

One of the most important works of religious art in the sixties — a period not immediately associated with its development — was the set of Stations of the Cross designed by the young woman painter Leslie MacWeeney. She reduced the usual complexities of the Way of the Cross to a series of life-size line drawings of the principal figures, the whole conception being direct, bold, and tender, with no hint of the sickening perversity and sentimentality of the mass-produced religious accoutrements so beloved of the Irish Catholic. Neither was there any hint of the Renaissance or even Gothic fondness for the exaggeration of grief.

The feeling was a totally correct one of infinitely restrained, infinitely deep understanding of real suffering, and of a miraculous serenity in its acceptance. There was no false note, nothing maudlin, nothing trite, but a powerful emotional content. The artist worked for years to produce a final work of staggering authority, beautifully rendered in a flat, dense woven black line

Fig. 43 Leslie McWeeney, *Stations of the Cross, 1963*. Corpus Christi Church, Knockanure, Co. Kerry.

Fig. 44 Anna Ritchie, *'Global Passage', 1961*. Kilkenny Design Workshops.

on saffron wool panels. The flat plane of the drawing reinforces the flat tapestry quality of the wool panel. While the drawing is tightly controlled, not distorted in the anatomical sense but rather stylised, there are nevertheless most skilful subtleties of expression: the difference, for example, of the faces of the women of Jerusalem and of Christ's mother, although both have the same archetypal face; the suffering progression of Christ falling the first, second, and third times. The Stations were designed and made for the new parish church of Knockanure, County Kerry, designed by Ronald Tallon, were they now hang (Fig. 43).

If I have given considerable attention to the work of sculptors, it is because the sculptors, in general, produced a body of particularly strong work. Even a very quiet artist, like Melanie le Brocquy, whose work was more classical than the ebullient experiments of more adventurous spirits, nevertheless held her own small space with insistence.

The younger artists who started to exhibit in the early seventies were, unusually, from Cork. Eilis O'Connell and Vivienne Roche were students of John Burke in the Cork School of Art and initially were very influenced by his painted steel abstraction. Both subsequently developed highly individual styles of their own, but they had been taught how to weld properly, how to finish their work impeccably and above all how to clarify their ideas.

A new talent, that of Aileen McKeogh, emerged just at the end of the period under discussion, an artist with a more organic turn of mind who was to signal the rise of a most interesting group of young women artists in the period 1975-85.

There were, of course, always more painters than sculptors, whether male or female. One of the interesting aspects of Irish women's art of the sixties and early seventies was the groundswell of decent work which sustained the major talents. There was indeed a whole orchestra of minor players who showed their work in the group exhibitions and from which the divas or great soloists arose. There were artists like Eileen Costelloe and Noreen Rice whose work I reviewed time and again but which has not left even the slightest trace on my memory. There were painters like Barbara Warren, Margaret Irwin, Beatrice Behan, Caroline Scally, Pamela Mathews, Cherith McKinstry, Anne King-Harman, Phoebe Donovan, Anita Shelbourne, Kitty Wilmer O'Brien,

whose work appeared faithfully year after year, and which was always of a certain quality, but never reached those levels of intensity which would lift it into exciting art. Anna Ritchie was one of those the quality of whose work was above average. Married at that time to the painter Basil Blackshaw, her work was in an abstract vein not unlike a softer William Scott (Fig. 44). It is many years since I have seen any new work of hers but throughout the sixties she was an artist of consistent quality and interest.

Yet among all the artists whose work stands out in the sixties, like Michael Farrell, Robert Ballagh, Barrie Cooke, the women artists are among the most intense and the most distinguished. Anne Madden, who married the painter Louis le Brocquy in 1958, had been showing work in Dublin and London since the early fifties, but really began to come into her own in the nineteen-sixties with her new paintings of rock-forms. She was awarded the first Carroll's Prize in 1964 by the New York-based Irish critic Brian O'Doherty who, as critic for the *New York Times*, was the first adjudicator of the newly instituted Prizes. In the following year she represented Ireland at the Paris Biennale for Young Artists where her five-part rock painting of white forms on a black ground was deemed by the American poet-critic John Ashbery, writing in the *New York Herald Tribune*, to be the best painting in the Biennale.

She is an artist whose work has consistently come in peaks, easily identifiable. The large rock paintings of the mid-sixties, some in diptychs and triptychs or even more numerous assemblies of canvases, were her first peak, quite beautiful abstract paintings, based in rock and land formations, painted with superb nervous verve in a colour range of purple and white, or red, or a grainy white and sand (Fig. 45). Luckily many of these works are in public collections, in Trinity College, in the Hugh Lane Municipal

Fig. 45   Anne Madden, *Diptych, 1967*. Allied Irish Banks Collection.

Gallery of Modern Art, in the Ulster Museum and in Carroll's Factory in Dundalk.

The second peak was around 1970 with the very strong series of *Megaliths* and *Standing Stones*, those druidic monumnts which are still to be seen around the countryside. Anne Madden has painted them as giant forms emerging from the darkness of pre-history, simply outlined by a thin white line on dark brooding backgrounds of purple, black, navy-blue, and wine-dreg red. The paintings, again often diptychs, are sombre, with a fresh, rough and thriving gloom. The surface, while freely and sometimes wildly painted, holds together as absolutely as granite. 'For me, the image', she says, 'is important as an emotive charge, as in the megalith series, even though it often became abstracted to the point of disparition. What interests me in painting is the articulation of the pictorial space — or void. Painting only works, whether it be figurative or abstract, if the elements of which it is constructed — colour, light, form, space — are rendered eloquent. Whether the image disappears behind the canvas or whether it remains visible is not very important to me, as long as the painting functions as a pictorial space.'

One of the most moving of this series of 'Stone' paintings was the single panel *Menhir*, related in the artist's mind to a sacrificial stone, but surfacing on the canvas in a storm of red forcing its way through veils and layers of white, behind which the white lines of the original stone outline are just visible, as indeed the original reasons and justifications for war recede in the horrors of violence and terrorism.

These paintings emerged from an area of expression where vastly more powerful feelings are capable of being visibly created and tolerated than is possible in the medium of language. Such forceful expression was not fashionable at the time they were painted, a time of minimalism and reductivist painting, but this was not a seasonal art.

Menhir was one of the last of the megalith series and she has spoken of what happened: 'When I felt I was coming to the end of the megalith series, I introduced a horizontal line at the top of the vertical form, making an opening — for me an opening in my painting as well as an exit from these vertical canvases. These openings, doorways, windows, are metaphors of the artist's vision as well as openings into possible space, psychic and physical, interior and exterior, of the mind and of matter.'

While Anne Madden was exploring the possibilities of large-scale treatment of the landscape and of archaic monuments in it, old stones, tracks, walls, immemorial witnesses to the human presence, another artist Camille Souter was intensifying her more domestic view of the land. In the late fifties, Camille Souter was one of the best *tachiste* painters in the abstract expressionist manner, then almost at saturation point. She gained an Italian Government scholarship and spent some time in Italy which, curiously, did not have the effect of broadening or extending the range of her painting, but sent her back to a late-Impressionist Bonnard style of painting which suited her temperament extremely well. She gained a Carroll's Hon. Mention in the first series of prizes in 1964, and again in 1965 (Fig. 46).

Her popularity is understandable at many levels: her painting is small in scale, fitting easily into the normal domestic interior, its subject matter of man-managed nature, ordinary fields, still lives, makes no demands, and what saves the paintings from a slack or banal character is a very subtle intensity held right down to a perfect pitch of epiphany. The paintings are as ordinary and as memorable as a perfect walk in the country on a summer day.

At certain periods, the artist has dived off into pools of curious subject matter, series such as the joints of meat, the spines of fish from which the flesh has been eaten, paintings from the air of aeroplanes on the ground — she has completed over 40 hours of flying lessons — and other by-ways of interest, but her main concern has been the land, the ordinary out-of-town countryside, nothing heroic or dramatic, as profound, as lyrical, as eloquent as Horace or Heaney.

Maria Simonds-Gooding's work has been like a combination

Fig. 46 Camille Souter, *Washing by the Canal, 1964*. Limerick Municipal Gallery of Art.

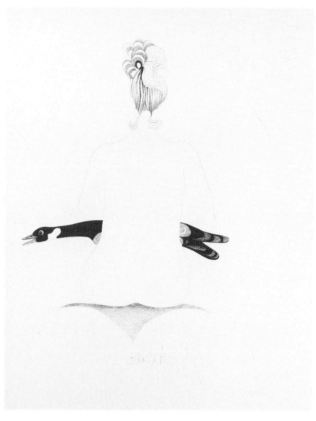

Fig. 47 Pauline Bewick, *Canada Goose and Girl, c.1965*. Private collection.

of Madden and Souter in her concern with archaic habitations as if seen from the air. From a built-up base on her canvases, she constructs ring-forts and other ancient signs of human presence. She won the Carroll's Prize for under-40's in 1970. She has gradually eliminated all colour from her reliefs. Although I believe that her preoccupation with the forms of ring-forts and ancient sites arose quite independently, the early work bears a striking resemblance to the painted reliefs of the Danish artist Jagemaker, shown in The Rosc Exhibition of 1967.

Following Maria Simonds-Gooding into County Kerry, the graphic artist Pauline Bewick, whose mother Harry Bewick was a witty and resourceful contriver of *objets trouvés* all through the sixties, set up house at Caragh Lake with her husband and childen, and incorporated her surroundings into her fluidly drawn, romantic water-colour illustration (Fig. 47). Many of these had fairy-tale echoes of swans, frogs, and miraculous fowl, set in a landscape of lakes, reeds, and rivers; the location was transported in the summer to Tuscany.

In spite of her work being so graphic, Pauline Bewick has never gone seriously into print-making. Reproductions of her very popular drawings have been made commercially, but not, so far as I am aware, original prints. I recall an exhibition of oil monographs which represented an attempt at oil-painting and at printing, but she was happy with neither, and returned to her favourite medium of water-coloured drawings. There have been, however, outstanding women print-makers who, again, have been leaders in the medium. Mary Farl Powers has been the most original and inventive of the many women print-makers, using mixed techniques of etching, relief etching, lithography and other media in largely abstract works with a most subtle use of colour (Fig. 48). Alice Hanratty was prominent in the revolutionary changes in the National College of Art & Design at the turn of the seventies when the stranglehold of the Royal Hibernian Academy over the school was finally loosened and abolished. She has largely concentrated on print-making, although I find that her large water-colour images are always more immediate and more satisfying than her prints. Nevertheless, she has produced a

considerable body of serious work in a Post-Modernist idiom, using Renaissance images of single portraits. Sara Horgan's mixed media prints and collages have a special sensibility, almost an early nineteenth century character of delicacy, charm, and wry resignation, although her aesthetic means are quite modern. Ruth Brandt, and Constance Shortt, while working in a more modest, conventional style, have provided, along with many others, that undemanding, pleasant body of work which underpinned the more outstanding talents, as did the women painters.

In the graphic medium of drawing, the Irish-American artist Kathleen Cooke held several solo shows of her work at the Hendriks Gallery during the period. Her animal drawings best showed her skill at conveying the bulk of a large beast in an almost continuous single line. She was able to express her respect for the animal while making an amusing image of its bulk.

Finally, among the many foreign artists who settled in Ireland in the period, including the American Minimalist Jo Baer — the subject of the opening exhibition in the new Douglas Hyde Gallery in Trinity College in 1978 — one of the most outstanding was the ceramic sculptor Sonja Landweer. Her ceramic objects, bowls, pots and sculptural pieces, were beautifully made and also had the quality of simple forms won at great cost from a multitude of possibilities. Her simplicity was subtle in the extreme, tuned to a feminine sensitivity in the exercise of the highest art and skill (Fig. 49). Her method of using a batik glaze was unprecedented in ceramics. Her work embodied the purest expression of fine art in one of its most ancient forms, with no scruples about it being

Fig. 48 Mary Farl Powers, *Cloud Torso 1, 1979*. Collection of the artist.

Fig. 49 Sonja Landweer, *Bowl*. Collection of the artist.

brazenly beautiful, useless, pure art. She concentrated entirely on beauty of form for its own sake, on achieving the most delicate thinness of texture and astonishing glazes. Her art was infinitely quiet, using sombre colours which did not, however, produce sombre effects but rather a profound subtlety and peace which

seemed to have genetic origins in the oriental forms of her pots and bowls, generally supported on a tiny round base.

Her later work included *Feathered Demons*, fetishistic objects combining feathers and pottery in dark shades of black and brown.

It will be seen that the core of Irish women's art in the period 1960-75 was still involved with basic concerns of landscape and nature, not particularly with family or personal relationships, nor with feminist policies and that these concerns were pushed very far beyond the conventional treatment of these subjects.

The imagination and vision of artists like Anne Madden and Camille Souter in painting, and of Gerda Frömel and Alexandra Wejchert in sculpture, injected new life and spirit into all women working in the arts, so that this period of the sixties and early seventies carried through, very strongly, into another generation the inimitable pioneering work of Mainie Jellett and Evie Hone, Mary Swanzy, Norah McGuinness, and Nano Reid. So many women, so much fine art.

Contemporary women artists

Aidan Dunne

The years between the mid-seventies and mid-eighties made up a revisionist decade. They saw the first serious eclipse of Modernism as the prevalent artistic orthodoxy, the acceptance of pluralism as a *fait accompli*, the meteoric rise of the New Painting. At the same time, pluralism has, by definition, allowed the continuing diversification of experimental arts practice and the consolidation of novel forms and media.

The high proportion of young women artists active in Ireland has ensured that any account of their work throughout the last ten years is central to any discussion of Irish art, or of the perpetual contemporary debate about what art is and what it might be.

Numerical value, the quality of work and the fact of successful careers clearly suggest a practical equality of the sexes in Irish art. Yet it is undoubtedly true that a history of recent events in the South, including the Anti-Abortion and Divorce referenda campaigns, indicate that the role of women in Irish society is still hidebound by a deeply entrenched conservatism. Women artists, no more than women of any other status or vocation, cannot but be affected by prevailing social conditions, and they must still face many of the pitfalls outlined in Germaine Greer's *Obstacle Race*.

It is notable, for example, that women have been conspicuous by their absence in two large group exhibitions selected by men in recent years: Making Sense and Directions Out. Could it be that the criteria of selection employed hinge on specifically male attitudes? In any case, this curious imbalance is often reflected in international terms. While it is easy to think of many internationally renowned artists who happen to be women, big survey exhibitions like Zeitgeist and A New Spirit in Painting boasted few female exemplars — a fact perhaps indicative of the underlying machismo of expressionist painting.

In Ireland, younger artists have come to terms with, or choose to ignore, the indigenous modern visual arts tradition. This might be briefly summarised as a half-assimilated Modernism; what has been described as romantic landscape painting, and expressionist figuration. A whole host of other, outside issues, socio-political, environmental, and formal, press for attention, together with immediate problems of personal expression.

While the Irishness of Irish art is a disputed commodity, there is no doubt that the country has, North and South, remained an insular pocket in relation to the international art world. Attempts to promote Irish art abroad have been sporadic and, with a few notable exceptions, only marginally successful. Influences have been felt and absorbed here, but it is a predominantly one-way traffic.

There is nothing new about this. The vein of international Modernism that gained currency here was, in most cases, steeped in a kind of local vernacular. It was diffidently embraced, cautiously practised. It is certainly true however, that by the mid-seventies, educational developments and the cumulative dispersion of visual arts information through the mass media meant that younger artists and students were exposed to a much broader range of arts practice than their predecessors, and arguably felt, to a greater extent, pressures to come to terms with it in their own work.

Art in Ireland had, however, retained a basically conservative character. The precarious dominance here of any prevalent international orthodoxy cannot be compared with the situation in any corner of the truly cosmopolitan art world. So that, for example, when Susan Rothenberg decided one day that the time had come to describe the outline of a horse, with oil paint, on canvas, an event that as much as any other signalled the general move to painting, such a move, while meeting with some enthusiasm here, certainly lacked the taint of heresy it held elsewhere. It meant something quite different as seen through the filter of Irish caution.

The Modernist enterprise in Ireland was but one element in a complex pattern of activity, a regionalised, greatly attenuated version of international holy writ. It is not an overstatement to say that before Irish artists ever seriously came to terms with Modernism, they were told that they dwelt in a Post-Modernist environment: tear up the rule book, catch as catch can, it's anybody's game. In a way, this meant nothing more than a licence to go on doing precisely what they had been doing all along.

Many critics and historians have documented and elucidated the role of women in the history of western painting as passive possessions, there to be displayed, regarded by male patrons and viewers as desirable objects. The majority of images of women projected in the mass media today are similarly passive, dependent on male-determined notions of glamour, desirability or domesticity. The proliferation of such images, it has been argued, leads to a compliant narcissism in the female audience. Women are persuaded to look, act and respond in certain predetermined ways, ways that gratify male expectations.

It is reasonable to expect that women artists will approach the received images of their sex in both art history and consumer culture critically, that they will set out to counter and reconstruct those images. Such a programme inevitably involves grappling with a much wider range of issues than might at first be apparent. It entails dealing with such areas as individulity, male-female relationships and individual roles within social groups. We are, essentially, talking about constructing an alternative image of a world we have come to take for granted.

The Women's Movement has changed the general perception of female experience, investing major aspects of it with a significance and validity previously denied. Younger artists have, whether concurrently or as a consequence, been able to reassess in their work the quality and nature of previously obscured levels of experience, and perhaps to make a truer image of both women and the world they inhabit.

Sometimes this reassessment is completely straightforward. Sculptress Joan Smith's work, for example, is a celebration of the female. Rounded, egglike forms suggest pregnancy, motherhood, and her *Earthmother* is a large-scale, outdoor sculpture of a nude woman, half submerged, face down, as if swimming in the earth itself. The artist, incidentally, is by no means alone in eschewing any hint of a radical feminist perspective. This seems like a reasonable wish to indicate that her work is in no sense special pleading, that it is general in its scope.

Dublin artist Pauline Cummins has similarly been interested in expressing the maternal experience in terms of exuberant sensuality. Paintings of women dancing, high-keyed and loosely made, gave way to work in other media. Nine Months and After, an exhibition on pregnancy and childbirth which she organised, has as its centrepiece a photographic slide-tape presentation made by her about her own pregnancy. This installation focussed on the fullness of sensual experience engendered by pregnancy and was, primarily, a celebration of the richness of life and the creativity. A more recent slide-tape project, *Inis t-Oirr*, sees a woman proprietorially projecting (figuratively and literally) herself onto the body of her husband or lover through the personalised pattern of an Aran gansey. In drawing on such cultural references, and exploring the nature of a sexual relationship in genuinely novel terms, Cummins has considerable broadened the reach and sophistication of her work.

Louise Walsh, a Limerick-born artist, has aggressively tackled conventional images of woman in savage, life-size figures made from recycled natural and synthetic materials. These roughhewn, *bricolage* beings are recognisably human and female, but have horses' heads: woman as 'a beast of burden'. The violence of her technique, and the often pointed cruelty of her choice of materials

Fig. 50 Louise Walsh, *Harvest Queen, 1986.* Collection of the artist.

Fig. 51 Cathy Carmen, *'There's a Woman Phase, whose wounds cry out like stones from a sling'*, 1986. Collection of the artist.

Fig. 52 Eithne Jordan, *Study for three heads, 1986.* The Hendriks Gallery.

— for example, domestic objects forcefully displaced, colander as buttock, baby's bottle as breast — demonstrate and indict women's social position and give her sculptures an abrasive edge. Often they seem to castigate the passivity of their subjects as well as pointing out the injustice of their position. It is worth noting Walsh's considerable technical skills and the awareness of conservation issues that her employment of found materials implies.

Cathy Carman's figures, sculpted in wood and stone, and cast in bronze, are also roughly treated. Whether gouged with a chainsaw, or chiselled, hacked and generally savaged, their stubbornness, intractability and determination to survive is emphasised. They are durable female spirits, battered by fats and circumstances but vital, solid and outward looking. Rhythmic patterns of movement and the use of bold colour suggest buoyancy and underline this openness. Despite apparent vicissitudes, the dominant impression is one of optimism and immense durability, a durability rooted in earthy contact.

Eithne Jordan came by way of aerial, expansive, abstract expressionist landscapes to figurative painting. Her series of swimmers were loosely made, generalised beings that blended with the rhythm of the current and, by extension, of their world. Gradually she began to treat allegorical themes — Beauty and the Beast, notably — in terms of flattened, vague drawing and a sombre palette. Descriptions of motherhood and family life were made in this vein: the child as a small, clinging beast, the husband or lover as a towering, overwhelming presence, the woman weighed down, smothered. There is a sculptural monumentality

to her figures, who move sluggishly, as if still underwater. The mood in her pictures is often mellow and positive rather than oppressive, expressing, for example, the affirmative aspects of friendship and solidarity, co-operation as opposed to exploitation. That descriptive vagueness endures, as if she still distrusts the apparatus of naturalism.

Vivien Burnside and Ann Timony both deal with individual figures and with more complex groups. Burnside's wall drawings, distinctive cut-outs with a characteristic umber, burnt complexion, flow freely across the wall, evading the strictures of rectangular format. There is an exuberance in their inveterate, dancing motion. The drawing is relaxed, freely naturalistic, and emancipation seems to be equated with energy and movement. Timony's figures and sculptural tableaux, indebted to George Segal and Ed Keinholz, can be theatrical and have the air of illustrating given ideas — perceptual prisons, the difficulty of personal communication, self-image, alienation. A certain roughness of handling is evident, and can work against the mood of the pieces, but her energy and ambition augur well.

Where Timony illustrates directly, Gabby Dowling, who has worked in stage and prop design for several years, created, in Animal, her highly theatrical exhibition of sculpture and drawings, and allegorical world in which the cosy anthropomorphism of fables and fairy tales is turned on its head, its exemplars given real teeth and applied to the realm of human emotional life. Like Louise Walsh, Dowling employs materials pointedly and precisely. Her vision of an aggressive, predatory set of creatures was genuinely unsettling and effective.

Joanna Robertson is a painter whose deadpan, precise realism and liking for the dark side of domesticity suggests the influence of Lucian Freud. Her portrait drawings and paintings display a desire to deal directly, nakedly with their subjects. This aspiration to emotional honesty is a major virtue of her work, though it has yet to result in a truly individual style or vision, (in this she is comparable to another figurative painter of considerable ability, Geraldine O'Reilly). Vicki Olverson's less differentiated female figures, whether sculpted in ceramic or vigorously painted and drawn, are repositories of energy, virtual amazons, sometimes juxtaposed with land or seascapes that are equally tempestuous.

Rita Duffy's subjects are invariably differentiated. Her subject matter is the city life of her native Belfast, from her immediate circle to the wider social context. In its depiction she addresses immediate issues: the practical difficulties of coping with poverty and unemployment, the police presence on the streets, civil strife. The expressionist distortion of her work can slide towards caricature.

Duffy's crowded social panorama, with its discordant vitality, its urgency, contrasts with the blandness of the domestic spaces outlined in the work of two other painters, Carol Graham and Diana Kingston, though, like Mary Roden, who employed photo-realist images drawn from advertising to illustrate the position of women in contemporary society, Kingston began to incorporate advertising imagery in her work in a quizzical, interrogative way.

Dublin painter Mary Burke has explored the urban world with a curious impersonality. This generally uninhabited, highly synthetic environment, is depicted in terms of heightened, unnatural colours and textures. The spaces — bedrooms, bathrooms, driveways, buses — seem as if they have just been vacated. The effect recalls Edward Hopper's night-time city scenes, lonely yet inviting. Burke seems similarly ambivalent about the anonymity and strangeness of her immediate environment. The emotional spareness of her work contrasts with Veronica Bolay's domestic world, a comfortable place of reassuring certainties. Bolay's pleasantly decorative, modest depictions of workaday scenes and events have won her an enthusiastic public and critical following.

Eilish McCarrick is an artist who has worked in a variety of media and shown a preference for photography. Her photographs, particularly, treat the received image of Irish domesticity harshly. Even the mundane is given an edge of menace, and she has an eye for jarring, surreal detail. There is a Hitchcockian obsessiveness and morbidity to her explorations of both the domestic and the hard urban worlds, and an implicit suggestion that the pressures of family life and early experience engender the atrophied emotional life, the defensive coldness of a harshly delineated, alternative, darklit culture. Like Louise Walsh, she is a cruel observer of convention. McCarrick's fragmentary, atmospheric images suggest echoes of Cindy Sherman's photographs, charged with drama, like single frames from imaginary films. Julie Murray has, in videos and installations, used the narrative and pictorial conventions of the thriller to create an atmosphere of anxiety and menace, lending the familiar an unsettling strangeness.

Claire Donnelly's video *Doll* chronicles the punishment of a woman who renounces her doll-like role and dares to express her own, autonomous sensuality. Called to order by a mechanical soldier drummer, there is no room in her world for individual, female expression. The theme is perhaps developed from an installation piece which implied that the expression of such sensuality was fallaciously controlled by religious institutions, a reversal of true priorities. Margaret Magee, another performance and video artist, now working in America, has critically explored

the relationship between institutional and individual priorities.

'We were spiritually mugged, verbally raped, placed under constitutional threat,' Nell McCafferty later wrote of women's experiences during the Anti-Abortion Referendum campaign in 1983. Three years later, the Referendum on the proposed change in the constitution in relation to Divorce was defeated by a majority of two to one, recreating the moral split of this Anti-Abortion vote. A number of individual incidents in between the two events ominously corroborated McCafferty's aggrieved view.

The horrific death of schoolgirl Ann Lovett while giving birth in a field in Granard, in 1984; the protracted Kerry Babies Tribunal and the experience of Joanne Hayes; the dismissal of teacher Eileen Flynn (because she had a baby out of wedlock) and the expulsion of girl pupils from Catholic schools on similar grounds, all indicated the circumscribed, embattled position of women in Irish society.

'We conducted a debate on male-defined terms and we lost the debate', McCafferty said of the Anti-Abortion Referendum. Equally, the Kerry Babies Tribunal reflected a male-dominated society in its constitution, its underlying attitudes and in its eventual judgement. Against the background of specific, tragic and traumatic personal experiences like those of Ann Lovett or Joanne Hayes, the bitterness of Louise Walsh's imagery, Cathy Carman's figuratively scarred figures, Eilish McCarrick's mordant view of domestic life, or painter Jacinta Feeney's early paintings, which took a grotesque view of the same subject, do not look like extreme responses — which is not, of course, to claim that they responded to individual events.

Rather, these events, and the ethos of which they are symptomatic do graphically demonstrate just why individual artists should need to find their own space, to shape their own worlds — a common feature of artistic expression, but one given particular urgency and relevance in the case of Irish women.

'I would like my work to be seen as some kind of evidence of a private world,' Kathy Prendergast has said. 'It is a separate reality which is inspired by, drawn from, parallel to and yet very distant from our own world.' The writer and critic Denis Donoghue, in his *Arts Without Mystery* lectures, views this access to another reality, beyond the *realpolitik* of daily life, as one of art's major strengths.

Prendergast's work has employed some of the mechanics of exploration and archaeology in describing her own world. Her series of map-drawings, of a woman's body as landscape, and her *Concise History of the World,* had a conceptual completeness and originality. Other projects have provided more fragmentary, but still compelling glimpses of separate realities: the Egyptian-like tomb hoard of *Homage,* the mythic implications of the twining serpents in *Lick Your Own Wound Mate* and the chariot of *Scuttle.* These implications are picked up in a ghostly series of watercolours in which ephemeral male and female figures engage in bizarre couplings and juxtapositions. They resemble accounts of some strange creation myth. It is notable that Prendergast moves freely from one medium to another, that what counts for her is the quality of the vision she is trying to express.

Anne O'Regan's world comes to us complete. Arcane and

Fig. 53 Kathy Prendergast, *Untitled, 1982-83.* Private collection.

Fig. 54 Anne O'Regan, *Pandora's Smiling Again, 1986.* Collection of the artist.

remote, fanatically detailed, it is another lost civilisation, a kingdom of the Incas or an Ancient Egypt, with its own grandiose, decorative architecture. An interior space of massive vaulted ceilings, texturally dense, it is inhabited by animal and human creatures who blend imperceptibly into the background complication. Such materials as a weathered, badly oxidated panel from a car door, or tin cans flattened and collaged in place, fit seamlessly into this archaeological framework: an imaginative glimpse back into the past of the present. O'Regan avoids the risk of being taken for a whimsical, Tolkien-like fantasist through her assiduous refusal to settle for cute effects. Instead, she presents us with a world that is genuinely strange and compelling.

Jane Proctor in her Licata-like drawings uses the idiom of ideograms and hieroglyphics and the classical languages to create her own hermetic script. Antiquity is also implied in the frequently fragmentary presentation, as if the image is but a ragged scrap of papyrus salvaged from a greater whole. A wariness, an unease, is implied in this distancing of self from the here-and-now, but at the same time her work functions primarily on a decorative level.

Jacinta Feeney's early paintings, wild, loosely made images of sexual and emotional violence, were set in a claustrophobic domestic world, a Beckettian, Baconian nowhere overseen by crucifixes on the walls, faces peering though the windows as distorted women underwent varieties of torment. The force packed into these grotesque images was like a cry of anguish, but the *Grand Guignol* effects tended to drown out the message. Feeney has subsequently refined her vision considerably, with mixed results. She has invented a personal mythic realm, a lotus-eating, Mediterranean island world she explores at a langorous pace. Attempts to marry this soft focus setting with a sharper, referential style of realism have been uneasy. The dominant impression of her work to date is one of escape from repressive domesticity to a rich, imaginative inner life.

In a way, escape is also the dominant theme in Anita Groener's paintings. A Dutch expatriate, Groener, like her compatriot Karel Appel in the 1950's and '60's, is obsessed with a child's vision of the world, that is, with an innocent vision, visually and emotionally innocent, untainted by knowledge of the trials and tribulations of adult life. Children's drawings, her own and others', are obviously an important source, but the pictures have their own gestural, spiky language. In them, flight is usually a metaphor for escape and freedom. Crows flutter around ubiquitously, harbingers of both good and bad. Groener's work superficially resembles mainstream New Painting, but in fact its roots are elsewhere and the resemblance is purely incidental.

If Groener obsessively explores a childhood world, Alice Maher in her drawings and paintings repeatedly returns to a dreamscape wherein is enacted a violent, surreal drama. No element in this nightmare vision is neutral: everything is in the grip of traumatic

Fig. 55   Jacinta Feeney, *Untitled, 1979/80*. Collection of the artist.

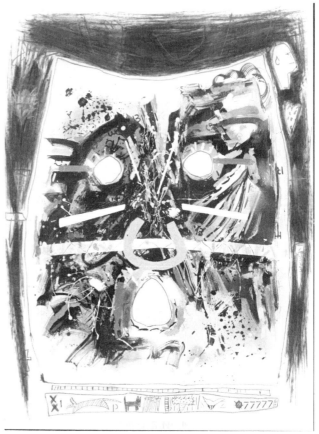

Fig. 57   Anne Carlisle, *Sing Sing II, 1983*. Private collection.

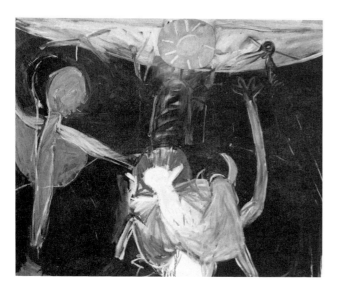

Fig. 56   Anita Groener, *Dionysus Fell, II, 1987*. Collection of the artist.

metamorphosis, is attacked or attacking, consuming or consumed. It is, like Gabby Dowling's fictional creation, a predatory realm. The imagery is often sexual: aggressive phalli and vaginae dentatae. As with Feeney's early paintings, however, there is a cumulative sense of excess, a sense that the horror-story imagery uses surrealistic method to achieve easy effects.

Anne Carlisle is an artist with a brilliant decorative instinct,

unrivalled in handling flat colour and pattern, who has never settled for mere decoration. The bulk of her work to date has fleshed out her own personal world, for example a series of still lifes devoted to favourite objects, or *naif,* fond celebrations of animals and animal imagery. There is generally a tension present between the figurative subject and the abstract, spontaneous nature of the marks used to describe it. As if to emphasise this, she inclines to indirection, preferring images of things to the things themselves — masks rather than faces, for example, or gardens as visual expressions of human personality. The flat colour, abstracted patterns, naive drawing and cut-outs all repeatedly underline the flatness of the picture plane. *Rag Trade,* 'a pictorial analysis of a various levels of involvement that women have in relation to (the textile industry)', a mixed media piece exhibited at the Fenderesky Gallery in 1986, was notably different.

Anna O'Sullivan, now working in the United States, has, in a variety of media, including performance and film, worked from the basis of often painful personal experience to make statements of general relevance. Her video *Fat Aggie Sings*, took an Orbach-like look at weight, as a personal and a feminist issue, in terms of devastating, self-deprecating humour — such self-honesty has become a hallmark of her work.

In some respects Eilis O'Connell's work, like Kathy Prendergast's, seems to relate to some alternative world. Its obsessiveness, its formal complexity, its imaginative leaps all suggest an attempt to provide a precise description of some

Fig. 58   Anna O'Sullivan, *Two stills from video, "Fat Aggie Sings", 1984*. Collection of the artist.

difficult, intractible reality. Like Vivienne Roche, she began as a hard-edge steel abstractionist. But whereas Roche has remained forthrightly Modernist in her concerns, linking her work to the masses and forms of modern architecture, O'Connell has progressively admitted more and more references into her sculpture, perhaps influenced by her interest in archaeology and primitive art. Some of these references, to source materials, natural and synthetic (feathers, for example, or a fragment of a skillet) are allowed to stand in the finished pieces. There is an enduring tension between organic and geometric forms. The finished, fetishistic objects always have an air of being fastidiously, painstakingly formed, and much of the effort seems devoted to turning them

in on themselves — lately they are protected with multiple layers of burnished colour. Mask-like wall pieces exemplify this trait.

Landscape has long been a central area of preoccupation for Irish artists. Younger artists have been continually drawn to it without accepting given terms. For many, landscape is actually something more, a way into the world of nature, and the whole problematic issue of our perception of and relationship to the natural world. In the work of an artist like Pauline Cummins, as well, there is an implicit suggestion that through specifically female experience, women are instinctively closer to nature than men, that the female sensibility is more in tune with the natural order than the male. It is a perception that informs, or can be logically deduced from the work of a number of artists, including Alanna O'Kelly, Una Walker, Helen Comerford, Joan Smith, Eithne Jordan and Vicki Olverson. Yet it would be wrong to imply that every landscape made by a woman is inspired by the notion of embodying the female principle. The work simply tackles too broad a range of issues for that to be the case, often working from an existing tradition and in the process transforming and renewing it.

Cecily Brennan's paintings and drawings are firmly rooted in landscape. Her formidable drawings of Wicklow in 1982 used the full reach of her body. Their viewpoint enabled us to soar birdlike over the mountains and valleys, the forestry plantations, bogs and lakes. All this weight of physical detail was hungrily absorbed and described with urgent, gestural strokes in images that were brimming with energy.

More recently, Brennan has narrowed the focus of her gaze and become absorbed in swirling, vibrant pictures precipitated by visits to Howth's Rhododendron Gardens. Sonorous, soft-focus colours arranged in subtle, spiralling patterns draw the spectator deep into the paintings. Immersed, so to speak, in the painting, one is free to absorb associations. The neutral, flexible beauty of her work has a great deal to do with its considerable popularity. Monet's Giverny is the indispensible point of reference, and perhaps Pollock's voyages of spiritual discovery. Brennan is, by comparison, a cautious painter, carefully circumscribing the limits of her world, not as ready to let herself go as she was in those Wicklow landscapes.

Fig. 59   Eilis O'Connell, *Bee Mask, 1985*. Private collection.

Aileen McKeogh's relief sculptures are fantastically elaborated accounts of landscape, abstracted like cross-sections, allowing us to see the tree roots twining below, mirroring the spread of branches above. They have something of the air of scale models, but models of nature as a composite of interacting processes, ecological works that note human influence on the land. These works follow on a prolonged interest in wood and forests which led to sculptures and installations that set out to encapsulate something of the spirit of a forest as a hallowed, special place, an harmonious, self-sustaining ecosystem. At an early stage, McKeogh moved from traditional materials and processes to direct use of wood and wood products. Found natural materials play an important part in the more recent work as well.

Painter Jackie Cooney also treats landscape in dynamic terms, but in a way that tends towards formalist abstraction. Her spare, careful paintings suggest layered strata. She treats basic details and patterns analytically, and individual elements, precisely observed, rather than an ecological overview, form the basis of her work.

The same holds for Theresa McKenna, whose tapestries and constructions employ a wide range of materials in robust investigations of natural form and pattern. Often her imagery includes specifically male and female elements. McKenna's use of materials draws on a host of traditional female skills, likewise Vivienne Bogan, whose collaged watercolours of handmade paper are often sewn together, as if she is literally stitching the landscape.

Fig. 60   Cecily Brennan, *Bog Drawing, 1982*. Bank of Ireland Collection.

Fig. 61   Aileen McKeogh, *Treescape, 1985*. Collection of the artist.

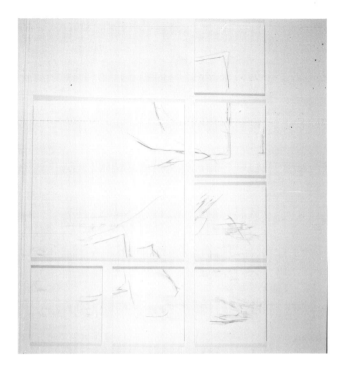

Fig. 62   May Fitzgerald, *The Drawing Room 1, 1986*. Collection of the artist.

Fig. 63   Gwen O'Dowd, *Summers Evening, 1985*. Collection of the artist.

Mary Fitzgerald's analytical methodology compares, on some levels, with Jackie Cooney's, though her forms are more abstracted, organised on organic/geometric poles. Her work is based on the grid, and its tensions derive from the balance of opposites: light and dark, geometric and gestural shapes, blankness and clutter. Essentially, free gestural marks are bounced off a grid in a way reminiscent of the work of Felim Egan. Fitzgerald has made increasingly elaborate arrangements of composites that allow her to establish complex sequences and inter-relationships.

Though she began by concentrating on the details of decay in Dublin's Inner City, Gwen O'Dowd has steadily moved to a more general treatment of the theme of decay and seasonal regeneration. Her large abstract paintings present rich, densely textured surfaces, suggesting, at first, sources like the exposed inner walls of half-demolished buildings, weathered paintwork and so on. There was a certain ambivalence towards this subject matter. It was treated almost exclusively in aesthetic terms: beauty in decay. The problems posed by this have eased since she broadened her range of references. Her pictures are by no means sentimental in their view of nature. They have a brash vigour, a take-it-or-leave-it roughness. Thick varnish binds many unruly layers of diverse texture together. A younger painter, Rachel Kerr, focusses on rocks by and under water to produce comparable if less sophisticated, more heavy handed textural images.

By contrast, air and water, in Bernadette Kiely's fluid compositions are in a state of constant flux, swirling in buoyant, spiralling patterns of movement. Sculptress Sally Houston has also examined the flowing patterns of water in drawings and, surprisingly, perhaps, in wood-and-steel sculptures. These pieces resemble conventional abstract constructivist works, but are exceptionally energised, rushing their planes and volumes through

tangles of intersections and collisions, bearing a figurative relationship to the hectic mobility of flowing water.

A sense of natural flux also informs Helen O'Toole's large, gestural canvasses. Abstract Expressionist in feeling, they have an authentically earthy colour range and an excellent sense of space. Their expansive, watery freedom suggests an Eastern influence. Lorraine Wall's landscapes are part of a quieter world, much of it bounded by hedgerows, farmed but flourishing, unsubdued. Unemphatic but persuasive, her paintings, often composites to facilitate panoramic views, have a patient, enlightened appreciation of the land.

The basis of Alanna O'Kelly's work in many media is the whole question of the relationship between humans and their natural environment. Sensitive to the nature of materials, and eager to link artistic practice to the natural cycle ('Materials that I bring together, weave together, take their energy from the earth. It is not removed,' i.e., the work does not disturb the natural order of things), she has made flax sculptures and installations employing natural and primitive craft forms, by implication indicating their virtue and appropriateness. Her repertoire of forms, skills and ideas was broadened through wide travel, but her concerns certainly originate along the Wexford coastline of her childhood. These enduring interests have led her to address her work to contemporary issues, and to utilise a growing variety of means, including live performance and video installation. *Chant Down Greenham,* for example, counterpoints her own voice with a tape of heavy machinery in a graphic demonstration of the conflict between human (obviously with particular reference to the female sensibility) and technological values. O'Kelly is both committed in the partisan sense, an issues artists, and technically adventurous, a resourceful investigator of her physical environment.

As with Pauline Cummins, she has sought out ways of discovering and applying her own cultural heritage as an Irishwoman. Una Walker's installations also use a wide range of materials and cultural references in works that relate to the myriad manifestations of the natural cycle, and the human (and particularly woman's) place in it, often with reference to folk tradition or mythological beliefs. Julie Kelleher's paintings and, more recently, installations, have evidenced an enthusiasm for the Dionysian side of nature, its prodigality, its spontaneity, implicitly identifying with this vision of enlightened chaos.

Many individuals who have been discussed here as practising artists have also been active in related administrative areas. Cecily Brennan and Eithne Jordan were responsible for establishing the Visual Arts Centre Ltd., designed to provide studio and workshop space for young artists at affordable rents, now located at Strand Street in Dublin. Nearby, the New Art Studios, founded by Mary Burke and Maria Keating in 1983, fulfils a similar function. On the other side of the Liffey, Jenny Haughton has been the administrator of Temple Bar Studios since its inception, and a driving force behind its service and exhibition activities.

Anne Carlisle and Deirdre O'Connell are both practising artists involved in the founding and running of *Circa*, the Irish contemporary art journal, and clearly see this involvement as a vital aspect of their arts activities.

Women have been, and continue to be, instrumental in the functioning of the network of regional arts centres and galleries. Brid Dukes, for example, was for many years a remarkably energetic presence as administrator of the Belltable Arts Centre. She is currently engaged in establishing a private gallery in Limerick; while Blaithin de Sachy, now director of the Hendriks Gallery in Dublin, was, as co-director of her own Lincoln Gallery, a tireless advocate of work by gallery artists in a way that went beyond notional professional responsibilities.

Circa has been enormously important in opening up the discussion of arts practice in Ireland at a time when, with the waning of a dominant Modernist ideal, the field is necessarily uncertain and fragmented. Initiatives have been taken in recent times in the direction of community arts, with localised administrative structures and efforts towards communal involvement in anything from exhibitions and arts weeks to mural projects. Nevertheless, a gallery-oriented system of state and private patronage still dominates the art world, and the contemporary arts audience remains very much a minority. The major reforms in the basis of art education needed to change this state of affairs seem more remote than ever at a time of budgetary cutbacks.

What can be said is that many Irish artists, female and male, have shown exceptional energy and commitment to artistic practice over the last decade, and that they have been consistently active in areas beyond the immediate scope of their own creative work, in administration, publishing and education: that they have not passively accepted their role in a given order but have, in their work and outside of it, sought to question and change that order.

Contemporary women artists

Practices and issues into the future

Joan Fowler

If at the turn of the twentieth century women artists were, with very few exceptions, regarded as little more than happy amateurs, the closing decades of the century indicate a substantial increase in the numbers of professional women artists who regularly exhibit their work. Attendant upon this development are the questions: Is strength in numbers a sign of equality? Are there significant differences between the concerns of women artists and those of their male counterparts? The questions at least warrant an attempt to trace the course of contemporary art by Irish women, to locate their work within an Irish art context, to compare their position with trends abroad, to pinpoint directions into the future.

At the outset it is necessary to state that to discuss women's art exclusive of men's art is to run into immediate reactions. Many feminists will argue the dangers of ghettoization, that is, that focussing on women's work can reinforce women's marginal position(s) in relation to the power structures in society, rather than activate change. There are the facts that, for all the success of contemporary women's art, it is usually men who educate women artists, their work is usually selected by men, whether for public or private galleries or commissioned, and within these processes the artist may have very little control over her work. Alternatively, the mention of women's art can conjure up all sorts of pre-conceptions about supposedly feminine qualities, for example, handcraft related practices. And indeed, in contemporary Irish art there are several prominent women artists who engage with hand-made paper and/or delicate surface qualities in their painting. But the equation between women artists and notions of feminity is not particularly productive. To disentangle psychological — 'natural' — considerations from social conditioning and women's traditional roles is, in many respects, a red herring.

The second point to be made is that this is the first large scale exhibition of women's art in Ireland.[1] Because it is necessarily exploratory it would be wrong to be overly programmatic about the contemporary situation and to pretend cohesion where cohesion does not exist. Whether or not there should be a specifically 'women's angle' is a separate question, and one for the future. As it is, we have a selection of women's art which reflects a range of contemporary art practices and media, and what amounts to the beginnings of differing responses to the women's movement of the seventies and eighties. This is not to be disparaging, but to say that feminist issues are only just beginning to take effect and inevitably will be a major factor in determining the shape(s) of women's art in the decade to come. If anything, this exhibition may act as a catalyst simply because it is the first forum of its kind.

When we look to group show catalogues of the early 1970's as indicators of the numbers of women artists exhibiting along with men artists, we find they are a very small minority. This was true of the annual shows, the Irish Exhibition of Living Art and the Independents, which represented the more progressive elements in Irish art.[2] Cecily Brennan has argued that the influence of post-World War II Modernist art was sufficient in Ireland for the pervasive model to be that of the male artist.[3] The Independents group was, and by and large still is, best known for somewhat aggressive expressionist painting or printmaking and a rough-and-ready life style. There is an element of living out male artist stereotyped roles within the group. In IELA, after the retirement of Mainie Jellett, Brian King became Chairman in 1972 and he helped inaugurate a period of more experimental art media, though again male artists tended to pre-dominate.

By the late seventies at least two forces helped to increase the representation of women. Art education was changing and expanding, and the development of the economy in the sixties created a situation where private galleries could be established. The modernization of the art schools and the introduction of new art departments initiated greater potential in higher education and allowed the enhancement of the number of women students who also intended to develop their careers after college. Opportunity was also aided by more public galleries in the mould of the Project Arts Centre in Dublin (opened 1966) which specifically encouraged young artists. Arts Centres outside Dublin were developed and, with new or newly vamped galleries such as the Taylor, the Hendriks and Oliver Dowling, these facilities and exhibition spaces were essential to the development of the visual arts, particularly, it so happens, to women artists, since their arrivals coincided.

Outside Ireland, the seventies were distinguished by extreme forms of artistic experimentation within *avant-garde* circles. For a long time prior to this a debate was forged around the question, 'is photography art?', but by the seventies the issue had lost most of its pertinence as artforms became more and more extreme. Photography was an important medium for artists committed to process over product, since photographic documentation was in many cases the only record of the work. It was a decade of reaction against the art object (especially painting) and its projected role in the art market as a unique object of high investment value. Art, it was thought, was not reducible to monetary considerations. Conceptual art was especially strong in Italy, West Germany, France and England, while in the United States installation work devolved from Minimalism and was adopted in western Europe. The installation was site specific work which operated in a particular space, often could be reassembled in a different location, and had ramifications for both indoor and outdoor sites.

By the mid-1970s, however, performance art was the most dominant avant-garde force. While its reign is regarded as short-lived, giving way to the 'return' of painting by the late seventies, it is worthwhile referring in this context to its precursor in the United States — body art. Body art was partly stimulated by American women artists, for example Lynda Benglis, who used their own body as a means of highlighting men's sexual and economic authority over women. Body art was therefore the first art movement to be directly informed by the resurgence of feminism and, as we trace the developments in women's art in the 1980's when women's issues extend to other art mediums, there continues to exist forms of protest art in the United States which have antecedence in body art.

These movements were comparatively insubstantial in Ireland. It should be borne in mind that the philosophies which generated Modernism were articulated elsewhere in Europe and North America earlier in the century and by this time, just after their arrival on these shores, they were already spent forces. Irish radicalism in art in the 1970's was as much a continued reaction to the oppressive fifties as anything else. This is not to ignore the contributions made by artists who for example exhibited with the Independents and the Irish Exhibition of Living Art, but because the eighties are a time of major reassessment and realignment, in retrospect it might be said that Modernism arrived in Ireland too late to make a sustained impact. It was a moral victory, however, that the Modernists displaced the hegemony of the Royal Hibernian Academy as part and parcel of a modernization process in Ireland.

Another view of the advance of the modern movement since the sixties is that Ireland is essentially too conservative to assimilate fundamental change, and that modernity is only skin deep. Such arguments relate to the development of a greater consciousness of women's art because the pattern in centres abroad is that radical feminist art, predictably enough, emerges within avant-garde art or 'advanced' art. (However unfashionable the concept of progress might be, we are still dealing with art which is perceived to be radical.) But in the 1970's radical art was synonymous with medium. In Ireland there is not one single action by a woman

artist that is comparable to the performance of Brian O'Doherty or Robert Ballagh in their respective reactions to the events of 'Bloody Sunday' in Derry in 1972. It is indicative rather than surprising. Most likely there was not the same sense of 'artistic licence' for women as for men.

Since 1972 Brian King and then, from 1984, Aileen McKeogh, as Chairpersons of the Irish Exhibition of Living Art, have actively attempted to encourage less conventional artforms that have included performance, video and more recently billboards and banners.[4] Despite their efforts, and despite the contribution of third level education as well as the evolution of other open Submission exhibitions such as the Limerick Exhibition of Visual Art, (EVA), the support system is in this respect very poor and even in decline because of recent financial pressures. Most galleries continue the preponderance of painting, drawing, print and sculpture. We do not know, therefore, if performance in Ireland has the same potential for women artists as occurred in the United States and Europe. For instance, Derry-born artist Roberta Graham, who is based in London, has developed audio-slide presentations that explore her own sexuality. Whether these presentations actually counteract the long-standing prerogative of male artists to express their sexual fantasies through art is a moot point, but in so far as there is nothing comparable in Ireland there is a question mark, even though Kathy Prendergast and Alice Maher *have* approached these issues through drawing and painting.

Eilish McCarrick is a photographer who has little respect for the more traditional visual art practices. Her world is encapsulated into stark black and white prints, an urban world of youthful fantasy where 1950's American movies are re-played, and humans are objectified in much the same way as the inanimate fetishes which dominate. The images are often quite brutal in their effect, and while they may seem unreal, even surreal, the realities of the poverty and unemployment of the 1980's underpin the ostensibly fantastic subjects. McCarrick herself is in some respects similar to fifties heroes like Joe Orton, operating on the fringes of the society but observing the low-life and the night-life with an almost black humour. Her attitudes seem negative, but negativity has always been present in modernist thinking—life is often unpleasant, society uncharitable or worse towards its rejects. McCarrick, in

Fig. 64 Eilish McCarrick, *Untitled, 1987*. Collection of the artist.

Fig. 65 Maggie Magee, *Discontinent, 1985, Still from Video Mural.* Collection of the artist.

short, utilizes themes common in mainstream twentieth century art which rarely have exposure in Irish art where romantic subjects are so often to the forefront.

Maggie Magee's references have been more explicitly Dadaist, but as a video artist she had drawn from a number of strands in performance art because Time rather than the still image is the uppermost theme in her video work. After graduating from the National College of Art and Design in Dublin she went to Chicago for post-graduate studies and she continues to live there. Opportunities in Ireland for video artists and performance artists are limited, if not non-existent, with only the Triskel Arts Centre in Cork running a regular programme; the United States offers possibilities, both artistic and technical, that are unavailable at home. Just over half the women artists who contributed to the Douglas Hyde Exhibition have received all or part of their formal art education abroad, and all have spent formative periods abroad. The stimulus of art practices outside Ireland is still seen as an essential part of one's art education despite the upsurge in art that ·has occurred in the last decade, and this seems to apply as much to painters as to video and performance artists.

Alanna O'Kelly first arrived at performance art through sculpture while a student in Dublin in the mid-seventies; then slide installation and other art media attracted her. Her direction echoes the increasing disillusionment with the hard, abstract, impersonal forms of Late Modernism by her conscious choice of natural materials at an early stage in her career, and her later evocation of primitive ritual in a piece for the Independents' sculpture exhibition at Marlay Park in 1983 which included a performance. She reflects that which the American artist Robert Smithson had articulated in the years before his death in 1973, which was the rejection of the synthetic in favour of environmentalist concerns.

Smithson's influence is particularly relevant to American women artists whose commitment to natural materials culminated in a desire to feature traditional women's crafts in a fine art context, which was unprecedented. Alanna O'Kelly has, however, taken her work a stage further. Since childhood, she had been appreciative of traditional keening, something she came into contact with again

Fig. 66 Alanna O'Kelly, *"Dancing with my shadow"*, 1986. Pentonville Gallery, London.

at Greenham Common. The combination of those background experiences and her studies at the Slade School of Art in London, where her earlier romantic tendencies have become a good deal more structured partly through direct contact with feminist art practices, is a significant development.

The argument that two generations of Irish artists had to, as it were, attempt to catchup with post-World War II Modernism is countered with the argument that Irish art cuts its own path with or without the latest in international trends.[5] Whichever position one adopts, socio-economic considerations inform us that, while art students *do* refer to international art the art, market in Ireland *is* conservative in avant-garde terms. In a small, marginal country such as Ireland, the art audience is limited, and will continue to be so unless there is a major shift in educational policies. The advent of Postmodernism has, however, brought an apparent compatibility between the concerns of young artists and their potential audience. But this should not lull us into a sense of complacency because there is a good deal of thinking to be done about where Irish art is, and where it is going. Within this new situation, the directions for women's art pose particularly acute questions.

Differences between what are now portrayed as art historical periods, 'Modernism' and 'Postmodernism' (however unsatisfactory the term which demarcates Modernism), are often discussed in stylistic terms: Modernism is abstract, 'cool' art (i.e., Minimalism), and Postmodernism is figurative, 'hot' art (i.e., New-Expressionism). Such characteristics describe some features but of course not all. Twentieth century art is much too complex to be subsumed into general tendencies and the usefulness of these terms is only in a broad, and therefore vague, sense. It is in this sense that we can say there is a carry-over of formalist, typically 'Modernist', features in the work of Eilis O'Connell, Dorothy Cross, Deirdre O'Connell, as well as Maggie Magee and Eilish McCarrick. Not coincidentally, none of these artists engages in painting, which is often the standard bearer for 'Irish' art. There is, however, another and important way of understanding Modernism in terms of general cultural drives and aims with which art styles may or may not coincide. Modernism reflected the desire for a cohesive culture throughout the capitalist nations, the so-called International Style (architecture) and formalism (visual art) being the high water mark. None of the artists referred to would subscribe to this world-view and are to a greater or lesser extent evolving a content or social meaning in their art beyond the 'empty content' that was the pre-eminent mode of art styles in the sixties and seventies.

Of these three sculptors, Eilis O'Connell is the least self-conscious in the way the work assumes its form. She has used a wide array of materials from metals to feathers in her standing sculpture and wall reliefs. The materials seem to dictate the forms though in all her work both non-contemporary and contemporary international sculpture have mediated and provided reference points. In this respect she has been eclectic. Dorothy Cross and Deirdre O'Connell on the other hand have developed their sculpture in tighter, thematic ways. There is a conscious, enigmatic quality about both which is heightened by subdued hues or, effectively, the absence of colour.

Dorothy Cross has developed her post-college work from a series, started while still a student in the United States, about concepts of Ireland to a series which uses architectural representations of two and three dimensional space, to work resulting from a visit to India. It should be said that, while her work assumes three dimensional form, she is also a printmaker, and not only does she make constructions in flat planes but she creates distance between the viewer and the piece by emphasizing clean, precise lines. Just as an etcher's image may seem to operate on a different level to the viewer by the visibility of the edge of the plate on the paper, and the white space of the white paper to the picture frame, Cross's sculptures, like her prints, establish their own unencroachable space. The import seems to be that of personal space and identity (or lack thereof). Even the work in the *Ireland* series, not all of which has these hard edges, is apparently about place — Ireland — but yet is about non-place, because the viewer cannot relate to anything familiar. *Ireland* is a representation of Ireland, serving a symbolic function but without substance.

The drawings of Deirdre O'Connell are also flat and impenetrable. Often they suggest their object but do not reveal it. Instead they predict through mark-making, alluding to a corner of a solid object which lies off the the picture frame. Her three-dimensional pieces go some way towards fulfilling the absence in the drawings. These are often casts of plaster of paris forms that remain ghostly and are not relatable to the real world. They have their own existence and appeal to the unconscious, or are a representation of concepts of the unconscious.

In terms of mainstream art, sculpture or 3-D work in the

Fig. 67   Dorothy Cross, *Toll, 1986*. Collection of the artist.

seventies and eighties has been very potent and influential, encompassing installation, performance and 'the return of the art object'. Many internationally established installation artists and conceptual artists of the seventies have adapted their work to the demands of the 'new art' of the eighties. The keynote is the issue of Postmodernism. With the wisdom of hindsight we can observe an element of freneticism in the Isms of Late Modernism; there was outrageousness for the sake of outrageousness even while the art world was long since past the point where it could be truly outraged. In other words, there was in-built decadence, (strains of which are to be found in Postmodernist art). However, we have also come to recognize that the Postmodern is not lodged within any particular type of art, but has much wider and deeper implications. Critics and theorists from a variety of backgrounds and interests cite the decline of the economy of the United States, and its cultural hegemony, as a root cause of a major shift affecting our perceptions of the Western world.

In visual art, where the United States had ruled supreme for two decades, the changes were assumed in survey exhibitions such as Zeitgeist (1982) and Documenta VII where European art was celebrated over American. The new 'philosophy', post-structuralism, suggested not only the fragmentation of society but the fragmentation of the sense of self. English language words such as 'difference' and 'other' assumed new significance as 'WASP' mentality was challenged and issues of race and gender were pushed up the agenda. There are two consequences that are relevant here. In several European countries (and further afield), local art is being re-evaluated in terms other than the dictates of the international, that is American, style, and, women's art has come into its own, informed by feminist theory, and seemingly with ideology, motivation and direction, patently seen to be lacking in men's art. The critique of (male) new-expressionism is but one instance where the women's movement has showed its strength.

While it is clear Irish art has always adopted a watered-down version of art trends, and has misunderstood the import of many developments, it nevertheless takes stock. This particular juncture

Fig. 68   Deirdre O'Connell, *No Fire in the Hearth, No Sun in the South, X and XI, 1987.* Collection of the artist.

is very vital because for the first time in this century models exist by which the history of Irish art may be explored, not according to the standards of Paris, London or New York, but according to the particular historical context of Ireland. The so-called postmodern condition has led British, Italian and German art historians, critics and artists to a re-examination of their own presumptions about standards and contexts, and may have the same effect on their Irish counterparts. If this follows in line with outside examples the objective is to establish greater appreciation of our links with and differences from other national groupings, (in these days isolationism is not an option), as well as to understand better local differences. It is a basis for a more mature assessment of Ireland's position(s) and direction(s) in regard to the visual arts.

The second possibility arising from this historical juncture is in regard to women's art. Ireland has suffered from colonization — many would argue it is still colonized in its dependence on Britain and Europe — and women have been doubly colonized in that sense. Republicanism was and, perhaps still is, a force for liberation and therefore has its parallels with contemporary feminism. Both are inescapable in today's Ireland, and one tends to lead to the other where there is pursuit of radical alternatives. Yet few visual artists have explored these relationships although they are central to the work of Pat Murphy, an important contemporary film-maker, who has close affiliations with the visual arts. If access was the question for Irish women artists in the last

decade, content and social meaning are the questions for the years ahead. It is no longer a matter of numbers, it is what women artists are doing and saying in their practices.

At its simplest level there is a tradition of fine art which has always been male dominated. That is to say, men have determined what it is that constitutes 'fine art'. Contemporary women artists are educated in that tradition and the question which follows is, can they or should they (re)educate themselves in another way? This is a far-reaching question and there are grounds for arguing that the answers might well have lasting consequences for women's art in Ireland. The impact of the women's movement presents not just another art practice but affords an insight into the relationships between men and women, attitudes and power structures, that will effect change. It relates to the way things are in Ireland, and perceptions of what these should be. The outcome of two recent referenda on the Republic's Constitution, which directly affect women's rights, make the question all the more unavoidable. Where fine art was once seen as an autonomous practice, we now tend to see it more as a social practice alongside others, and as such it is implicated.

Kathy Prendergast, Eithne Jordan, Alice Maher, Viv Burnside and Louise Walsh have all, to a greater or lesser extent, used woman or woman's sexuality as a theme in their work. Between 1982 and 1983 Kathy Prendergast did a series which literally mapped a female body using ink and watercolour on paper. The

Fig. 69 Vivien Bunside, *Wall drawing, Mixed Media*. Fenderesky Gallery, 1986.

Fig. 70 Alice Maher, *Braque, 1986*. Collection of the artist.

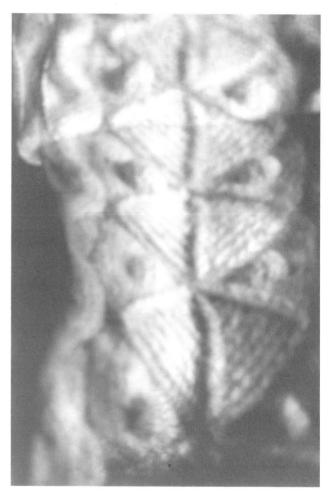

Fig. 71 Pauline Cummins, *Male Torso from Inis t'Oirr/Aran Dance*. Slide sound piece, 1985-86.

association, made by men, between the contours of landscape and contours of woman was made graphic, consciously deflating the titillation factor. Meanwhile Eithne Jordan began her series of drawings and paintings depicting a female form which was not quite whole or solid — sometimes more fish-like than 'human'. The meanings and associations of these works were ambiguous, perhaps intended to represent the transforming powers of creation, as if between gases and matter. In her paintings, Alice Maher also depicts forces but of a psycho-sexual kind which have rarely been explicit in women's art. Maher's collages (which exist independently) indicate how such paintings can be constructed,

how the juxtaposition of images can fuel the imagination. The wall drawings and cut-outs on paper of Viv Burnside and the sculpture of Louise Walsh are, respectively, a celebration of womanhood and woman as 'beast of burden' (Walsh's words) — a horse. These are not necessarily contradictory; it is as necessary to challenge Irish puritanical attitudes to nudity as it is to challenge the working status of the majority of Irish woman.

All this work shows a range of possibility for fine art concerns. Of contemporary Irish women artists, Pauline Cummins is particularly articulate in pointing out the restrictiveness of 'serious', i.e. male, concepts in the visual arts.[6] If we look at the prevalent artistic subjects of recent times, we see that these happen to exclude a good deal of our experience, and banish women's specific experiences such as motherhood to the outer reaches of trivia. Pauline Cummins's view questions who is to say what is worthy of consideration in an art context. Male sexuality is legitimate but childbirth isn't? Seen in this light, a hierarchy of fine art values looms before us, narrow, prejudiced and sexist.

While much of the 'advanced' art of the eighties is seen to represent a shift from the abstract to the figurative — from the assertion of 'pure' artistic emphases to attempts to gain socio-political revevance — art in the eighties is also interpreted as a time when different styles and attitudes can co-exist, where there isn't the same pressure for a dominant artform. The creed of Pluralism is very pervasive but in fact the sense of choice is about as deep as the advertising for any form of commodity on the commercial market. Whereas in the 1960s there may have been a time-lag between the latest art style in New York and its currency in Ireland, today the news is instantaneous thanks to developments in our communications networks. Fashion overlaps with fashion at ever-increasing speed. There are artists who respond to changing perceptions of meaning and relevance in art, and there are those who prefer to remain consistent and develop within their own frames of reference. Mary Fitzgerald's paintings are abstract although she is as much informed by Japanese traditions in art as by western, modernist practices. What determines validity in contemporary art practice is not whether abstract or figurative art is uppermost, but whether it is capable of intercepting the crucial concerns of the day. The perpetuation of abstract art undermines the claim that figurative art is now the relevant art. The validity of work within these groupings is another matter.

Although sculpture, installation and performance have gained in significance in the last decade, painting continues to be the most widely regarded and perhaps the most commercially successful medium in the visual arts in Ireland.[7] When painting once again resumed its position in the United States and Western Europe between the late seventies and early eighties, the response in Ireland was that the 'new' painting already had a strong basis in Ireland, specifically through the bedrock of the Independents. It would be more accurate to say Ireland had not felt the full impact of post-painting tendencies, and the continued presence of expressionist-type painting was a case of art fashions catching Ireland on the rebound. But the painters Eithne Jordan and Cecily Brennan have exhibited regularly in the Independents' annual show, and neither of these artists was essentially concerned with the now standardized expressionist motifs or gestures. Where Eithne Jordan has developed her 'Woman' theme, thereby embarking on subject possibilities that have not been tapped before in this way in Irish art, Cecily Brennan takes on the oldest subject of all in fine art in Ireland: landscape.

Brennan is therefore confronted with the full might of art history and as a feminist she will not be content to adopt this as 'hers', yet she cannot totally ignore it. Her response in the first instance has been to develop a 'personal' vision of the Wicklow mountains and of the Rhododendron Gardens at Howth. The intervening years between these series mark a change in her approach from the great expanse of the mountains to the enclosed space of the gardens. She is only too well aware that the paintings of the latter, with their swirling in-turning shapes, can be associated with the womb and can be stereotyped as typically female. Her task then is to negotiate a difficult course between a well established landscape painting tradition on the one hand, and her identity as a woman artist on the other. As a landscape painter, she is in a most central position to explore and challenge some of the most cherished aspects of Irish art.

The challenges for Irish women artists lie in this grey area of identity, though their responses need not necessarily conform to

Fig. 72 Cecily Brennan, *Garden in Autumn, 1985.* Allied Irish Banks Collection.

that which has occurred with women's art elsewhere. Ireland has a relatively conservative record in the visual arts which is not simply the result of a generally conservative society but, (linked as these might be), it is also the result of a less affluent society than in other parts of Europe. By definition, avant-garde art requires a substantial support as a sub-set of a larger support system which in Ireland is not great. While there may be an equation of sorts between radical ideas including feminism with radical artforms, this should not blind us to the most conventional of artforms. There was a time, in the sixties and early seventies, when the distinction between Irish art and International art had a purpose. This no longer prevails, and with access to ideas and artforms from other places we ought to have the confidence and competence to overcome the separate histories of the conservative and the modern in order to understand better the actual and potential contexts for art in Ireland. The revolution in attitudes about the role of women is likely to be a quiet one in Ireland; changes are almost imperceptible but changes there are.

1. Predecessors in contemporary women's art exhibitions include, Anne Carlisle, Dorothy Cross, Aileen McKeogh and Kathy Prendergast, Hendriks Gallery, Dublin, 1984, and, *Women on Women,* six women artists, Fenderesky Gallery, Belfast, 1986.

2. In 1971, for example, there were six women and twenty-eight men in the *Independents* exhibition. And in 1973, there were six women and forty-six men in the *Irish Exhibition of Living Art.*
3. Notes for a lecture at the Battersea Arts Centre, London, as part of a seminar on Irish Women's Art, 22-24 March 1986.
4. The billboards and banners, introduced in 1984 and 1985, were intended to reach the non-gallery-going public rather than to indicate a pre-occupation with experimental forms.
5. Brian O'Doherty, 'The Irish Imagination, 1959-71', catalogue essay for an exhibition of Irish art as part of *Rosc '71.*
6. For example, Cummins's seminar in Temple Bar Studios, Dublin, 5 February 1987.
7. Drawings are increasingly popular, presumably because they are less expensive.

Catalogue

Overleaf: Caroline Hamilton, *'Domestic Happiness as acted in this city, a tragi-comic farce',* (detail), (cat. no. 9).

Henrietta Dering, *Portrait of a Lady,* (cat. no. 1).

Henrietta Dering, *Portrait of a Gentleman,* (cat. no. 2).

Henrietta Dering (fl.1694-1728/29)

1   Portrait of a Lady, 1704

Pastel on paper, 35.8 × 26.8 cms.

PROVENANCE: collection of the Earl of Erne.

INSCRIBED: on reverse, *Henrietta Dering Dublin 1704*

This delicate and charming pastel portrait of a Lady seen in half-length, forms a pair with the *Portrait of a Gentleman,* (cat. no. 2). Though the painting has been carefully finished and the details naturalistically rendered, it is not known who the sitter was. However the inscription on the back of the painting notes that it was painted in Dublin in 1704 at a time when the artist had a large fashionable practice there.

Henrietta has endowed this quite simple portrait of a beautiful woman, with both life and movement, as seen in the head gently turned to one side, and also with character as the sitter seems to look at the spectator with a somewhat quizzical expression in her eyes. The soft, grey background which the artist has chosen, admirably sets off the various textures in the painting: the rich golden satin of the dress with its luminous highlights against the warm rosy flesh tones of the skin and the soft curls piled up on

the Lady's head which fall gently and indeed sensuously, over her bare neck.   KMM

Lent by the Earl of Erne.

Henrietta Dering

2   Portrait of a Gentleman

Pastel on paper, 35.8 × 26 cms.

PROVENANCE: collection of the Earl of Erne.

This half-length pastel portrait of a gentleman in a suit of armour with his head slightly turned to one side, is a pendant to cat. no. 1. As with the latter, it is unfortunately not known who the sitter was. Though not dated, the portrait was undoubtedly made at the same time as the *Portrait of a Lady* in 1704.

Despite the artist's use of a single silvery-grey pigment, she has managed to impart a varied tonality together with very fine nuances of light throughout the portrait. As with its pendant, the texture of each surface — the suit of armour, the pale flesh tones and the soft powdered hair — has been finely rendered with interesting juxtapositions.   KMM

Lent by the Earl of Erne.

Susanna Drury, *The East Prospect of the Giant's Causeway,* (cat. no. 3).

Susanna Drury (1733-1770)

3 The East Prospect of the Giant's Causeway

Gouache on vellum, 34.3 × 68.6 cms.

SIGNED: on stone, bottom left, *Sus. Drury / pinx*

PROVENANCE: Carton, county Kildare; private collection, Ireland.

VERSIONS: another pair, *(East and West Prospects of the Giant's Causeway),* very similar, is in the collection of the Ulster Museum, Belfast, Art Department cat. nos. 1652 and 1653; what may have been a third pair was in the sale of the effects of Dr. John Barrett's ('Jacky' Barrett 1753-1821) the eccentric vice-provost of Trinity College, Dublin; Samuel Jones, Trinity Street, Dublin, 20 May 1822, 2nd part, lot 272; 'View of the Giant's Causeway, marked Susanna Drury, 4½ feet long, and 15 inches wide', bt. Alderon £1.10,0.' These dimensions would accommodate one of the two known pairs mounted together in one frame.

ENGRAVED: François Vivarès, London, line-engravings, published by Susanna Drury 1 February 1743/4. *The West Prospect* is dedicated to Alexander McDonnel, Earl of Antrim; *The East Prospect* is dedicated to John Boyle, Earl of Orrery. Long and detailed descriptions, answering to numbers on the engraving, are engraved at the base. The engravings contain details which appear on one or other of the two versions, neither version corresponding exactly with the engravings. The Vivarès engravings were reworked and republished by Boydell in 1777 and reprinted again in 1837.

LITERATURE: Strickland, *A Dictionary of Irish Artists,* (1913), p. 305; Anne Crookshank and the Knight of Glin, *The Painters of Ireland* (1978), pp. 62, 67 (ill. in colour); Lady Llanover, ed. *Autobiography and Correspondence of Mary Granville, Mrs. Delany,* (1861); Martyn Anglesea and John Preston, 'A Philosophical Landscape: Susanna Drury and the Giant's Causeway', *Art History,* vol. 3, no. 3, (September 1980), p. 252.

Susanna Drury's views, painted before 1740, were the first trustworthy views of the Giant's Causeway ever produced, and were preceded only by two very misleading engravings after Christopher Cole (1694) and Edwin Sandys (1696). Mrs. Delany wrote to her sister on 8 October 1758 'Mrs. Drury, who took draughts (of which you have the prints) lived three months near the place, and went almost every day. I can do nothing so exact and finished.'[1]

The technique of gouache on vellum is more associated with miniature painters, though there was a strong Dutch and Flemish tradition of landscape in this medium going back to the sixteenth century (e.g. Hans Bol). In England at the beginning of the eighteenth century gouache painting was particularly associated with Joseph Goupy (1680?-1768), yet another London artist of French extraction.[2]

The groups of fashionably-dressed figures in both of Susanna Drury's *Prospects* show that as early as 1740 the Giant's Causeway had become a tourist attraction. MA

1. Llanover, vol. 3, p. 519.
2. See M. Anglesea and J. Preston, 'A Philosophical Landscape: Susanna Drury and the Giant's Causeway', *Art History,* (September, 1980), vol. 3, no. 3, p. 252.

Private collection.

Letitia Bushe (fl.1731-d.1757)

4 View of the village of Bray, 1736

Pen and grey wash on paper, 20.4 × 28.4 cms.

PROVENANCE: Guildhall Bookshop where purchased by the present owner.

INSCRIBED: *View of the village of Bray from the riseing ground near the Malt House taken in 1736 in a morning by L.B.*

This delightful and charming topographical drawing by Letitia Bushe executed in 1736 'in one morning' is one of the earliest known views of Bray. To the left of the view is Old Bray framed

Letitia Bushe, *View of the Village of Bray, 1736,* (cat. no. 4).

Letitia Bushe, *View from the Well-House at Hampstead, 1743,* (cat. no. 5).

by the Little and Big Sugarloaf Mountains while on the high ground overhanging the river, can be seen the Protestant church of St. Paul, built in 1609 (today used as a pipe and organ works) and in front of it are some of the houses situated in the Main Street. Further off behind the bridge, are buildings perhaps relating to the Mill which had existed there since the beginning of the 18th century. In the centre of the drawing is the Old Bridge crossing the Dargle or the Bray River as it was originally called. Built in 1666, it connected the portions of the town Old Bray and Little Bray which lay on different sides of the river while also linking the main Dublin to Wexford road on which the coaches travelled. The artist has included a coach crossing this bridge which, in 1741, collapsed after a storm. To the right can be seen a cluster of cottages in Little Bray in the Connagh parish — an area where the land was 'chiefly laid out in villas and ornamental plantations' and which was a favourite place of residence (S. Lewis, *A Topographical Dictionary of Ireland,* 1837, p. 392). The walls of one of these estates are seen here with an unusual and intriguing newly planted circle of trees at its entrance. This could either be the estate of Corke Abbey or the Old Castle of Little Bray.

Since the beginning of the century there was an extensive brewery and malting store and the 'Bray ale was considered a celebrity'. Perhaps the Malt House, from where the artist drew the view, was related in some way to this industry?

In this landscape the artist has treated her subject in a natural as well as anecdotal fashion. She has depicted herself, accompanied by a friendly looking dog, drawing the view on the Dargle as so many of the Romantic artists such as George Barret, James Arthur O'Connor and Thomas Roberts were to do sometime later. The anecdotal details of the figures and animals and even the smoke billowing out of the cottages, enliven her composition and also add a touch of humour.

Letitia has handled her drawing with a delicate touch and has used light washes of the ink, while details such as the trees are painted in a distinct, soft and feathery style.   KMM

Lent by Dudley Snelgrove.

Letitia Bushe

5   View from the Well-House at Hampstead, 1743

Pen and grey wash on paper, 19.3 × 28.5 cms.

SIGNED, DATED AND INSCRIBED: *View from the Well-House at Hamstead 28th July 1743 by L. Bushe*

PROVENANCE: Guildhall Bookshop, Kingston, where purchased by present owner.

Letitia Bushe has drawn this fine annotated panoramic view of London from Hampstead Heath, a place which was not only favoured by writers and poets but which was also a popular sketching point among artists from the 18th century. Furthermore it was famous and fashionable as a spa from the early part of the 18th century when the medicinal value of its spring water was discovered, and it was probably from Well-Walk, near the entrance to the present day Gainsborough Gardens, that Letitia drew this scene in 1743.

The drawing is an interesting record of the city at this date, outlining as it does the main landmarks. After the Great Fire in 1666 many city churches and houses were built and some of these can be seen here. The well-known silhouette of St. Paul's cathedral by Christopher Wren (1632-1723) with its cruciform plan and high-colonnaded drum topped by the lofty, elegant classical dome and lantern, structurally completed in 1710, is seen on the far left. To the right of this is St. Bride's Church in Fleet Street which since the 15th century always had close links with the Press. Originally on the site of the first Irish settlement in London and where St. Bridget, the 6th century Irish saint from Kildare, founded the first Christian church, it was rebuilt by Wren after the Great Fire. The unusual spire consisting of four octagonal arcades capped by an obelisk was added in 1703. Unfortunately the church was bombed during the Second World War, though it was later restored. In the centre of the drawing is the elegant Montagu House in Bloomsbury built by Robert Hooke (1635-1703) in 1674-80 for Ralph, the 1st Duke of Montagu who was Charles II's ambassador in Paris and whose love of all things French led to his house being constructed on lines similar to the French *Hôtels* in the style of Lemercier. Though damaged by fire in 1686 and rebuilt immediately it remained substantially Hooke's work. In 1755 it was sold for the newly established British Museum and finally demolished in the 1840's. Behind it is Nicholas Hawksmoor's (1661-1736) church of St. George with its extraordinary steeple crowned by a figure of George I in Roman dress, noted by Walpole as being 'a masterpiece of absurdity', and which was only completed in 1731. Finally to the right is the Gothic Westminster Abbey. The Abbey's West Towers, seen in the drawing, were also built by Hawksmoor though only completed in 1745. Letitia has outlined the whole city against the hazy range of the Surrey hills in the background and throughout the drawing she has used a light feathery but detailed touch which seems to be typical of her style.   KMM

Lent by Dudley Snelgrove.

Mary Delany (1700-1788)

6 'The dargel belonging to Lord Powerscourt in Ireland', 1765

Pencil, ink and wash on paper, 26 × 37 cms.

SIGNED: in monogram, *MD; 1765*

INSCRIBED: *The dargel belonging to Lord Powerscourt in Ireland.*

PROVENANCE: Francis Wellesley; his sale, Sotheby's, London, 1920, lot 209; National Gallery of Ireland, cat. no. 2722.

EXHIBITED: 1973-74, *Pen and Pencil Exhibition,* International Cultural Centre, Antwerp and Bibliothèque Royale, Brussels, no. 8; 1986, *Finest Prospects,* Kenwood House, London.

LITERATURE: Hilary Pyle, 'Artist or Artistic? The Drawings of Mary Delany', *Irish Arts Review,* vol. 4, no. 1, (Spring 1987), pp. 29 (ill.) — 31.

Mary Delany's book of drawings, now in the National Gallery of Ireland, consists of loose drawings and drawings on the page, compiled by her over thirty years. Many are landscapes sketched

Mary Delany, *'The dargel belonging to Lord Powerscourt in Ireland',* 1765, (cat. no. 6).

at the places she visited, and finished off in her studio at home. This view of the foot of the waterfall in the Powerscourt estate, in county Wicklow, is one of her more lyrical compositions. She lays emphasis on the romantic height of rocks and trees, and the luxuriance of foliage, in preference to the dramatic drop of water that attracted Barrett and Carver. The mood is pastoral, as is common with her figure scenes. She was always on the look out for 'improved', wild, pretty places. But this late drawing is unusually well finished and pictorial.   HP

Lent by the National Gallery of Ireland.

Florence Cole, *Crom Castle,* (cat. no. 7).

Lady Florence Cole (1778/9-1862)

7 Crom Castle

Pencil on paper, 15 × 19.2 cms.

SIGNED: *Florence Cole.*

PROVENANCE: Prof. F. Mitchell, Townley Hall, county Louth, by whom presented to the National Trust; Rowallane, Saintfield, county Down.

This drawing represents Old Crom Castle, a plantation fortification of c.1611. This was situated on the Crom estate, the seat of the Earls of Erne, not many miles from Florence Court, the home of Florence Cole. Crom had been the scene of a bitter conflict in 1689 between Protestant Enniskillen forces and the Jacobites, the latter losing over two thousand men. The view depicts the picturesque ruins of the castle, which overlooks Lough Erne, the structure having been destroyed by fire in 1764.   CM

Lent by the National Trust for Northern Ireland.

Caroline Hamilton, *Society, 1801*, (cat. no. 8).

Caroline Hamilton (1771-1861)

8   Society, 1801

Watercolour on paper, 35.6 × 48.2 cms.

INSCRIBED: *Society, 1801*

PROVENANCE: by descent to the present owner.

LITERATURE: Anne Crookshank and The Knight of Glin, *The Painters of Ireland c. 1660-1920*, (1978), pp. 173-74 (ill.).

In *Society, 1801* Caroline Hamilton shows the *ennui* of a Dublin drawing room after the Union, which reduced Dublin's social world to a shadow of its former self. All the participants of this card party are portrayed in a state of complete and utter boredom, yawning and scarcely managing to stay awake.   KOG

Private collection.

Caroline Hamilton, 'Domestic Happiness as acted in this city, a tragi-comic farce', (cat. no. 9).

Caroline Hamilton

9   'Domestic Happiness as acted in this city, a tragi-comic farce'

Pencil and wash on paper, 29 × 44 cms.

INSCRIBED: *Domestic Happiness as acted in this city, a tragi-comic farce.*

PROVENANCE: by family descent to the present owner.

The Methodist influence of Caroline's mother and her own Evangelicalism distanced her from the usual attitudes of the Irish 'Ascendancy'. In her privately printed memoirs of 1851 she talks of the worldly and corrupting set she lived in as a girl in Dublin up for the 1798 rebellion: 'They seemed to have very little or no religion, and very little happiness in domestic life, bad husbands and still more extravagant wives, all wildly in pursuit of pleasure!' *Domestic Happiness as acted in this city, a tragi-comic farce*, sums up the effects of this dissipation.   KOG

Private collection.

Caroline Hamilton, *The Kingstown to Holyhead Packet*, (cat. no. 10).

Caroline Hamilton

10   The Kingstown to Holyhead Packet

Pencil and wash on paper, 17.8 × 22.3 cms.

SIGNED: *CH*

PROVENANCE: Slane Castle sale, June 1979, where purchased by the present owner.

Caroline gives us a rare insight into the trials and tribulations of travel in the early years of the nineteenth century. She describes in her characteristically satirical style the embarkation of passengers at Kingstown for their trip to Holyhead. Ladies in long dresses are being carried on board in a rather undignified manner via a precarious looking ladder, while an extremely reluctant horse is being lowered in the direction of a stationary carriage. The attitudes of the passengers already safely on deck varies from the complete indifference of the lady devouring a hearty lunch on the left to the despondency of the lady slumped on the table in the foreground.   WR

Lent by the Hon. Desmond Guinness.

Caroline Hamilton, *'Mal de Mer' on the Irish Sea*, (cat. no. 11).

Caroline Hamilton

11   'Mal de Mer' on the Irish sea

Pencil and wash on paper, 17.8 × 22.3 cms.

INSCRIBED: *'Mal de Mer' on the Irish sea, presented by Caroline Hamilton to George Dodd, Master of the Holyhead Packet.*

PROVENANCE: Slane Castle sale, June 1979, where purchased by the present owner.

'Mal de Mer' on the Irish sea, a sequel to Caroline's *Kingstown to Holyhead Packet*, illustrates the ghastly fate that befalls the unfortunate passengers on their journey to Holyhead. As in the embarkation scene, Caroline compares and contrasts with her keen wit the behaviour of the passengers; some are violently ill while others are completely oblivious to the horrors surrounding them. It is obvious from the gruesome vividness with which Caroline records the scene that it was based on personal experience.

WR

Lent by the Hon. Desmond Guinness.

Elizabeth McCausland, *Charlotte Edgeworth*, (cat. no. 12).

Charlotte Edgeworth died at the age of twenty-four at her home in Edgeworthstown, county Longford. McCausland's miniature of Charlotte dates from the year of her death which suggests that it was a posthumous work and that the artist was an acquaintance of the family. In it Charlotte appears as an intelligent young woman of strong character.

WR

Lent by the National Gallery of Ireland.

Elizabeth McCausland (fl.1806-1807)

12   Charlotte Edgeworth, 1807

Watercolour on ivory, 6.8 × 5.3 cms.

PROVENANCE: Mrs. H. Colvin, by whom presented, 1970; National Gallery of Ireland, cat. no. 7550.

One of a pair of miniatures by Elizabeth McCausland of Charlotte Edgeworth (1783-1807). Charlotte Edgeworth was the fifth daughter of Richard Lovell Edgeworth (1744-1817), author and inventor of various agricultural and other machinery including one of the earliest schemes for a telegraph. Charlotte was the daughter of Edgeworth's third wife Elizabeth, who was the sister of his second wife Honora. Edgeworth in fact had four wives and numerous children, one of whom was Maria Edgeworth the novelist.

Elizabeth May, *Basaltic pillars near Fairhead, Co. Antrim*, (cat. no. 13).

Elizabeth May (fl.1810)

13   Basaltic pillars near Fairhead, Co. Antrim

Oil on canvas, 76 × 109 cms.

INSCRIBED: on the stretcher, *Basaltic Pillars near Fairhead, Co. Antrim from a coloured drawing taken on the spot by Donald Stewart 1810;* on label on reverse, *View of the Giant's Causeway Ireland painted by Miss Sinclair, afterwards wife of the Rev'd Sir Edward May from a watercolour by Donald Stewart.*

PROVENANCE: collection of Lady Goff.

Stewart's wash drawing of Benmore or Fairhead is in the Armagh County Museum and was engraved as Benmore or Fairhead for William Hamilton Drummond's *The Giant's Causeway, A Poem,* (Belfast 1811) and again, though not credited to the artist, was published in William Hamilton's letters concerning the North Coast of the County of Antrim, (Belfast 1822).   COC

Lent by Lady Goff.

Maria Taylor, *Mrs. Henry Grattan,* (cat. no. 14).

Maria Taylor (1777-c.1823)

14   Mrs. Henry Grattan

Oil on canvas, 43 × 34 cms.

PROVENANCE: Mrs. Lecky, by whom presented, 1904; National Gallery of Ireland cat. no. 567.

LITERATURE: W. G. Strickland, *A Dictionary of Irish Artists,* (1913), p. 434.

Mrs. Grattan was born Henrietta Fitzgerald and was descended on her father's side from the Desmonds and on her mother's from the Stevensons of county Down. She married Henry Grattan when he was already a prominent figure in Irish politics. They had two sons, James and Henry, both of whom became Members of Parliament, and two daughters, Mary Ann and Harriet.

Henrietta outlived her husband by eighteen years; he died in 1820 aged seventy-four and it seems likely, judging by her sober and somewhat melancholy appearance, that her portrait was painted a short time after Grattan's death.

The artist paid particular attention in the portrait to the background details. Among the pictures hanging in the interior is the drawing by Alexander Pope (1763-1835) of Henry Grattan which refers to his famous moving of the 'Declaration of Rights' in the Irish House of Commons in April 1782 (see E. Scriven's engraving after Pope, N.G.I. cat. no. 10,437). The Irish house of Commons showed its gratitude to Grattan in May of the same year by bestowing on him a grant of £50,000 for the purchase of an estate at Moyanna near Stradbally, county Offaly. Significantly, 1782 was the year of Grattan's marriage to Henrietta.

                                                        WR

Lent by the National Gallery of Ireland.

Cecilia Margaret Nairn, *Landscape with two women by a waterfall,* (cat. no. 15).

Cecilia Margaret Nairn (1791-1857)

15   Landscape with two women by a waterfall

Pencil and watercolour on paper, 18.9 × 29.6 cms.

PROVENANCE: The Neptune Gallery, Dublin, from whom purchased, 1967; Ulster Museum, Belfast, art dept. cat. no. 1227.

EXHIBITED: June 1967, *J. H. Campbell and his School*, Neptune Gallery, Dublin, no. 26.

The landscape exhibits a fair degree of competence, containing both a sense of spatial recession and a realistic depiction of the vegetation and foliage of the trees. The figures near the water are rather crudely painted, however, as is the waterfall itself.

EB

Lent by the Ulster Museum, Belfast.

been endowed with life and movement. The darker figures surrounding them form a swirling frieze that leads the spectator's eye into the hazy blue distance in the background. Grace has cleverly, yet naturally handled the different picture planes with each one linked to the next through the placement of the figures. This scene is painted with such competence and confidence that one is left to wonder what Grace St. Albans might have achieved had she pursued painting as a career rather than as a pastime.

KMM

Private collection.

Grace, Duchess of St. Albans, *My Mother's Coming of Age*, (cat. no. 16).

Charlotte Augusta, Duchess of Leinster, *A group of children by a heath-side*, (cat. no. 17).

Grace, Duchess of St. Albans (1848-1926)

16   My Mother's Coming of Age, 1840

Watercolour on paper, 19.5 × 37.7 cms.

PROVENANCE: by descent in the artist's family.

INSCRIBED: on label at back, *Coming of age of my mother at Newtown Anner. To remain at Newtown Anner Grace St. Albans*

This small but beautifully finished watercolour depicts the celebration of the coming of age of the artist's mother, Catherine Isabella Osborne (1819-1880). Catherine, probably born in Newtown Anner, was the daughter of Sir Thomas Osborne (1757-1821) of Newtown Anner, M.P. for Carysfort and Sheriff of Waterford, and Catherine Rebecca Smith (d.1856). This celebration took place in Newtown Anner in 1840, four years before Catherine married Ralph Bernal, M.P., who assumed the surname of Osborne.

In the foreground to the right, on a piece of high ground, which serves as a bridge between the spectator and the main subject, some people, spectators like us, are watching the festivities. Dressed in white, the dancers in the centre, reeling round the pole, have

Charlotte Augusta, Duchess of Leinster (1793-1859)

17   A group of children by a hearth-side

Pencil and watercolour on paper, 20 × 24.1 cms.

PROVENANCE: from an album belonging to the 3rd Duchess of Leinster.

The attribution of this work to the Duchess of Leinster is very secure; it came in an album of drawings and watercolours which once belonged to her, in which there still remains a similar work depicting a mother and child signed by the Duchess with her monogram *CAL*. In both are the same colours in the watercolour embellishments and the handling of the anatomical passages is extremely like.

This drawing must be among the best works of the Duchess: the very complicated arrangement of the children is made into a convincing composition; the depiction of the interior with its modest furnishings is well handled, while some of the details are very precisely drawn. Several well known contemporary Irish professional artists were not as competent as this. The children may well be in the kitchen of a house on the Carton estate. Unfortunately there is no means of dating this work.

MW

Private collection.

The Hon. Frances Charlotte FitzGerald de Ros, *Jane Repton at a writing table,* (cat. no. 18).

The Hon. Frances Charlotte FitzGerald de Ros (d.1851)

18   Jane Repton at a writing table

Pencil and watercolour on paper, 27.2 × 20.8 cms.

INSCRIBED: *Jane Repton*

PROVENANCE: from an album belonging to the 3rd Duchess of Leinster.

The reason for attributing this work to the Hon. Frances Charlotte FitzGerald de Ros is due to the fact that it came from the album of drawings and watercolours which belonged to the third Duchess of Leinster; moreover, on the original mount in the Duchess's hand it is inscribed: *by F C F de Ros.*

The sitter in this work may well be Jane Seymour FitzGerald, daughter of the third Duke and Duchess of Leinster, who in 1848 married George William John Repton. If this hypothesis is correct,

the drawing must have been executed after Lady Jane's marriage and the artist's premature death in February 1851.

While there are defects in the draughtsmanship in certain areas, notably in the line of the right shoulder and neck and in the drawing of the left hand, the overall effect is rather charming. There is a feeling for colour in the sketch-like treatment, while the Regency period writing table and its cluster of accessories is well handled. Had the artist not died so young she might have become a really talented practitioner.

MW

Private collection.

Elizabeth Still Stanhope, Countess of Harrington, *Wheelbarrow with six of the artist's children,* (cat. no. 19).

Elizabeth Still Stanhope, Countess of Harrington (c.1819-1912)

19   Wheelbarrow with six of the artist's children

Pencil and watercolour on paper, 11.3 × 16.5 cms.

PROVENANCE: by descent in the family of the Earls of Harrington; consigned in a portfolio by a member of this family to an auction conducted by Wm. B. Fitt & Co., Ltd., in the Village Hall, Adare, county Limerick, 13 April 1984, lot 504, where bought by Miss Phillippa Quinlan, Dublin, from whom purchased, October 1984; National Gallery of Ireland cat. no. 19,226.

EXHIBITED: 1986, *Acquisitions 1984-1986,* National Gallery of Ireland, Dublin, no. 34.

The children so charmingly grouped around the wheelbarrow are six of the artist's own children; Philippa Leicester (b.c.1842), Fanny Joanna (b.c.1847), Caroline Margaret (b.c.1840), Fitzroy William (b.1845), Lincoln Edwin (1849-1902), and Charles Augustus Stanhope (1844-1917), later 8th Earl of Harrington. Elizabeth was fond of using her children as subjects for her genre sketches and she was clearly never short of willing models as she had altogether twelve children. This watercolour, like much of Elizabeth's work is not dated, however the age of the children suggests that it was painted in c.1850.

WR

Lent by the National Gallery of Ireland.

Lady Charleville, *A view of Bangor with the late 18th century Gothick Penrhyn Castle, Wales,* (cat. no. 20).

Clementina Robertson, *Arthur Lefroy,* (cat. no. 21).

Lady Charleville (1762-1851)

20   A view of Bangor with the late 18th century Gothick Penrhyn Castle, Wales

Gouache on paper, 43.2 × 66 cms.

PROVENANCE: private collection, Ireland.

It is probable that this painting was executed after Lady Charleville's son, Charles William Bury (1801-51), later 2nd Earl of Charleville, became Member of Parliament for Penrhyn although it must predate Thomas Hopper's Norman Revival castellated alterations to the Castle which is visible in the distance. Although her son also represented Carlow and Falmouth in Parliament and was the Sheriff of the King's County, he was deemed 'the greatest bore the world can produce'. Lady Charleville is best known for her carefully observed and sensitive pencil studies of trees in the park at Charleville Forest, where she lived. These show the romantic sensibility she brought to her observation of nature. Examples can still be seen in the Castle at Charleville Forest. Here she favours a medium which readily allows her to capture the romantically atmospheric scene before her and shows her, unusually, working in colour in tones reminiscent of Cozens.

NGB

Private collection.

Clementina Robertson (1795-c.1853)

21   Arthur Lefroy

Watercolour on card, 19 × 15.4 cms.

PROVENANCE: Mr. E. S. Robertson, by whom presented, 1905; National Gallery of Ireland cat. no. 2556.

There is some doubt about the traditional identification of the sitter as Arthur Lefroy. Although nothing is known of Arthur Lefroy, the Lefroy family, who were of Flemish descent and had settled in Newton Perry in county Limerick, were prominent in Ireland. The most famous member of the family was Thomas Langlois Lefroy (1776-1867) who became Lord Chief Justice of Ireland in 1852.

Clementina Robertson's careful training as a miniature painter is well reflected in the Lefroy portrait. The main emphasis is on the face which is finished in a detailed and pleasing manner. Lefroy's expression conveys an air of sincerity and honesty. The informal pose of the sitter, his arm resting on the back of a chair is very similar in feeling to another watercolour drawing by Clementina Robertson of the Reverend J. D. Hastings (National Gallery of Ireland cat. no. 2557).

WR

Lent by the National Gallery of Ireland.

90

Elish Lamont, *Miss O'Hara*, (cat. no. 22).

Margaret Stokes, *Ireland's Eye*, (cat. no. 23).

Margaret Stokes (1832-1900)
23   Ireland's Eye

Watercolour on paper, 16 × 21 cms.

SIGNED: in monogram, centre foreground Ⓜ

PROVENANCE: the artist; by descent to W. N. Stokes (the artist's grand nephew); and then by descent to the present owner.

EXHIBITED: 1970, *Watercolour Society of Ireland, Centenary Exhibition 1870-1970*, The Hall, Molesworth Street, Dublin, no. 122.

LITERATURE: Sir Samuel Ferguson, *Cromlech on Howth*, (London 1861), pl. 7.

Elish Lamont (1816-1870)
22   Miss O'Hara

Watercolour on ivory, 9 × 7 cms. (sight).

SIGNED: *Elish La Mont*

PROVENANCE: purchased, 1927; Ulster Museum, Belfast, art dept., no. 1891.

LITERATURE: John Hewitt and Theo Snoddy, *Art in Ulster: 1* (1977), p. 165; Eileen Black, 'Of Art and Artists' in J. C. Beckett *et al, Belfast, The Making of the City*, (1983), p. 90, ill.

There is little information available on the sitter, Miss O'Hara of Crebilly House, Ballymena, county Antrim, afterwards wife of General Wardlow.

Judging from the standard of this portrait, Elish appears to have had rather limited artistic ability. Although she has painted the sitter's dress and fine detail with skill, she has not breathed life into her subject — note how Miss O'Hara looks somewhat wooden and doll-like in appearance, not made of flesh and blood. The fact that Elish had a reputation by the mid-nineteenth century probably stems — it must be said — not from the standard of her work, but from the scarcity of competition from other women artists, particularly in the North of Ireland.   EB

Lent by the Ulster Museum, Belfast.

This view of Ireland's Eye was executed by Margaret Stokes as part of a series of seven landscapes which she did as illustrations for a poem, *The Cromlech on Howth* by Samuel Ferguson. This publication when it appeared in 1861 also contained illuminations based on those in the *Book of Kells* and the *Book of Durrow* accompanied by notes on Celtic ornamental art revised by George Petrie. In Ferguson's poem Ireland's Eye is described as 'Aideen's Briery Dell'.

This appropriately poetic view demonstrates Stokes' artistic qualities more clearly than many of her archaeological drawings which were generally of a purely documentary nature. One of the most striking aspects of the series of views for *Cromlech on Howth* is the colouring which shows great strength and variety and ranges from fresh daytime greens as in *Ireland's Eye* to glowing sunset reds and golds. In *Ireland's Eye* the island itself is seen in the distance beautifully framed by a delicate fairy-tale like tree.

WR

Lent by Mrs. R. H. O'Hanlon.

Mary Herbert, *The Lakes of Killarney from the slopes of Mangerton*, (cat. no. 24).

Mary Herbert (1817-1893)

24 The Lakes of Killarney from the slopes of Mangerton

Watercolour on cartridge paper, 97 × 32 cms.
PROVENANCE: Office of Public Works, Muckross House, Killarney.

The picture, a panoramic view of Killarney's Middle and Lower Lakes and the surrounding mountains encompasses, in the middle and foreground, the Estate of Muckross, home of Mary Herbert. Muckross was Mary's favourite subject. Indeed her artistic preoccupation with the estate found expression not only in painting but also in an extensive programme of building and landscaping carried out after her marriage. The rooftops, glimpsed through the trees in the middleground, are those of Muckross House. Designed for the Herberts by William Burn and completed in 1843, it formed part of a building programme that reached its apogee with the preparations for Queen Victoria's visit to Muckross in 1861.

In contrast to her earlier works, which could be over elaborate, this picture displays a confident, almost sketchy, style. The hazy tones of the distant mountains, lake and sky are picked up and intensified in the strong blues of the shadowed forest and river gulley and complimented by the blue-white leaves in the break of windblown trees on the right.

Mary weights the picture to one side by using stronger tones in the left middle and background and greater detail, including the rather rigid deer, in the left foreground. The effect of this is to emphasis, by contrast, the sense of sweeping spaciousness in the rest of the picture.

Though undated, this painting is identical to a sepia drawing in the National Library of Ireland which is dated 1861. NS

Lent by the Office of Public Works, Muckross House, Killarney, county Kerry.

Lady Alicia Parsons, *The Harbour at Kingstown, Co. Dublin*, (cat. no. 25).

Lady Alicia Parsons (1815-1885)

25 The Harbour at Kingstown, Co. Dublin

Watercolour on paper, 28.5 × 38.8 cms.
PROVENANCE: by descent to the present owner.

One of a series of watercolours painted in a fresh, almost naive style, using clear washes of colour. This is particularly effective in the representation of the sea and the sky. In companion studies of Portmarnock Strand and a red-sailed yacht drifting on the sea, she achieves a semi-abstract effect by offsetting small touches of strong colour against a limpid deep jade sea.

This view of the harbour at Kingstown (now Dun Laoghaire) must have been painted after 1859, when the Carlisle Pier and Wharf, which are depicted here, were built for the Mailboat. It must also have been painted before the mid 1860's, when the Club house of the Royal St. George Yacht Club (built in 1843) was extended. Daniel Gilman has furthermore pointed out that the guardship shown nestling in the harbour wall is the *Ajax*, whose former captain, Captain Boyd, is commemorated in the monument at the entrance to the jetty in the foreground. Howth Head is visible beyond on the horizon. Valuable topographical observations can also be made in a detailed view the artist painted of the town of Birr, probably around the same time. NGB

Lent by the Earl and Countess of Rosse.

Maguire presents herself as a respectably dressed person of leisure, so conforming to Victorian expectations of a woman artist. Her draughtsmanship is as yet unsure. The colouring and use of hatched strokes show her knowledge of watercolourists William Henry Hunt and Myles Birket Foster, probably through the work of her sister Adelaide Agnes Maguire (1852-1876), who in her short career was similarly influenced by them. ALH

Helen Maguire, *Self-Portrait while sketching,* (cat. no. 26).

Harriet Osborne O'Hagan, *Eugenie O'Hagan,* (cat. no. 27).

Helena J. Maguire (1860-1909)
26   Self-Portrait while sketching

Watercolour and pencil with white highlights on paper, 27.3 × 21.6 cms.

SIGNED: *H J Maguire. Sept. 18. . .*

PROVENANCE: Cynthia O'Connor and Co. Ltd., from whom purchased, 1987; National Gallery of Ireland, cat. no. 19,335.

EXHIBITED: 1987, *10th Annual Exhibition of topographical views and Irish subject paintings,* Cynthia O'Connor Gallery, Dublin, no. 5.

The final digits of the date on this watercolour have been almost erased, but from the sitter's appearance, this self-portrait would convincingly date from the early 1880's. The artist is shown against the bank of a river while making a pencil sketch. Germaine Greer in *The Obstacle Race* (1979) noted a tendency for women artists in the past to paint self-portraits, partly due to lack of models to study from, but also to record their lives and aspirations. Helena

Harriet Osborne O'Hagan (1830-1921)
27   Eugenie O'Hagan

Charcoal with white highlights on paper, 57 × 45.5 cms.

PROVENANCE: M. Garbaye and J. de L'Etre, by whom presented, 1948; National Gallery of Ireland cat. no. 3011.

Harriet's drawing of her sister Eugenie may belong to the same date, 1869, as the study of her other sister Marguerite Lemercier O'Hagan (National Gallery of Ireland cat. no. 3012). It is a charming portrait of a girl, with romantic expression, and large dreamy eyes looking into the middle distance. Although firmly modelled, the technique is loose, with soft shading around the eyes, mouth and chin, and deep shadowing in the wavy lustrous hair. The drawing is similar to some of Couture's portraits (Harriet studied with Couture in France), while the soft cross-hatching recalls Millet's charcoal technique. She uses white chalk highlights on the necklace. JC

Lent by the National Gallery of Ireland.

Harriet Osborne O'Hagan, *A Farm in Normandy, 1880*, (cat. no. 28).

Lydia Shackleton, *Pitcher-plants (sarracenia hybrids), 1885*, (cat. no. 29).

Harriet Osborne O'Hagan

28   A Farm in Normandy, 1880

Charcoal and watercolour with white highlights on paper, 30.3 × 43 cms.

SIGNED AND DATED: *H. Osborne O'Hagan 1880*

PROVENANCE: M. Garbaye and J. de L'Etre, by whom presented; National Gallery of Ireland cat. no. 3014.

EXHIBITED: 1984, *The Irish Impressionists*, National Gallery of Ireland 1984 (cat. no. 37).

Harriet O'Hagan may have recently been studying with Couture at Villiers-le-Bel but, like her contemporary, Helen Mabel Trevor, she took time off to visit Normandy. Although primarily a portraitist, here she shows a sensitivity to landscape, with the farmhouse in a clearing viewed through trees. The tall roof and wood-beamed façade are characteristic of the Normandy region. A small figure can be glimpsed just inside the open doorway. O'Hagan enjoyed using charcoal, in this drawing rubbed against the grain of the paper to great effect. Sometimes she used white highlights, but it was also common practice to scuff the surface of a drawing or watercolour to gain broken white surfaces. The picture was presented to the National Gallery by M. Garbaye and J. de L'Etre of Savigny-sur-Oise.   JC

Lent by the National Gallery of Ireland.

Lydia Shackleton (1828-1914)

29   Pitcher-plants (Sarracenia hybrids), 1885

Watercolour on paper, 38 × 26 cms.

PROVENANCE: National Botanic Gardens, Glasnevin, Dublin. Commissioned by Frederick Moore, 1885.

LITERATURE: B. Morley, *Lydia Shackleton's paintings in the National Botanic Gardens, Glasnevin,* (1979); *Glasra*, vol. 2, pp. 25-26.

Pitcher-plants are carnivorous — in the beautiful trumpet-shaped leaves hapless insects drown and their body-tissues decompose forming a nutritious soup that the plants absorb. Natives of the United States and Canada, they were popular greenhouse plants during the late nineteenth century and the Botanic Gardens at Glasnevin had one of the best collections in the world. In the wild, the pitcher-plants inhabit bogs and one American species has become naturalized in Irish peatlands.

More importantly, however, the first artificial hybrids of these strange plants were raised in Glasnevin, and Lydia Shackleton was engaged by the Keeper, Frederick Moore, to paint the hybrids. In each painting a single leaf ('pitcher') and a single flower are portrayed life-size. The leaves are remarkable, shaped like a long tapering flask with a hood over the mouth. The flowers are equally complicated — in these two the petals are rich crimson.

On the left is *Sarracenia x patersonii*, on the right *Sarracenia x chelsonii*; both are artificial hybrid, deliberately raised by gardeners.
                    CN

Lent by National Botanic Gardens, Glasnevin.

Jane Morgan (1831-1899)

30   Is that all?, 1898

Oil on canvas, 129 × 194.5 cms.

SIGNED: *Jane Morgan*

PROVENANCE: Lt. Col. W. A. C. H. Morgan, Banalun, Skibbereen, county Cork; probably his sale, 12-13 April 1961, where purchased by Mr. Cohen of Dublin, by whom sold to Trafalgar Galleries, London; sale, Christie's, London, 8 November 1974, lot 206; bought by P. J. Ward, London, by whom sold at Christie's, 16 April 1980, lot 77, where purchased by Ulster Museum, Belfast, art dept., cat. no. 2560.

Jane Morgan, *Is that all?*, (cat. no. 30).

LITERATURE: Eileen Black, 'Jane Morgan: A Forgotten Irish Artist.' *Irish Arts Review*, vol. 3, no. 4, (Winter 1986), p. 23, ill. p. 22.

The painting shows the interior of a pawnbroker's shop and a woman pawning a lamp — for which she has been offered only fifteen cents, judging from the broker's ticket, inscribed '7557 I. Harlem Licensed Pawnbroker No 6 Eighth Ave. New York. Nov 4 1898 15c.' The jewels on the broker's desk are, in fact, the artist's family heirlooms and not inexpensive studio props. According to the *New York Herald,* 5 April 1899, Jane's home was robbed on 10 December 1898 and jewellery and mementoes stolen. At the time of the robbery, Jane was working on *Is that all?* and had removed many of her jewels from the bank, to use in the picture. Luckily, much of the stolen property was recovered in New York on 3 March 1899. The little lamp (also a prized family possession) is at present in a private collection in Ireland.

The standard of the picture (painted only six months before Jane's death) is uneven, probably a consequence of the artist's increasing years and declining health. EB

Lent by the Ulster Museum, Belfast.

Edith Osborne, Lady Blake (1845-1926)

31 Jamaican butterflies

Watercolour on paper, 50 × 24 cms.

PROVENANCE: Department of Entomology, British Museum (Natural History), London (Blake paintings nos. 13, 17).

LITERATURE: P. Gilbert, *Butterflies,* (forthcoming).

This pair of watercolours depicts all the stages (from eggs, through caterpillars, to chrysalis, and finally the flying adults) in the life-cycle and the food-plant of two native Jamaican butterflies. The caterpillars of both species feed on the foliage of a passion-fruit vine *(Passiflora laurifolium)* whose marvellous hanging blossoms are

Edith Osborne, Lady Blake, *Jamaican butterflies,* (cat. no. 31).

vividly portrayed in the two paintings. Plants and animals are depicted life-size.

The butterfly *Heliconius charithonia,* with one of its caterpillars, was painted in December 1893. The caterpillar formed into a chrysalis on 5 December and on 15 December the adult butterfly emerged. The chrysalis is shown hanging from one of the vine's tendrils in the top right.

On 25 December 1892, the caterpillar of the Gulf fritillary *(Agraulis vanillae* — right-hand painting) formed itself into a chrysalis, and ten days later (on 5 January 1893) the beautiful adult emerged. Lady Blake has painted two caterpillars, and the chrysalis can be seen at the tip of the hanging shoot (bottom right).

In these fine compositions, it is worth noting that Lady Blake has shown such details as the chewed leaves of the plant. These watercolours thus provide valuable scientific information; the portrayal of the plants and the insects is accurate in all respects. CN

Lent by the Trustees of the British Museum, (Natural History).

Helen Mabel Trevor (1831-1900)

32 The fisherman's mother, 1892

Oil on canvas, 65 × 53 cms.

SIGNED AND DATED: *Helen Mabel Trevor f.1892.*

PROVENANCE: Helen Mabel Trevor Bequest, 1900. National Gallery of Ireland cat. no. 500.

EXHIBITED: 1893, as *La Mère du Marin,* Paris Salon, no. 1716; 1895, as *La Mère du Marin,* Royal Academy, London, no. 323; 1896, as *La Mère du Marin* (£150),

Helen Mabel Trevor, *The fisherman's mother*, (cat. no. 32).

Royal Hibernian Academy, Dublin; 1980, *The Peasant in French 19th Century Art*, Douglas Hyde Gallery, Dublin, no. 82; 1984, *The Irish Impressionists*, National Gallery of Ireland, Dublin, no. 40.

LITERATURE: J. Campbell, *The Irish Impressionists*, exhibition catalogue, National Gallery of Ireland, Dublin, (1984), p. 179; J. Campbell, 'Les Irlandais en Bretagne 1860-1914', *Pont-Aven et ses Peintres*, (Rennes 1986), p. 40, ill.

Trevor's figure subjects of the 1880's, of school-children and street urchins, are appealing but sentimental. After re-entering Carolus Duran's atelier in 1889, her drawing became tighter, and her subject-matter more realistic. Here the firm draughtsmanship is evident in the modelling of the face and hands of the aged widow but there is an oppressive quality in her closeness to the viewer, forward gaze, and the dark background. Her hunched pose, weathered face and heavy clothes tell of the hardship of her life, but the clasped rosary beads show the deep religious faith of the Breton people. The stooping pose of the woman who rests her hands on her stick recall some of Millet's Social Realist paintings or Bastien-Lepage's *Père Jacques*. The wrinkled face, the bonnet and heavy cloak are close to Frank O'Meara's *Old woman gathering leaves*, 1887. (O'Meara was also a student of Duran's). Trevor's study may appear conventional if compared with Roderic O'Conor's brightly coloured painting of an old Breton woman knitting, painted at the same time yet.

More than other Irish artists in Brittany, she took a keen interest in Breton life, and traditions, the villages and the fishing people, even a sense of involvement with the Norman and Breton widows in interiors. A painting entitled *A Breton widow* was shown at

the Royal Hibernian Academy in 1889. This painting was exhibited at the Paris Salon in 1893, and subsequently in London and Dublin. JC

Lent by the National Gallery of Ireland.

Helen Mabel Trevor, *Interior of a Breton cottage*, (cat. no. 33).

Helen Mabel Trevor

33   Interior of a Breton cottage, 1892

Oil on canvas, 63 × 46 cms.

SIGNED AND DATED: *Helen Mabel Trevor f.1892.*

PROVENANCE: Helen Mabel Trevor Bequest, 1900; National Gallery of Ireland cat. no. 501.

EXHIBITED: 1898, as *Interior Breton* (H. M. prize, see below), Paris Salon, no. 1972; 1904, *Irish Painters*, Guildhall, London, as *Interior of a Breton cottage*, no. 4; 1980, *The Peasant in French 19th Century Art*, Douglas Hyde Gallery, Dublin, no. 83, ill.; 1984, *The Irish Impressionists*, National Gallery of Ireland, Dublin, no. 41, ill.

LITERATURE: J. Campbell, *The Irish Impressionists*, exhibition catalogue, National Gallery of Ireland, Dublin, (1984), p. 180; J. Campbell, 'Les Irlandais en Bretagne 1860-1914', *Pont-Aven et ses Peintres*, (Rennes 1986), p. 39, ill.

Interior scenes were popular in this period, particularly among the Flemish and Dutch schools, and were represented by a number of Irish artists, including Thaddeus, Osborne, Allan and O'Brien. The pose in Trevor's picture recalls Osborne's tiny study of an old woman peeling potatoes, *Moderke Verhoft* (NGI cat. no. 1929). 'Dutch Interior' is sometimes a general rather than a strictly geographical term, and it is possible that this picture was exhibited under this title on one or two occasions, (e.g.: *The Evening of Life — A Dutch Interior*, Royal Hibernian Academy, 1897 £35). Trevor also showed *Interior de pêcheur en Normandie* at the Royal Academy in 1894.

Compared to the contemporary *The fisherman's mother* (National Gallery of Ireland cat. no. 500), it is more relaxed and open, the whole figure of the woman contained within the room, with light shining through the casement window, falling on the wall and floor of the simple interior, and modelling the lady's sleeve and hands. Elderly women were good models for Realist painters; they had a lot of time on their hands, and they sat still. However, Trevor was particularly interested in the lives and dwellings of the fishing and village people. At Douarnenez, for example, she observed that the villagers had few necessities in their houses. But they had unexpected luxuries, probably brought home by sailors from foreign lands.

Trevor's picture is shown among other canvases in a photograph of the artist in her studio (reproduced in *The Ramblings of an Artist*). The painting won honourable mention at the Paris Salon in 1898, thus enabling Helen to join the 'Liste des Artistes Recompensées'.

JC

Lent by the National Gallery of Ireland.

Helen Mabel Trevor, *Self-Portrait*, (cat. no. 34).

Helen Mabel Trevor

34   Self-Portrait

Oil on canvas, 66 × 55 cms.

PROVENANCE: Miss R. Trevor, by whom presented, 1900; National Gallery of Ireland cat. no. 502.

Helen Mabel Trevor depicts herself with cap, smock and palette, as a mature lady artist at the height of her powers. Her self-portrait was probably painted in the 1890's, when she was in her sixties and resident in Paris. It is interesting to compare this picture with the photograph of Helen in her studio, clasping her great palette and brushes, and surrounded by canvases, (see *Ramblings of an Artist*). The looseness in the painting of the garment and the viridian tones give an attractive touch to the picture. The painting was presented to the National Gallery by her sister Rose immediately after Helen's death in 1900.

JC

Lent by the National Gallery of Ireland.

Mary Kate Benson, *Breton Girl beside river*, (cat. no. 35).

Mary Kate Benson (d.1921)

35   Breton Girl beside river, 1891

Pastel on paper, 58.5 × 43 cms.

SIGNED AND DATED: *M.K. Benson 1891* (in pencil).

PROVENANCE: Elizabeth Guinness; private collection, Ireland.

EXHIBITED: 1892, Royal Hibernian Academy, Dublin, no. 229, (probably exhibited as *Prayer, en route to Market* — study in pastels).

Walter Osborne, in Quimperlé in 1883, may have encouraged younger artists such as Mary Benson to visit Brittany too. She was in Quimperlé in 1891, making several figure studies of local girls (e.g. *A Brittany Milk Girl* and *A Brittany Maiden*), and street scenes of the town. Here, a child in simple Breton costume, bonnet, apron and clogs, pauses on a small wooden bridge beside the river, in front of a dark wood and a château. She holds an umbrella and basket under each arm, and her hands are clasped. The presence of the umbrella, and the approaching grey clouds, suggest the onset of rain. As in many contemporary peasant paintings, the girl is viewed in close-up. But the sharp contrast of light and shadow on her face and dress seem too sharp for a 'plein-air' scene. The pastel is sensitively treated, particularly in the apron and dress of the girl, and the reflections in the river. There is a small touch of orange in her apron pocket, perhaps a posy of flowers.   JC

Private collection.

Sarah Henrietta Purser (1848-1943)

36   A visitor, 1885

Oil on canvas (cleaned 1944 and 1974), 76 × 50.5 cms.

PROVENANCE: the artist's collection; her sale, Dublin, Mespil House, 1943; Mrs. V. Ganley; the present owner.

EXHIBITED: December 1885, *Dublin Sketching Club annual exhibition,* Dublin, no. 233.

LITERATURE: *Dublin Sketching Club catalogue* (1885); *Daily Express* (15 December 1885), review of Dublin Sketching Club exhibition: 'A young lady dressed in a light gown is seated in the shadow of a window on a sofa, the light falling on her dress. The position is easy, yet very much foreshortened, and the tone that pervades the penumbra of the room is exceedingly true, if a little bleak and cold'; J. O'Grady, *Sarah Henrietta Purser* (Ph.D. thesis, National University of Ireland, 1974).

At the Mespil House sale this picture was knocked down to the late Mrs. Ganley for £1 because it was unattributed and very dirty. She considered it to be by Purser until about 1970 when she decided it was 'too good'. Her doubts were unjustified; the mode and bravura handling are typical of early Purser, and the Daily Express reviewer was clearly referring to the present picture. The 1974 thesis therefore identified it with *A visitor.* This identification was proved correct a year later when the National Gallery of Ireland acquired *A lady with a rattle,* cat. no. 4131, signed by Purser and dated 1885, on a canvas from the same maker, with the same model wearing the same hat, and painted with even greater verve.

The N.G.I. picture is dedicated with a mock-serious flourish

Sarah Henrietta Purser, *A visitor,* (cat. no. 36).

to Julian Sturgis, member of an expatriate Bostonian family of writers living in England, and himself a journalist who was especially interested in the land question in Ireland. He was a friend of the benevolent Irish landlord Sir Henry Gore-Booth of Lissadell, one of Purser's earliest patrons. Their common interests were complemented through the artist's friendship with Michael Davitt, founder of the Land League.

Purser spent the first week of July 1885 in Surrey executing at least six pictures for members of the Sturgis family, including a portrait of Julian which was exhibited the following year at London's Grosvenor Gallery. Surviving correspondence suggests that he and his wife had commissioned her portrait in pastel to mark their recent wedding. He wrote of his delight at receiving the gift of an oil painting as well, and his amazement; when could she have done it? Obviously the rapidly painted N.G.I. picture with its dedicatory inscription was that gift, and furthermore it bears the legend 'Mrs. Sturgis' on the reverse. The new Mrs. Sturgis was an Irishwoman, Mary Maud de la Poer Beresford.

This, then, is the identity of the young woman posing here as *A visitor.*   JOG

Private collection.

Sarah Henrietta Purser, *The Cooper's Shop, James' Gate Brewery,* (cat. no. 37).

she went to sketch in the Coopers' Shop she was to a modest degree in the family tradition of part ownership of the vast enterprise. She had to sell her shares after four months and it was more than a decade before she could afford to renew her small investment.

The cooperage was appealingly craftsmanlike, and arguably the most exciting department in the brewery especially when casks were being blazed. This sterilization process is going on in the centre of the present scene. Industrial genre was a novelty in Irish art, adding rarity value to the purely aesthetic qualities of this well composed, atmospheric, and dramatic picture.   JOG

Lent by the Guinness Brewery Museum.

Sarah Henrietta Purser, *The Circus Encampment,* (cat. no. 38).

Sarah Henrietta Purser

37   The Cooper's Shop, James' Gate Brewery, c.1887

Oil on canvas (relined), 61 × 50.8 cms.

PROVENANCE: the artist's nephew, Jack Geoghegan, by whom presented, 1950, to Arthur Guinness Son & Co. (Dublin) Limited; lodged in the Brewery Museum.

EXHIBITED: January 1889, *Dublin Art Club Exhibition,* Dublin, no. 110; 1957, *Art et Travail,* Geneva.

LITERATURE: Dublin Art Club catalogue (1889).

A sketchbook inscribed 'SHP 1887' now in a private collection in Limerick contains two pages with slight pencil drawings of coopers at work. Some of the poses recur in this painting.

The artist had strong family ties with the Dublin brewing industry. Her great-great-grandfather helped introduce porter brewing to Ireland 1776; her great grandfather became brewmaster at St. James's Gate Brewery in 1799 when its founder Arthur Guinness decided to concentrate on porter and the stronger stout; her grandfather joined the Guinness staff at the same time, aged sixteen; and both became partners in the firm which otherwise consisted only of Guinness family members. This partnership gave the artist's grandfather the means to buy Rathmines Castle and estate in 1834. On his death his eldest son refused a partnership but continued as general manager of the great brewery as long as it remained a private firm. It became a public company in 1886. The artist invested all £200 of her savings in shares, so that when

Sarah Henrietta Purser

38   The circus encampment

Oil on board, 25 × 30 cms.

SIGNED AND DATED: *SP* (in monogram) *1901*

PROVENANCE: bought from a Dublin art dealer by the present owner's mother; by descent to the present owner.

EXHIBITED: 1974, *Friends of the National Collections of Ireland Golden Jubilee exhibition,* Municipal Gallery, Dublin (not in catalogue).

LITERATURE: J. O'Grady, *Sarah Henrietta Purser* (Ph.D. thesis, National University of Ireland, 1974); J. O'Grady, 'Sarah Purser.' *Capuchin Annual* (1977).

Sarah Purser had used the 'SP' monogram since 1875 but gradually discarded it, and this is its last known appearance. In 1901 she gave her time and energy to promoting other artists and art projects, so that this gemlike evocation of summertime and circus magic is her only picture from that year. Perhaps that is why it is so joyful, and so painterly.   JOG

Private collection.

Sarah Henrietta Purser, *Summer flowers*, (cat. no. 39).

Sarah Henrietta Purser, *The drawingroom at Mespil House, c.1923*, (cat. no. 40).

Sarah Henrietta Purser

39 Summer Flowers

Oil on canvas, 76.7 × 63.5 cms.

PROVENANCE: given by the artist to Miss Hilda Alexander, county Tipperary, 1903; by family descent to her grandson, by whom sold to present owner.

LITERATURE: J. O'Grady, *Sarah Henrietta Purser* (Ph.D. thesis, National University of Ireland, 1974).

Throughout her career Sarah Purser painted flowers. Her strong and vigorous manner prevails in the independent flower-pieces and where the blooms are part of genre scenes. However, where the flowers are compositional or atmospheric adjuncts to portraits she displays a rarer skill, a delicate and subtle touch. The present picture has the merit of combining these qualities of strength and delicacy. It also shows an attractive tension between the traditional and the 'modern', with an age-old composition applied to an informal arrangement where delphinium and roses, crocosmia and chrysanthemum daisies are jumbled together.

In 1903 Miss Alexander visited Miss Purser and admired this beautiful picture. Because she liked it and it had been 'cluttering up my studio for years' the artist promptly gave it to her. It was typical of Sarah Purser to be generous, and to make light of her generosity with a good humoured remark. JOG

Private collection.

Sarah Henrietta Purser

40 The drawingroom at Mespil House c.1923

Oil on canvas, 46 × 35.5 cms.

PROVENANCE: by descent in the artist's family to the present owner, a grandniece.

EXHIBITED: 1974, *Friends of the National Collections of Ireland Golden Jubilee exhibition*, Municipal Gallery, Dublin, no. 10.

LITERATURE: *Friends of the National Collections of Ireland*, exhibition catalogue, (1974); *The Irish Times*, (15 February 1974); J. O'Grady, *Sarah Henrietta Purser*, (Ph.D. thesis, National University of Ireland, 1974).

By 1909 Miss Purser was not only an established artist but an increasingly public personality whose penetrating mind and formidable debating powers had been recognised for over thirty years. Now she left her Harcourt Terrace studio which had been a centre of Irish cultural, intellectual and nationalist life, and joined her eldest brother in leasing Mespil House. For over thirty more years she held a monthly salon there — 'my day of wrath' — where a welcome awaited anyone with talent or ideas, especially if they could talk.

The locus of these gatherings was the ᵇ ⱼt double drawingroom on the *piano nobile*. The present picture catches the lofty room in a quiet moment. More importantly it displays again a true painter's joy in shape and surface, colour and light.   JOG

Private collection.

on her time, a fact which she later deeply regretted. Her later oils are therefore smaller in scale, mostly landscapes of the countryside in West Cork.   FG

Private collection.

Edith Œnone Somerville, *Retrospect,* (cat. no. 41).

Edith Œnone Somerville (1858-1949)

41   Retrospect

Oil on canvas, 81 × 122 cms.

SIGNED: *Edith Œ Somerville '87*

INSCRIBED: on label on back, *'tis I indeed but grief doth changes show'*

PROVENANCE: by descent to the present owner.

EXHIBITED: September 1984, *Edith Œ Somerville 1858-1949,* Castletownshend, county Cork; October 1984, *Edith Somerville 1858-1949,* The Crawford Municipal Gallery, Cork.

LITERATURE: Edith Somerville, *Diary,* 1887; Frances Gillespie, *Edith Œ Somerville 1858-1949,* (Castletownshend 1984).

The picture was painted in 1887 at the time when Edith Somerville was visiting Paris regularly and was devoting most of her time to painting while she was at home. The large isolated image and the 'square brush' style indicate her awareness of French painting. The picture was painted in Castletownshend and the diary entries for the early part of the year chart its progress and identify the sitter as a local Cork woman — 'began on a canvas 5 × 3½, Mary Norris regarding herself with melancholy disfavour in a looking glass . . . went to work early, madly interesting. Began to paint and mostly got her head in — thundering good model — she never stirs'.

   This was Edith Somerville's first serious painting on an ambitious scale and the labels on the back suggest that this was the painting she brought to Paris later in the year to submit to the Salon. It was not accepted. *The Goose Girl* in the Crawford Municipal Gallery was painted the following year and is her only other painting on a similar formal vain. The onset of her literary career and her continuing involvement in hunting put many limits

Edith Œnone Somerville, *She drifted rudderless,* (cat. no. 42).

Edith Œnone Somerville

42   She drifted rudderless, (ill. for *In the State of Denmark,* 1894).

101

Wash with white highlights on paper, 26.5 × 10.5 cms.

SIGNED: *ŒSomerville*

PROVENANCE: by descent to Sir Patrick Coghill; Sir Patrick Coghill Gift, The Queen's University of Belfast.

EXHIBITED: September 1984, *Edith ŒE Somerville 1858-1949*, Castletownshend, county Cork, no. 24; October 1984, *Edith ŒE Somerville 1858-1949*, The Crawford Municipal Gallery, Cork.

LITERATURE: Frances Gillespie, *Edith ŒE Somerville 1858-1949*, (Castletownshend, 1984).

During the 1890's Edith Somerville and Violet Martin together undertook a number of tours on which they based articles for the *Ladies' Pictorial*. These were later published as travel books illustrated with wash sketches such as this. The tours themselves were fraught with complications and in the books the authors give frequent and scathing accounts of their problems. This sketch supposedly shows the artist herself, fleeing lost and angry along the deserted streets of Hamburg.

The bold swaying lines of the figure stand out against the plain background in a style similar to contemporary Parisian posters. There is also an Impressionistic handling of the distant streets with large blots and dabs of white laid over soft wash. Small scale sketches such as this, because of the speed with which they could be carried out, suited her ability to capture quickly the effects of movement and atmosphere.   FG

Lent by The Queen's University of Belfast.

Edith Œnone Somerville, *The Parapet of the wooded precipice from whose edge we were looking back*, (cat. no. 43).

Edith Œnone Somerville

43   The Parapet of the wooded precipice from whose edge we were looking back (ill. for *Beggars on Horseback*, 1895)

Wash with white highlights on paper, 21 × 33.1 cms.

PROVENANCE: by descent to Sir Patrick Coghill; sale, Sotheby's, 1968, where purchased by the Queen's University of Belfast.

EXHIBITED: September 1984, *Edith ŒE Somerville 1858-1949*, Castletownshend, county Cork, no. 33; October 1984, *Edith ŒE Somerville 1858-1949*, The Crawford Municipal Gallery, Cork.

LITERATURE: Edith Somerville, *Diary*, 1894; Frances Gillespie, *Edith ŒE Somerville 1858-1949*, (Castletownshend 1984).

On a more peaceful tour in Wales the two travellers are seen, umbrellas poised, stopping to survey the sweeping view beyond. Diary entries for 1894 describe afternoons spent in Castletownshend with Violet Martin modelling for the sketch on Marquise, one of Edith Somerville's horses. Horses and hunting were later to become the most frequent subject for her illustrations and she is brilliant at capturing their character and movement. She was a noted horsewoman herself and from 1903-1909 was Master of the West Carbery Hounds.

Many of Edith Somerville's illustrations are simple line drawings dashed off at speed. The medium of wash was used, as here, when she wished to obtain more atmospheric effects. An interest in French methods is evident in the decorative effect of the segmented planes and the influence of Japanese prints can be seen in the way the tree cuts off the corner on the left.   FG

Lent by The Queen's University of Belfast.

Rose Barton, *Ha'penny Bridge*, (cat. no. 44).

Rose Barton (1856-1929)

44   Ha'penny Bridge, 1892

Pencil and watercolour on paper, heightened with bodycolour, 29.5 × 51 cms.

SIGNED AND DATED: *Rose Barton 1892*

PROVENANCE: private collection, Ireland.

EXHIBITED: 1987, *Rose Barton*, Crawford Municipal Art Gallery, Cork; Fine Art Society, London; Ulster Museum, Belfast; Butler Gallery, Kilkenny.

Rose loved to capture the bustling life of fin-de-siècle Dublin. *The Ha'penny Bridge* is one of her most successful compositions. The quays and figures, though loosely worked, are instilled with great movement and fluidity. The bridge itself and the industrial background have a dramatically Whistlerian quality, the sunset achieving a hazy, romantic atmosphere.

Rose successfully returned many times in her career to the banks of the river Liffey, particularly the busy environs of the Custom House.

Another version of the Halfpenny Bridge is illustrated in *Picturesque Dublin, Old and New*, (1898) as *The Penny Bridge*.

RR

Private collection.

Rose Barton was born into the privileged Anglo-Irish gentry; at the age of eighteen in 1874 she was presented at Dublin Castle during Lord Spencer's first term of office as Lord Lieutenant. *Going to the Levée at Dublin Castle*, painted some twenty-three years after her presentation, shows us a traditional formal occasion of Dublin upper-class society. This carefully balanced composition is full of movement and atmosphere; through the dusky evening haze we sense the anticipation of the waiting crowd and the excitement of the occasion.

The same composition was reproduced from a grey wash drawing on page twenty-one of *Picturesque Dublin, Old and New* (1898).

A similar, smaller version of *Going to the Levée* of 1906 exists; it is a more intimate view but lacks the solemnity of this 1897 watercolour.

RR

Lent by the National Gallery of Ireland.

Rose Barton, *Going to the Levée at Dublin Castle*, (cat. no. 45).

Rose Barton, *Hop Pickers in Kent Returning Home*, (cat. no. 46).

Rose Barton

45 Going to the Levée at Dublin Castle, 1897

Watercolour on paper, 35.6 × 26.6 cms.

SIGNED AND DATED: *Rose Barton 1897.*

PROVENANCE: Miss R. Havericks, by whom presented, 1947; National Gallery of Ireland cat. no. 2989.

EXHIBITED: 1987, *Rose Barton*, Crawford Municipal Art Gallery, Cork; Fine Art Society, London; Ulster Museum, Belfast; Butler Gallery, Kilkenny.

Rose Barton

46 Hop pickers in Kent returning home, 1894

Watercolour on paper, 34.7 × 26.7 cms.

SIGNED AND DATED: *Rose Barton.1894*

PROVENANCE: by descent to Raymond F. Brooke, by whom bequeathed, 1952; National Gallery of Ireland cat. no. 325.

EXHIBITED: Winter 1894-5, *Royal Society of Painters in Water-Colours*, no. 154; January 1987, *Rose Barton (1856-1929)*, The Crawford Municipal Gallery, Cork, no. 18; March 1987, *Rose Barton (1856-1929)*, Fine Art Society, London, no. 18; May 1987, *Rose Barton (1856-1929)*, Butler Gallery, Kilkenny, no. 18.

LITERATURE: *Rose Barton (1856-1929)* Cork, London, Kilkenny, 1987.

The subject of this small sketch is less familiar than Rose's landscapes and cityscapes but it is very close to plein-air paintings by her contemporaries. In the countryside as in the city she is drawn to the working people and the women are seen returning through the fields, tired and peaceful at the end of the day. Any hint of sentimentality in the charming group is avoided by the omission of detail and the figures are conceived as part of the overall soft colours of the landscape.

The watercolour is handled with the artist's usual delicacy and freedom. All the outlines are blurred and the figures are seen as if through a haze of light, warm and heavy, redolent of lazy summery afternoons. FG

Lent by the National Gallery of Ireland

Mildred Anne Butler (1858-1941)

47 Among the woods, 1898

Watercolour heightened with white on paper, 72.4 × 52 cms.

SIGNED AND DATED: *Mildred A. Butler Jan. 1898*

INSCRIBED: on reverse, *Among the Woods*

PROVENANCE: the artist's studio; consigned by the Executors of Mrs. Doreen Archer-Hoblon to Christie's, 19 October 1981, lot 168, where purchased by the present owner.

Among the woods is an excellent study of pigeons in flight and must surely have been the result of long periods of study from nature. However, given the extremely detailed rendering of the birds, the artist may well have resorted to studying from models; indeed she is known to have had a collection of stuffed birds of the more common varieties at Kilmurry. She has chosen an unusually low viewpoint which helps to draw the viewer into the world of the pigeons who are caught making a sudden departure through the trees. The formula of rendering detailed close-ups of birds clearly defined and silhouetted against hazy atmospheric backgrounds is one which she used repeatedly.

Among the woods was most probably painted at the artist's home in Kilmurry. Kilmurry provided the most constant source for her paintings and was noted for its profusion of birdlife, particularly the larger varieties like crows, jackdaws and pigeons. WR

Private collection.

Mildred Anne Butler, *Among the Woods*, (cat. no. 47).

Mildred Anne Butler, *A preliminary investigation*, (cat. no. 48).

Mildred Anne Butler

48 A preliminary investigation

Watercolour heightened with white on paper, 65.6 × 97.5 cms.

SIGNED AND DATED: *Mildred A. Butler 1898*

INSCRIBED: on reverse, *A preliminary Investigation*

PROVENANCE: formed part of the contents of the artist's studio; consigned by the

Executors of Mrs. Doreen Archer-Houblon to Christie's, 13 October 1981, lot 47, where purchased; National Gallery of Ireland, cat. no. 7952.

EXHIBITED: 1899, Royal Academy, London, no. 1116; 1981, *Mildred Anne Butler,* Dublin and Kilkenny, no. 41 (ill. in colour).

As the title suggests this picture records the first tentative approaches of a group of doves to an open bag of corn, Mildred Anne must have planted the bait herself for the unsuspecting birds. She was very keen on studying directly from nature, so much so in fact that she was known to have regularly tethered one of the Kilmurry cows in order to study it at close quarters and also to have let it go hungry for quite some time so as to observe its bone structure. Despite these acts of over enthusiasm, Mildred Anne had a great affinity with the creatures she painted and always managed to capture the endearing and often humorous qualities of their personalities. WR

Lent by the National Gallery of Ireland.

PROVENANCE: formed part of the contents of the artist's studio; consigned by the Executors of Mrs. Doreen Archer-Hoblon to Christie's, 13 October 1981, lot 17, where purchased by the present owner.

Watercolours of gardens in flower abound in Mildred Anne's *oeuvre* though many of these with their over abundance of highly coloured blossoms in neat little borders are slightly garish. However, *Wisteria,* a theme repeated on several occasions, is one of the best examples of her garden studies.

The open upper-storey window and doorway beneath serve as an effective backdrop for the encroaching sundrenched wisteria. The beauty of the various creepers is admirably captured by the artist's fresh and vivid treatment of the colourful blooms and lush foliage.

Wisteria is not signed or dated but is of a similar style to two other watercolours of the same subject, one of which was exhibited at the Old Watercolour Society in 1923. WR

Private collection.

Beatrice Gubbins, *Flowers in vases with a Chinese Figurine,* (cat. no. 50).

Mildred Anne Butler, *Wisteria and other blossoms outside an open window,* (cat. no. 49).

Mildred Anne Butler

49   Wisteria and other blossoms outside an open window

Watercolour heightened with white on paper, 36.9 × 26.6 cms.

Beatrice Gubbins (1878-1944)

50   Flowers in vases with a Chinese figurine

Watercolour on paper, 24 × 34 cms.

PROVENANCE: by family descent to the present owner.

EXHIBITED: April-May, 1986, *Beatrice Gubbins (1878-1944),* Crawford Municipal Art Gallery, Cork, no. 8.

LITERATURE: Francis Russell, *Beatrice Gubbins 1878-1944,* exhibition catalogue, Crawford Municipal Art Gallery, Cork, 1986.

This was probably painted at Dunkathel and, like many of the watercolours there, it is unsigned and virtually impossible to date. There is no marked stylistic development in her work but a typical feature throughout is a delicate poise and simplicity in the composition. Here this is used to create a quiet, peaceful air.

She handles watercolour well and knew how to exploit different techniques for various effects. Here the simple washes give a good impression of the light playing over the polished surfaces of the table and the figurine.   FG

Private collection.

Gwendolen Herbert, *An old Irish Woman,* (cat. no. 51).

Gwendolen Herbert (1878-1966)

51   An old Irish woman

Plaster, ht. 27 cms.

PROVENANCE: Mr. Peter Lamb, Dublin, from whom purchased June, 1985; National Gallery of Ireland cat. no. 8306.

EXHIBITED: 1986, *Acquisitions 1984-86,* National Gallery of Ireland, Dublin, no. 73.

LITERATURE: Adrian Le Harivel and Michael Wynne, *Acquisitions 1984-86,* (1986) no. 73, p. 81 (ill.).

The attribution to Herbert of the statuette *An old Irish woman* is based on the illustration of a very similar work in *The World's Art,* (1907), p. 611.   MW

Lent by the National Gallery of Ireland.

Jane Service Workman, *Ombre et Lumière,* (cat. no. 52).

Jane Service Workman (1873-1943)

52   Ombre et Lumière

Watercolour on paper, 40 × 53 cms.

PROVENANCE: by family descent to the present owner.

EXHIBITED: 1901, Paris Salon, no. 2940 (under Mlle. Janey Workmann).

This evocative study was also known as *Afternoon Tea* because of the blue and white china and copper tea pot catching the light through the half open door in the hall beyond. The picture may well have been painted in the reputedly dark house which Charles Rennie Mackintosh had built for the artist's uncle, Willy Workman in University Gardens in Glasgow. A wealthy shipowner (he owned the City Line), he collected pictures by the Glasgow School and used to take his extended family up the West coast of Scotland in his yacht. The house is now part of Glasgow University.   NGB

Private collection.

Helen O'Hara, *Evening*, (cat. no. 53).

Gladys Wynne, *Glenbeigh, Co. Kerry*, (cat. no. 54).

Helen O'Hara (1881-1919)

53   Evening

Watercolour with chinese white on white paper, 36.7 × 54 cms.

SIGNED: *HOH* (in monogram).

PROVENANCE: bequeathed by Miss Alice Finley, Kells, Abbots Langley, Hertfordshire; Ulster Museum, Belfast, Art Department cat. no. 1320.

EXHIBITED: 1894, Belfast Art Society, Belfast, no. 158, (priced at 3 gns.).

LITERATURE: Martyn Anglesea, *Royal Ulster Academy of Arts, A Centennial History*, (1981), p. 33 (ill.).

This is an open seascape with two gulls, presumably painted at Portstewart. It is very competent and professional.   MA

Lent by the Ulster Museum, Belfast.

Gladys Wynne (1878-1968)

54   Glenbeigh, Co. Kerry, c.1900

Watercolour on paper, 28.6 × 45.8 cms.

SIGNED: *Gladys Wynne.*

PROVENANCE: by family descent to the present owner.

Gladys Wynne's watercolours sometimes manifest a warm, mottled density, whose colour tones are analogous with the superb tweeds the Wynne sisters used to design from nearby Tigroney

House in Avoca. The later, usually landscape, views for which she became known when they were on exhibition at Combridge's Gallery in Dublin, rarely show the spontaneous, airy sense of space, light and air captured in this early watercolour. The light on the lone cluster of blackthorn blossom is echoed in the sparkling whitewash of the cottage with its loosely painted mountainy backdrop and fleeting clouds.   NGB

Lent by Patrick Wynne.

Sarah Cecilia Harrison (1863-1941)

55   Sir Hugh Lane, Director of The National Gallery of Ireland (1875-1915)

Oil on panel, 41 × 31 cms.

PROVENANCE: J. Gorry, Dublin, from whom purchased, 1954. National Gallery of Ireland cat. no. 1280.

EXHIBITED: 1965, *W. B. Yeats. A Centenary Exhibition*, National Gallery of Ireland, Dublin, no. 144; 1980, *Ireland's Literary Renaissance: Twentieth Century Portraits*, Marshall Fields, Chicago, no. 5.

LITERATURE: M. Wynne, *Fifty Irish Painters*, (1983), p. 43.

Hugh Lane, son of the Rev. James William Lane, rector of Ballyblack, county Cork and later, of Redruth, Cornwall, was a noted art collector, dealer and critic. Most of his youth was spent in travelling on the Continent, with his mother. In 1893, he entered the art trade, and five years later, commenced in business on his own, with rapid success. His interest in Ireland and Irish art began in 1901 and became the driving force of his life. In 1914, he was appointed Director of the National Gallery of Ireland (he had served as a Governor and Guardian for ten years) and during

Sarah Cecilia Harrison, *Sir Hugh Lane, Director of The National Gallery of Ireland (1875-1915),* (cat. no. 55).

Hazel Lavery, *The Brown Baby,* (cat. no. 56).

the eleven months of his management, presented twenty-four paintings to the Gallery. His desire to found a modern gallery in Dublin and Dublin Corporation's inability to provide it, led to his bequeathing, in 1913, an important collection of modern paintings to London, and not to Dublin, as planned. Complications arising from an unwitnessed codicil to his will (whereby he restored the paintings to Dublin) have resulted in both cities sharing the collection since 1959. Knighted in 1909, he was drowned when the *Lusitania* was torpedoed on 7 May 1915.

The painting shows Lane in a reflective mood, his thin artistic hands clasped in front of him. The portrait's crisp handling and rather taut controlled brushwork, is typical of Cecilia's style.

EB

Lent by the National Gallery of Ireland.

Hazel Lavery (1887-1935)
56   The Brown Baby, 1905

Oil on canvas, laid on board, 36 × 25.5 cms.

SIGNED AND DATED: *Hazel Martyn 1905*

PROVENANCE: from the artist by descent to the present owner.

EXHIBITED: 1909, *Salon d'Automne,* Paris.

The Brown Baby, a portrait of Hazel's daughter Alice, is so called because of the baby's sallow skin. It was painted in 1905, the year after Hazel had been tragically widowed. She did not exhibit it, however, until her return trip to Europe in 1909, when she met again and married John Lavery. Although Hazel spent much time in France this is the only painting she exhibited at the Salon. Painted 'en plein air' — directly out of doors — a style of painting much favoured by the revolutionary artists of the time, Hazel here successfully creates an atmosphere of space and airiness. The pretty baby, extravagantly dressed in a billowing gown, is carefully protected from the sunshine by the dense foliage on the left. *The Brown Baby* is a rare and interesting example of Hazel's early work in oils before she came under the influence of John Lavery.

BMG

Private collection.

Constance Markievicz (1868-1927)
57   Portrait of Susan Mitchell c.1905

Oil on canvas, 42 × 32 cms.

PROVENANCE: Kitsy Mitchell, London.

Susan L. Mitchell (1866-1929) was assistant editor to Æ (George Russell) on the *Irish Homestead* and later on the *Irish Statesman.* Her best known works are a book of mystic verse, *The Living Chalice,* and her lampoons of Dublin literary and political figures in *Aids to the Immortality of Certain Persons.* She knew Constance Markievicz after her return from Paris, but became particularly friendly with her in 1916, during her imprisonment and trial, when she looked after her personal affairs. Though not signed, this portrait has always been ascribed to Markievicz by the family, and resembles her style during the period when she exhibited with Æ. Æ portrayed Susan Mitchell in a similar, but more vigorous,

Constance Markievicz, *Portrait of Susan Mitchell*, (cat. no. 57).

Evelyn Gleeson, *Self-Portrait wearing a shoe buckle*, (cat. no. 58).

Her tiny frame (she was only five feet tall) is almost engulfed by the deep blue 'Aesthetic' dress she wears, while her distinctive pince-nez glasses do not mask the determined but dreamily idealistic nature of the artist.   NGB

Lent by Patrick Kelly, Dublin.

profile image, in a drawing in the National Gallery of Ireland; whereas John Butler Yeats's portraits of her tend to be more intimate.   HP

Lent by Kitsy Mitchell.

Evelyn Gleeson, *View from Benown, near Athlone, Co. Westmeath*, (cat. no. 59).

Evelyn Gleeson (1855-1944)

58   Self-Portrait wearing a shoe buckle, c.1890

Pastel on paper, 49.5 × 39.4 cms.
PROVENANCE: Catherine MacCormack (artist's niece); Patrick Kelly.

Evelyn Gleeson was best known as a portrait painter when, in 1902, plans were being discussed for the setting up of the Dun Emer Guild. There are several very competent pastel portraits by her which show a muted velvety richness echoed only in her few extant watercolour designs for needlework. Used in the Rosalba manner, it was not a medium favoured as a rule by artists of this period.

Evelyn Gleeson

59   View from Benown, near Athlone, Co. Westmeath, c.1891

Watercolour on paper, 20.2 × 34.9 cms.
PROVENANCE: Catherine MacCormack (artist's niece); Patrick Kelly.

Painted from Benown, the house her father had bought outside Athlone, the painting depicts the parkland sweeping past an eccentric hedgehog-like clump of trees in the foreground, to reveal the creeks of Lough Ree and the spire of St. Peter's, Athlone visible in the distance. Evelyn Gleeson painted several watercolour views at this period, some in the company of Caroline Orridge, a competent watercolourist, who was to become the first wife of her old friend, the botanist Augustine Henry. She favoured conventional views of trees, fleeting shadows and the watery landscape of the midlands, painted with an affectionate familiarity. Later, her watercolours are less sweeping and seem mostly to focus on arrangements of wild and garden flowers.   NGB

Lent by Patrick Kelly, Dublin.

Frances Beckett, *Hill of Howth,* (cat. no. 60).

Frances Beckett (1880-1951)
60   Hill of Howth, 1909

Oil on canvas, c.60.9 × 91.4 cm.

INSCRIBED: *F. SINCLAIR 1909*

PROVENANCE: Seán O Criadain; Mrs. D. Hamilton, Monkstown, Co. Dublin.

Though it has no title, this is thought to be a view of the Hill of Howth from the back of the Red Rock. It was painted shortly after the artist's marriage and her name and the date were added to the painting some time later. The treatment reflects an interest in Nathaniel Hone, who also painted the coast north of Dublin; but the broad fluid brushstrokes and vivacious handling of light and shade create an immediate effect which is typical of Beckett.

HP

Lent by Deirdre Hamilton, the artist's daughter.

Harriet Hockley Townshend, *Winter,* (cat. no. 61).

Harriet Hockley Townshend (1877-1941)
61   Winter, 1911

Pastel on paper, 108 × 75 cms.

SIGNED: *HHT*

INSCRIBED: on labels on reverse, *Winter by Miss H H Townshend/ Parmerstown Park/ Dublin* and *Miss Theodosia Townshend/ aged 19/ 1911.*

PROVENANCE: on loan to the Castletown Foundation.

Painted in 1911, this portrait of Miss Theodosia Townshend illustrates Harriet's accomplished and confident style. The pose is formal yet the expression on the young woman's face and her dashing costume with ostrich feather hat lends a lightness and sense of gaiety to the composition. Although it is not known from whom Harriet received tuition at the Metropolitan School of Art in Dublin in 1910, it is clear from the style of this portrait that she was either directly or indirectly influenced by the work of William Orpen who taught at the School between c.1908 and 1912.   WR

Lent from a private collection courtesy of the Castletown Foundation.

Marjorie Robinson,, *Reverie, 1914,* (cat. no. 62).

Josephine Webb, *Dora Sigerson (Mrs. Shorter),* (cat. no. 63).

Marjorie Robinson (1858-1924)

62   Reverie, 1914

Watercolour on ivory, 9 × 7.5 cms. (sight).

SIGNED AND DATED: *M. Robinson 1914*

PROVENANCE: one of twenty-two miniatures, donated by the artist's brother, John B. Robinson, in 1925, as a memorial. Ulster Museum, Belfast, art dept. cat. no. 4517.

The excellence of Marjorie's talent as a miniaturist is clearly obvious in this portrait. Beautifully modelled and delicately handled, it displays an arresting realism, full of introspection and tinged with wistfulness.   EB

Lent by the Ulster Museum, Belfast.

Josephine Webb (1853-1924)

63   Dora Sigerson (Mrs Shorter)

Pastel on paper, 59 × 47.7 cms.

PROVENANCE: presented by the artist, 1919. National Gallery of Ireland cat. no. 6026.

Dora Sigerson was born in Dublin, August 16, 1866, the eldest daughter of Dr. George Sigerson, a surgeon and Gaelic scholar.

Her mother Hester Sigerson, was the author of a successful novel, *A Ruined Race,* as well as a number of poems.

The Sigerson family, who lived at No. 3 Clare Street, were prominent members of the circle of writers and artists who were deeply involved in the Gaelic Revival. Dora Sigerson married Clement Shorter, the editor of the *Illustrated London News,* in 1896 and thereafter lived in England.

In a tribute to Miss Sigerson after her death in 1918, Katherine Tynan described her heavy dark hair, beautiful brow and eyebrows, fine grey eyes, short nose and red lips, '. . . singularly beautiful, with some strange hint of storm in her beauty'.

Though the dark hair is partly hidden by a hat in Miss Webb's portrait, it is an excellent likeness, judging by other portraits and photographs. Miss Webb has also captured the melancholy air which often appears in Miss Sigerson's poetry. Miss Sigerson received no formal education or training, but she had a strong poetic sense and could express the sadness and desolation which were intensified by what she felt was her exile in England. Douglas Hyde pointed out that she became more Irish because she had left Ireland: not an uncommon situation. According to Miss Tynan, Dora Sigerson Shorter died of a broken heart, after what she felt was the failure of the 1916 Rising.

'The soft little hands of the rain stroked my pale cheek,
The kind little feet of the rain ran by my side'.

— from *The Comforters,* by Dora Sigerson Shorter.

SAD

Lent by the National Gallery of Ireland.

Helen Colville, *St. Stephen's Green,* (cat. no. 64).

Helen Colville (d.1953)

64   St. Stephen's Green

Pencil and watercolour on paper, 28 × 38.1 cms.

PROVENANCE: presented by the artist to the present owner, 1946.

There is a pleasant feeling of tranquillity and of times gone by in Colville's idyllic rendering of St. Stephen's Green in the summer. Particularly attractive are the figures of the young girl in a pink dress and wide brimmed hat and the small boy in blue who gaze languidly at the ducks in the pond. On the far side of the park beyond the strolling figures, there is a clear view of the tall houses of St. Stephen's Green North, a view which today is much obscured by the now equally tall trees that surround the park.   WR

Lent by Mrs. R. H. O'Hanlon.

Sadhbh Trinseach, *Nymphs and Satyrs,* (cat. no. 65).

Sadhbh Trinseach (1891-1918)

65   Nymphs and Satyrs, 1917

Conte crayon on paper, 73.6 × 104.2 cms.

PROVENANCE: by family descent to the present owner.

A particularly abandoned study at a time when shivering nude studies were more common. It reveals the strong, energetic nature of the artist, whose tragically early death was greatly lamented in Dublin literary and artistic circles. It is all the more remarkable when compared with the formal graphic work, broad painterly canvases and sensitive drawing which are contemporary with this.

NGB

Lent by the Coffey family.

Sadhbh Trinseach, *Self-portrait with Diarmuid Coffey,* (cat. no. 66).

Sadhbh Trinseach

66   Self-portrait with Diarmuid Coffey

Oil on canvas, 61 × 45.8 cms.

PROVENANCE: by family descent to the present owner.

This unfinished sketch, surprisingly modern its loose, painterly treatment, shows the artist at work as she looks into a mirror. On the left hand side, as though painted on a wall, is a profile portrait of Diarmuid Coffey, whom she had just married. She also drew a pensive charcoal sketch of him smoking a pipe at this time. He was the author of the first biography of Douglas Hyde, who was a close friend and as profoundly involved in the Celtic Revival as she was.   NGB

Lent by the Coffey family.

Margaret M. Sherlock, *Street scene in Serenaga, Kashmir,* (cat. no. 67).

Margaret M. Sherlock (1886-1966)

67   Street scene in Serenaga, Kashmir, c.1917

Watercolour on paper, 26.7 × 19 cms.

PROVENANCE: by family descent to the present owner, Beatrice Somerville-Large.

As was the custom, the Sherlocks used to spend the summer months in the hills and the winter on the plains of India. Margaret Sherlock particularly loved Kashmir and did a number of delightful watercolours of mountainy meadows full of wild mimulus, temples, house boats and village life. She painted from whatever wooden house they had taken for the season. She painted an exquisite portrait of the family ayah on one occasion, using a similar palette to the loose chocolate tones of this painting. Its composition and strongly orchestrated juxtaposition of planes of shadow and light are particularly successful.   NGB

Lent by Beatrice Somerville-Large.

Alice Jacob, *Coelogyne valida,* (cat. no. 68).

Alice Jacob (1862-1921)

68   Coelogyne valida, 1918

Watercolour on paper, 20 × 33 cms.

SIGNED: *AJ June 1 '18*

PROVENANCE: commissioned by Frederick Moore, June 1918, National Botanic Gardens, Glasnevin, Dublin.

LITERATURE: E. C. Nelson, 'Orchid paintings at Glasnevin', *Orchid Review,* vol. 89, (1981), pp. 373-77; E. C. Nelson & E. M. McCracken, *The Brightest Jewel, a history of the National Botanic Gardens, Glasnevin, Dublin,* (Kilkenny 1987).

This watercolour portrays a single inflorescence of a tropical orchid *(Coelogyne valida)* from the collections grown in the Botanic Gardens, Glasnevin, in 1918; details of parts (lips) of the individual flower are also depicted.

Orchids were very fashionable indoor plants during the last century and Ireland has a special and very significant place in the history of orchid cultivation. At the Glasnevin Botanic Gardens an unequalled collection of orchids were assembled by David and Frederick Moore, and it was Sir Frederick Moore who

113

commissioned this painting, one of a series of more than 1,500 orchid portraits (all are preserved in the National Botanic Gardens today). Other artists, including Lydia Shackleton, worked for Moore between 1894 and 1920, painting the Gardens' plant collections   CN

Lent by the Hugh Lane Municipal Gallery of Art, Dublin.

Kathleen Fox, *Science and Power*, (cat. no. 69).

Kathleen Fox (1880-1963)

69   Science and Power, 1911

Oil on canvas, 40.6 × 31.8 cms.

INSCRIBED: on back, *Fireworshippers by K. Fox, 20 Rue Chalgrin, Ave. de Bois de Boulogne, Paris ·*

PROVENANCE: by family descent to the present owner.

EXHIBITED: 1911, Royal Hibernian Academy, Dublin, no. 110.

One of two versions of this painting with its punning title (the other is in the Dublin Municipal Gallery) which shows the sculptor, Albert Power (1882-1945) at work on the great stone figure of Science which was shortly to adorn the new College of Science in Merrion Street. A contemporary critic wrote that he had 'seen this picture in actual execution and can testify to the difficulties experienced by the clever artist owing to causes beyond her control.'

Power had set up a makeshift studio against the wall of the building, in which the night watchmen are seen here warming their hands over a brazier (hence the alternative title, *Fireworshippers* on the back). Kathleen Fox much appreciated the sculptor's skill, unaffected Dublin charm and unconventional attitudes. She secured for him a commission to sculpt Cardinal Mannix in marble. He also sculpted Yeats, James Stephens, Lord Dunsany, St. Oliver Plunkett and the facade of Mullingar Cathedral among his many and various works.   NGB

Lent by Susanna Pym.

Kathleen Fox, *Peace or the Hungarian Princess*, (cat. no. 70).

Kathleen Fox

70   Peace or The Hungarian Princess, c.1914

Oil on canvas, 117 × 81.2 cms.

SIGNED: *K. Fox*

PROVENANCE: by family descent to the present owner.

It is not recorded exactly when this portrait was painted, or why, but it was painted in London shortly before the First World War.

In mood and treatment it reflects Whistler, but uses a loose, broken brushwork technique on the large scale the artist often employed. The sitter, who gazes up reflectively from her book, set against an embroidered silk hanging, was a Hungarian princess whom the artist knew in London, and who was deported at the outbreak of War as an 'undesirable alien'. Kathleen Fox painted many portraits, particularly in the early 20's, notably Grace Gifford (as *The Fish Wife*), Lord and Lady Powerscourt, Cardinal Mannix, Albert Power, the Earl of Kimberley, mostly on a similar scale.

NGB

Lent by Master Thurston Pym.

The symbolism in the painting has not been recorded, of the starling perched on the fortune-telling paraphernalia beside the scarlet robed artist and the ominous bird spreading its wings before the ill-fated sitter, reminiscent of the bird of death in Rossetti's *Beata Beatrix*.

NGB

Lent by Miss Hilary Pym.

Kathleen Fox, *The Fortune Teller*, (cat. no. 71).

Wilhelmina M. Geddes, *Portrait of Ethel Geddes*, (cat. no. 72).

Kathleen Fox

71   The Fortune Teller

Oil on canvas, 86.4 × 96.5 cms.

PROVENANCE: by family descent to the present owner.

This self-portrait of the artist with her adored eldest brother and mentor Colonel Charles Fox (Scots Guards) was painted shortly before his premature death from cancer in 1926. When she painted his portrait in 1922, he had been awarded a D.S.O. and was Deputy Inspector-General Native Levies, I.R.A.Q. Both he and his youngest brother, who had died aged twenty-nine in 1910, were extraordinarily brave and distinguished soldiers and sportsmen. Charles Fox was a champion Oxford rowing Blue and won the Diamond Sculls, for which he set a long-standing world record in 1901. He was the first British Officer to escape from a POW camp in Germany and founded the Escapers Club with the King as Patron.

Wilhelmina M. Geddes (1887-1955)

72   Portrait of Ethel Geddes, c.1910

Watercolour on paper, 15.9 × 11.4 cms.

PROVENANCE: by family descent to the present owner.

This painting shows the positive influence of Orpen on Geddes' work, although she had produced competent drawings and oil and watercolour paintings before she came down to Dublin to attend his classes. She made a number of fine studies of herself, her younger two sisters and brother in charcoal, pencil and watercolour as well as the Art School models, particularly a sinewy old man. Orpen apparently much admired her work. This study shows a much fuller faced Ethel than subsequent smaller watercolours, which are reminiscent of Gwen John in their poignant intensity and rich, glowing colour. Ethel Geddes, who was born in 1889, sometimes stayed with her older sister in Dublin and later in London. She effectively embroidered a number of her sister's designs in needlework, some for the Yeats sisters' Cuala Industries. She died in 1966.   NGB

Lent by E. M. F. Kerr.

Wilhelmina M. Geddes

73   a) Cinderella dressing her ugly sister for the ball, 1910
b) Cinderella's ugly sisters trying the glass slipper for size, 1910

Both watercolour and ink on paper.
a) 24.8 × 14.6 cms.
SIGNED: *W.M.G.*
PROVENANCE: purchased by Sarah Purser and then by family descent to the present owner.

EXHIBITED: 1910, *Fourth Exhibition,* Arts and Crafts Society of Ireland, Dublin, no. 212; 1985, *The Dublin Arts and Crafts Movement 1885-1930,* Edinburgh, no. 68.

b) 26 × 14.6 cms.

PROVENANCE: by family descent to the present owner.

There are three illustrations in this series, of which those exhibited here are the first and third. The middle one (not exhibited) is in a woodland setting where an aged fairy prepares to transform the pumpkin into a magic coach for Cinderella. Geddes sent a) down from Belfast for exhibition at the Arts and Crafts Society Exhibition in Dublin in 1910. Rosamund Praeger advised Sarah Purser to go and see it. She did, bought it, urged Geddes to take up stained glass and invited her to join An Túr Gloine, the Tower of Glass Cooperative. The artist had not hitherto taken seriously suggestions that she take up stained glass, for which these watercolour illustrations demonstrate she was eminently suitable; b) even includes some notably Arts and Crafts stained glass behind the two sisters. Both illustrations show how effectively Geddes

Wilhelmina M. Geddes, *Cinderella dressing her ugly sister for the ball,* (cat. no. 73a).

Wilhelmina M. Geddes, *Cinderella's ugly sisters trying the Glass Slipper for size,* (cat. no. 73b).

could offset richly glowing washes of colour against expressive, velvety black lines. The graphic artists she most admired at the time were the Beggarstaff Brothers, but there are also elements of Brangwyn. a) was described in an interview with the artist as showing 'the beautiful, poor and scornful Cinderella winding ribbons in the hair of an unwieldly dame. It is finished with a menacing sense of irony.' Cinderella is based on Geddes' youngest sister Florence. NGB

a) *Private collection.*
b) *Lent by E. M. F. Kerr.*

It is not recorded why or exactly when this enchanting picture was done but the modelling of the child's face, the sharp angular lines describing the forms and th anatomical treatment of the three intently fiddling gnomes in feathered caps walking down a moonbeam would suggest a date in the early 20's. Another factor is the cat, a subject Geddes much enjoyed depicting, which is a fusion of Orange Billy, c.1916-22 and his successor, Jenkins, c.1922-25. Although known as *Jacob's Ladder* in the family, the subject remains unclear. The glowing candle appears similarly treated in a number of Geddes' illustrations in the mid 20's, several of them reproduced as book jackets or frontispieces. There is no record that this picture was ever reproduced or published. NGB

Lent by E. M. F. Kerr.

Wilhelmina M. Geddes, *A Dream or Jacob's Ladder,* (cat. no. 74).

Wilhelmina M. Geddes

74   A dream or **Jacob's Ladder,** c.1923

Ink and watercolour on paper, 22.9 × 40 cms.
SIGNED: *W.M. Geddes*
PROVENANCE: by family descent to the present owner.

Estella F. Solomons, *Self-Portrait,* (cat. no. 75).

Estella F. Solomons (1882-1968)

75   Self-Portrait, c.1910

Oil on canvas, 69.2 × 56.2 cms.
PROVENANCE: by family descent to the present owner.
LITERATURE: H. Pyle, *Portraits of Patriots,* (1966), (ill. facing p. 10).

An early likeness, worked with typical spontaneity. The sketch-like quality, and subdued colouring, still reflect the artist's interest in Rembrandt, as does the unusual effect of light breaking up the picture plane into spaces of arresting shape. Estella Solomons was never interested in background, only in the personality she painted, and often attempted a peremptory thrust of the figure so as to create a moment of immediacy. That is particularly successful in this case, where it promotes an intimacy with the artist, caught in an instant of self realization, without her brushes.   HP

Private collection.

Estella F. Solomons, *A gay day in Donegal,* (cat. no. 76).

Estella F. Solomons

76   A gay day in Donegal, 1915

Oil on canvas, 43 × 55.5 cms.

SIGNED: in monogram, *EFS*

PROVENANCE: purchased c.1936 by the present owner, D. A. O'Liaháin.

EXHIBITED: 1915, Royal Hibernian Academy, Dublin, no. 55.

Estella Solomons visited Holland to paint landscape in 1911, and at home continually explored the vicinity of Dublin. But it was not until 1914 or 1915 that she went to Donegal and here she developed her sense of colour. She was to return to Donegal repeatedly. Æ was already there, painting the more settled area around Marble Hill Bay, but Estella Solomons was drawn to the wild headlands and depths of sea. Her manner is rapid and expressionist, using wedges of gleaming colour, with brilliant highlights. The whole view is vivacious, full of moving sea, shifting light and clouds, capturing the essence of a sunny day on the Donegal coast.   HP

Lent by D. A. O'Liaháin.

Kathleen Isobel Mackie, *The Market,* (cat. no. 77).

Kathleen Isobel Mackie (b.1899)

77   The market

Oil on canvas, 76.2 × 50.8 cms.

PROVENANCE: Royal Ulster Academy Diploma Collection.

EXHIBITED: c.1926-7, *The Salon,* Paris; 1981, *Royal Ulster Academy Diploma Centenary Exhibition,* Ulster Museum, Belfast; 1985, *A Retrospective Exhibition of Kathleen I. Mackie,* Castle Espie Gallery, county Down, no. 37.

LITERATURE: Martyn Anglesea, *Royal Ulster Academy of Arts, A Centennial History* (1981), facing p. 110 (ill. in colour).

VERSIONS: a detailed oil sketch on canvas (45.8 × 35.7 cms.) of the right hand half of this composition, signed *K. I. Metcalfe,* is still in the artist's possession and was exhibited in 1985, *A Retrospective Exhibition of Kathleen Mackie,* Castle Espie Gallery, county Down, no. 1.

The form of the signature in the final composition, *K. I. Metcalfe Mackie,* is that used by the artist in the years immediately following her marriage in 1926. While absorbing the influences of Degas and Forain in the handling, this vivid Irish market scene contains a mild element of near-caricature which is reminiscent of Phil May.

Kim presented this as her diploma work to the Ulster Academy of Arts (now the Royal Ulster Academy) on her election as an associate in 1936.   MA

Lent by the Royal Ulster Academy of Arts.

Jessie Douglas (1893-1928)

78   Cherry Ripe

Watercolour on smooth white paper, 32 × 26 cms.

INSCRIBED ON VERSO: *'painted / by Miss Jessie Douglas / Belfast / A Real Artist!/ The portrait of a niece of hers / a daughter of Dean Seaver'.*

PROVENANCE: found in store, unrecorded, in 1968 and absorbed into collection; Ulster Museum, Belfast, art dept. cat. no. 1023.

LITERATURE: Martyn Anglesea, *Royal Ulster Academy of Arts, A Centennial History,* (1981), p. 45 (ill.).

Jessie Douglas, *Cherry Ripe*, (cat. no. 78).

Rosalie Franks, *Henry Street, Dublin in 1924*, (cat. no. 79).

In *Cherry Ripe*, Douglas portrays the head and shoulders of a young girl wearing a white blouse, grey gym-slip and bunches of cherries hanging behind her ears. MA

Lent by the Ulster Museum, Belfast.

Rosalie Franks (fl. c.1921-1929)

79 Henry Street, Dublin in 1924

Pencil and watercolour on paper, 19 × 10.5 cms.

SIGNED: in monogram, ℟

INSCRIBED: *Henry Street Dublin in 1924 / Rosalie Franks / Tir na n-oga / Malahide / £2.2.*

PROVENANCE: private collection, Dublin.

Rosalie Franks depicts a busy 1920's Henry Street through an impressionistic haze of blue. Although some of the then familiar features like the beautifully scrolled iron lamps, the 1920's automobiles and Nelson's Pillar (just visible at the end of the street) are indicated, Franks has largely concentrated on rendering the atmospheric effects. All details are blurred and the whole scene is covered by the watery veil which glistens here and there with reflected light. WR

Private collection.

Lady Dobbin (1868-c.1948)

80 Afterglow, c.1920?

Watercolour on paper, 27.9 × 38.1 cms.

SIGNED: *K. Dobbin*

PROVENANCE: Máirín Hope.

Here Lady Dobbin has used a loose washy palette with small dabs of local colour to evoke the dying embers of a dewy summer's evening. It is unrecorded whether this is a garden in Cork and who the small group of people are in their smart Twenties evening clothes, bestirring themselves from the garden seat opposite a deep yew-backed herbaceous border, before night falls.

The soft, smoky watercolour technique is reminiscent of that

Lady Dobbin, *Afterglow,* (cat. no. 80).

of a number of artists of the period, like Mildred Anne Butler and Rose Barton.

NGB

Lent by Máirín Hope.

Grace Gifford, *Edward Martyn 'having a week of it' in Paris,* (cat. no. 81).

Grace Gifford (1888-1955)

81 Edward Martyn 'having a week of it' in Paris

Pen and ink on paper, 20.9 × 26.6 cms.

SIGNED: *Grace Gifford*

PROVENANCE: Hugh Lane Municipal Gallery, Dublin.

EXHIBITED: 1975, *Irish Art 1900-1950,* Rosc Exhibition, Crawford Municipal Gallery, Cork, no. 28.

Edward Martyn (1859-1923), with Yeats and Lady Gregory, founded the Irish Literary Theatre in 1899, and wrote his play *The Heather Field* for it. He was also one of the founders of An Túr Gloine, Sarah Purser's stained glass studio; and was instrumental in bringing leading contemporary artists to the new Cathedral in Loughrea, in the early years of this century, to design windows, banners and sculptures. A shy, retiring man, who lived on his own at Tullyra Castle, county Galway, he was satirized by George Moore in *Hail and Farewell,* as well as by Gifford.

HP

Lent by the Hugh Lane Municipal Gallery of Art, Dublin.

Kathleen Quigly, *Father Time,* (cat. no. 82).

Kathleen Quigly (1888-1981)

82 Father Time, 1920

Woodcut on paper, 6.4 × 6.4 cms.

SIGNED: *Kathleen Quigly June 1920.* From an autograph book inscribed to Harry Clarke.

PROVENANCE: the Harry Clarke Studio's book keeper, Miss O'Sullivan and family descent; Hugh Iremonger, from whom purchased by the Municipal Gallery, Dublin.

One of a series of woodcuts by the artist done at this period, it demonstrates her strong use of line, exemplified in the few extant examples of her work. NGB

Lent by the Hugh Lane Municipal Gallery of Art, Dublin.

Kathleen Cox, *Portrait of Brian Boydell,* (cat. no. 84).

Kathleen Cox (1904-1972)

84 Portrait of Brian Boydell, 1922

Oil on canvas, 53.3 × 43.1 cms.

MONOGRAMMED: *KC*

PROVENANCE: Brian Boydell.

Painted in 1922 when the composer was five years old at his parents' house, Kilrock in Howth, where the Coxes were neighbours up the hill. Kathleen Cox was only eighteen at the time and was soon to abandon painting for sculpture. NGB

Lent by Brian and Mary Boydell.

Ethel Rhind, *The Archangel Michael and the Dragon,* (cat. no. 83).

Ethel Rhind (c.1878-1952)

83 The Archangel Michael and the dragon, 1921

Pencil, ink and watercolour on paper, 20.2 × 14.8 cms.

INSCRIBED: in pencil, *St. Michael/ In Memory of those who fought and fell in the Great War 1914-1918/ 2' 4" × 4' 6"*

PROVENANCE: Patrick Pollen, Esq., by whom presented, 1966. National Gallery of Ireland, cat. no. 18,453.

EXHIBITED: 1985, *The Dublin Arts and Crafts Movement 1885-1930,* Edinburgh.

This, the only extant design for *opus sectile* by the artist, shows Michael standing with his shield on top of the vanquished dragon, whose head lolls forward out of the picture frame. The large panel for which this is the sketch is secured into the exterior surface of the south wall of All Saints Church, Grangegorman in north Co. Dublin. There, a much more anthropomorphic dragon is still alive and the Archangel dramatically poised on the edge of a cliff, one foot on its head as he raises his sword for the final thrust. NGB

Lent by the National Gallery of Ireland.

Kathleen Cox

85 Crouching girl with a tray, c.1929

Glazed earthenware, 23.5 × 28.7 cms.

STAMPED: with the artist's colophon

PROVENANCE: by family descent to the present owner.

EXHIBITED: 1985, *The Dublin Arts and Crafts Movement 1885-1930,* Edinburgh.

Kathleen Cox's glazed ceramic sculpture was unique in Ireland for its notably high standard of modelling and original design,

Kathleen Cox, *Crouching girl with a tray*, (cat. no. 85).

often of a Symbolist nature. She seems only to have worked on a small scale and cast some pieces a number of (unrecorded) times. Sometimes they were painted in strong, washy colours. They are always marked with her colophon. Here she has modelled the arched body of her fellow art student, Doreen Dickie, in lithely flowing lines. She also modelled masks of friends, like the painter Brigid O'Brien and the writer Norris Davidson. She used the naked form of her husband in reverie as an evocative bookend. Other figures depict Dublin 'shawlies' and flower girls (e.g. those in the National Museum, Dublin collection).   NGB

Lent by Ms Gráinne Palmer (daughter of the artist).

Eileen Murray, *'This or Emigration'*, (cat. no. 86).

French tradition of Bastien Lepage and like the painters of Brittany preferred simple subjects of peasant life and the local community.

EB

Lent by the Ulster Museum, Belfast.

Eileen Murray (b.1885)

86   'This or Emigration', c.1926

Oil on canvas, 91.5 × 61 cms.

SIGNED: *E. Murray*

PROVENANCE: sale, Belfast Art Society's Exhibition, where purchased, 1926. Ulster Museum, Belfast, art department, cat. no. 648.

Unusual for an Irish picture of this period in the strength of its social realism and political comment. It shows strongly the influence of her period at the remote Cornish village of Newlyn and the colony of artists there including Stanhope Forbes and Norman Garstin, who had established *plein air* painting in the

Eileen Reid (1894-1981)

87   A young black boy in boxer shorts

Oil on canvas, 76 × 50 cms.

SIGNED: on revrse, *Oulton*

PROVENANCE: the artist's family.

EXHIBITED: December 1984, *The studio of Eileen Reid 1894-1981*, Cynthia O'Connor Gallery, no. 27.

LITERATURE: Cynthia O'Connor Gallery catalogue, 1984, no. 27.

It is assumed that this painting is a study done at the Royal Academy during Eileen's student days. She was greatly benefited by Sir William Orpen, who, apart from being a family friend was

Eileen Reid, *A young black boy in boxer shorts*, (cat. no. 87).

also her master. This somewhat unusual and risqué subject must owe a great deal to her tutor's cosmopolitan influence.   COC

Lent from a private collection courtesy of Cynthia O'Connor Gallery.

Georgina Moutray Kyle, *The lifting of the fog at the gasworks, Belfast*, (cat. no. 88).

Georgina Moutray Kyle (1865-1950)

88   The lifting of the fog at the Gasworks, Belfast, c.1926

Oil on canvas, 55.1 × 73.5 cms.

SIGNED: *G Moutre Kyle*

PROVENANCE: bequeathed by the artist, 1950. Ulster Museum, Belfast, art department, cat. no. 342.

EXHIBITED: 1926, Belfast Art Society, no. 147; 1928, Royal Glasgow Institute of Fine Arts, no. 145; 1930, *Irish Art Exhibition*, Brussels, no. 61 as *Fin de Brouillard, (Belfast)*; 1945-46, *The Work of Miss G. Moutray Kyle*, Belfast Museum and Art Gallery, no. 13.

LITERATURE: Sam Hanna Bell, Nesca A. Robb, John Hewitt, (eds.), *The Arts in Ulster* (1951), p. 86.

The scene was painted from a spot on the Ormeau Embankment, looking across the Lagan, towards the Belfast Gasworks.

   The painting, with its broad areas of pale colours, heavy outlining of every detail and strong emphasis on pattern, is typical of Georgina's style. The picture is a striking image of a relatively mundane urban scene and is probably the artist's best work.EB

Lent by the Ulster Museum, Belfast.

Clare Marsh, *View of rooftops*, (cat. no. 89).

Clare Marsh (1874-1923)

89   View of rooftops

Oil on canvas, 56 × 43.2 cms.

PROVENANCE: Mrs. Bernard Mullin, Dublin.

This view from the artist's window at evening must be *Automobile Club*, exhibited posthumously in the St. Stephen's Green Gallery in June 1923. The studio, shared with Mary Swanzy from autumn 1920, looked over the back of the Royal Automobile Club in Dawson Street. Clare Marsh painted other night studies, and in city and landscapes of this period developed her sense of colour in an objective impressionist way, without drama or emotion. The delicate blue of half-light draws the private rambling aspect of the Dublin Georgian houses together, the lamplight adding a faint lustre.   HP

Lent by Mrs. Bernard Mullin.

Florence Ross, *Old mill, old trees,* (cat. no. 90).

Florence Ross (1870-1949)
90   Old mill, old trees

Watercolour on paper, 26.8 × 36.9 cms.
SIGNED: *F.A. Ross*
PROVENANCE: presented by Mrs. Jacob to Waterford Municipal Collection.

This liquid study looks as though it was painted during one of the summers Florence Ross spent with her cousins at Annamoe, county Wicklow. In style it resembles views of the house and gardens and picturesque old bridge there, still in the family collection. She was with them in 1925, 1931 and 1941, 1943 and 1944, when she would go out sketching with her cousin, Elizabeth Synge. She also ran a successful sketching club in the Glendassan Valley, near Glendalough. Her work is characterized by loose washes of evenly laid colour, reflecting her sense of place and love of nature, often contrasting areas in deep shade with those caught in the sun.   NGB

Lent by the Garter Lane Arts Centre.

Lily Williams, *Portrait of Ethel Montgomery*, (cat. no. 91).

Lily Williams (1874-1940)
91   Portrait of Ethel Montgomery

Oil on canvas, 50.8 × 66 cms.
SIGNED: *lily Williams*
PROVENANCE: Niall Montgomery; private collection, Dublin.

Ethel Montgomery was wife of James Montgomery of the Irish Censorship Board, and the centre of literary and musical circles in Dublin in the 1920's and 1930's. Both are mentioned by Gogarty in *As I was going down Sackville Street,* Montgomery described as 'a trim figure in a blue reefer jacket who looked like a sea-faring man, censors films and compensates for this by making jokes.'

The portrait, somewhat formal, is in the Lavery style of impressionism, making a lively image in harmonious light colouring. An emphasis is laid on the cultured and imaginative — somewhat dreamy — character of the sitter, as well as on her obvious pleasure in elegant dress.   HP

Private collection.

Grace Henry, *Nightfall over mountain village,* (cat. no. 92).

Grace Henry (1868-1953)

92 Nightfall over mountain village

Oil on canvas, laid on board, 25.3 × 19 cms.

SIGNED: *E.G. Henry*

PROVENANCE: sale, James Adam and Sons, Dublin, 8 December, 1983, lot 189; J. G. Cruickshank collection.

In style and subject, the painting almost certainly is from Grace Henry's period in Achill with her husband Paul Henry, 1912-1920. The form of the signature, *E.G. Henry,* was used in the early time of the artist's career and would confirm a date probably between 1915 and 1920. Other similar paintings of night scenes in tones of Prussian blue and also depicting village settings in Achill are known to have survived from this period of the artist's work.

Within the very small space of the picture, Grace Henry has compressed the detail of an extensive landscape of village houses and peatstacks rising to distant hills, in a thickly painted style of few and confident brush strokes. The bold, curved lines of the central lane lead the eye into the landscape, which is both simple and yet congested with detail. Most of all, this is a painting of the eerie atmosphere of moonlight, achieved by muted tones of grey and blue, and offset with surprising touches of colour like the magenta of the peatstacks and in the hills. JGC

Lent from the Collection of J. G. Cruickshank.

Grace Henry, *The Red House at Mougins,* (cat. no. 93).

Grace Henry

93 The Red House at Mougins

Oil on board, 27 × 35 cms.

SIGNED: *G. Henry*

PROVENANCE: J. G. Cruickshank collection.

The work seems to be one of a number painted by Grace Henry at the village of Mougins, which is about 5 miles inland of Cannes in the South of France, and probably dates from the early 1930's when the artist was painting most frequently in France and Italy.

The painting is constructed on two planes. In the background, but dominating in colour and area, is the three-dimensional cubic shape of the house in vibrant red with its complementary blue of closed shutters and drawn blinds, while in the foreground the curving branches of two almond trees, white in full blossom, seem to move in the breeze. The scene is full of colour, even to a range of greens and ochres in the garden and flashes of magenta and alizarin in the shadows, in the trees, and along the line of the roof, the colour creating the effect of heat in the afternoon sun. It is a picture of atmosphere, of the Mediterranean early summer, achieved by the use of strong colour, and of contrasting gentle movement of the almond blossom where Grace Henry's painterly brushwork is best seen. JGC

Lent from the Collection of J. G. Cruickshank.

Lilian Lucy Davidson (d.1954)

94 Night in Claddagh

Oil on hardboard, 21.5 × 22.8 cms.

PROVENANCE: by family descent to the present owner.

EXHIBITED: 1933, Royal Hibernian Academy, Dublin, no. 33.

Lilian Lucy Davidson, *Night in Claddagh,* (cat. no. 94).

Lilian Davidson portrayed the Claddagh, the Irish-speaking district of Galway, at a time when she was involved with the Torch theatre for which she had been writing a play.   HP

Lent by Miss Anne Yeats.

Lilian Lucy Davidson
95   Night

Oil on panel, 27.9 × 39.4 cms.
SIGNED: in monogram, ┗D
PROVENANCE: Lillias Mitchell, Dublin.

A painting of moonlight. Though inscribed on the reverse, 'Night in a Dublin . . .', the romantic atmosphere is reminiscent of

Lilian Lucy Davidson, *Night,* (cat. no. 95).

Galway. Both Lillias Mitchell and Anne Yeats were pupils of Lilian Davidson.   HP

Lent by Miss Lillias Mitchell.

Eva Hamilton, *Tobar Padraig, Co. Mayo,* (cat. no. 96).

Eva Hamilton (1876-1960)
96   Tobar Padraig, Co. Mayo, 1925

Oil on board, 21.2 × 25 cms.
PROVENANCE: bequeathed by Dr. R. I. Best, per the Friends of the National Collections of Ireland, 1959; Ulster Museum, Belfast, art dept. cat. no. 315.

County Mayo's bleak, grim rather forbidding but beautiful and remarkably varied coastline has been admirably captured here by Eva Hamilton with just a few purposeful brushstrokes and a strong sense of colour.

Though she trained under Orpen and in the Slade School of Art, Eva appears in such works to have evolved a style of her own, though she must have been aware of the work of Roderic O'Conor who painted similar rocky coastal scenes. Painted in 1925, this small but striking landscape is unusual for Eva at this time as she mainly painted portraits and it was not until the 1930's that she began to concentrate on landscapes.   KMM

Lent by the Ulster Museum, Belfast.

Letitia Hamilton (1878-1964)
97   Fiesole Hill, Florence

Oil on board, 17.7 × 22.9 cms.
PROVENANCE: bequeathed by Dr. R. I. Best, per the Friends of the National Collections of Ireland, 1959; Ulster Museum, Belfast, art dept. cat. no. 314.

Letitia Hamilton, *Fiesole Hill, Florence,* (cat. no. 97).

Letitia Hamilton, *Rhododendrons,* (cat. no. 98).

The view in this painting of Fiesole, a picturesque hilltown on the outskirts of Florence, celebrated for its beautiful landscape and panorama was a particularly popular sketching point among artists and no doubt Letitia Hamilton was drawn here on one of her many painting trips to Italy.

The landscape in this painting has been treated in an 'expressionist' manner as the artist attempts to capture the atmosphere of a cool summer's day and the impression this has on her, rather than portraying the scene realistically. The thick impasto typical of this artist's style also adds to this effect. The hills, most probably of S. Francesco, which loom over the houses and which cover more than three-quarters of the canvas, are broken up by the meandering tributary of the river Mugnone. The brightly painted house to the right counterbalances the darker hills while such details as the washing hanging out to dry in the breeze and the lady standing to one side add a lively and nearly anecdotal element to this landscape.   KMM

Lent by the Ulster Museum, Belfast.

Letitia Hamilton

98   Rhododendrons

Oil on canvas, 51 × 41 cms.

SIGNED: *L.M.H.*

PROVENANCE: Purser-Griffiths Collection; Miss A. Griffiths; private collection, Ireland.

The treatment of this unusual still-life of rhododendrons, with its strong vibrant colouring and rich, luscious texture of the paint combined with the swirling brushstrokes, is very 'expressionist' in effect. Letitia Hamilton has handled her medium in much the same manner as Roderic O'Conor who obviously had a strong influence on her and she has used the bold brushstrokes and the

effect of impasto as an inherent part of the composition. O'Conor's influence can also be seen in her choice of strong, positive colours.

The slightly off-centre positioning of the vase, with the blooms billowing out over to the left, relieves what would otherwise be a static and traditional composition.   KMM

Private collection.

Letitia Hamilton

99   Snow in Co. Down

Oil on canvas, 50.5 × 60 cms.

SIGNED: *LMH*

PROVENANCE: Hugh Lane Municipal Gallery, Dublin.

In *Snow in Co. Down* the artist relies, as usual, almost solely on her brush and on the expressive manipulation of paint in rich impastoes to create the desired effect. The whole landscape, and particularly the boughs of the broad pine tree, have been thickly spread with snow as if with a spatula, while the bare branches of the tree in the middle distance have been given a densely frosted appearance.

The wintry tones of snowy whites, tinged with icy hues of

Letitia Hamilton, *Snow in Co. Down,* (cat. no. 99).

blue and pink, conjure up a sense of mystery and stillness, so typical of the season.   WR

Lent by the Hugh Lane Municipal Gallery of Art, Dublin.

Margaret Clarke (1888-1961)

100   Self-Portrait, c.1914

Oil on canvas, 40.6 × 30 cms.

SIGNED: *M. Crilley*

PROVENANCE: the artist; Mrs. Michele Whelan.

EXHIBITED: 1979, Taylor Galleries, Dublin, no. 44.

Painted shortly before her marriage in October 1914, this may be the self-portrait exhibited in the Royal Hibernian Academy (1918, no. 83), though at least one other self-portrait is known. In a simple direct manner, she presents her own forthright character, the strong face, the clear eyes. The brushes represent her profession, but she is as candid in dwelling on the blue cardigan and feminine shirt. Colour, in background and garments, plays a dominant part in creating the sense of realism and freshness.

HP

Lent by Mrs. Michele Whelan.

Margaret Clarke

101   Strindbergian, 1927

Oil on canvas, 127 × 101 cms.

SIGNED: *Margaret Clarke 1927*

Margaret Clarke, *Self-Portrait,* (cat. no. 100).

Margaret Clarke, *Strindbergian, 1927,* (cat. no. 101).

PROVENANCE: by family descent to the present owner, the artist's son.

EXHIBITED: 1962, Royal Hibernian Academy, Dublin, no. 68; 1979, *Margaret Clarke,* Taylor Galleries, Dublin, no. 1.

LITERATURE: 'Drama Notes by SLM', *Irish Statesman,* vol. 4, no. 7, (25 April 1925), p. 212.

Margaret Clarke, *Ann with cat,* (cat. no. 102).

Margaret Clarke painted a few large scale fantasy pictures in the train of Orpen and Augustus John, *Strindbergian* being based on Strindberg's *The Ghost Sonata,* first performed in January 1908. This was staged by the Dublin Drama League, as *The Spook Sonata,* in April 1925, with Shelah Richards as the Colonel's Daughter, Paul Ruttledge as the Student, and Gabriel Fallon as the Old Man. The play is gloomy and introspective, lamenting 'this world that is for ever changing, for ever erring, for ever in pain', using various types of humanity as characters. The final scene dissolves away to reveal Bocklin's *The Island of the Dead.*

In the play, the Old Man, who has spent his life squeezing life out of others, is exposed by the Mummy (wife of the Colonel who has been ruined by the Old Man) and Bengtsson (the Colonel's footman). He is put in the cupboard — which the Mummy has occupied for years — and forced to kill himself with the same rope with which he strangled the Dead Man, or Consul. Margaret represents the main characters and events, but widens the theme by using personalities of her own choice — Lennox Robinson, for example as the Student; her maid Julia (who was frequently her model) as the Colonel's Daughter; Julia's brother Dan as the Old Man; Mrs. Gavin (a cleaner in the Harry Clarke studios) as the Mummy — thus extending the specific story into a tragedy of personal and world dimensions.

The composition is skilfully organised so as to contrast the dreamy idealistic characters gathered about the Dark Lady, in the foreground, against the gross materialism of the world, in mid-distance, dominated by the figure of the Cook — a vampire who sucks food and blood from those she serves. In this background scene, the Colonel's Daughter is drawn into the Dance of Death, near the Death Screen — a crucial symbol in Strindberg's drama. In this painting, Margaret Clarke shows her attraction to Gauguin and the romantic symbolists, while not departing from her own distinctive realism, with its rich harmonious colouring.   HP

Lent by David Clarke.

Margaret Clarke painted her daughter Ann several times; the portrait of Ann aged between six and eight, in the Hugh Lane Municipal Gallery, has a quality of decorative formality, together with a strong sense of human presence. This adolescent portrait aims at greater naturalism, while at the same time is indebted to the symbolic backdrops of Van Gogh's late portraits and is a reminder that in more personal paintings Margaret Clarke was constantly experimenting and seeking freer expression. The stylised landscape suggests the range of thoughts of the pensive girl, as well as something more esoteric and complex.   HP

Lent from the Estate of the artist's daughter.

Margaret Clarke

102   Ann with cat, c.1930

Oil on canvas, 75.5 × 63.5 cms.

SIGNED: *M. Clarke*

PROVENANCE: Mrs. Ann Bourke; Sara Bourke, Bray, county Wicklow.

EXHIBITED: 1932, Imperial Institute, London; 1962, Royal Hibernian Academy, Dublin, no. 66; 1975-76, *Irish Art 1900-1950,* Rosc Exhibition, Crawford Municipal Art Gallery, Cork, no. 12; 1979, *Margaret Clarke,* Taylor Galleries, Dublin, no. 41.

Moyra Barry (1886-1960)

103   Self-Portrait in the artist's studio, 1920

Oil on canvas, 30.4 × 25.5 cms.

SIGNED: *M.B.*

INSCRIBED AND SIGNED: on reverse, *Moyra Barry 1920 "In the Studio"*

PROVENANCE: the artist's estate; bequeathed to the artist's family, by whom sold to The Gorry Gallery, Dublin, from whom purchased, 1982. National Gallery of Ireland, cat. no. 4366.

EXHIBITED: 1982, *Moyra Barry 1886-1960,* The Gorry Gallery, Dublin, no. 40; 1984, *Acquisitions 1982-83,* National Gallery of Ireland, no. 2.

LITERATURE: Adrian Le Harivel and Michael Wynne, *Acquisitions 1982-83* exhibition catalogue, National Gallery of Ireland (1984).

Moyra Barry, *Self-Portrait in the Artist's Studio,* (cat. no. 103).

In this self-portrait the artist is seated by a brightly coloured canvas, dressed in a smock and with a black scarf tied in a flat bow high on her forehead. Her face with its delicate features is carefully executed and contrasts with her smock and the background areas which are painted in a free and expressive manner. In many ways Barry has treated the interior of her studio as an abstract composition of varying shapes and colours. WR

Lent by the National Gallery of Ireland.

Rosamond Praeger (1867-1954)
104 Portrait bust of Miss E. M. McCormick

Cast bronze, 49.5 × 26.5 cms.
PROVENANCE: donated to the Ulster Folk Museum by the sitter's family.
EXHIBITED: 1975, Memorial Exhibition, Queen's Hall, Holywood, county Down.

Little is known of the sitter for this portrait except that she was a relative of the Kennedy family who lived at Cultra Manor before the house and park were sold to the Folk Museum. It has been selected for its extraordinarily sensitive modelling and skill at capturing the softly rounded features and composed but abstracted gaze of the young girl. A bronze cast portrait head of the artist's brother, the botanist and scholar Robert Lloyd Praeger (1865-1953), in the National Gallery of Ireland (cat. no. 8035) is much more stiff and formal. NGB

Lent by the Ulster Folk Museum.

Rosamond Praeger, *Portrait bust of Miss E. M. McCormick,* (cat. no. 104).

Rosamond Praeger
105 The Dolphin Race, c.1938

Painted plaster plaque, 19 × 33 cms.
SIGNED: *S.R. Praeger*
PROVENANCE: Seán O'Criadain.
EXHIBITED: 1938, Royal Hibernian Academy, Dublin, no. 378.

This is a particularly successful colouring of a design which is known to have been used, uncoloured, inset into a mantelpiece. It is one of her most carefree and delightful sculptural reliefs, in its suggestion of playful abandonment and, despite its breakable nature, is unusual in that it has survived intact. Praeger's skill at capturing the softly rounded grace and mobility of small children's bodies is shown nowhere better than in her low relief plaques. Ten years earlier she had sculpted three small boys in *Bathers,* another very popular design. She does not seem to have numbered her plaster casts from an initial design, rather produced them on demand.

This panel can be compared to a relief panel depicting the moulded figures of cavorting young water nymphs, designed by Ellen Mary Rope and coloured by Alice Louise James in 1906 for the Della Robbia Pottery at Birkenhead. Rope was also noted for

Rosamond Praeger, *The Dolphin Race,* (cat. no. 105).

her work representing groups of young children. There are plaques in the Ulster Museum, the Ulster Folk Museum and Methodist College, Belfast.   NGB

Lent by Mr. Seán O'Criadain.

Mabel Young, *Landscape with dry stone wall,* (cat. no. 106).

Mabel Young (c.1890-1974)

106   Landscape with dry stone wall

Pencil and watercolour washes on paper, 27.9 × 38.1 cms.
SIGNED: *Mabel Young*
PROVENANCE: inherited from the artist by the present owner.

An obituarist of the artist wrote that she was 'devoted particularly to the painting of trees . . . the character of the wind-torn Wicklow trees which even in the valleys assume distinctive and sometimes distorted personalities. . . . Also she caught that white light you get in the Wicklow hills, quite different from the sombre, ocean-charged atmosphere of the West.'   NGB

Private collection.

Angela Antrim, *The Siege of Dunluce,* (cat. no. 107).

Angela Antrim (1911-1984)

107   The Siege of Dunluce, c.1934/35

Pen, ink and watercolour on paper, 55.9 × 76.2 cms.

INSCRIBED: *Dunluce Castle/The Capture of the Castel by the McDonnells from the MacQuillans (Circa 1550). Respectfully Presented to Lady Rose and Mr. Francis Baring by the engraver and painter Angela Antrim.*

PROVENANCE: as inscription.

The artist had been drawing sharply observed, mercilessly witty caricatures ever since she was a girl, revealing a ruthless streak on occasion. She especially enjoyed a scene like this which she could people with readily identifiable characters. She has gathered here an assortment of relations, like a great-great-uncle Alexander, known as 'The Fox' and great uncle Angus, who weighed twenty stone. Another comparable scene is *The Charity Ball,* drawn around the same time.

In 1930 she collaborated on an illustrated children's book, *The Little Round Man,* with Alice Lindley (only published recently by Warne) and shortly before her death Ulster Television published her witty and graphic *McDonnells of Antrim.*

She signed her work 'A.A.'   NGB

Lent by Lady Rose Baring.

Angela Antrim

108   Samson, c.1934/35

Carved limestone, 76.2 × 38.1 cm.
PROVENANCE: by family descent to the present owner.

This piece may date from an exhibition the artist held before the war, as it does not appear to have been a commissioned work. It depicts Samson straining to pull the pillars down and is sculpted

Angela Antrim, *Samson,* (cat. no. 108).

Violet McAdoo, *Tiled Roofs (Spain),* (cat. no. 109).

Painted not long after the artist left the Royal College of Art, this bold watercolour with its strong sense of structure shows influences from Cezanne, the Fauves and the Cubists.   MA

Lent by the Ulster Museum, Belfast.

from a hunk of limestone full of pieces of fossil. He is rough hewn and the pillars are polished. There are stylistic echoes of Epstein, Gill and Gaudier-Brzeska, as well as mediaeval carving in the elemental pathos of the features. The artist was happiest when carving and a lot of her best work was on this sort of scale, if not smaller.   NGB

Lent by the Viscount Dunluce.

Kathleen Bridle, *Lough Erne from Rossfad,* (cat. no. 110).

Violet McAdoo (fl. c.1925-1965)

109   Tiled roofs (Spain), 1933

Watercolour over pencil on heavy white wove paper, 38.7 × 56.2 cms.

SIGNED AND DATED: *V. McAdoo 1933*

PROVENANCE: the artist, 39 Rugby Road, Belfast, from whom purchased, 1944, by the Ulster Museum, Belfast, art dept. cat. no. 1566.

EXHIBITED: 1944, *Two Artists,* Belfast, no. 76; 1981, *Royal Ulster Academy Diploma Centenary Exhibition,* Ulster Museum, Belfast.

LITERATURE: Martyn Anglesea, *Royal Ulster Academy of Arts, A Centennial History* (1981), p. 78 (ill.).

Kathleen Bridle (b.1897)

110   Lough Erne from Rossfad, 1945

Watercolour on white paper, 36.3 × 46.7 cms.

SIGNED AND DATED: *Kathleen Bridle / September 1945*

PROVENANCE: purchased from the artist, 23 Eastbridge Road, Enniskillen, 1951. Ulster Museum, Belfast, art dept. cat. no. 994.

EXHIBITED: 1973, *Arts ·Council of Northern Ireland,* Belfast, no. 8.

LITERATURE: Martyn Anglesea, *Royal Ulster Academy of Arts, A Centennial History,* (1981) facing p. 71 (ill. in colour).

As early as 1935 Kathleen Bridle's work was praised for perfecting 'that indescribable grey-green that lies on the Irish countryside in the rainy season'.[1]   MA

1. *The Northern Whig,* 15 October 1935.

Lent by the Ulster Museum, Belfast.

Beatrice Glenavy, *Self-Portrait with Shelah Richards in Pittsburgh,* (cat. no. 111).

Beatrice Glenavy (1883-1968)

111   Self Portrait with Shelah Richards in Pittsburgh, 1925

Pencil, pen and watercolour on paper, 30.5 × 20.3 cms.

INSCRIBED: *"Isn't he lovely, Shelah"?!/ "Isn't he beautiful, Beatie"?! U.S.A. Pittsburgh July 1925*

PROVENANCE: given by the artist to Shelah Richards; then by family descent.

Ever since she was a student, Beatrice Glenavy had drawn spirited deftly humorous caricatures, often including her own merciless self-portrait (she was regarded in Dublin artistic circles as a beauty). Many of these are in letters to friends, others were published in contemporary magazines like *The Irish Review.* Two she gave to her friend, the actress Shelah Richards. The other, dated 1925, is entitled *Shelah takes her Mother for a Run in the Standard.* The Richards family and Beatrice Glenavy's in-laws had known each other during seaside summers at Greystones for a long time when, during the war years, Beatrice and Gordon Campbell took a house

opposite the Richards and the artist saw how the young girl longed to become an actress. She introduced her to Lennox Robinson at the Abbey Theatre, despite Lady Gregory's reservations about her not being sufficiently 'peasant stock'. She subsequently appeared in the original cast of O'Casey's *The Plough and the Stars* (1926) and as well as a long career as an actress, worked in Irish television and as an independent producer. She married the playwright Denis Johnston while on tour with the Abbey Company in America.   NGB

Lent by Pat and Michael Johnston.

Beatrice Glenavy

112   The Intruder, 1932

Oil on canvas, 69.9 × 95.3 cms.

SIGNED: in monogram, *BG*

PROVENANCE: acquired by Professor Fearon from the artist; passed to his executor and then by family descent to the present owner.

EXHIBITED: 1932, *Aonach Tailteann Exhibition of Irish Art,* Dublin, no. 133; 1932, Royal Hibernian Academy, no. 37; 1933, Royal Academy, London, no. 12; 1955, Waddington Gallery, Dublin.

LITERATURE: Beatrice Lady Glenavy, *Today we will only gossip,* (London 1964).

Described by *The Irish Times* in 1932 as 'reminiscent of an 18th century French theme, in which a golden-haired female centaur startles a picnic and bathing party beneath formalized foliage', this unusually large and richly coloured painting for the artist is more reminiscent of Rex Whistler's satirical mural, *In Pursuit of Rare Meats,* executed in the Restaurant of the Tate Gallery in London (1926-27).

   The artist wrote in her autobiography, 'I painted a picture which I liked very much, called "The Intruder". It portrayed an imaginary woodland scene with people having a picnic; a female centaur has galloped through the wood and beckons to a young

Beatrice Glenavy, *The Intruder,* (cat. no. 112).

man in the picnic party who is leaping madly forward to follow her. . . . Richard Orpen . . . was very keen that my picture should be bought by the Haverty Trust. . . . Unfortunately some of the members of the committee considered that it was "obscene" so they did not buy it. My meaning, if any, had been that the unknown was more interesting than the known. Next year I sent the picture to the R.A., where it was hung on the line, got good notices, and was caricatured by George Morrow in *Punch* under the title "The Home Wrecker".'

The Intruder incorporates a number of themes the artist had used and would continue to explore in her work.   NGB

Private collection.

Beatrice Glenavy, *Still-life with garlanded china hound and hare ornament,* (cat. no. 113).

Beatrice Glenavy

113   Still-life with garlanded china hound and hare ornament

Oil on canvas, 40.6 × 50.8 cms.

SIGNED: *BG* (in red).

PROVENANCE: Shelah Richards and then by family descent.

EXHIBITED: Royal Hibernian Academy 1970 (In Memoriam), no. 5 as *The Huntress.*

After 1933 the artist painted a number of imaginary scenes where she made surrealistic juxtapositions of real life and inanimate objects so that reality and illusion became blurred. She wrote how much pleasure she got from 'painting still-life arrangements with romantic backgrounds of forests and distant figures.' She particularly admired Mark Gertler's paintings in which he instilled a china figure with 'profundity and mystery'; she marvelled at 'the beauty of the paint, the queer sense of eternity that it contained . . .' The glaucous tones of this sylvan setting highlighted by soft rose pink and beige, where a broken or cracked china figure is set beside a rose, dead bird, cactus, paper cut-out

or shell, are also found in her *Birth of Venus* and *Roses* in the Dublin Municipal Gallery and *Enigma* in The Ulster Museum.   NGB

Lent by Jennifer Johnston.

Beatrice Glenavy, *Mother and Child,* (cat. no. 114).

Beatrice Glenavy

114   Mother and Child

Oil on canvas, 61 × 41 cms.

SIGNED: *BC,* in monogram.

PROVENANCE: Sir John Purser-Griffith; by family descent to his great niece, Miss A. Griffith, from whom purchased by the present owner, 1986.

Beatrice Glenavy painted and sculpted a number of interpretations of the mother and child theme throughout her career. As this painting is inscribed with the BC monogram, it must have been painted after she married Gordon Campbell in 1912 and by 1931, after which, on her husband's succession to his father's title of Lord Glenavy, she began signing herself BG. A label on the reverse side bears the address of Sarah Purser's stained glass workshop, where the artist resumed work briefly on her return to Ireland after the First World War. Unfortunately, the book in which the artist meticulously recorded all her work is (hopefully temporarily) untraced and the painting is undocumented. A *Mother and Child* was exhibited at the Royal Hibernian Academy in 1934 (for sale at 7 gns. which would tally with the number 7 on the reverse) but the mother's 'Aesthetic' dress would suggest an earlier date. Behind the absorbed foreground figures and painted on a backdrop of paler glaucous tones, the ethereal mythological figures rising regally from the mist above a sea monster, a Viking ship and a turreted island keep are reminiscent of those the artist had illustrated in 1913 for Violet Russell's *Heroes of the Dawn*. Perhaps the mother is telling one such story to the rapt child and the haunting scene behind them is an evocation of her words.

NGB

Private collection.

Dorothy Isabel Blackham (1896-1975)

115   House painting in Paddington

Pencil and watercolour on paper, 56.8 × 51.5 cms.
SIGNED: *D. BLACKHAM*

Dorothy Isabel Blackham, *House Painting in Paddington*, (cat. no. 115).

PROVENANCE: presented by Mrs. Thea Boyd, by whom presented, 1977 to the Hugh Lane Municipal Gallery, Dublin.

In this view, presumably from the artist's studio in London, the main focus is on the neo-classical style building across the road. House painters are at work on the façade, some are on ladders while others are on the roof busily painting the pillars of the balustrade. Dorothy's rendering of the architecture is realistic and detailed while her treatment of the figures is highly stylized. The colours used are the muted greys of the cut stone enlivened somewhat by the green of the vegetation below. A striking contrast is created by the silhouetting of the dark ornamental iron balcony against the pale grey of the cut stone.   WR

Lent by the Hugh Lane Municipal Gallery of Art, Dublin.

Mainie Jellett, *Seated Nude*, (cat. no. 116).

Mainie Jellett (1897-1944)

116   Seated Nude, 1921

Oil on canvas, 56.3 × 46.2 cms.

PROVENANCE: Miss Bay Jellett, by whom acquired from the artist's estate for the Neptune Gallery, Dublin, 1975, where purchased, Ulster Museum, Belfast, art dept. cat. no. 2293.

EXHIBITED: 1974, *Mainie Jellett*, Neptune Gallery, Dublin, no. 21 (ill.).

In the short but intense period of study under André Lhote, Mainie Jellett produced a large number of paintings of the nude, both male and female, in which the essentials of Analytical Cubism were followed. This work, for which she made numerous studies, is an outstanding example.

Yet in 1921, which is the date of this and other related works, the mood among art students in Paris, and with other colleagues attending the Lhote Académie, must have been somewhat retrospective. Cubist painting along the lines Lhote was teaching was felt to have run its course, and the direction being taken by the leading painters, including Braque and Picasso, indicated a break either towards their return to realism, or towards a much more austere examination of form and colour as an expression of canvas surface. BA

Lent by the Ulster Museum, Belfast.

Mainie Jellett, *Abstract*, (cat. no. 117).

Mainie Jellett

117   Abstract, 1922

Oil on canvas, 59.7 × 48.2 cms.

PROVENANCE: from the artist's family; private collection, Dublin.

EXHIBITED: 1974, *Mainie Jellett*, Neptune Gallery, Dublin, cat. no. 23 (ill. front cover).

One of the earliest of the artist's pure abstract works, and painted during 1922, the first full year during which she worked with

Albert Gleizes, to whom she went from Andre Lhote in December, 1921. Recently, a gouache study of this painting came to light, but none of the preparatory pencil drawings have survived.

The boldness and simplicity of the composition, with the rich and assured colours, exemplifies the confidence with which Mainie Jellett absorbed all the technical essentials of pure abstract art in the first year of her studies under Gleizes. Her output during 1922-23 was prodigious, and included a large number of abstract studies developed on the principles of 'translation' and 'rotation', as taught by Gleizes. The earliest were single-element works, the rotation being from one axis. By 1924 she had developed more complex compositions with four elements, and by the late twenties this had further evolved into seven- and eight-element figures. With the introduction, in the thirties, of semi-abstract religious subject matter she moved further away from the initial austerity of impact of her earliest works, making canvases such as this one extremely rare, and of seminal significance in assessing her importance in the evolution of abstract principles. BA

Private collection.

Mainie Jellett

118   Abstract composition, 1927

Oil on canvas, 111.7 × 56 cms.

SIGNED: *M. Jellett '27*

PROVENANCE: bought from the artist in 1928; private collection, Dublin.

EXHIBITED: 1962, *Mainie Jellett. A Retrospective Exhibition of Paintings and Drawings*, Hugh Lane Municipal Gallery, Dublin, cat. no. 64.

Painted on rough, 'French' canvas, almost of the texture of sacking, though not the roughest she used, the painting was probably done in France during the summer visit that year to Gleizes. The work is a two-element abstract composition. Many studies and sketches for work from this period have survived.

From 1924 on, Mainie Jellett developed a number of different compositional structures, and her abstracts, which still adhered to the technical principles of 'translation' and 'rotation', were at times extremely complicated, both in the inter-relationship of the elements, as many as eight being contained in a single work, and in the colours which were involved. Relatively speaking, *Abstract composition* is straightforward and direct, using two primary colours in a bold fashion that she favoured at the time, and which occurs in a number of paintings of this date.

BA

Private collection

Mainie Jellett, *Abstract composition,* (cat. no. 118).

Mainie Jellett

119   A Composition

Oil on canvas, 92 × 62 cms.

SIGNED: *Mainie Jellett*

PROVENANCE: Dawson Gallery, Dublin, where purchased in 1968. National Gallery of Ireland, cat. no. 1875.

When the large gouache study for this was exhibited in the 1962 Mainie Jellett retrospective exhibition (cat. no. 41) it was dated c.1930. Yet a smaller gouache study exists, dated 1922, and the later date must be taken as speculative, as must association with the main period of semi-abstract, religious figurative paintings of the 1930s.

Mainie Jellett, *A Composition,* (cat. no. 119).

The top corners of the painting contain decorative additions to the main, single-element composition, which may derive from one of the early Italian Masters. Even before becoming an abstract artist, Mainie Jellett, as André Lhote's pupil, had been engaged in drawing and painting Cubist works derived from Old Master paintings, her best-known example of this being *Homage to Fra Angelico.*   BA

Lent by the National Gallery of Ireland.

Mainie Jellett

120   Achill Horses, 1944

Oil on canvas, 61 × 92 cms.

SIGNED AND DATED: on the back, *M. Jellett 1944*

PROVENANCE: Miss R. Kirkpatrick Bequest, 1979, National Gallery of Ireland, cat. no. 4320.

EXHIBITED: 1962, *Mainie Jellett. A Retrospective Exhibition of Paintings and Drawings,* Hugh Lane Municipal Gallery, Dublin, cat. no. 68 (ill.).

LITERATURE: *Ireland,* no. 593, 1962 (ill. p. 7).

Mainie Jellett, *Achill Horses*, (cat. no. 120).

The return to realism, throughout the 1930's, was occasioned by a number of factors, including the range of her teaching and the various commissions she received, for decorative and symbolic work expressive of Ireland, notably for international fairs in Glasgow and the United States. Chinese art was a third factor of great importance in shaping her style and inspiration in the late thirties and early forties, and particularly with this and related paintings of horses.

There was a strongly religious theme to many of these later works, but landscapes and seascapes, as well as genre paintings showing the works and crafts of people in the West of Ireland, came from her studio at the time. She was also teaching life drawing regularly.

BA

Lent by the National Gallery of Ireland.

Evie Hone, *Abstract Composition*, (cat. no. 121).

Evie Hone (1894-1955)

121   Abstract composition

Gouache and pencil on paper stuck on board, 34.3 × 43.8 cms.

SIGNED: bottom right, *E. Hone*

PROVENANCE: Dawson Gallery, where purchased by the family of the present owner.

This small but beautifully finished abstract composition, probably an early work by Evie Hone which displays the strong influence of her training under Lhote and particularly Gleizes, is very similar to the work Mainie Jellett was producing at this time. Hone however, unusually enough here, uses a subtle range of colour tones, confidently mixing soft pastel hues of pinks, mauves and pale greens. Though the actual subject matter is not known, Evie, who was devoutly religious, often based her abstract studies on religious subjects.

The artist has very carefully and harmoniously built up her single composition, and the bright core, surrounded by the fragmented circles which create an ordered rhythm, draws the spectator into the centre of the painting.

KMM

Private collection.

Evie Hone, *A landscape with a tree*, (cat. no. 122).

Evie Hone

122   A landscape with a tree, 1943

Oil on board, 69 × 69 cms.

SIGNED AND DATED: *E. Hone 1943*

PROVENANCE: Miss R. Kirkpatrick Bequest, 1979. National Gallery of Ireland, cat. no. 4322.

EXHIBITED: 1943, *Irish Exhibition of Living Art*, National College of Art, Kildare St., cat. no. 128.

This is one of numerous oils on a larger scale which Evie Hone exhibited throughout her later career, and like *Snow at Marlay* it shows a clear enjoyment of the lyrical colours and shapes of landscape. The vivid tones are laid on thickly, bringing out the structural discipline inherent in the composition. She has turned the background hills into rectangular screens to make a foil for the central groupings of fields and stones. Against this array of flattened shapes the tree stands out in a bold and decorative pattern.

FG

Lent by the National Gallery of Ireland.

Evie Hone, *Snow at Marlay*, (cat. no. 123).

Evie Hone

123   Snow at Marlay

Oil on board, 37 × 49 cms.

SIGNED: *E. Hone*

PROVENANCE: Friends of the National Collections of Ireland, by whom presented, 1957; National Gallery of Ireland, cat. no. 1371.

EXHIBITED: 1955, *Irische Kunst der Gegenwart Iserlohn*, no. 4; 1958, *Evie Hone 1894-1955*, University College, Dublin, no. 30; 1966, *1916 Jubilee Exhibition*, St. Joseph's Hall, Nenagh no. 7; 1980, *Exhibition of Irish Painting*, Town Hall, Dun Laoghaire.

LITERATURE: Michael Wynne, *Fifty Irish Painters* (1983), p. 49 (ill.).

Snow at Marlay is full of expression and demonstrates a freedom of brushwork and an independence of style which tells of Evie Hone's Parisian training.

Marlay was a familiar subject for Evie, as it was there that she established her stained glass workshop in the 1940's after the closure of the stained glass co-operative An Túr Gloine of which she had been an active member. Today some two hundred and fifty acres of parkland at Marlay in Rathfarnham make an attractive and much admired public park.

WR

Lent by the National Gallery of Ireland.

May Guinness, *A Religious Procession in Brittany*, (cat. no. 124).

May Guinness (1863-1955)

124   A religious procession in Brittany

Oil on canvas, 127 × 102 cms.

SIGNED: *M. Guinness*

PROVENANCE: Mrs. M. Lloyd, Executor of the late May Guinness, by whom presented, 1956; National Gallery of Ireland, cat. no. 1339.

EXHIBITED: 1966, *1916 Jubilee Exhibition*, St. Joseph's Hall, Nenagh, no. 8.

Also known as *Procession à Joscelyn* this painting, although figurative, comes near to abstraction in its simplification of detail. Its main strength lies in the striking contrast between the black and white of the traditional Breton costume and the white of the first holy communion dresses. A claustrophobic and eerie effect is created by the forcefulness of the crowd surging down the hill, hemmed in on either side by the tall houses of the narrow winding village street.

The theme of religious processions was a fairly common subject matter among the artists who visited Brittany and this clearly illustrates the deeply rooted religious faith which characterised the region.

WR

Lent by the National Gallery of Ireland.

May Guinness, *Golden Wedding in Belgium*, (cat. no. 125).

May Guinness

125   Golden Wedding in Belgium

Oil on canvas, 61 × 91 cms.

PROVENANCE: purchased from the artist or from the artist's retrospective exhibition, April 1956, by the present owner.

EXHIBITED: 1943, *Irish Exhibition of Living Art,* National College of Art, Dublin, no. 101.

May Guinness often depicted scenes of traditional life in the villages of Brittany and Belgium (see *Religious Procession,* cat. no. 123), recording a way of life which was fast disappearing in so many other areas in France at the turn of the century. It was a theme which was popular among artists working in Brittany who were attracted by the picturesque and rural nature of the unspoilt villages. This painting, representing a typical Belgian celebration of a golden wedding in a simple rustic interior with the figures wearing the costumes of the time, was made on one of the artist's late trips to the continent.

The striking linear composition of a family seated around a table, displays the influence of Cubism on May's work. While the composition is quite flat and stylised, though not quite as fragmented as a Cubist work, it has been carefully built up on a series of triangles which create a dramatic tension within the picture and all the lines seem to converge in diagonal shafts on to the centre of the canvas and of the table. This is the brightest area in the picture and, conveniently, there is an empty place here, so that everything combines to draw the spectator into the heart of the composition. The unusual combinations of colours, the pinks, blacks and blue-greys contrast in a striking and nearly shocking manner with the bright white areas of the canvas.

KMM

Private collection.

May Guinness, *Still-life with Tulips,* (cat. no. 126).

May Guinness

126   Still-Life with tulips

Oil on canvas, 62.5 × 76 cms.

PROVENANCE: purchased from the artist or from the artist's retrospective exhibition, April 1956, by the present owner.

This still-life with tulips in a vase has been painted with incredible verve and ease. The delicacy with which May Guinness has treated some of the blossoms betrays the influence of Raoul Dufy. It is through her fluent and strong brushstrokes, however, that she has practically given 'life' to the flowers which appear to be blooming on the canvas.

The cool palette and the free abstract, decorative use of colour found in May's paintings, which again shows the influence of Dufy as well as of Marie Laurencin, is here relieved by the strong splashes of crimson in the tulips. Rather interestingly, she has also picked out the colours of the flower arrangement and used them for the background, making the whole canvas a visual kaleidoscopic delight. This freer, decorative style, which owes a lot to the Fauves, is more typical of May's later work.

KMM

Private collection.

Harriet Kirkwood (1880-1953)

127   Still life with Fruit and Flowers, c.1940

Oil on canvas, 79 × 63 cms.

PROVENANCE: Mr. Collinson, by whom bought from the artist in 1940 or 1941; bequeathed to his daughter Miss Renee Collinson, by whom presented, in memory of the artist, 1983; National Gallery of Ireland, cat. no. 4470.

EXHIBITED: 1984, *Acquisitions 1982-83,* National Gallery of Ireland, Dublin, no. 11.

LITERATURE: Adrian Le Harivel and Michael Wynne, *Acquisitions 1982-83,* (1984) p. 24 (ill.).

Harriet Kirkwood, *Still-life with fruit and flowers,* (cat. no. 127).

Hilda Roberts, *Portrait of George Russell (AE),* (cat. no. 128).

Although a still life in the traditional manner Harriet Kirkwood's use of colour is very personal. A fresh and delicate blend of shell pink, pale blue and orange is achieved in the abundant display of flowers. There is a distinct lack of precise detail throughout the painting which reflects in a small degree the artist's *avant-garde* training in Paris.

The whole composition is filled with light and there is a sense of natural continuity between the interior space and the landscape beyond. The view is of the Wicklow Mountains from the artist's own house, Collinstown Park, Clondalkin, county Dublin.

WR

Lent by the National Gallery of Ireland.

Hilda Roberts (1901-1982)

128 Portrait of George Russell (Æ), 1929

Oil on canvas, 76.2 × 63.8 cms.

SIGNED: *Hilda Roberts / 1929*

PROVENANCE: purchased from the artist, 1936; Ulster Museum, Belfast, art. dept. cat. no. 392.

EXHIBITED: March 1930, Hackett Gallery, New York; 1931, Dublin Painters' Gallery, no. 35; 1932, *Aonach Tailteann,* Exhibition of Irish Art, Dublin, no. 19;

1933, Royal Hibernian Academy, Dublin; 1965, *Portraits of Great Irish Men and Women,* Ulster Museum, no. 193; 1975, *Irish Art 1900-50,* Rosc, Cork, no. 62.

LITERATURE: *Dublin Magazine,* vol. 10, no. 4, (1935) (frontispiece).

Painted when she was only twenty-eight, at Russell's home in Dublin, during the course of six Sunday morning sittings, this portrait justifiably received much critical acclaim when it was exhibited in New York and subsequently Dublin. The picture had been suggested by the Hackett Gallery for their exhibition of *Twelve Irish Painters,* as they were enthusiastic sellers of Æ's paintings. The *New York City Times* said it 'tells us more about [Æ] than we learn from his paintings. Under the brow of a thinking man, furrowed and somewhat anxious with his thoughts, the eyes bend upon us the steady unseeing gaze of the mystic, quite remarkably rendered'. An Irish critic felt she had 'caught that sort of stern pixiness about him which reveals her as something of a psychologist'.

Set against one of his own Symbolist paintings, determinedly transcending his habitual dishevelment, the artist/writer/poet/visionary and economist is depicted in characteristic pose, as though about to jump up and expound on a new idea.

NGB

Lent by the Ulster Museum, Belfast.

Hilda Roberts, *Achill Boy*, (cat. no. 129).

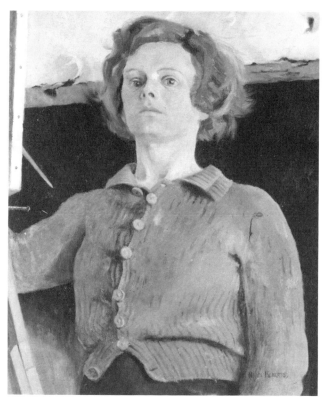

Hilda Roberts, *Self-Portrait in red cardigan*, (cat. no. 130).

Hilda Roberts

129   Achill boy

Oil on canvas, 61 × 49.5 cms.

SIGNED: *H. Roberts*

PROVENANCE: by family descent to the present owner.

EXHIBITED: 1931, St. Stephen's Green Gallery, Dublin; 1979, Taylor Galleries, Dublin, no. 1.

When she exhibited in 1932 in a group show of the Dublin Painters, Hilda Roberts' work was singled out as unique in its promise of genius: 'Of all the recent individual exhibits her collection of child portraits was easily the most outstanding'. She was able to capture the unaffected ingenuity and native curiosity of the children who gathered around her in Achill clamouring to be painted but becoming shy and slightly awkward when confronted with the artist's attention. Usually they are single portraits. She tried to depict as many different facial types as possible and set great store on getting the child's likeness, after doing a careful drawing or so. The background shapes are an important part of the composition.   NGB

Lent by Mrs. Eithne Clarke.

Hilda Roberts

130   Self-Portrait in red cardigan

Oil on canvas, 55.9 × 45.8 cms.

SIGNED: *Hilda Roberts*

PROVENANCE: by family descent to the present owner.

EXHIBITED: 1979, Taylor Galleries, no. 17.

The only extant self portrait by the artist, although she painted many portraits, some formal commissions and some people whose features especially appealed to her e.g. Elizabeth Rivers, Patrick Tuohy, her brother-in-law, Lyle Donaghy (Ulster Museum), her aunt Lizzy, her husband, a charwoman in Waterford, Brinsley McNamara, Mrs. Jellett, Maurice MacGonigal, Robert Barton, Mr. Justice Reddin, Mrs. Liam O'Flaherty and Pat Mullen of Achill.

Her concentration has given her an unaccustomedly stern gaze here. Austin Clarke recalled that she was known in Dublin as 'Cinderella' as she flitted enchantingly from subject to subject.

NGB

Lent by Mrs. Eithne Clarke.

Frances Kelly, *Portrait of George Furlong*, (cat. no. 131).

Frances Kelly (fl. from 1929)

131 Portrait of George Furlong, 1935

Oil on canvas, 88.8 × 74.3 cms.

PROVENANCE: gift from the artist to Dr. G. Furlong.

George Furlong, born in 1898, was educated at Clongowes and University College, Dublin. After a period of study abroad, in Paris and Munich, and in Vienna where he received a doctorate for his work on Anglo-Saxon manuscript illumination of the tenth and eleventh centuries, he went to London to lecture at the National Gallery and the Tate Gallery. In 1935, he was appointed Director of the National Gallery of Ireland. His period of office during the War was fraught with frustrations, including the temporary evacuation of some of the more valuable works in the collection into safe-keeping in Tourmakeady, county Mayo, and the uncooperative attitude of the Board in matters of purchase. However he was responsible for some important acquisitions, such as the Castiglione allegory and the Tintoretto portrait of a Venetian senator. He resigned in 1950 when the Board refused to purchase Murillo's *Christ healing the paralytic at the Pool of Bethesda*, now in the National Gallery, London. He died in 1987.

Frances Kelly's sympathetic three-quarter length portrait blends the outward appearance of her sitter with his surroundings of flowers, books and space, in a psychological way, so as to emphasise the inner qualities of scholarship and imagination. The capricious light dwells on tulips, Dr. Furlong's forehead and the opened pages. The darkened side of his face expresses both disappointment and strong determination. The painting is in constant motion,

creating a striking dichotomy between the diagonal flow of light and the contemplative quiescence of the sitter. It was painted in 1935, the year of his appointment as Director. HP

Lent by Mr. Rex Britcher.

Frances Kelly, *Still-life with Pièta*, (cat. no. 132).

Frances Kelly

132 Still-Life with Pièta, 1943 or 4

Oil on canvas, 127 × 152.4 cms.

PROVENANCE: Clongowes Wood College.

Painted from a Pièta belonging to Evie Hone. In still life, Frances Kelly shared much in common with the older artist, Moyra Barry, who was showing her expansive impressions of flowers in the Academy in the 1930's and 1940's; but Frances Kelly's muted palette, and the broken surface of the picture plane create a more reflective mood. HP

Private collection.

Mary Swanzy (1882-1978)

133 Young woman with flowers

Oil on canvas, 76 × 63.5 cms.

SIGNED: *Swanzy*

PROVENANCE: artist's studio collection; Pyms Gallery, London, where purchased, 1986; private collection.

EXHIBITED: 1986, *Mary Swanzy ARHA (1882-1978)*, Pyms Gallery, London, no. 3.

The dark eyes and pursed scarlet mouth of the young woman are similar to those in '*Young woman with white bonnet*', (exhibited Pyms

Mary Swanzy, *Young woman with flowers,* (cat. no. 133).

Mary Swanzy, *Red roofed villages and hilly landscapes,* (cat. no. 134).

Gallery, 1986, no. 2) and could be the features of the artist herself. Probably painted in Paris (there is a photograph extant, taken in studios at No. 229, Bvd. Raspail), the two pictures show Swanzy's early efforts at Cubism, influenced by Picasso and Delaunay, perhaps just before the First World War. She exhibited with Delaunay and other experimental artists at the Salon des Independants in 1914. The sad face of the girl, shown in three-quarter view, floats like a disembodied mask in the midst of geometric shapes. Diagonal splinters of light cut across the canvas. An exquisite bouquet of flowers, red, yellow and green, stylised in curling arabesques, is suspended before her, and blood red flowers cover her heart. The floating face and breast, flowers and heart and the shafts of light, give a tender religious symbolism to the dynamic Cubist composition, suggestive of the artist's vulnerability, or wounded love. Similar themes appear in Swanzy's later allegorical work.   JC

Lent by Mr. and Mrs. L. Quinn.

Mary Swanzy (1882-1978)
134   Red roofed villages and hilly landscape

Oil on canvas, 40.5 × 40.5 cms.

PROVENANCE: artist's studio collection; Mrs. Mary St. Clair Swanzy Tullo (the artist's niece); Pyms Gallery, London, where purchased; private collection.

This richly-coloured Mediterranean or Eastern European landscape shows Mary Swanzy's painting at its most pure and 'painterly'. The mountain landscape is confidently built up with cheerful reds and greens, mauves and ochres, reminiscent of Cezanne. Swanzy first saw paintings by Cezanne in Gertrude Stein's collection in Paris in 1906-07, and learned from him a firmness of modelling and understanding of the structure of nature. Here, horizontal and diagonal lines lead our eye up to the red-roofed hilltop village. Thomas McGreevy remarked that Swanzy was probably the first Irish painter to show the influence of Cezanne.[1] This could easily be a Provençal or Italian landscape, painted after the First World War, but it probably belongs to a group of Balkan canvases, painted during her Czechoslovak visit in 1920.   JC

1. Thomas McGreevy, *Fifty Years of Irish Painting,* Capuchin Annual (1949).

Private collection.

Mary Swanzy
135   Samoan scene, c.1924

Oil on canvas, 152 × 92 cms.

PROVENANCE: Allied Irish Banks Collection.

EXHIBITED: 1924, Honolulu; 1924, Santa Barbara, California; 1925, Galerie Beruheim Jeune, Paris (probably entitled, *Scène dans la Foret*); 1968, *Mary Swanzy Retrospective Exhibition,* Municipal Gallery of Modern Art, Dublin (as *Samoan Scene I,* no. 12 or *Samoan Scene II,* no. 13); 1986, *Allied Irish Banks Collection,* Douglas Hyde Gallery, Dublin (no. 12).

LITERATURE: Litti Paulding, 'Irish Artist finds work in vicinity for her brush', *Santa Barbara Daily News,* (18 November 1924); Peta Cullen, 'Mary Swanzy: a major Irish painter', *The Irish Times* (24 May 1968), ill.; Dr. Frances Ruane, *The Allied Irish Banks Collection,* exhibition catalogue, (1986), p. 26, ill.; Julian Campbell, *Mary Swanzy H.R.H.A. (1882-1978),* Pyms Gallery exhibition catalogue, p. 22 (1986).

Mary Swanzy, *Samoan scene*, (cat. no. 135).

bright flowers and large-leaved trees, the blue skies and brown-skinned native women in cheerful cottons. The bare brown back and colourful garments of the native girl, the garland of flowers around her thick black hair, invite comparison with Gauguin's Tahitian canvases. But Swanzy's Samoan paintings lack his symbolic overtones, and are a more direct response to the sunny world around her. She works in the shadowy forest interior of royal palms and coconut, banana trees and papaya.

Our eye is always lured into the warm shimmering pool, in which the naked women and child bathe, enclosed by the verdant wall of the forest. If we look closely we can see hanging fruits, cheerful red and yellow parrots, gorgeous green and blue leaves (on the left), and the blue of a mountain face glimpsed above the forest. Although painted with obvious rapidity and freshness, close inspection also reveals the variety of brushstrokes in different areas of the canvas, and something of Swanzy's creative processes: the bold modelling of the bathers' figures, the broad sketchy strokes of the girl's dress and the forest floor, the crisp outlines and flat modelling of the broad leaves, the roots of the foreground plant, and the thin, 'impressionistic' sketching of the criss-crossed forest ceiling. Her painting methods reflect the colour and growth of the jagged-leaved plants, as if the painting itself is symbolic of the forest. Yet the result is spontaneous, rich and joyful.   JC

1. Pro-Quidnunc, 'An Irishman's Diary', *The Irish Times*, (April 1976).
2. L. Paulding, *op. cit.*

Lent from the Allied Irish Banks collection.

Mary Swanzy, *The Message*, (cat. no. 136).

Mary Swanzy

136   The Message

Oil on panel, 45.1 × 53.3 cms.

Upon her arrival in Honolulu and Samoa in 1923-24, Mary Swanzy was stunned at how many greens there were in the world.[1] A contemporary review probably refers to this particular painting: 'One sees first a wilderness of banana trees, a veritable nest of great green leaves. Soon the remarkable draughtsmanship is apparent. The interlacing of the leaves, the tonal play of green is very decorative. The repetition of the tree trunks is an interesting note. There are always figures in all her paintings. The dark brown squat figures with bright coloured flowers in their hair are fascinating'.[2] This *Samoan Scene* is one of the largest and finest paintings in her South Sea series. We are witness to a quiet forest scene, the back view of the native woman in the foreground leading our eye to the pool of water and bathers in sunshine. The curving palm leaves at the top of the canvas and the shadowy bank in the foreground successfully frame the pool of sunshine in the centre of the picture, and there is a pleasing contrast between vertical trunks and arching leaves.

Away from the confines of Europe, the art schools and galleries, the sensuous side of Swanzy's nature is given free rein and responds with exuberance to the sunshine and colour of the tropics, the

EXHIBITED: 1968, *Mary Swanzy Retrospective Exhibition*, Municipal Art Gallery, Dublin, no. 25; 1975, *Irish Art 1900-1950*, Rosc Exhibition, Crawford Gallery, Cork, no. 138.

LITERATURE: Hilary Pyle, *Irish Art 1900-1950*, (1975) ill. facing p. 67; Julian Campbell, *Mary Swanzy A.R.H.A. (1882-1978)*, Pyms Gallery catalogue (1986) ill. p. 25.

The Message, presented to the Municipal Gallery in 1945, was probably painted during the War years when Mary Swanzy was living in Dublin. Although not religious in a strict sense, a 'religious' element is present in many of her paintings. *The Message* is more directly Christian than many of her allegorical paintings, and lacks the savagery of some of her other war-time pictures. Nevertheless, there is still a characteristic sense of enigma in the juxtaposition of Christian tenderness and human stupidity, in the separation between the Virgin and Child, on the left, and the group of shepherds on the right, the expressively-clasped hands of the Madonna, and the mysterious arched rocks and barren landscape. As a student in Paris, Swanzy had encountered Picasso and the early work of the Cubists, who had opened her eyes to Cézanne, and to the structure underlying Nature, and led her back to a new appreciation of Early Italian Renaissance painting. The hard outlines of the figure, the angular folds of drapery, and rocky, slightly 'Cubist' landscape are reminiscent of some Florentine and Northern Italian paintings (e.g. by Mantegna and Bellini, which she could have studied in the National Gallery in London; or, for instance, Granacci's *Holy Family with St. John in a landscape*, in the National Gallery, Dublin cat. no. 98); her madonna has a similar statuesque quality, seeming to grow out of the rocky landscape.

The influence of William Orpen's draughtsmanship, the satire of his First World War paintings, reappear in her caricature-like studies of the Second World War. Here, for example, the foolish-looking shepherds with simple faces and open mouths, are close to the frightened, ignorant crowd in Orpen's *Fire Bomb at Picardy* (Pyms Gallery collection).   JC

Lent by the Hugh Lane Municipal Gallery of Art, Dublin.

Mary Swanzy

137   The gardener and the bluebird

Oil on canvas, 71 × 63.25 cms.

PROVENANCE: Dawson Gallery, Dublin, from whom purchased, c.1969; private collection, Dublin.

EXHIBITED: 1968, *Mary Swanzy Retrospective Exhibition*, Municipal Gallery, Dublin, no. 57.

LITERATURE: J. Campbell, *Irish Artists in France and Belgium, 1850-1914*, (Ph.D. thesis, Trinity College, Dublin, 1980).

Many of Swanzy's war-time canvases were satirical and grotesque, but there is a new contentment in her later painting which became increasingly personal and lyrical. *The gardener and the bluebird*, 1965,

Mary Swanzy, *The gardener and the bluebird*, (cat. no. 137).

shows her at her most imaginative and poetic, the gardener and the bluebird in an idyllic 'Italianate' landscape seeming to share the joy of Spring in a moment of joyous communion. Coarse and powerful male figures appeal in several of her paintings, (e.g.: *The queen and the labourer*, Pyms Gallery, 1986 [no. 61], and *A figure study*, [NGI cat. no. 1312]), and the gardener here may suggest a 'Lawrentian' theme. Yet there is a gentleness in the way he holds the pot of flowers, and whistles to the bird, who sings its heart out on a silvery twig. The magical atmosphere is enhanced by the glowing, dream-like landscape, with its wood and terraced fields, its gate and mysterious staircase leading to a blue hilltop village. The distant blue mountain peaks are reminiscent of Venetian painting. Many elements of her experience and imagination come together in her later painting: memories of sunny lands in which she had travelled, an admiration for Renaissance painting, a book read or a dream, some incident in her youth remembered. Birds and flowers, trees and woods, appear in other paintings and each may have a personal symbolism for the artist. Yet its meaning remains private for her; she did not encourage literal interpretation of her work. The tentative drawing style in the arms and hand of the gardener, the transparent lines around flower pots and watering can add to the ethereal effect, and suggest that the subject developed out of her imagination as she was painting.

The joyous colouring, silvered cerulean blues, warm pinks and glowing greens, reds and ochres, maroons and silvers, give a rich and jewelled effect, characteristic of her later painting when she seemed to return to the School of Paris with whom she came of age: to Marie Laurencin, Picasso's 'rose' period and, particularly, Chagall.   JC

Private collection.

Dictionary of Irish women artists

Acheson, Anne Crawford (1882-1962)

Anne Acheson was born in Portadown and educated at Victoria College, Belfast, Belfast School of Art and the Royal College of Art, London where she studied sculpture under Lanteri. She exhibited at the Royal Academy and internationally, and was awarded a CBE in 1919. She lived in London and Glenavy, county Antrim.   MA

Adams, Vikki (b.1961)

Born 1961; 1984 BA degree, Fine Art, National College of Art & Design, Dublin; 1986 MFA Degree, Slade School, London.

Exhibitions: 1985, 'Of Desire' — Temple Bar Studios, Dublin; 'When the shit hits the fan', Houghton St. and N.E. London Polytechnic; 'Ponophobia', October Gallery, London and London Film Makers Co-op; 1986, NCAD Decade Show, Guinness Hop Store.

Alment, Mary Martha (1834-1908)

Mary Martha Alment was born in Derry and later studied in Dublin under Henry McManus. McManus was appointed head master of the newly constituted Schools of the Dublin Society which became the School of Design in 1849, and it was during his term that women were first admitted as students.

Alment was chiefly a landscape painter though she also did some portraiture. She was a frequent exhibitor at the Royal Hibernian Academy (from 1858 to 1908), at the Watercolour Society of Ireland and at the Dublin Sketching Club. The majority of her exhibited works were views in Wicklow and Dublin with a particular emphasis on the Dargle and Dodder rivers, and from 1882 views of North Wales occur frequently.

None of these works have been located.   WR

Annesley, Lady Mabel (1881-1959)

Lady Mabel Annesley was the daughter of Hugh, the 5th Earl of Annesley of Castlewellan, county Down.

She attended the Frank Calderon School of Animal Painting in 1895. In 1920-21 she studied wood engraving at the Central School of Arts and Design under Noel Rooke. Mainly interested in wood engraving, Annesley illustrated a number of books in this medium, including a limited edition of *Songs from Robert Burns* for the Golden Cockerel Press.

She was a prominent member of the Belfast Art Society and one of the earliest members of the Society of Wood Engravers. She exhibited in Belfast at her studio in Lombard Street; in Dublin at the Watercolour Society of Ireland in 1923; in London, where she held a one woman show at the Batsford Gallery in 1933 and in Manchester where her engravings were exhibited posthumously in a memorial show at the Whitworth Art Gallery in 1960.

Her work can be seen in the Ulster Museum, Belfast and in the British Museum.   WR

Antrim, Countess of (Angela) (1911-1984)

Lady Antrim was born Angela Sykes, youngest daughter of Sir Mark Sykes, the 6th baronet of Sledmere in Yorkshire. He drew excellent caricatures and wrote a humorous book about military manoeuvres which the Germans took seriously. Although he died when she was only ten, she and her brother Christopher continued this family tradition. She was privately educated until she went to Belgium to train under the sculptor D'Havlosse. She returned to him after a period at the British School in Rome. She then sculpted in a studio near Regent's Park, mostly in stone, and often on a very large scale. A huge anti-Fascist figure she made of a helmeted figure was smashed before the War. In 1934 she married the 8th Earl of Antrim and, at the outbreak of War, the family moved over to Glenarm Castle in county Antrim, where she lived for about thirty years. Towards the end of the war, on a rehabilitating mission for over a year in the Low Countries, she made a disturbing sculpture of a skeletal Mother and (bouncing) Child at Belsen.

From Ireland she carried out a number of public commissions in stone (e.g. St. Joseph's Church, Ballygally, Larne, county Antrim and Parliament Buildings, Newfoundland), portrait busts and painted an extensive series of imposing murals at Glenarm from 1939 onwards. She exhibited with the Royal Hibernian Academy and the Irish Exhibition of Living Art. An accident in 1962 affected her hand so she could no longer carve, only model and have her work cast in bronze.   NGB

See cat. nos. 107-08

Armstrong, Anna Langley, see Nairn, Anna Langley

Bagwell, Lilla see Perry, Lilla

Balfour, Lady Florence see Cole, Lady Florence

Balfour, Mary see Herbert, Mary

Ball, Anne Elizabeth (1808-1872)

Anne was the elder of the two daughters of Bob Stawell Ball and Mary Green; she was born in Cobh, county Cork, and moved with her parents to Youghal in 1815 and thence to Dublin. With her sister Mary, who was born in 1812, Anne shared a passion for natural history, Anne concentrating on plants (especially seaweeds), and Mary on insects and molluscs. They collected specimens which frequently ended up in the natural history cabinets of other prominent Irish naturalists. The Ball sisters were encouraged by their elder brother, Robert, who was widely respected as a natural historian and was a Member of the Royal Irish Academy and a Fellow of the Royal Society of London.

Anne's interest in seaweeds brought her into contact with contemporary botanists, particularly William Henry Harvey — after 1844 Harvey and Robert Ball were both on the staff of Trinity College, the former as Keeper of the Herbarium, the latter as Director of the Museum. Anne contributed records for Harvey's account of Irish seaweeds, which was published in 1836 as part of James Townsend Mackey's *Flora Hibernica,* and she continued to collect during the 1840's.

Miss Ball drew and occasionally painted the seaweeds that she collected; she also used fungi and microscopic organisms as subjects. Several hundred drawings and pen sketches have survived in the National Botanic Gardens, Dublin. ECN

Barry, Moyra A. (1886-1960)

Moyra Barry was born in Dublin, where she trained at the Schools of the Royal Hibernian Academy. Her talent was recognised while she was still a student and she was awarded a number of prizes for drawing and composition including the Taylor Prize. She continued her studies in London at the Slade School and following this she moved to Quito in Ecuador where she taught for some time.

Returning to Dublin, Moyra soon gained recognition as a painter of still-life, landscape, genre and portraiture. Flower painting, however, was her speciality, with chrysanthemums, hydrangea and rhododendrons being her favourite subjects.

She frequently exhibited at the Royal Hibernian Academy between 1908 and 1958 and occasionally at the Watercolour Society of Ireland in the 1940's and 1950's. She also held a number of one-man shows in Dublin and contributed to various international group shows in England, Holland, America and Canada.

Examples of her work are in the National Gallery of Ireland, the Limerick City Art Gallery and the Ulster Museum, Belfast. WR

See cat. no. 103

Barton, Mary Georgina (fl. late 19c.-early 20c.)

Mary Barton was born at Farndreg, Dundalk and studied at the Westminster School of Art and in Rome. She lived in England where she became an associate member of the Society of Women Artists in 1909 and a full member in 1911. She painted landscapes in oils and watercolour. Between 1883 and 1914 she exhibited with the Watercolour Society of Ireland, she also exhibited at the Paris Salon and in England. In 1911 she illustrated and published *Impressions of Mexico with Brush and Pen.* Her work is represented in the Hugh Lane Municipal Gallery, Dublin. SAD

Barton, Rose (1856-1929)

Rose Barton was born in Ireland, the daughter of Augustine Barton, a lawyer of Rochestown, county Tipperary. In 1874 Rose travelled to Brussels with her mother and sister where she received drawing and painting lessons. On her return she studied under Paul Naftel R.W.S. in London and thence went to Paris in the early 1880's where she trained under the popular salon artist Henri Gervex.

The recurring traits that characterise her watercolours are a preoccupation with simple subjects with a sketchy impressionist finish and a preference for bright colours. One of her greatest achievements was the depiction of changing weather conditions; she loved to capture the reflections of objects in the rain or the effect of bright sunlight and especially the mystrerious atmosphere of a fog. Her watercolours were clearly influenced by Turner and Whistler but always remained personal and fresh. The atmospheric and sensitive quality of the paintings can be seen in the context of other Irish women artists of the period, notably Mildred Anne Butler (her lifelong friend), Beatrice Gubbins, Lady Dobbin and Edith Somerville (her cousin).

Rose exhibited widely during her long professional career. She exhibited for the first time in Dublin in 1878 at the Royal Hibernian Academy and thereafter she moved freely between Dublin and London, exhibiting in both capitals. The 1880's was a period of development for Rose, during which time she showed her work at the Society of Lady Artists, the Royal Institute and the Royal Academy. Following her election as an Associate of the Royal Watercolour Society in 1893, she exhibited mainly with that body.

In 1898 Rose illustrated the book *Picturesque Dublin, Old and New,* by Francis Gerard, with ninety-one reproductions of grey wash drawings of views in and around Dublin. She embarked on a far more ambitious task in 1904 — the text and illustration of her own book, *Familiar London.* The book remains an impressive achievement, with over fifty colour illustrations of charming, atmospheric views of London. The text, though somewhat sentimental, gives us a fascinating insight into the working methods and attitudes of the artist.

By 1906 Rose was firmly established in London. In 1911 she was elected the first lady member of the Royal Watercolour Society. She died at the age of seventy-three at her home in Knightsbridge.

Examples of her work are in many public and private collections including the National Gallery of Ireland, the Crawford Municipal Art Gallery, Cork, the Ulster Museum and Hugh Lane Municipal Gallery, Dublin. RR

See cat. nos. 44-46

Beckett, Frances (1880-1951)

Known as Cissie Beckett, she was born in Dublin, daughter of William Beckett. Her father built many fine houses around Dublin, including the family home, Earlsfield, the present British Embassy. She studied at the Metropolitan School of Art, a contemporary of Beatrice Elvery (later Lady Glenavy), Estella Solomons and Lily Williams, with whom she exhibited at the Young Irish Artists' Exhibition in Dublin, in 1903. The following year she went with Elvery and Solomons to Paris, and attended life classes at Colarossi's. She exhibited in the Royal Hibernian Academy as Fannie Beckett; first in 1897, and then from 1901-1908, showing mainly portraits, including one of Estella Solomons. In 1908, she married William Abraham Sinclair, an art dealer and friend of

Orpen, whose father was a painter. They lived at Baily, Howth, gathering painters and literati around them for the next thirty years.

Her early work shows much in common with that of Estella Solomons, in its Rembrandtish introspection, and psychological use of light, though she worked with a broad brush, and used less detail. After her marriage she painted little.   HP

See cat. no. 60

Benson, Charlotte E. (1846-1893)

Charlotte Benson was born in Dublin, the daughter of a well-known surgeon Dr. Charles Benson who was president of the Royal College of Surgeons (1854-5), and the sister of Mary Kate Benson.

Although listed as an amateur by Strickland, she did attend the Dublin Society's School for two years where she distinguished herself by winning a number of prizes. She was a frequent exhibitor at the Royal Hibernian Academy from 1873 to 1891, at the Watercolour Society of Ireland in 1879 and 1882 and at the Dublin Sketching Club from 1888 to 1892. Her work included views in Wicklow, Kilkenny and Connemara as well as views from the continent and England. In 1887 she exhibited a view of the Nilgiri Hills following a visit she had made to her brother in India.

None of her works have been located.   WR

Benson, Mary Kate (d.1921)

Mary Kate Benson and her sister Charlotte were both painters and regular exhibitors at the Royal Hibernian Academy. Mary went to England and studied under Herkomer and Calderon; then to Paris, where she studied with Lazare. At home she and Charlotte lived at 42 Fitzwilliam Square in Dublin. She did some portraits of her family, but was principally a landscapist, painting in a variety of locations in Ireland, Wales and England. In the 1870's she painted Waterloo Bridge and St. Paul's Cathedral. She first exhibited at the Royal Hibernian Academy in 1873 and continued to show there every year (except on three occasions) until 1906. She also showed at the Amateur Art Society, and the Nineteenth Century Art Society.

She travelled much on the continent. She and Charlotte were in Belgium in the late 1880's, painting in the Ardennes, and also near Grindelwald, and in common with many Irish artists of this period, she painted a 'Belgian Interior'. In c.1892 she was in Brittany, painting interiors, figure studies, village and market scenes there. Paintings of Quimperlé and other Breton scenes were shown at the RHA, 1892-93. After Charlotte's death in c.1892, she continued travelling, to Cornwall in c.1893 (painting at St. Ives), and in c.1896, to Normandy (for example at Montreuil). At home she painted scenes along the River Liffey, and at Renvyle in Connemara.

In c.1899 she moved from Fitzwilliam Square to Howth, and in 1906 she seems to have been living in Bath. Her final painting at the RHA (as her first exhibit there, thirty years earlier) was a scene in Donegal. She died on 21 March, 1921.   JC

See cat. no. 35.

Bewick, Pauline (b.1935)

Born in 1935, in Northumbria, England; 1938-1946 brought up on a farm in Kenmare, county Kerry. Then she and her mother travelled Ireland and England, living in caravans and house boats. Constantly moving, her early education focussed more on art than other subjects; 1952 she completed her studies at the National College of Art and Design, Dublin. She continued to paint and also design stage sets.

In 1973, she moved with her husband and two children from Dublin to county Kerry.

Exhibitions: 1957, Clog Gallery, Dublin; 1959, Parkway Gallery, London; 1960, Parkway Gallery, London; 1965-1977, Dawson Gallery, Dublin; 1968, New Gallery, Belfast; 1972, Italian Cultural Institute, Dublin; 1974, Cork Arts Society Gallery, Cork; 1976, Kennys Gallery, Galway; 1978, Cork Arts Society Gallery, Cork; 1980, Taylor Galleries, Dublin; 1981-82, selected to represent Ireland at the European Graphic Art Biennial (Biennale Europäische) Baden Baden. Exhibition also went to Art Bureau Charlottenburg, West Berlin; 1986, Retrospective Exhibition, Guinness Hop Store, Dublin; Crawford Municipal Art Gallery, Cork and Ulster Museum, Belfast.

Collections: Arts Council of Ireland; Arts Council of Northern Ireland; Bank of Ireland; Coras Tráchtála; P.J. Carroll & Co. Ltd., Dublin; EEC Brussels; The Haverty Trust; Municipal Art Gallery, Cork; Overseas Publications, Ireland; Office of Public Works, Dublin; Trust Houses, Dublin Airport.

Blackham, Dorothy (1896-1975)

Dorothy Isabel Blackham was born in Dublin on 1 March 1896, the daughter of the Chief Cashier at Kingsbridge. She trained in Dublin at the Royal Hibernian Academy with Dermod O'Brien from 1916 to 1921, and at the Metropolitan School of Art and in London at Goldsmith's College from 1921 to 1922. The Tailteann Festivals of 1928 and 1932 saw her awarded medals for her works. She also taught, but never gained a large following. During the 1939-1945 war she worked in Gibraltar, amongst refugees. After the war she married Elsner Stewart, but she continued to paint under her maiden name. At first they lived in London, but then moved to Donaghadee, county Down. She painted nearly until her own death in 1975, in spite of being severely crippled by arthritis.

While at the Royal Hibernian Academy she took particular interest in the design of posters. Her subjects tend to be firmly rooted in Ireland, especially the West and the North, although she also took inspiration from scenes in London, as, for example, *House Painting in Paddington,* in England, in Scotland and on the Continent. She also did scraper-board drawings for *The Bell* magazine and Christmas cards, as well as work in oils, watercolours and tempera. Mary Swanzy said of her work: 'she knows everything,' a great compliment from such an artist. Amongst her friends were Mainie Jellett, by whom she was considerably influenced, and the Yeats sisters, Lily and Lolly, for whom she did a number of designs, for the Cuala and Clune Presses.

She exhibited widely, at the Royal Academy, the Royal Society of British Artists, the Ulster Academy, the Ulster Women Artists' Group, the Royal Hibernian Academy, the Watercolour Society of Ireland and the Arts and Crafts Society of Ireland.

Examples of her work are in the Hugh Lane Municipal Gallery, Dublin.   NA

See cat. no. 115

Blake, Lady (Edith) (1845-1926)

Edith Osborne, born at Newtown Anner, Clonmel, was the elder daughter of Ralph Bernal who assumed the surname Osborne on his marriage in 1844 to Catherine Isabella Osborne, the only child of Sir Thomas Osborne of Newtown Anner, county Tipperary. She was the sister of Grace Osborne, who became Duchess of St. Albans and her childhood influences are discussed in her sister's biography. In 1874 Edith married Henry Arthur Blake who served in the British Colonial Service; he was knighted in 1888, and served as Governor of the Bahamas, Newfoundland, Jamaica, Hong Kong, and finally Ceylon.

As she accompanied her husband on his overseas postings, Edith Blake lived in various different parts of the British Empire and had opportunities to paint the flora and fauna of subtropical and tropical regions. Among other places, she lived in the Bahamas (1888-1887) and Newfoundland (1887-1888) and was in Jamaica from 1889 to 1897, Hong Kong from 1897 to 1903, and in Ceylon from 1903 to 1907.

Edith Blake began painting about 1865 and certainly continued into the early 1900's. She was keenly interested in the plants and the insects of the various countries where she lived. She painted a beautiful series of watercolours showing the Lepidoptera (butterflies and moths) of Jamaica at various stages during their individual life-cycles and with their foodplants.

Most of Lady Blake's numerous watercolours of the flowers of Jamaica and Hong Kong are in private collections; none have been published. There are also 195 paintings of Jamaican Lepidoptera in the British Museum (Natural History), London.
                                                                          ECN

See cat. no. 31.

Bogan, Vivienne (b. 1951)

Born in Limerick. 1979, completed her studies at Limerick School of Art. She moved to King Street Studio, Glasgow and then to Yerewaw, Armenia, where she had her first one woman show. She returned to Ireland in 1981.

Selected Exhibitions: 1981, Guinness Peat Aviation Emerging Artists, Tulfarris EVA, Limerick; Irish Exhibition of Living Art, Douglas Hyde Gallery, Dublin; Six Limerick Artists, AIB, Limerick; Women's Exhibition, Belltable, Limerick; Group Exhibition, Valerie Porter Gallery, Galway; 1982, Belltable Foursight, Arts Council Touring Exhibition; Oireachtas, Bank of Ireland, Dublin; Limerick Artists, Castle Gallery, Kilkenny and Tulfarris; GPA Emerging Artists, Douglas Hyde Gallery, Dublin; 1983, Beltaine, Limerick Artists, Limerick and Quimper, Brittany;

1984, Ennistymon '84; Wexford Arts Centre, 10th Anniversary; Arnotts Landscape Exhibition, Dublin; 1985, Group Show, Grafton Gallery, Dublin; Two-Woman Show, Wexford Arts Centre; The Mustard Seed, Four Artists, Adare; Group Show, Ballycasey Gallery, Shannon.

Collections: Allied Irish Bank; An Chomhairle Ealaíon/The Arts Council; NIHE, Limerick; Council of Europe; Guinness Peat Aviation; Museé des Beaux Arts, Quimper; Gilbey Ireland Ltd.

Bolay, Veronica (contemp. artist)

Born in Hamburg, West Germany. National College of Art and Design, 1958-1963, Diploma; 1964-69, worked as a theatre-costume designer in Cuxhaven, Hamburg, Aachen (Aix-la-Chapelle); 1971, settled in Dublin, Ireland.

Solo-Shows: 1975, Lantern Theatre, Dublin; 1977, Setanta Gallery, Dublin; 1977, Setanta Gallery, Dublin; 1981, Lad Lane Gallery, Dublin; 1983, Lincoln Gallery, Dublin; 1984, Sligo Arts Gallery, Yeats Building; 1987, Grafton Gallery, Dublin.

Group Shows: 1975, Creative Women, Arts Council Gallery, Belfast; 1978, Women-Show, Project Gallery, Dublin; Brucker Gallery, Munich; SADE — Cork; 1979, Vierlanden Gallery, Hamburg; 1982, CAN — Cork, Cork Arts Society (Two-person Show) Amsterdam, in conjunction with the Treasure of Ireland Show; 1976-1986, participated in all shows of the Independent Artists, Oireachtas, Figurative Image. Showed at EVA Limerick. Open Exhibition Claremorris; 1985, Festival celtique, Lorient, France representing Ireland; Graphic-Show, Milwaukee, USA; 1986, The Artist and the Bomb, Dublin, Cork and 87 Moskau.

Collections: GPA Collection, Jurys Hotel Dublin and Cork; Vincent Ferguson; NIHE, Dublin; Oliver Dowling; Regina Mundis College, Cork; Cork Arts Society; Melanie le Broquy and private collections in Ireland, Berlin, West Germany, England, France and Brazil. 1986: 4 large stained-glass windows for 'Hotel Imperial', Dundalk, commission.

Others: 1985 TV-film made by West German TV.

Boyle, Alicia (contemp. artist)

Born in Bangkok of Irish parents. Childhood in Ireland and London. Earliest painting made in Limavady, county Derry. Studied in London, won two Scholarships at Byam Shaw School of Art. Guest artist at School of Fine Art in Greece.

One Man Exhibitions: in Ireland: Arts Council of Northern Ireland, Belfast, 1950, 1952, 1959, 1963, 1967; North West Arts Trust, Derry, 1967. In England: Peter Jones Gallery, London; Leger Galleries, London; Walker's Galleries, London; Midland Group of Artists, Nottingham, Northampton Art Gallery.

Works also shown at: Leicester Galleries, London; Roland, Browse and Delbanco, London; etc.

Prizewinner: Open Painting Competition, Arts Council of Northern Ireland, 1962.

Collections: Ulster Museum, Belfast; Arts Council of Northern Ireland; North West Arts Trust, Derry; Northampton Art Gallery; Nottingham Castle Art Gallery; Herbert Art Gallery, Coventry; Lake District Art Gallery Trust, Kendal and in private collections in Ireland, England, USA, Sweden etc., also for Education Committees and Schools in England.

Boyle, Mary see Darby, Mary

Bradford, Martha see Wilmot, Martha

Brandt, Ruth (b.1936)

Born 1936 and educated in Dublin. Her mother Muriel Brandt ARCA, RHA, was a portrait, landscape and mural painter, her father a graphic designer. She studied painting at the National College of Art and Design in Dublin, where she was awarded a three-year scholarship. Subsequently spent a year in Florence on an Italian government grant. For a number of years after this her career was divided between free-lance illustration and lettering, and part-time teaching at the National College of Art. During these years she exhibited at various group exhibitions including the Royal Hibernian Academy and the Irish Exhibition of Living Art; was occasionally associated with Dolmen Press publications; was commissioned for various architectural lettering projects by Liam McCormick and Associates, Derry, which included work in his churches in Creeslough and Glenties, county Donegal and the new Meteorological Offices, Glasnevin, Dublin, and stained glass windows at Artane Oratory, Dublin.

In 1973 gave up most free-lance work and returned to etching at the Graphic Studio, Dublin. Became a member of the Independent Artists Group, and since 1976 lectures full-time at the National College of Art and Design, Dublin.

She has had one woman exhibitions in the Setanta Gallery in 1978 and the Lincoln Gallery in 1982.

Brennan, Cecily (b.1955)

Born in 1955 in Athenry, county Galway; 1978, graduated from the National College of Art & Design, Dublin.

One woman exhibitions: 1982, Project Arts Centre, Dublin; 1985, Taylor Galleries, Dublin.

Group Exhibitions: 1978, Best Graduate Show, Project Arts Centre, Dublin; NCAD Staff/Student Show, Douglas Hyde Gallery, Dublin; 1979, Limerick Exhibition of Visual Art; 1980, Independent Artists, (82, 83); 1983, Graphic Studio Touring Print Exhibition; Cibeal Cincise, Kenmare, county Kerry; Figurative Image, Bank of Ireland, Dublin; Black Church Print Studio Exhibition, Triskel Arts Centre, Cork; University Collage, Collection of University College, Dublin; 1984, International Exhibition of Painting, Cagnes-sur-Mer, France; 1986, NCAD Decade Show, Guinness Hop Store.

Collections: An Chomhairle Ealaíon/The Arts Council, Dublin; University College, Dublin; Bank of Ireland; Allied Irish Bank; Allied Irish Investment Bank; Algemene Bank Nederland; Contemporary Irish Arts Society; P. J. Murphy; V. A. Ferguson.

Brett, Rosa (1829-1882)

Rosa Brett was born in Dublin and although her parents were Irish the family went to live in Kent while Rosa was still a child.

Judging from her early sketch books she appears to have started painting in earnest around the time of her twenty first birthday in 1850. She exhibited at the Royal Academy from 1858 to 1862 under the pseudonym of Rosarius, where according to her brother John (also an artist) her work was enthusiastically received by the Pre-Raphaelites. Indeed her detailed realistic style had much in common with theirs. She continued to exhibit, though only occasionally, during the 1860's and 1870's at the Royal Academy and at various provincial exhibitions, for example in Liverpool and Manchester.

Her preferred subject matter was landscape and natural still life of which over eighty examples are known. Despite the competent and professional quality of her work she never gained any official recognition or much public acclaim.

Information on her career and work has only recently come to light (see Pamela Gerrish Nunn, 'Rosa Brett, Pre-Raphaelite', *The Burlington Magazine,* (October 1984), p. 630).

All of her existing works are in private collections in Britain.

WR

Bridle, Kathleen (b.1897)

Having studied at the Metropolitan School of Art, Dublin, and the Royal College of Art, Kathleen Bridle settled in Fermanagh in 1926. An active and popular art-teacher for many years, her pupils included William Scott and T. P. Flanagan. She is an academician of the Royal Ulster Academy. MA

See cat. no. 110

Le Brocquy, Melanie (b.1919)

Born in Dublin in 1919; she studied at the National College of Art, Dublin, the Royal Academy School and the Ecole des Beaux Arts, Geneva; 1981, became a member of Aosdana.

1937, exhibited with the Royal Hibernian Academy, and subsequently in 1938, 1939, 1941, 1968, 1974, 1975, 1982, 1983, 1984; 1942, joint exhibition with Louis le Brocquy, Dublin; 1943, exhibited with the Irish Exhibition of Living Art, and subsequently in 1965, 1967, 1971; 1962, 3rd Biennale Christlicher Kunst der Gegenwart, Salzburg; 1968, Art in Worship, Belfast and Dublin; 1972, Oireachtas, Dublin, and subsequently 1972, 1973, 1975; 1973, joint exhibition with William Scott, Dawson Gallery, Dublin; 1974-75, Contemporary Irish Sculpture, Dublin; 1975, Creative Women, Belfast; 1976, joint exhibition with Patrick Heron, Dawson Gallery, Dublin; 1978-84, Taylor Galleries Group Exhibition, Dublin; 1982, International Art Auction for Amnesty, Dublin; 1984, EVA, Limerick; 1986, One-woman show, Taylor Galleries, Dublin.

Collections: National Self-Portrait Collection; Arts Council of Ireland; Dublin Corporation; Municipal Gallery of Modern Art, Dublin; Crawford Municipal Gallery, Cork.

Brooks, Sarah Theresa (1850-1928)

From 1874 Miss Brooks lived in one of the most remote parts of Western Australia. With her mother and older brother, John Paul, she set up home at Balbinia, twenty-five miles from Mount

Ragged near the coast of the Great Australian Bight and over five hundred miles east of the capital of Western Australia, Perth. 'They were gentle-folk and totally unfitted for such a venture in that harsh, waterless country.' The Brookses survived — just — and Sarah lived the rest of her life in that isolated, scrub-encircled homestead. She died in Norseman in September 1928 aged 78.

Sarah Theresa Brooks arrived in Australia before she was one year old; her parents had emigrated from Ireland and settled at Geelong, Victoria, in eastern Australia. Sarah's father, Henry Ferby Brooks was a graduate of Trinity College, Dublin, and her mother was Emily Henrietta Donovan from Cobh, county Cork.

Henry Brooks died within a few months of the family's arrival at Geelong, leaving his young widow to look after two very small children, Mrs. Brooks decided to establish a small school which flourished for a time, and she ensured that her son and daughter both received excellent education. Sarah had art lessons from Edmund Sasse — these cost £1. 6. 6d. per term — and her accounts show that she subscribed to such periodicals as *Nature and Art*; she also learned to speak at least seven languages.

Details of Sarah Brooks' artistic work are scanty but several of her paintings, including at least one landscape, survive in private collections in Western Australia. Whe she was living at Balbinia in Western Australia, Miss Brooks collected the local plants for Baron Ferdinand von Mueller, the government botanist in Melbourne, and she is commemorated in two Australian wildflowers, *Scaevola brooksiana* and *Hakea brooksiana*.   ECN

Brown, Deborah (b.1927)
Born 1927 in Belfast; 1946, Belfast College of Art; 1947-50, National College of Art & Design, Dublin and subsequently Paris; 1966-69, Member of the Women's International Art Club; Member of the Free Painters and Sculptors, London.

One Woman Exhibitions: 1951, CEMA Gallery, Belfast; 1955, British Council, Glasgow; 1956, Ulster Museum, Belfast; 1959-64, New Vision Centre Gallery, London; 1962, Arts Council Gallery, Belfast; 1964, New Gallery, Belfast; 1966-77, David Hendriks Gallery, Dublin; 1974, Tom Caldwell Gallery, Belfast.

Group Shows: 1948, Royal Hibernian Academy, Dublin; 1949, Royal Society of Women Artists, London; Royal Ulster Academy, Belfast; 1951, Royal Society of British Artists, London; 1960, Painting by Ulster Artists, Arts Council; 1961-75, Irish Exhibition of Living Art, Dublin; 1965, Arnolfini Gallery, Bristol, Four Painters; 1966-69, Women's International Art Club, London and Bradford; 1966, Modern Irish Painting, Ulster Museum, Belfast; 1967, Women's International Art Club Exhibition, Galerie Greuze, Paris; 1968, Ulster Painting '68, Arts Council Gallery, Belfast; 1969, Contemporary Irish Painting, Park Square Gallery, Leeds; 1969-79, Modern Irish Painting Exhibition in Europe; 1971, Irish Imagination, Rosc 71, Dublin, Boston, Philadelphia, Washington; 1972, Gordon Lambert Collection, Municipal Gallery of Modern Art, Dublin and Ulster Museum, Belfast; 1974, Irish Directions, USA tour; 1980, A Sense of Ireland, London; 1984, Rosc 84, Dublin.

Collections: Arts Council of Northern Ireland, Ulster Museum,

Belfast; Municipal Gallery of Modern Art, Dublin; An Chomhairle Ealaíon/The Arts Council; BBC, N. Ireland; RTE, Dublin; Great Southern Hotels; P. J. Carroll & Co. Ltd., Bank of Ireland, Dublin; Lombard & Ulster Bank, Dublin.

Burke, Mary (b.1959)
Born 1959; 1982, BA Degree, National College of Art & Design, Dublin.

One Woman Exhibitions: 1984, Lincoln Gallery, Dublin; 1985, Belltable Arts Centre, Limerick.

Group Exhibitions: 1980, Independent Artists, Dublin, and 1982; Oireachtas, Dublin, and 1982, 83, 84, 85, 86; 1981, Claremorris, and 1982, 83, 84; 1982, Royal Hibernian Academy, Dublin, and 1983, 84, 85, 86; 1983, GPA Exhibition, Dublin; 1984, EVA, Limerick; 1986, Four Views, Touring Exhibiting; NCAD, Decade Show, Guinness Hop Store.

Collections: Adshel; CIE; Ulster Breweries; Irish Pension Fund; Property Unit Trust; Tony Ryan (GPA).

Burnside, Vivien (b.1958)
Born 1958 in county Derry; 1981, BA Fine Art, Ulster University; 1982, Artist in Residence, Maysfield Leisure Centre; 1982-85, Secretary, Artists Collective of N. Ireland. Since 1983 working in Arts Council Gallery, Belfast.

One Woman Exhibitions: 1983, Drawings, Riverside Theatre, Coleraine; Wall Installations, Grapevine Arts Centre, Dublin; 1984, 'Figures', Crescent Arts Centre, Belfast; 1987, Grafton Gallery, Dublin (in August).

Group Exhibitions: 1981, Aspects of Drawing, Maysfield Leisure Centre, Belfast; 1982, Four Artists, Newcastle-upon-Tyne, England; Six plus Two, Queen's University, Belfast; Exhibition of Visual Art, Limerick; 1984, Irish Graduates, Visitor's Centre, Enniskillen; Irish Exhibition of Living Art, Dublin; 1985, Figureworks, Bluecoat Gallery, Liverpool; 1986, Collective Images, touring N. Ireland; 1987, 'Artists from Queen Street Studios Belfast', Limerick; Two person show, Newry Arts Centre.

Bushe, Letitia (fl.1731-d.1757)
She was the youngest daughter of Arthur Bushe of Dangan, county Kilkenny, Secretary of Commissioners of Revenue. Since she is described on 25 November 1731 by Mrs. Delany as 'a gay, good-humoured, innocent girl, without the least conceit of her beauty; . . . she paints delightfully', it may be surmised that she was born about 1710. Letty was a close friend of Mrs. Delany's from her first visit to Ireland in 1731. Later when Mrs. Delany married Dean Delany and came to live near Dublin from 1744-45, Letty Bushe frequently stayed with her for weeks or months on end. It appears from Mrs. Delany's letters that she stayed regularly with other families as well, though from time to time it appears she lived alone in an apartment in Dublin. Her company was clearly in demand. On 19 January 1744/45 Mrs. Delany remarks to her sister: '. . . for besides her ingenuity, she has a turn for conversation that is not common, and her good-humour is inexhaustible'.

She painted in both oils and watercolours and also did miniatures but from all accounts landscape painting appears to have been her prime interest. Her work was much in demand in the circle of her friends. Lady Knapton of Abbeyleix wrote, probably sometime in the mid-1750's, saying: 'I am afraid E. Roden will be very angry wth. me for a request I have to make her, wh is that she will let me keep the Drawing Letty is doing for her as it is the only thing of consequence she has attempted. I cannot think of parting with it and it will be no Loss to Ly R. as she is just going to begin a Landscape in Colors which will be prettier'. (Northern Ireland Public Record Office).

It is not known where Letty Bushe learnt her art but it has been suggested on stylistic grounds that she learnt from Bernard Lens (1682-1740) or one of his sons, Andrew Benjamin (1713-1770) or Peter Paul. He was in Dublin about 1737, though there is no evidence that he taught when in Ireland, and a view of Bray by Letty dated 1736 does not show any marked difference in style from her later work.

She had visited England in 1743 when she painted a very competent view of London from Hampstead and views in Bath and Bristol. It is not clear whether her plans for other visits to England ever came to fruition. In 1751 two of her drawings were engraved as frontispieces for Richard Barton's *Lectures in Natural Philosophy . . . on Lough Neagh* and his *Some remarks towards a full description of Upper and Lower Lough Lene, Near Killarney, in the County of Kerry.* Of the latter engraving, Mrs. Delany in February 1751, remarks that 'the engraver hath not done justice to the delicacy of her pencil' and it has a claim to be the earliest depiction of Killarney known.

Letty Bushe died on 17 November 1757 in Dawson Street, Dublin. AOC and KOG

See cat. nos. 4-5.

Butler, Lady (Elizabeth) (1846-1933)

Elizabeth Thompson was born at Lausanne in 1846. Her family travelled a great deal, and she spent her youth between England and the continent of Europe. She and her sister Alice (the poet Alice Meynell) were educated by their father, who encouraged Elizabeth in her passion for drawing. She trained at South Kensington and in Florence under Giuseppe Bellucci. Her painting, *Calling the roll after an engagement, Crimea* (known as *The Roll Call*) was hung on the line at the Royal Academy in 1874, and brought her almost instant success. From then on she concentrated on military subjects., She was converted to the Roman Catholic Church in 1873, and in 1877 she married the Irish Catholic Major William Butler, later General Sir William Butler, GCB, KCB. She accompanied her husband on campaigns abroad as he pursued a distinguished military career, bore him six children, and continued to achieve enormous success as a painter. Lady Butler spent the last years of her life at Gormanston, county Meath, the home of her youngest daughter.

From the time of her marriage Elizabeth Butler seems to have kept up a close relationship with Ireland, and to have stayed frequently at Bansha Castle, county Tipperary, the family home.

She exhibited at the Royal Hibernian Academy from 1892, and, in 1907 she became a trustee of the National Gallery of Ireland, having retired with her husband to Bansha in 1905. She painted two major works with Irish subjects. *Listed for the Connaught Rangers* (RA 1879), shows two vigorous young peasants under rather casual military escort. The scene is set in a broad mountainy landscape, with a ruined cottage in the foreground, and one of the young men looks wistfully back at a cluster of cabins in the valley. Though the scene is set in Connaught it was painted in Kerry, and the rainwashed landscape is vividly evoked. It is an anecdotal picture, perhaps rather sentimental. Her most important Irish picture, *Evicted* (RA 1890, RHA 1892, now in University College, Dublin) is neither. A woman, bare-headed and bare-footed stands starkly highlighted against the gable walls of a ruined cottage, while the eviction party disappears down the valley. The setting is stark and inimical, and is treated, like the figure, in free and energetic brushwork. Lady Butler said of her military pictures that she did not wish to portray the glory of war, but its pathos and heroism. The same could be said of *Evicted,* which has a strong expression of romantic nationalism surprising in the wife of a general in the British army, but perhaps explained by the fact that the Butlers were Catholic. *Evicted* was painted in Ireland in 1889, and hung over the chimney piece at Dover Castle where they lived when Sir William was Constable of Dover, 1896-1905. Examples of her work are found in the Tate Gallery, Leeds City Art Galleries and the National Gallery of Victoria, Melbourne. JS

Butler, Mildred Anne (1858-1941)

Mildred Anne Butler was the youngest daughter of Captain Henry Butler, a grandson of the 11th Viscount Mountgarret. Mildred Anne was probably encouraged to paint from an early age by her father, who was himself an interesting amateur artist favouring subjects from nature and, in particular, exotic plants and animals which he encountered during his periods abroad.

Mildred Anne's own artistic training began in the 1880's in London where she studied with Paul Jacob Naftel the English watercolourist. She continued her studies with William Frank Calderon who specialised in animal painting and later opened a school of animal painting. In the summers of 1894 and 1895 Mildred Anne was in Newlyn in Cornwall where she studied under the Irish artist Norman Garstin. Newlyn at that time was the centre for a group of artists interested in *plein-air* subjects many of whom had previously studied in France. Mildred Anne's contact with the Newlyn School was to remain an important influence on her work throughout her life.

Following her stay at Newlyn, she returned to her family home at Kilmurry, county Kilkenny where she remained, apart from frequent trips to England and the continent, until her death.

Her range of work was very much dominated by the theme of nature. Views of pasture land with cows, and gardens with colourful borders of flowers predominate. She also did genre views of villages and towns on the continent. It was Kilmurry, however, the house, its garden and surroundings that was her great passion and some of her best paintings are of birds and animals which she observed at Kilmurry. These she depicted with an uncanny degree of realism and expression.

She first exhibited at the Dudley Gallery in Piccadilly and continued to exhibit throughout her life, though she had virtually stopped painting by the 1930's due to arthritis. She exhibited in both Ireland and England in various galleries and institutions including the Royal Hibernian Academy, the Watercolour Society of Ireland, the Belfast Ramblers, the Royal Academy and the Royal Watercolour Society of which she became an associate in 1896 and a full member in 1937.

During her career, Mildred Anne proved herself to be not only a skilled artist but also a keen business woman capable of marketing her watercolours successfully. Among her patrons were Queen Mary, the Grand Duke of Hesse and in 1896 her exhibit at the Royal Academy *The Morning Bath* was the first work by a woman artist to be purchased by the trustees of the Chantry Bequest. This painting is now in the Tate Gallery. She is also represented in the National Gallery of Ireland, the Ulster Museum and the Hugh Lane Municipal Gallery, Dublin.   WR

See cat. nos. 47-49.

Campbell, Beatrice see Glenavy, Lady (Beatrice)

Carlisle, Anne (b.1956)

Born in 1956 at Templepatrick, county Antrim, Northern Ireland; 1976-79, Ulster College of Art and Design, Belfast; 1979-80, Chelsea College of Art, London; 1980-81, Travelling in USA and Canada on Arts Council Award. Alice Berger Hammerschlag Travel Scholarship; 1980-84, based and working in Belfast.

One Person Shows: 1981, Recent Work, Octagon Gallery, Belfast; 1983, 'Winging It', Octagon Gallery, Belfast; 1984, Recent Work, Arts Council Gallery, Belfast.

Group Shows: 1979, Five Ulster Artists, Arts Council Touring Exhibition. Interaction Project Arts Centre, Dublin; 1980, Brunel University, Cooper's Hill, Middlesex; Irish Living Art, Douglas Hyde Gallery, Dublin; John Moore's XII, Walker Gallery, Liverpool; Crossing, Forebank Gallery, Dundee; 1981, Irish Living Art, Douglas Hyde Gallery, Dublin; Aspects of Drawing, Maysfield Leisure Centre, Belfast; 1982, Contemporary Irish Drawing, The Robert Hull Fleming Museum, University of Vermont, USA; SADE Sculpture and Drawing Exhibition, Crawford Municipal Gallery, Cork; Small Works, Anderstown Leisure Centre, Belfast; Artists Incorporated, St. Paul's Gallery, Leeds; Ulster Places, Arts Council Touring Exhibition; Douglas Hyde Gallery, Dublin; EVA Exhibition of Visual Art, Municipal Gallery, Limerick; The Long Acre, 8 Weeks 8 Works, Installation, Art and Research Exchange, Belfast; 1983, EVA Past Prizewinners, Arts Council Gallery, Belfast; Municipal Gallery Pery Square, Limerick; Guinness Peat Aviation Exhibition for Emerging Artists, Douglas Hyde Gallery, Dublin; 1984, Works on Paper, Triskel Arts Centre, Cork. Hendriks Gallery, Dublin; 1986, Woman on Woman, Fenderesky Gallery, Belfast.

Collections: Arts Council of Northern Ireland; Arts Council

of Ireland (An Chomhairle Ealaíon); The Ulster Museum; Stokes Kennedy Crowley; Guinness Peat Aviation; Gordon Lambert; Northern Ireland Housing Executive; also in private collections in the UK, USA and Ireland.

Carmen, Cathy (b.1952)

Born 1952 in Portlaoise; 1969-73, studied National College of Art & Design, Dublin; 1976-77, studied Dun Laoghaire Arts School.

Group Exhibitions: 1977, Oasis Sculpture Exhibition, St. Anne's Park, Dublin; 1978-79, Lincoln Gallery, Dublin; 1978-81, Independent Artists Annual Exhibition, Dublin; 1982-84, Independent Artists Annual Sculpture Exhibition, Marlay Park, Dublin; 1981, Shape Exhibition for the Blind, Dublin; 1984, October Exhibition, Temple Bar Gallery, Dublin; 1985, Temple Bar Gallery, Dublin.

One Woman Exhibitions: 1984, Project Arts Centre, Dublin; 1986, Grafton Gallery, Dublin.

Collections: Marlay Park, Dublin; Bank of Ireland, Dublin; Vincent Ferguson, Dublin.

Caulfield, Mrs. (fl. 1774-1778)

Mrs. Caulfield is mentioned as being a most gifted artist by the Rev. Dr. Campbell in his *Philosophical survey of the South of Ireland* (1778). According to him, she excelled in drawing, painting in oils and watercolour, modelling in clay and wax and embroidery. She received a silver palette from the Dublin Society in February, 1774 for her 'ingenious needle-work'; this, however, is the only other known reference to her artistic abilities.   WR

Charleville, Countess of (Catherine Maria) (1762-1851)

Born Catherine Maria Dawson, she was brought up at 54 Marlborough Street in Dublin by her grandmother, and educated at the Collège Royal, Toulouse between 1778-81. In 1787 she married James Tisdall in county Louth. He died ten years later and in 1798 she married Charles William Bury, Baron Tullamore, a graduate of Dublin University, who became the 1st Earl of Charleville of the 2nd Creation in 1806, and subsequently a Fellow of the Royal Society and President of the Royal Irish Academy. His accomplished amateur designs for the Gothick revival castle they began to build c.1800 near Tullamore, county Offaly can be compared with watercolour designs for windows at Charleville Castle by Lady Charleville in the Murray collection (Irish Architectural Archive, Dublin).

Professor Warwick Bond (*Marlay Papers*, 1937) remarks that she was respected for her strong intellectual tastes and that she 'painted a good deal'. Apart from the Murray collection, a collection of her pencil drawings, including views of the park at Charleville with its ancient oak trees, is to be seen at Charleville in the collection of Michael McMullen, Esq. Lady Morgan wrote imploring Lady Charleville for a picture, 'I have my boudoir full of the offerings of foreign artists; but nothing of nature, of Irish talent'. She was a close friend of Lady Louisa Conolly of Castletown and corresponded frequently with Lady Morgan, Maria Edgeworth, Henry Grattan and his uncle, Dr. Marlay. Her manners were described by a contemporary as 'Irish and not exactly the sort that pleased . . . but after many years' acquaintance the excellence of her heart, her sense, her wit, and friendship, has compleatly attached us to her for her own sake. . . . She is in love with her lord . . . They are very rich, tolerably recherché in London, and want no help in worldly affairs'.

Her grandson, Brinsley Marlay, endowed the Fitzwilliam Museum at Cambridge. NGB

See cat. no. 20.

Chatterton, Nora S. (20th century)

Nora Chatterton, a landscape painter working in both oils and watercolours exhibited at the Royal Hibernian Academy between 1936 and 1939 a number of views of county Wicklow (including *Looking North towards the Scalp* and *Glencullen*) and other parts of Ireland.

She is represented in the Hugh Lane Municipal Gallery, Dublin. WR

Chenevix-Trench, Francesca see Trinseach, Sadhbh

Chester, Eileen see Murray, Eileen

Chewett, Jocelyn (1906-1979)

Born in 1906 near Toronto, Canada; 1913, came to England with her parents; 1927, entered Slade School of Fine Art, London, to study painting under Henry Tonks, but later returned to sculpture; 1931, left the Slade and went to Paris to work with Brancusi and Zadkine; 1935, returned to England and married the painter Stephen Gilbert; they settled in France in 1938; 1940, came to Ireland with her husband and spent the war years there exhibiting with the White Stag Group; 1945, returned to Paris and settled there for the rest of her life; c.1950, she was influenced by the Russian Suprematist painter Kasimir Malevich and, later, by the Belgian sculptor Georges Vantongerloo whom she met in about 1952.

Exhibitions: c.1935, at the Artists' International Association, London; at the Salon des Artists Français, Paris and at the Salon de Tuileries, Paris; 1940-44, with the White Stag Group, Dublin; 1945, Paris, frequently in group exhibitions from this date onwards; 1979, June, died in London.

Christen, Madame see Thompson, Sydney Mary

Christian, Clara see McCarthy, Clara

Clarke, Margaret (1888-1961)

Born Margaret Crilley, in Newry, county Down, she and her sister, Mary, trained at the technical school, and came to Dublin in 1905, to study under Orpen at the Metropolitan School of Art. Margaret Crilley became Orpen's student assistant, and he bought her work when she was twenty-two. She won Board of Education medals for painting from the nude in 1911, and for oil painting in 1912. She first exhibited at the Royal Hibernian Academy in

1913 — some portraits. With Harry and Walter Clarke, and her sister Mary, she visited Aran to paint about this time.

In 1914, she and Harry Clarke married. She continued to paint, using their children, and their maid Julia and her brother (who ran the kilns in the stained glass studio) as models in subject paintings, such as *The wife* and *Pierrot and Columbine* (1925). In the latter, Thomas McGreevy, later Director of the National Gallery, appears as Pierrot. She rapidly made a name for herself with her rich coloured realist portraits, and received many commissions from the 1920's onward, including the painting of St. Patrick in the Mansion House, for the Haverty Bequest, in 1932. Sitters included Lennox Robinson (whose portrait is now in the Crawford Municipal Art Gallery, Cork), President de Valera, Dermod O'Brien PRHA and Archbishop McQuaid.

She taught in the Dublin School of Art and the RHA Schools, and won further medals and a trophy in the Tailteann festivals of 1924, 1928 and 1932. She exhibited landscapes, portraits and flower paintings at the RHA for nearly fifty years, becoming ARHA in 1926 and RHA in 1927. In 1939, she held her first one-man show at the Dublin Painters' Gallery. After the death of her husband in 1931, she directed the Harry Clarke Stained Glass Studios with her daughter, and her son David, also a painter. She is buried in Redford Cemetery, Greystones, county Wicklow.

She is represented in the National Gallery of Ireland, the Hugh Lane Municipal Gallery, Dublin, in the Crawford Gallery, Cork, the Ulster Museum and in Limerick Art Gallery. HP

See cat. nos. 100-02.

Clayton, Caroline see Millard, Caroline

Clayton, Eleanor Creathorne (1834-1900)

Eleanor was born in Dublin, the daughter of Benjamin Clayton III (1809-1883) an engraver. From an early age she contributed drawings to various publications, first in Dublin and later in London including *Chat, London* and *Punchinello*. Books which she illustrated and published herself include *Notable Women,* (1859) and *Female Warriors* (1879). WR

Coffey, Sadhbh see Trinseach, Sadhbh

Cole, Lady Florence (1778/9-1862)

Lady Florence was the third daughter of the 1st Viscount Enniskillen (created 1st Earl of Enniskillen in 1789). In her youth from her home at Florence Court, near Enniskillen, she did abundant sketches. She is also noted for her cut-out work with paper. Several sketchbooks containing drawings by her were presented recently by Professor G. F. Mitchell of Townley Hall, county Louth, to the National Trust for Northern Ireland, for display at Florence Court.

In 1797 Lady Florence married Blaney Townley Balfour, of Townley Hall, county Louth. Not much is known about her life there. She died 1 March 1862. MW

See cat. no. 7.

Colthurst, Annie Cope (d.c.1930)

Born in Ireland the daughter of Sir George Colthurst, Bart., Annie was educated in Ireland and France. She studied art at Pau, Paris and London.

Her subject matter was extremely varied and ranged from landscapes and cityscapes to still lifes and subject paintings and portraits. Her subject paintings were largely on Irish themes, for example, *An Irish Wake* (exhibited at the Royal Hibernian Academy, 1903, cat. no. 121, now in the Hugh Lane Municipal Gallery, Dublin) and *Kitty O'Callaghan, the flowerseller* (exhibited RHA, 1908, cat. no. 221), however she also produced works of a more topical nature like her *Votes for Women* (exhibited RHA, 1913, cat. no. 340). Her landscapes and cityscapes included views in Ireland, Britain and on the Continent. She had a very active exhibiting career, both in Ireland, where she exhibited forty-three works at the RHA between 1902 and 1929, and in England, where she exhibited works at numerous galleries in London and the Provinces, including the Walker Art Gallery, Liverpool, the Royal Society of Portrait Painters, and the Royal Academy.   WR

Colville, Helen (d.1953)

Helen Colville was presumably born in Dublin where she lived for all of her adult life. Her home was at Baily in Howth. Judging from her hectic exhibiting career, her charming and easy style was much appreciated by the public. She started exhibiting with the Watercolour Society of Ireland as early as 1892 and continued to do so almost every year until her death. That she was one of the most prominent members of the Watercolour Society is clear from her inclusion in the Society's Centenary Exhibition in 1970. She also exhibited both oils and watercolours at the Royal Hibernian Academy from 1920 to 1947, at the Royal Society of Artists, Birmingham and at the Society of Women Artists. Her subject matter was landscape and themes from nature in general with a strong preference for trying to capture in her work the changing effects of the seasons and the times of the day.

Her watercolours are in private collections and in the collection of the Hugh Lane Municipal Gallery, Dublin.   WR

See cat. no. 64.

Comerford, Helen (b.1945)

Born 1945 in Thomastown, county Kilkenny. Studied at the National College of Art & Design, Dublin; Belfast College of Art & Design, Akademie Voor Beeldende Kunst, Utrecht, Netherlands; post-graduate studies, Utrecht Akademie.

One Woman Exhibitions: 1980, Taylor Galleries, Dublin; 1984, Taylor Galleries, Dublin; 1985, Wexford Art Centre.

Selected Group Exhibitions: 1977, Project Arts Centre, Dublin; EVA, Limerick; 1978, Irish Exhibition of Living Art, Dublin (80, 81, 84); Women's Show '78; 1979, Contemporary Irish Artists; 1981, Independent Artists, Dublin; EVA, Limerick; GPA Emerging Artists, Tulfarris, county Wicklow; Oireachtas; 1982, Sculpture and Drawing Exhibition, Crawford Art Gallery, Cork; James Joyce Centenary Exhibition, The Ulysses Project, Douglas

Hyde Gallery, Dublin; GPA Emerging Artists, Douglas Hyde Gallery, Dublin; Four Kilkenny Artists, Butler Gallery, Kilkenny; 1984, October Show, Taylor Galleries, Dublin; 1985, Divisions, Crossroads, Turns of Mind: Some New Irish Art, selected by Lucy Lippard, touring USA.

Collections: Municipal Gallery of Modern Art, Dublin; Bank of Ireland; Allied Irish Finance; An Chomhairle Ealaíon/The Arts Council; Kilkenny Art Gallery Society; Fitzwilton Ltd., Dublin.

Cooke, Kathleen (contemp. artist)

Born in Ireland. Lived in Canada. US citizen.

One-Man Shows: 1970, Betty Parsons Gallery.

Group Shows: 1969, Betty Parsons Gallery, 'The World of the Zoo'; 1969, Graham Gallery, 'Birds and Beasts'; 1969, Albright-Knox Art Gallery, Buffalo, New York; 1969-70, New School Art Center, New York, 'American Drawings of the Sixties'; 1970, Graham Gallery, 'Birds and Beasts'; 1970, David Hendriks Gallery, Dublin, Ireland; 1970, Hurlbutt Gallery, Greenwich, Conn. 'Mr. & Mrs. Joseph H. Hirschorn Select.'; 1970-71, Betty Parsons Gallery, 'Sculpture — The Artists Plus Discoveries'; 1971, Heckscher Museum, Huntington, New York, 'Paintings, Drawings and Sculpture for Acquisition'; 1971, Society for Contemporary Art, 31st Annual Exhibition, Art Institute of Chicago, 'Works on Paper'; 1971, Philadelphia Museum of Art, Rental Gallery; 1971, National Endowment for the Humanities Travelling Exhibition, 'Drawings by Living Americans'.

Cooney, Jackie (b.1947)

Born 1947 in Dublin. Studied at the National College of Art & Design, Dublin including post-graduate studies.

One-Woman Exhibition: 1984, Project Arts Centre, Dublin.

Group Exhibitions: 1981, Oireachtas, Dublin; Wicklow Group Show, Tulfarris Gallery, Wicklow; Exhibition of Visual Art, Limerick; 1982, Exhibition of Visual Art, Limerick; Sculpture and Drawing Exhibition, Cork; 1983, Oireachtas, Dublin and Limerick; 1984, Independent Artists, Bank of Ireland, Dublin; Oireachtas, Dublin; 1986, NCAD Decade show, Guinness Hop Store.

Corr, Fanny (1807-1883)

Isabelle Marie Françoise Corr, better known as Fanny Corr, was born in Brussels, the daughter of Erin Corr, an engraver of Irish parentage. Fanny trained under the Belgian artist François Joseph Navez (1787-1869) and later became, like her tutor, a well known portraitist, and painter of history and genre subjects. She kept up a strong link with Ireland, exhibiting seven times at the Royal Hibernian Academy between 1832 and 1865 and also gaining several commissions in Ireland for her husband William Geefs (1805-1883), who was sculptor to the Belgian King.

Examples of her work are in collections in Brussels, and an engraving after her painting *Young Mother* is in the *Art Journal* of 1867.   WR

Cox, Kathleen (1904-1972)

Kathleen Cox was born in Wo-Sung in China, where her father was a doctor. On the family's return to Ireland, to Howth in county Dublin, she studied sculpture under Oliver Sheppard. While a student at the Dublin Metropolitan School of Art she was awarded the Royal Dublin Society Taylor Scholarship in 1925, 1926 and 1927 for her modelling. She exhibited textile design at the 1925 Arts and Crafts Exhibition. Between 1929 and 1933 she ran a Pottery Studio with Stella Rayner and exhibited with the Royal Hibernian Academy. She specialized in portrait masks. Her own bohemian beauty was captured by Hilda Roberts in an oil portrait at this period. She moved to England on her marriage in 1933, where she later published a book on comparative religion.

NGB

See cat. no. 84.

Crampton, Selina (1806-1876)

Selina Crampton was probably born in Dublin. She was the daughter of Sir Philip Crampton, a noted Dublin surgeon, whose sister Anne married Charles Kendal Bushe. She was therefore a cousin of Edith Somerville. Selina was a talented amateur with a marked comic sense. Her best watercolours are of people rather than landscapes, though the latter predominate. As the unmarried sister of a diplomat, Sir John Crampton, who himself was only married for three years between 1860 and 1863, she travelled widely, visiting her brother whose work took him to the principal cities of Europe and America. He was also a painter, and unlike his sister had been taught.

AOC and KOG

Crilley, Margaret see Clarke, Margaret

Cross, Dorothy (b.1956)

Born 1956 in Cork; 1973-74, First Year Foundation Course, Crawford Municipal School of Art, Cork; 1974-77, BA Hons. Degree, Leicester Polytechnic, England, (3D Design); 1976, Guest Student Gerrit Rietueld Academy, Amsterdam, Netherlands; 1978-79, Non-Degree study at San Francisco Art Institute (Sculpture); 1980-82, MFA Degree, San Francisco Art Institute (Print), graduated May 1982; 1982-83, Art work in San Francisco; Travel within the U.S.A. and South America.

One Person Shows: 1980, Triskel Art Centre, Cork; 1984, Triskel Art Centre, Cork; 1985, Hendriks' Gallery, Dublin ('Contraptions').

Group Shows: 1978, Goldsmiths' Hall, London; New Ashgate Gallery, Surrey, England; 1979, Diego Rivera Gallery, San Francisco, USA; 1981, Diego Rivera Gallery, San Francisco, USA; Intersection Gallery, San Francisco, USA; 1982, Ancient Currents Gallery, San Francisco, USA; Emmanuel Water Gallery, San Francisco, USA; 1983, 'Artspace', Gutai, Koshienguchi, Japan ('Volm' Group); 1984, Hendriks' Gallery, Dublin (4 Gallery Artists); 'Volm', Tokyo, Japan; Living Art Exhibition, Dublin ('Irish Coronation Chair', Bank of Ireland); Guinness Peat Aviation (GPA) Exhibition for Emerging Artists, Dublin; 1985, 'Volm', Kid-ai, Luck Gallery, Tokyo, Japan; CAN '85 (Cork

Art Now), Crawford Gallery, Cork; 'Sculpture in the Chair', (Vogue, October), Smiths' Gallery, London; 'Irish Women Artists', Battersea Arts Centre, London; '23 Women', Triskel Art Centre, Cork; 'Irish Art Now', Marginalia della Forme d'Arte, Turin, Italy; 'Six-in-the-sticks', Butler Gallery, Kilkenny; Guiness Peat Aviation (GPA) Exhibition for Emerging Artists, Dublin; 'Figurative Image', Bank of Ireland, Dublin; 'Claremorris Open Exhibition'.

Cuffe, Lady (Charlotte) see Wheeler-Cuffe, Lady (Charlotte)

Cummins, Pauline (b.1949)

Born in Dublin in 1949. Graduated from the National College of Art and Design in 1969, having specialised in painting and ceramics.

Exhibitions: 1984, Irish Exhibition of Living Art, 'Celebration at the National Maternity Hospital' a mural/installation; 1984, One Woman Show, at Kvindegalleriet, Aarhus, Denmark; 1985, 'Anne Kelly — is a midwife', a slide/tape piece, Neighbourhood Open Workshop, Olympia Drive, Belfast; 1985, The Crescent Art Centre, Belfast; 1985, Illustrations from 'An t'ollamh agus an lucog' in 5 cities tour of Japan; 1985, Irish Exhibition of Living Art, 'Inis t'Oirr — a slide/tape installation; 1986, Irish Women Artists, 'Eye to Eye' Woman Artists Slide Library, Battersea Art Centre, London; 1986, '4 women 4 cultures' Mixed Media Exhibition, Hunter College, New York; 1987, American Women's Caucus for the Arts, Boston, 7 venue tour of Boston and New York, with Inis t'Oirr — slide/tape performance.

Awards: 1985, Bursary Award, Irish Exhibition of Living Art; 1986, The George Campbell Memorial Travel Award; 1986, Arts Council Commission for exhibition to tour second-level schools.

Curran, Amelia (1775-1847)

Amelia was the eldest daughter of the famous Irish orator John Philpot Curran. She is not known to have had any formal artistic training but was naturally gifted not only as a painter but also as a musician and a writer.

Her career as a painter seems to have started when she moved to Rome in 1818 after the death of her father. It is likely that this was not her first visit to the continent as her father had been travelling frequently to England and the continent ever since the Act of Union, to which he had been strongly opposed in spite of the fact that he held the post of Master of the Rolls in Ireland from 1806 to 1814. There were other family reasons why the Currans felt the need to escape from Ireland for long periods, chief among these was the elopement of Amelia's mother with a clergyman named Sandys and the early death of her youngest sister Sarah. Sarah had been deeply attached to Robert Emmet and shortly after his execution in 1803 she died of a broken heart in Sicily.

This unhappy family background seems to have affected Amelia's disposition as she is known to have suffered from severe bouts of depression. In Rome she made a living by portraiture and making copies from Old Masters. The only known example of her original work is in the National Portrait Gallery in London (cat. no. 1234). It is a portrait of Percy Bysshe Shelley whom she met in Rome in 1818. The work illustrates Amelia's talent as a portraitist admirably, despite the fact that it was the result of only one sitting (the Shelleys having departed from Rome suddenly due to the death of one of their children) and that she herself said of it in a letter to Mrs. Shelley 'it was so ill-done and I was on the point of burning it. . .'.

Amelia died in Rome in 1847 and in the following year Lord Cloncurry commissioned the Irish sculptor John Hogan to design and execute a tablet to her memory in the church of St. Isidore in Rome.

WR

Currey, Fanny (d.1912)

Fanny Currey came from Lismore and was a friend of Edith and Grace Osborne (Lady Blake and the Duchess of St. Albans respectively). She stayed with them at Newtown Anner when she was a girl and was involved with them in illustrating envelopes for letters sent to Mrs. Osborne. The Osborne family's interest in art is mentioned in the biography of the Duchess of St. Albans and it seems likely that Fanny learnt with the Osborne girls from visiting watercolourists. No formal education for her is known. She was involved in the first exhibition of drawings and watercolours held in Ireland in 1871 in Lismore organised by a local drawing society. Exhibitions were held annually and from 1878 the society was known as The Irish Fine Art Society. They exhibited at various venues, including Carlow, Cork and Belfast where c.1887 they showed under the name 'The Watercolour Society of Ireland'. They had been exhibiting annually in Dublin from 1877 when they held their tenth exhibition there. Fanny Currey took the lead in all these activities and The Watercolour Society of Ireland is still in existence; although it has not held provincial shows since 1891, it has an annual exhibition in Dublin. By the late 1880's Miss Currey's work was considered of such a high standard that it was said of her that she 'could not be considered an Amateur in any sense of the word save one, that she is not dependent upon the pursuit of Art for a livelihood'.

Miss Currey also exhibited at the Grosvenor Gallery and the Royal Institute of Painters in Watercolour in London between 1880 and 1896. She also showed in the RHA from 1877 to 1896, mostly flower pieces and landscapes. It is understandable that flowers formed a large part of her repertoire in view of her great interest in gardening. As the proprietor of the Warren Nursery, Lismore she was one of the earliest of Ireland's world famous daffodil breeders. From the titles of her exhibited works it is clear that she travelled on the continent and in England and Wales.

AOC and SAD

Darby, Mary (d.1869)

Mary Darby was the daughter of Alexander Boyle and Grace Vicars and married in 1817 the Rev. Christopher Lovett Darby of Kells Priory, county Kilkenny. Her brother-in-law, James John Hornby, rector of Winnick in Lancashire, was a cousin of the Earl of Derby, whose protegé, the great watercolourist Edward Lear, stayed at

Knowsley, the Earl's Lancashire seat in the early 1830's for some years. It is likely that she met Lear then, as his influence on her work is obvious. She is not known to have had any other training. Her earliest known work is a drawing of the interior of Holycross Abbey, county Tipperary, now in Indianapolis, USA.

AOC and KOG

Davidson, Lilian Lucy (d.1954)

Born in Wicklow, she later studied at the Dublin Metropolitan School of Art. She exhibited *The Student* at the Royal Hibernian Academy in 1914, and continued to exhibit at the Academy until the year of her death. She was a friend of Mainie Jellett, Stella Frost and Lily Williams; and of Pat Wallace, with whom she worked at the Torch Theatre, painting scenery and designing posters. In the early 1920's, she painted in Belgium, exhibiting urban views at the RHA, and for the rest of the decade she divided her time between France and the West of Ireland. Later she worked in Donegal, Mayo, Wicklow and Connemara. She painted portraits of Jack B. Yeats, Joseph Holloway and others. She taught at various Dublin schools, and also at her studio in Earlsfort Terrace, her aim being to encourage painting from nature, and out-of-doors. She contributed regularly to the Watercolour Society, and the Munster Fine Arts Club, and exhibited abroad. The main influence on her work was Jack B. Yeats, in his representational phase. She laid a similar emphasis on line, though she never developed colour as he did, and latterly she tended to be interested mainly in the abstract effects of light, though continuing to paint in a realist manner. She was elected ARHA in 1940. Examples of her portraiture are in the National Gallery of Ireland and Hugh Lane Municipal Gallery, Dublin.

HP

See cat. nos. 94-95.

Dawson, Catherine Maria see Charleville, Countess of (Catherine Maria)

Delany, Mary (1700-1788)

Born Mary Granville in Wiltshire, in 1700, niece of Lord Granville, who was a noted patron of all branches of the arts. At seventeen, she married Alexander Pendarves, of Roscrow, Cornwall, and, on being widowed seven years later, she left Cornwall to live in London. In 1743, she married the Rev. Patrick Delany, who was a close friend of Jonathan Swift — she had corresponded with the latter since her first visit to Ireland in 1731. Delany was a witty connoisseur, and popular member of Swift's literary circle. When he was appointed Dean of Down, they paid regular visits to Ulster, while living at Delville in Glasnevin, and staying frequently with relatives and friends around the midlands of England. Mary Delany's career as an artist coincides with her years in Ireland, when she was encouraged by her husband to draw landscape wherever they went. She had had lessons from Goupy, who instructed her to copy the family portraits in oil and some of these copies still survive. In her drawings she was influenced somewhat by Hogarth and Hayman. However, she never wholly amalgamated her topographical outline with the stylistic notions she adopted into a confident cohesive manner.

She was a competent musician, and experimented with various crafts, designing fabrics, grottos and a chapel at Delville. Her major original work, the *Hortus Siccus,* now in the British Museum, was commenced at the age of seventy-two, a botanical collection of nearly a thousand flowers cut from paper. This was exhibited, with some of her designs and her courtdress worked by herself, at the Pierpont Morgan Library, New York, in 1986.   HP

See cat. no. 6.

Dering, Henrietta (fl.1694-1728/29)

Henrietta's maiden name was de Branlieu and though no evidence of her parentage exists, it seems probable that she was a member of a French Huguenot family. Her birthplace and date of birth are unknown but the will of her daughter Mary Dering, dated 23 April 1746 and proved on 13 June 1747, identifies the artist as marrying on 23 March 1694, Robert Dering, son of Sir Edward Dering, 2nd Baronet, of Surrenden Dering in Kent. (Information kindly given by Philip Blake). Several members of the Dering family made their careers in Ireland and they were intermarried with the Southwell and Perceval families who had landed property in Ireland.

It is not known where she learnt her art though she apparently studied in 1707 with Simon Digby, Bishop of Elphin, her second husband's friend and superior, a well-known miniaturist. However, her style of 1703 had not changed appreciably in 1715 and presumably her early training must have been in the late seventeenth century.

Her earliest known pastels are dated Dublin 1703. She appears to have had a large practice in the fashionable Dublin world in the years 1703/04 and 1705. She drew portraits of several of her husband's relatives, including Philip Perceval and the 1st Earl of Egmont, who was President of the Trustees of the Colony of Georgia, who sent General Oglethorpe to establish a settlement in Savannah. Robert Dering's date of death is not known, but on 11 April 1705 Mrs. Dering married a widower, Gideon Johnston (1668-1716), an Anglican clergyman. In 1706 they went to London to apply for missionary service in Charleston, finally arriving there in 1708. Henrietta Johnston continued to work as a portrait painter. Her art was mentioned by her husband in 1709 in a letter quoted in the MESDA Catalogue of 1979: 'Were it not for the assistance my wife gives me by drawing of Pictures (which can last but a little time in a place so ill peopled) I shou'd not have been able to live'.

Henrietta visited England in 1711, returning to Charleston in 1713 where in 1716 her husband drowned in an accident. In 1725 she went to New York and continued to paint. She died on March 7, 1728/29.

Her works are in the collection of the Museum of Early Southern Decorative Arts in Winston-Salem, North Carolina, U.S.A.
                                                           AOC and KOG

See cat. nos. 1-2.

Dobbin, Lady (Kate) (1868-c.1948)

Born Kate Wise, the daughter of a solicitor in Clifton, Bristol in 1887, she became the second wife of Alfred Graham Dobbin, J.P., a tobacco manufacturer and merchant of Cork. In 1900, as High Sheriff of the City of Cork, he was knighted on the occasion of Queen Victoria's visit to Dublin. She exhibited with the Royal Hibernian Academy from 1894 until 1947, showing one hundred and five paintings during that long period. She was also included in Crampton Walker's Exhibition of Irish Artists at the Fine Art Society in May 1927, organised as a sequel to his survey of Irish art, *Irish Life and Landscape,* published that year and the first exhibition of its kind to be held in London, representing as it did only Irish artists in oil and watercolour.

She seems to have painted mostly in watercolour and usually signed her work *K. Dobbin.* Her work ranges from evocative scenes with poetic titles in melted moody washes, to views of Cork, Shandon, the Lee and the countryside beyond, Roundstone and Kinsale. She particularly favoured the sea, water, mist and twilight. She also painted accurately observed and richly coloured flower studies.

By 1939 the Dobbins had given up their large house in Montenotte and had moved into the Imperial Hotel.

She is represented in the Cork Municipal collection and her work appears regularly at auction.   NGB

See cat. no. 80.

D'Olier, Helen Campbell (1829-1887)

Helen was born in Edinburgh where she received her initial training from William Simson (1800-1847) a landscape and genre painter. In 1849 she married an Irish barrister John Rutherford D'Olier and came to live in Dublin.

Her early works were copies of Old Masters as well as some original landscapes. However, she is remembered chiefly for her careful and detailed copies of pages from Irish illuminated manuscripts. The most important copies she did were those of pages from the *Book of Kells* which are today kept in the Manuscript room in Trinity College.

She exhibited various works including pencil drawings, paintings and lithographs at the Dublin Exhibition of 1861.   WR

Donnelly, Claire (b.1963)

Born in 1963. 1985, completed Diploma studies (ANCAD) at the National College of Art and Design, Dublin; 1980-83, Member of Committee, Grapevine Arts Centre, Dublin; 1983-85, worked in New Art Studios, Dublin; 1986, community arts tutor, Base 10, Ballymun, Dublin.

Exhibitions: Art on Video, Kilkenny; Women on Film Artists, Battersea Arts Centre, London.

Douglas, Jessie (1893-1928)

A Belfast painter by whom only one work is known, but who was evidently of some considerable ability, she may have been related to the painter Harry R. Douglas. She first appears as a member of the Belfast Art Society in 1893 when she exhibited a view of *Winchester, Petite Marie* and *Gossip,* from an address at 6 Chichester Street. In 1895 her address is given as 1 Donegall Square, but she did not exhibit that year. In 1896 she was elected one of the four vice-presidents of the Belfast Art Society, and has her address at 24 Garfield Chambers, Royal Avenue. That year she exhibited a view in Brittany, *Mischief* and *A Lacemaker.* She exhibited almost every year until 1914, sending views in the South of England, Donegal, Connemara, France, Holland, and fancy subject-portraits. In 1918 she was elected an honorary member of the Belfast Art Society. She exhibited one work, *Love in a Mist,* in 1920, still from 24 Garfield Chambers. She was still at the same address in 1928, though she had not exhibited since 1920 at the BAS. Her name never appears on the lists of the Ulster Academy of Arts which started in 1930.   MA

See cat. no. 78.

Drury, Susanna (1733-1770)

A mysteriously obscure but very able painter whose views of the Giant's Causeway are landmarks both in Irish topographical painting and in European scientific illustration. Her birth and death dates are not known, but she was the sister of the Dublin miniature painter Franklin Drury (d.1771). It is also not known where she was trained, but it might have been London as her only dated work is a *View of London from One-Tree Hill,* 1773 (sold Dublin 1905; with Frank Sabin, London, 1954, present whereabouts unknown). A pair of landscapes or perspectives of the Giant's Causeway won the £25 premium of the Dublin Society in 1740, and Susanna Drury's identity was disclosed to the Society by Dean Gabriel Maturin, a prominent Dublin Huguenot. This raises the question whether Susanna Drury had Huguenot connections and may have been trained on the continent. Her style also has affinities with Joseph Tudor (?1696-1759) who was one of the unsuccessful candidates for the 1740 Premium. Her views of the Giant's Causeway were engraved in London by François Vivares (another Huguenot) in 1743-4. The engravings were circulated throughout Europe and provided the French geologist Nicholas Demarest (1725-1815) with evidence to support his 'vulcanist' theory of the origin of basalt as against the then commonly held 'neptunist' theory. Susanna Drury's family was Anglo-Irish and contained soldiers and clerics. Her married name was probably Warter as a 'Susanna Warter' is mentioned in Franklin Drury's will of 1770.   MA

See cat. no. 3.

Duffy, Rita (b.1959)

Born 1959 in Belfast. 1978-82, BA Degree in Fine Art, Ulster Polytechnic, Belfast. Currently studying for an MA Degree.
One Woman Exhibitions: 1983, 'Rathlin Remembered', Queen's University, Belfast; 1985, 'Portuguese Drawings', Corridor Gallery, Lurgan; New Paintings, On the Wall Gallery, Belfast.
   Group Exhibitions: 1981, Irish Exhibition of Living Art, Douglas Hyde Gallery, Dublin; Tom Caldwell Galleries, Dublin

and Belfast (1983, 1984); 1982, Solomon Gallery, Dublin; Ulster Academy Exhibition, Ulster Museum, Belfast (1982-85); Exposure III, ILAC Centre, Dublin; 1984, Percy French Watercolour Competition, Tower House, Bangor, county Down; Altona Gallery, Lisburn; Seagoe Gallery, Portadown; Nova Exhibition, Arts Council Gallery, Belfast; 1985, Young Artists, On the Wall Gallery, Belfast; Percy French Watercolour Exhibition, Bangor; Solomon Gallery, Dublin; Group Show, On the Wall Gallery, Belfast; 1986, Octagon Gallery, Belfast; Four Women Artists, Newcastle; N. Irish Artists, Singapore; Print Exchange Exhibition, China; Fresh Art, Barbican, Concourse Gallery, London; Claremorris Exhibition, county Mayo; GPA Exhibition, Dublin.

Duncan, Mary (1885-1960)

A landscape painter and etcher, Mary Duncan was born in Bromley in 1885, the daughter of John Kinmont Duncan. She first studied at the School of Art in Bromley, then at the Slade School and later in Paris. Though it is not known exactly when she came to Ireland, it was probably some time about 1908. She first exhibited at the Royal Hibernian Academy in 1910. While living in Dublin she formed a close friendship with Estella Solomons and Cissie Beckett. As a member of the Gaelic League, she adopted the Irish version of her name 'Maire Ní Dhonnchada' which she continued to use in the company of her friends until the end of her life.

Though she mainly painted landscapes and genre scenes she was also a prolific etcher. In about 1911 she made some portrait etchings of James Stephens and George Russell, and her etchings of the Custom House and The Old Houses of Parliament were used in *Saorstat Eireann — Irish Free State Official Handbook* (Dublin 1932, facing pp. 89 and 101). In these she manages to capture the atmosphere and character of the buildings while remaining topographically accurate.

Duncan returned to England sometime after the Rising though she kept a Dublin address until 1920. She eventually moved to Cornwall in the 1930's, settling at Mousehole near Penzance from where she continued to send her work to the Royal Hibernian Academy until 1953. She also exhibited her work at the Royal Academy from 1929-46, as well as in many provincial Galleries in England such as the Walker Art Gallery, Liverpool, Manchester City Art Gallery and the Glasgow Institution of Fine Arts. She is represented in the Hugh Lane Municipal Gallery, Dublin.

KMM

Elvery, Beatrice see Glenavy, Lady (Beatrice)

Fannin, Marianne Edwardine (1845-1938)

Marianne Fannin was born in Dublin. Her parents emigrated to the Cape of Good Hope in 1845 shortly after she was born. Two years later the family moved to Natal and settled at The Dargle, a property named by her father, Thomas Fannin, after the Wicklow river.

George Fannin, Marianne's older brother, developed a keen interest in the local flora and he collected innumerable specimens of the wild plants that flourished in this area of Natal. These were pressed by his sister, and then sent to William H. Harvey, Professor of Botany in Trinity College, Dublin; the herbarium in Trinity College retains many of the Fannin collections and there are a few duplicates in the national Botanic Gardens, Glasnevin. As well as pressing the specimens for later scientific analysis, Marianne painted the flowers of Natal.

In 1869, Marianne Fannin married the Rev. Eustace Wilberforce Jacob who died two years later. About this period Mrs. Jacob painted an album of the flowers of Natal. For a time she lived in England where she studied music and painting but she returned to South Africa in 1875, moving to Transvaal in 1878 where the following year she married the Rev. Alfred Roberts. Marianne continued painting while she lived at Potchefstroom; her subject were flowers and landscapes. She died at Heidelberg, Transvaal, in 1938.

There are some of Marianne Fannin's botanical watercolours in the School of Botany, Trinity College, Dublin, and her landscapes are in private collections in South Africa.   ECN

Feeney, Jacinta (b.1954)

Born 1954 in Donegal, Ireland. 1977-80, Preston Polytechnic, Lancashire; First Class BA (Hons.); 1981-84, Royal College of Art, London, MA.

One-Man Shows: 1980, Tom Caldwell Gallery, Dublin; 1986, Arts Council of Ireland Touring Exhibition; The Hendriks Gallery, Dublin.

Principal Group Shows: 1980, Bank of Ireland, Exposure II; Listowel International Print Biennale; Belltable, Limerick 'Women's Work'; Claremorris Open Exhibition; Guinness Peat Aviation, Tulfarris, Co. Wicklow; Harris Museum, Preston; 1981, Northern Young Contemporaries; Whitworth Art Gallery, Manchester; 1982, Listowel International Print Biennale; 1983, Brompton Gallery, Knightsbridge, London; Consort Gallery, South Kensington, London; 1984, Guinness Peat Aviation; Royal Academy Diploma Gallery; Stowells Exhibition; Christies Inaugural, London; Brompton Gallery, Knightsbridge, London; TSWA Touring Exhibition, England; 1985, Irish Group Show, Five Dial, Covent Garden; Lancashire Polytechnic; The Religious Spirit of Contemporary Art, Westminister Cathedral; 1986, Athena International Art Award, Mall Gallery; Fisher Fine Art, London, 'The Human Touch'; Royal Academy Summer Show, London; Bank of Ireland, 'Figurative Image', Dublin.

Fitzgerald, Dorothy (b.1888)

A painter and lithographer, Dorothy Charlotte Jellett Fitzgerald was the daughter of Prof. George Francis Fitzgerald. She was educated at Alexandra College, Dublin and she later studied art at the Royal Hibernian Academy Schools where she was awarded the Taylor Scholarship.

She exhibited frequently at the RHA from 1905 to 1930. Her subject matter was portraiture and figures and her style was bold and striking, often based on strong contrasts of black and white.

During her career she also exhibited at the Fine Art Society, the Walker Art Gallery, Liverpool, the Royal Society of Portrait Painters, the Royal Academy, and the Royal Institute of Painters in Watercolours. Two of her lithographs are in the Hugh Lane Municipal Gallery, Dublin.   WR

Fitzgerald, Mary (b. 1956)

1977, graduated from the National College of Art & Design, Dublin.

One Woman Exhibitions: 1982, Oliver Dowling Gallery, Dublin; 1984, Oliver Dowling Gallery, Dublin; 1986, Oliver Dowling Gallery, Dublin.

Group Exhibitions: 1981, MAKI Gallery, Tokyo; 1982, SADE, Cork; EVA, Limerick; 1983, Claremorris Open; Personal Choice, Butler Gallery, Kilkenny; 1985, Claremorris Open; Personal Choice, Butler Gallery, Kilkenny; Edinburgh/Dublin Exhibition; Irish Exhibition of Living Art, Dublin; Four Irish Artists, Touring Exhibition, Ireland, Brazil, Argentina; 1986, Personal Choice, Butler Gallery, Kilkenny; Celtic Vision Touring Exhibition; NCAD Decade Show, Guinness Hop Store; 1987, Irish Exhibition of Living Art.

Collections: An Chomhairle Ealaíon/The Arts Council; Arts Council of Northern Ireland; Contemporary Irish Art Society; Allied Irish Bank, New York and Brussels.

Forster, Miss (fl.1780)

Little is known of Miss Forster's life or career. She was a sister of the landscape painter John Forster and was herself a miniaturist. She exhibited with the Society of Artists in Ireland in 1780 and is recorded as having been a student of Thomas Boulger (fl.1761-1788).

No examples of her miniatures are known.   WR

Fox, Kathleen (1880-1963)

Kathleen Fox was brought up in an Anglo-Irish family in the outskirts of Dublin in a series of large houses. Her father was in the King's Dragoon Guards. She entered the Dublin Metropolitan School of Art in 1903, where her work attracted the attention of Orpen, with whom she subsequently studied in London and whose assistant she became at the Dublin Art School. Among the scholarships and prizes she won was a Gold Medal in the 1908 National Competition for her enamelling; her early versatility was also expressed in painted china, carved wood, silver, costume design and stained glass. She first exhibited with the Royal Hibernian Academy in 1911 before leaving to paint in Paris and then in Bruges. She was back in Dublin in 1916 to paint the Rising (e.g. *The Arrest* (1916) in Sligo). During the War she had a studio in London, where she met her husband, Lt. Cyril Pym, who was killed in action; she bore a daughter in 1918. She moved to Nice, where she continued to paint and exhibit in France, London and Dublin. In 1921 her work was shown at the New English Art Club in London, the National Portrait Society, the Royal Academy and the RHA; she also painted her well-known portrait of Cardinal Mannix in London (Hugh Lane Municipal Gallery, Dublin). She returned to Dublin in the mid 1920's as her beloved eldest brother was seriously ill. On her mother's death, she inherited Brookfield, a large house in Milltown, Dublin, of which she often painted interior views. She did not exhibit with the RHA between 1924 and 1943 but was a highly successful portraitist both in Ireland and England. She is now (perhaps unfairly) best known for the many very competent flower studies she painted in the 1940's and 1950's. She is represented in many public and private collections both in and out of Ireland and was one of Leo Smith's first artists at the Waddington Gallery in Dublin.   NGB

See cat. nos. 69-71.

Franks, Rosalie (fl. c.1921-1929)

Nothing is known of Rosalie's background or training; however, it is clear from the quality of her work that she had a good knowledge of the watercolour technique and was influenced by the work of the Impressionists.

Her style, characterised by atmospheric washes and muted watery tones, is most reminiscent of the style of Rose Barton with whose work she may have been familiar. Rosalie was a constant exhibitor at the Irish Watercolour Society from 1921. She also exhibited one painting at the Royal Hibernian Academy in 1928. Judging from the titles of her exhibited works, Rosalie was a keen traveller, producing views of places in France, Switzerland, Italy (particularly Venice and Florence) and England.

Her work is represented in private collections.   WR

Information supplied by KOG

See cat. no. 79.

Frömel, Gerda (1931-1975)

Born 1931 in Schonberg, Czechoslovakia, of German parents. After the war, her parents returned to Germany; 1948-52, she studied sculpture at the Art Schools in Stuttgart, Darmstadt and Munich; 1956, she came to Ireland and settled here; 1975, she died in her early forties in a drowning accident; 1957-75, Irish Exhibition of Living Art; 1960-62, Salzburg Biennale of Christian Art; 1962-63, Independent Artists Exhibition; 1964, one person show, Dawson Gallery, Dublin; Arts Council Exhibition of Graphic Art; 1967, joint exhibition with Michael Scott, Dawson Gallery, Dublin; 1970, Dawson Gallery, Dublin; 1976, Retrospective Exhibition, Municipal Gallery of Modern Art, Dublin.

Ganly, Brigid (b.1909)

Brigid Ganly was born in Dublin, the daughter of artist Dermot O'Brien. She studied at the National College of Art and at the Royal Hibernian Academy School in Dublin. She studied modelling under Oliver Sheppard and won many prizes for sculpture. Later Brigid continued her studies in Rome and Florence. Throughout her career Brigid has been a constant exhibitor of both oils and watercolours at the Royal Hibernian Academy of which she is a member.

Her works are included in the collections of the Dublin and Waterford Municipal Galleries.   WR

Geddes, Wilhelmina Margaret (1887-1955)

Wilhelmina Geddes was born at Drumreilly, county Leitrim but spent most of her childhood in Belfast, where she was educated at Methodist College and learned to draw on summer holidays in Scotland. From 1903 she attended the Belfast School of Art, where she won a number of prizes for her drawing illustrations and graphic design. In 1910 she began attending Orpen's classes at the Dublin Metropolitan School and exhibited at the Arts and Crafts Society. She returned to the Belfast School for part of 1911, and was given a travelling scholarship, most of which she spent in the British Museum. Her first unusually graphic work in stained glass also dates from this year, her first public window from 1912. She was included in the 1914 Exposition des Arts Décoratifs in the Louvre. She exhibited at the Royal Hibernian Academy in 1913, 1914, 1916 and 1930. Until she left for London in 1925, to work in a rented studio in the Glass House in Fulham, she divided her time between Belfast and Dublin, where she made a succession of extraordinarily powerful stained glass windows at An Túr Gloine, Sarah Purser's Tower of Glass studio, a number of whose preparatory designs are in the National Gallery of Ireland. She designed bookjackets, bookplates, stamps, posters, graphic and book illustrations some of which she translated into glass. In 1924 she held a joint exhibition in Belfast with Rosamond Praeger, an old family friend, of whom she drew a portrait (Ulster Museum). From London, among the many places she exhibited were the Society of Scottish Artists, the Ulster Academy (of which she became an Academician in 1933), the Arts and Crafts Societies of both Ireland and England, the British Empire Exhibition at Wembley. She is to be honoured by the Arts Council of Northern Ireland this year with a centenary exhibition.   NGB

See cat. nos. 72-74.

Geefs, Fanny see Corr, Fanny

Gifford, Grace (1888-1955)

She was born in Dublin, grand-niece of the painter Sir Frederick Burton. Her elder brother, Gabriel Paul Gifford, was also an artist, and exhibited in London and the United States. She was Orpen's pupil at the Metropolitan School of Art; his oil and pencil portraits of her in 1907 portray her strong humorous personality. She attended the Slade for a time. She was a member of the Dublin United Arts Club, drawing cartoons of writers and artists, the most celebrated being that of Susan Mitchell and George Moore, as 'Cupid and Psyche', published in *The Irish Review* (September-November 1914, facing p. 281). Her book of caricatures of Irish personalities, *To hold as 'twere,* was published in 1919, and two further collections in 1929 and 1930.

She joined Sinn Féin with her two sisters and took an active part in the republican movement. In May 1916, she married Joseph Plunkett, one of the leaders of the Rising, while he was awaiting execution, and she drew two posthumous portraits of him, one in June 1916, the other in 1935. In 1917, she became a member of the Provisional Republican Government, and used her artistic training to promote the nationalist cause with posters and banners. She opposed the treaty, in an article in *The Republic* (March 1922), and with her sister was imprisoned in Kilmainham Jail, where she decorated the walls of her cell with paintings. She is best remembered for her stylish cartoons, with their distinctive looped images, capturing in pen the essence of the anecdotal wit and literary bavardage of the Irish Renaissance.

She is represented in the Hugh Lane Municipal Gallery, Dublin.

HP

See cat. no. 81.

Gleeson, Evelyn (1855-1944)

Evelyn Gleeson was born in Knutsford in Cheshire where her father was a general practitioner. Persistent respiratory problems may have been a factor in her father's decision to move his young wife and three children back to Athlone, when she was fifteen. Here Dr. Gleeson philanthropically founded the Athlone Woollen Mills to stimulate local employment and bought Hill House in the town, before moving out to Benown, a large house near Portlick Castle.

His eldest daughter studied painting in London, at the studio of Ludovisi, and then in Paris. She also studied design in London, where she was praised for her sense of colour. She returned to Ireland, aged about forty, after an artistically and politically active life in London. She was a committed Suffragist, member of the Pioneer Club and the Gaelic League before ill health and nationalist interests motivated her to come back and set up the Morris-inspired Dun Emer Guild in Dundrum, county Dublin between 1902-04. Her watercolours and pastels are mostly to be found in the collection of her family. She worked her portraits in pastel and used watercolour for her smaller scale landscapes, still-lifes and flower and tree studies. She also designed rugs and carpets, about which she was extremely knowledgeable and lectured extensively.

NGB

See cat. nos. 58-59.

Glenavy, Lady (Beatrice) (1883-1968)

Beatrice Elvery was born into an artistic family who lived in Dublin and then Carrickmines. She followed her mother and aunt by entering the Dublin Metropolitan School of Art in 1896, where her versatile talents were soon recognised by John Hughes in the sculpture class and, later, Orpen, both of whom did portraits of her. She won a number of prizes and scholarships, including one for a summer course at South Kensington (1898-99) and the Taylor Art Scholarship 1902-04. She exhibited with the Young Irish Artists from 1902 and at the 1904 Arts and Crafts Exhibition; that year she studied at Colarossi's in Paris and then joined An Túr Gloine, Sarah Purser's Tower of Glass stained glass cooperative. Although her work in glass was as competent as her modelling, she was encouraged by Orpen to leave and study painting with Tonks and Steer at the Slade in 1910. In 1912 she married Gordon Campbell, a barrister and later statesman, and went to live in an artistic milieu in London until after the War, when they returned to Dublin. By 1931, when her husband became

Lord Glenavy, she had raised three children and begun to spend much more time painting. She exhibited regularly (except for a gap between 1908-12) with the Royal Hibernian Academy from 1902 until 1969, sending sculpture and paintings over from London during the War and changing her monogram from BE, to BC to BG. She was elected an RHA in 1933 and held her first one man show in 1934 at 7 St. Stephen's Green. She painted and designed furniture, illustrated books, designed posters and Christmas cards for the Cuala press and made plaster plaques, some of which appear in her later paintings. These later paintings are of a surreal nature, often setting dead or inanimate objects in woodland settings or, De Chirico-like, on abandoned sea shores in muted tones. Her work is represented in public collections in Dublin (Hugh Lane Municipal Gallery), the Ulster Museum, Belfast, Drogheda, Cork and Limerick.

NGB

See cat. nos. 111-14.

Gonne, Anne (1816-c.1876)

Anne Gonne was born in Devonshire and married Henry Gonne, a Dublin engraver, in 1840. She exhibited frequently at the Royal Hibernian Academy from 1840, chiefly flowers and fruit in watercolours. Mrs. Gonne also taught drawing and modelled flowers in wax.

WR

Gore-Booth, Constance see Markievicz, Constance

Granville, Mary see Delany, Mary

Greatorex, Eliza (1820-1897)

Born Eliza Pratt at Manor Hamilton, county Leitrim, she left Ireland with her family in 1836. Having settled in New York, she married Henry Greatorex, a prominent musician, in 1849. It was only after her husband's death in 1858 that Eliza began to study art in earnest, first with the Scottish born painters James and William Hart who were both members of the National Academy in New York. She continued her studies in Paris with Emile Lambinet (1815-1877) and later made study trips to England, Germany and Italy.

She is best remembered for her drawings and lithographs of New York City, though she also did many landscapes. Among her early exhibited landscapes (from 1855 to 1860) were many views of Ireland, including the *Gap of Dunloe*, the *Glen of the Downs, Ross Castle, Killarney* and *Homestead in the North of Ireland.* These suggest that she visited Ireland during this period. In 1864 she became the first woman artist to be elected an Associate Member of the National Academy.

Towards the end of her life she spent long periods working in Europe where she was accompanied by her daughters Kathleen Honora (b.1851) and Elizabeth Eleanor (b.1854) both of whom became artists.

The Metropolitan Museum, New York has a number of works by Eliza Greatorex.

WR and ECN

Griffith, Patricia (née Wallace) (1913-1972)

Born 1913 in Dublin; 1932-35, studied at the Royal Hibernian Academy school before spending a year at the Slade School, London, after which she returned to Dublin; c.1941, married the architect William Griffith and from about that time painted mainly in gouache, exhibiting regularly at the Watercolour Society of Ireland and with the White Stag Group. From about the mid-forties, due to domestic commitments, she more or less stopping painting; 1972, died in Puckane, near Nenagh, county Tipperary.

Groener, Anita (b.1958)

Born 1958 in Veldhoven, The Netherlands.

Art Education: 1975-80, Mollerinstitute, Tilburg (NL), BA in Fine Arts; 1980-82, Academy of Fine Arts, Arnhem (NL), MA Painting. Living and working in Dublin since 1982.

Group Shows: 1984, Independent Artists, Dublin; 1985, Independent Artists, Dublin/Belfast; 1986, GPA Awards for Emerging Artists, Dublin; Independent Artists, Dublin/Limerick; 1987, Two-woman show with Eithne Jordan, Pentonville Gallery, London; Wexford Arts Centre, Wexford; Irish Art for Holland, Amsterdam.

Solo Exhibitions: 1986, Work on Paper, Lincoln Gallery, Dublin; Work on canvas, Project Arts Centre, Dublin.

Awards: Large scale Bursary Awards, Independent Artists, 1985; Arts Council Bursary, 1986.

Collections: Irish Contemporary Arts Society; Vincent Ferguson; GPA; Nial Andrews MEP.

Gubbins, Beatrice (1878-1944)

Born in county Limerick, Beatrice Gubbins lived all her life at Dunkathel, a late-Georgian house in Glanmire just outside Cork city. It is not clear where she got her early training, but since her hand is not untutored, it is likely that she attended the Crawford School of Art. The registers there are not extant for the appropriate years but, her sister Frances Gertrude did attend there in 1885. Beatrice was a stalwart traveller throughout her life and many of her watercolours were carried out during her various trips. She visited Italy many times, worked as a nurse in London during the war and in her later years, after her mother had died, she travelled to Morocco (1929), The West Indies (1930), and Algeria (1931). She did not study art on the Continent but significantly she visited Barbizon in 1902.

Beatrice is among the best of the highly talented amateur watercolourists during the early part of the century. Her subject matter is varied: intimate genre and domestic scenes, still-life and landscapes. For many years she was secretary to the Queenstown Sketching Club, an enthusiastic amateur group whose rules are still preserved among the papers at Dunkathel. Unlike the Dublin Sketching Club, the Queenstown group do not appear to have exhibited together, but Beatrice did exhibit a number of pictures at the Royal Hibernian Academy in 1910 and 1911. For the purpose of anonymity within the highly critical Sketching Club she frequently signed herself either 'Greyhound', 'Jessamine' or 'Benjamin'.

Most of her pictures are still at Dunkathel, where they are on view to the public.

FG

See cat. no. 50.

Guinness, May (1863-1955)

Born in Dublin, Mary Catherine (May) Guinness was the daughter of Thomas Hosea Guinness of Tibradden House. She was educated at home by French and German governesses, and at Mrs. Power's school, which she left to teach her younger brothers and sisters. This extra burden is why she developed late as an artist. It was not until c.1905-07 that she went to Paris, where she studied art seriously for the first time. There she studied with Van Dongen, Lhote, and, later, the Spanish artist Aglada. She also visited Brittany, and *A Religious Procession in Brittany* draws its inspiration from this. During the first World War, she joined the French Army as a nurse, and was decorated. After the War, she continued to visit France every year for at least part of the year, and she pursued her studies while there. Later on, she tended to lead a rather withdrawn existence, staying most of the time at Tibradden.

Miss Guinness' early work had an 'Art Nouveau' quality. In this she was much influenced by Matisse. Her study under Lhote caused her to bring a much-needed discipline to her work. The religious pictures that she copied, such as those in the Louvre, show how the easy mastery that she seemed to possess was, in fact, the result of extremely hard work. She favoured the Post-Impressionists, and adapted her work to their technical methods. After such paintings as *Outside a Paris Café,* the colour textures became as important as the subject in the communication of the artist's vision. Her work also shows the influence of Picasso, Dufy and Marie Laurencin. During her 'Cubist' phase her work tended to be rather stiff and expressionless. It improved in quality when, under the influence of Dufy, it became somewhat more free. She particularly retained the gentleness of Marie Laurencin and the violent colours of Aglada. Her style varied a great deal, which makes it very difficult to date, and she adopted different styles of modern French artists without fully evolving a style of her own. She exhibited frequently, in London and Paris, alone, and at the Salon des Indépendants, especially still life and flower subjects.

Examples of her work are found in many collections, notably the National Gallery of Ireland, the Hugh Lane Municipal Gallery, Dublin, the Crawford Municipal Gallery, Cork, Limerick Art Gallery and Drogheda Municipal Art Gallery.

NA

See cat. nos. 124-26.

Hamilton, Caroline (1771-1861)

The daughter of William Tighe of Rossana, county Wicklow and Sarah his wife, daughter of Sir William Fownes of Woodstock, county Kilkenny, she was the cousin and sister-in-law of the poet Mary ('Psyche') Tighe and cousin and beneficiary of the last of the two 'Ladies of Llangollen', Sarah Ponsonby. She married Charles Hamilton of Hamwood, county Meath in 1801 and most of her and Sarah Ponsonby's papers are in Hamwood, (see Miss

Eva Bell, *The Hamwood Papers*, London 1930). A number of her drawings and watercolours are still in Hamwood and, as Anthony Malcolmson points out in his calendar of the Hamwood MSS, they show that she was a keen satirist and an acute observer.

Caroline Hamilton mentions in her diary (now mislaid in the National Library of Ireland but partially quoted in Bell *ibid.*, p. 333) that in 1795 her mother brought her family back to Rossana after an Italian sojourn and paid John Inigo Spilsbury, who had been art master at Harrow and who was the brother of Jonathan Spilsbury, the engraver and portrait painter, three hundred pounds a year to teach her daughters drawing. Caroline criticised Spilsbury's daughter Maria (later Mrs. John Taylor) 'for when she attempted to paint the passions she failed. . . I chose Mr. Hogarth for my model after Mr. Spilsbury had left us. Sometimes delighted with the effect of light and shade by candlelight I attempted it, and sometimes observing in company that muscles of the face were set in motion by such and such feelings, I came to express them, by recourse occasionally to Le Bruns *Passions* to convince me that I was right'. No better summary of her style need be attempted.

Other than those at Hamwood, further examples of her work are in the collection of the Hon. Desmond Guinness and the Hon. Garech Browne.   KOG

See cat. nos. 9-11.

Hamilton, Eva (1876-1960)
Eva Henrietta Hamilton, sister of Letitia, was born in 1876, daughter of Charles Robert Hamilton, of Hamwood, county Meath, and cousin of Rose Barton, the watercolourist. She studied at the Metropolitan School of Art along with her sister, and was much influenced by their teacher, Sir William Orpen.

She is particularly well-known for her portrait painting, and the influence upon her work of her teacher, Sir William Orpen, is emphasized by the fact that, early in her career, she earned her living by copying portraits by him. She had a career specialising in portraiture, for which she received commissions, and was most successful in her depiction of children. She also did many portraits of her own family. Due to economic necessity, however, she gave up her career as a portrait painter, to keep house for herself and other members of her family at Dunsinea, Castleknock. At this time she turned to landscape painting, especially of Irish scenes, of which *Tobar Padraig, Co. Mayo* is an example, and this is more typical of the latter half of her career.

She exhibited regularly, at the Irish International Exhibition (1907), the Royal Hibernian Academy (1904-45) and the Irish Exhibition of Living Art (1945).

Works by Eva Hamilton are to be found in the Ulster Museum, Belfast and the Crawford Municipal Art Gallery, Cork.   NA

See cat. no. 96.

Hamilton, Letitia (1878-1964)
Letitia Marion Hamilton was born in Dublin in 1878, sister of Eva. Educated at Alexandra College, Dublin, she then studied at the Metropolitan School of Art, her teacher being Sir William Orpen. From there she moved to London, studying first with Anne St. John Partridge, then at the London Polytechnic. Following that, she went on to study in Belgium, where her teacher was Frank Brangwyn. She was awarded medals: a silver medal in the Board of Education National Competition for an enamelled panel (1912) and a bronze medal in the Olympic Games Arts section. Like many young ladies of her time, Letitia travelled widely on the continent, especially France, Yugoslavia and Italy, as can be seen from her paintings, for example, *Fiesole Hill, Florence.*

Letitia was very much influenced by contemporary French artists, particularly Dufy, and also by Paul Henry and by Roderic O'Conor. Like other Irish artists who had continued their training on the continent, she gained a more down-to-earth approach to everyday subjects than was in evidence amongst Irish artists of an earlier generation. In this way she was typical of the manner in which the strong French influence on Irish painting, already much in evidence at the end of the nineteenth century continued into the twentieth. Her chief subjects were Irish landscapes and hunting scenes.

A founder member of the Dublin Painters Group, she was made a member of the Royal Hibernian Academy in 1944. She exhibited widely, at the RHA, her first appearance there being in 1909, the Royal Academy, the Burlington Art Gallery, the Kensington Art Gallery, the Paris Salon, the Scottish Society of Women Artists, and the Irish Exhibition in Paris.

Her works are to be found in the National Gallery of Ireland, the Hugh Lane Municipal Gallery, Dublin, and the Ulster Museum, Belfast.   NA

See cat. nos. 97-99.

Hanratty, Alice (contemp. artist)
Born in Dublin. Studied National College of Art, Dublin and Hornsey College of Art, London (Department of Post Graduate Studies).

One Man Exhibitions: 1962, 1971, 1976, 1979, Dublin (Davis Gallery, Capel Street; Setanta Gallery, Molesworth Street); 1978, Bangor, county Down, Pretani Gallery; 1967, Nairobi, Kenya.

International Biennales of Print: 1973, 1975, 1979, 1981, 1983, 1985, Ljublyana, Yugoslavia; 1978, Ljublyana, Yugoslavia, 'Homage to Marcel Duchamp'; 1974, 1976, 1978, Fredrikstad, Norway; 1978, Ostfold Kultursyre; 1973, 1976, 1987, Biella, Italy; 1981, Baden-Baden; 1982, 9th Triennale Grenchen; 1982/84, Interbep 82 Switzerland; 1984, 1987, Intergrafik '84 Berlin, German Democratic Republic; 1978, 4th Triennale New Delhi; 1980, Irish Government Promotion, Birmingham, Alabama; 1982, Irish Graphics (Department of Foreign Affairs Touring Exhibition); 1980, Irish Artists, Chicago; 1980, The Delighted Eye, London; 1979, Irish Printmaking (and international printers) Municipal Gallery; various years, Listowel Graphics; 1979, Orchard Gallery Belfast; Graphic Studio Retrospective Exhibition; 1964-70 (approx.), Living Art; 1962-82, Oireachtas; 1961-70 (approx.), Royal Hibernian Academy; 1969-70, Curwen Gallery, London.

Harrington, Countess of (Elizabeth) (c.1819-1912)

Elizabeth Still, daughter of Robert Lucas de Pearsall, of Wartensee Castle, St. Gall, Switzerland, was born about 1819. In 1839 she married Charles Wyndham Stanhope who became the 7th Earl of Harrington in 1866.

After her marriage, Elizabeth spent much of her time in Ireland, where she did many drawings and watercolours of her children and their activities and of landscape views of gardens and places where she visited and lived.

It appears that Elizabeth spent a lot of time visiting with her sister-in-law Charlotte Augusta, 3rd Duchess of Leinster, at Carton. The Duchess of Leinster, herself an accomplished amateur artist, seems to have encouraged those around her to paint and formed at Carton a circle of women artists which included the Duchess's sister Lady Caroline Stanhope and Frances Charlotte de Ros. WR

See cat. no. 19.

Harrison, Sarah Cecilia (1863-1941)

Portrait painter Sarah Cecilia Harrison (usually called Celia) was the daughter of Letitia and Henry Harrison, J.P., of Holywood House, county Down. She spent much of her youth and twenties in London, where her family settled after her father's death in 1873. From September 1878 until June 1885, she attended the Slade, winning a scholarship, various prizes and certificates, and a silver medal, for painting from the Antique. Despite living in England, she appears to have retained her links with Northern Ireland, as she exhibited with the Ladies' Sketching Club of the Belfast Government School of Art in 1879 (so too did Sydney Mary Thompson). In the late 1880's, she made Dublin her home. As with a number of other Irish artists of the period, she spent some time in France (in 1890), painting in Étaples and Brittany. She was a regular exhibitor at the Royal Hibernian Academy from 1889 until 1933, and was an Honorary Academician of both the Ulster Academy of Arts and its successor, the Royal Ulster Academy.

In addition to maintaining a successful portrait practice, she became involved, in 1912, in the attempt to find a suitable location for a gallery for Hugh Lane's pictures (she and Lane were close friends) and with fund raising to supplement Dublin Corporation's grant towards the building. She seems to have relished the political arena, for, in the same year, she became the first woman to serve on Dublin city council. There, she devoted her energies to the cause of the poor and did much to help improve their lot. Together with Alderman A. Byrne, T.D., she was instrumental in getting poor relief extended to include the able-bodied unemployed. For many years, she ran an advice centre for Dublin's needy, from a room in her home and helped countless numbers of the deprived and poverty-stricken (her work in this field being largely independent of any charitable organisation). She was also a tireless worker for women's rights and an ardent Nationalist (and a great grand-niece of Henry Joy McCracken). Her tall figure — she was 6 ft. 2 inches — was well-known in Dáil Éireann, where she was

a constant visitor until about 1940. She died on 23 July 1941.

Her work is represented in the National Gallery of Ireland, the Hugh Lane Municipal Gallery, Dublin, and the Ulster Museum, Belfast. EB

See cat. no. 55.

Hartland, Gertrude (1865-1954)

Gertrude Hartland was the daughter of Richard Hartland and Mary Walsh; she was born in Cork. Her father's younger brother, William Baylor Hartland; became a prominent Cork nurseryman.

Miss Hartland drew and painted flowers, principally daffodils, from her uncle's nursery between 1887 and 1897 at least. Her artwork was used as the basis for illustrations published in a variety of different places including Hartland's idiosyncratic bulb and seed catalogues. In 1897, William Baylor Hartland published a 'Special Jubilee Issue' of his daffodil catalogue. Its pages were decorated with engraved portraits of daffodils which Gertrude had prepared; the ordinary issue was available for a few pence but a limited number of hand-coloured copies was available costing one guinea each. The engraving was done by W. J. Welch who was the principal engraver for such horticultural periodicals as the *Gardener's Chronicle*.

Gertrude Hartland married Stephen Jackson; she died in 1954. ECN

Hayward, Phyllis (1903-1985)

Born 1903 in Portsmouth, England; c.1919, studied briefly at Portsmouth School of Art; c.1927, studied part-time at the Central School of Art, London, and also at this time became interested in the practice of psychology, becoming a member of Basil Rakocsi's Society for Creative Psychology. Married Donald Teale by whom she had one son, but separated in about 1939; 1940, went to Dublin where she remained until about 1950-51. During these years she exhibited with the White Stag Group, at the Contemporary Pictures Gallery and regularly at the Irish Exhibition of Living Art; 1948, became a member of the Society of Dublin Painters; c.1950, returned to England and later went to France where she remained until about the early sixties before settling permanently in London where she died in 1985.

Henry, Grace (1868-1953)

Grace Henry was born Emily Grace Mitchell, in Peterhead, Aberdeenshire, Scotland, the second youngest of ten children of a Church of Scotland minister, John Mitchell, and his wife Jane Garden (who was related to Byron). Grace Mitchell was born into a family of comfortable means helped by private income, and she was educated first at home by governesses, later at a London finishing school. Her mother's family had a house in Piccadilly, and she may have stayed on in London after her education. In the late-1890's, she was living in various lodgings in Aberdeen, exhibiting with the Aberdeen Artists' Society in 1898 and 1900. In the three years following, she studied in Brussels and at Paris ateliers, where she met and in 1903 married Paul Henry. She was by then 35, and yet her life as Grace Henry and her career as a painter was only just beginning. Both were to last for a further fifty years, though she later separated from Paul.

After their marriage, the Henrys returned to live and work outside London, in Surrey, for about eight years, but relatively little of their work survives from that time. In August 1912, they went for a short holiday to Achill and stayed on for another eight years! Much survives from this 'Achill' period, but while it established Paul Henry as a painter of Irish landscape and peasant life, it was less successful for Grace. She was already unsettled in her marriage, and experimented with various painting styles in those years of her early and mid-forties. She was frequently moving, visiting Dublin and London, but all the time she was developing a style using bold colour and fluid, painterly brushwork. Some of her 'Achill' landscapes were simplified almost to abstraction, depending only on outlines and flattened shapes. Others were outstanding in capturing atmosphere, like the Prussian blue and grey moonlight scenes of Achill.

After Achill, the Henrys settled in Merrion Row, Dublin, and with six others, founded the Dublin Painters' Society in 1920, exhibiting several times a year through the 'disturbed' 1920's. Grace Henry had a solo exhibition in the Magee Gallery in Belfast in 1923, and moved on to train under André Lhote in 1924-25. By this time, in the late 1920's, she had separated from Paul, but they were never divorced. She painted more and more in the South of France, and boats and sails in Italian harbours like Chioggio. Almost every year, and often several times a year, through the 1930's and 1940's, Grace Henry exhibited work in Dublin galleries and at the Royal Hibernian Academy. Her free and painterly style, heightened by the use of strong colours, seemed to be ideal for capturing the sunlit landscapes of the Mediterranean. By now an old woman, she was made HRHA in 1949 at the age of eighty-one. She had been living in Dublin hotels for several years, much reduced in the vigour of her painting style, when she died in Dublin in 1953. She is buried at Mount Jerome.   JGC

See cat. nos. 92-93.

Henry, Mabel see Young, Mabel

Henry, Olive (b.1902)

Olive Henry, painter and stained glass designer, is a native of Belfast. Her involvement with stained glass began when she was still a schoolgirl at Victoria College and attending night classes at Belfast School of Art. By good fortune, the owner of the Belfast glass firm of W. F. Clokey & Co. visited the art school, in search of a girl to train in his glass department. Olive, about to leave Victoria and attracted to the medium, was appointed to the post. She remained with the firm all her working life, from the autumn of 1919 until Easter 1972. Most of her time in Clokey's was spent designing windows, although, on a few occasions, she had the chance to produce the cartoons and paint the glass herself. However, despite the fact that this opportunity only seldom arose

(she relished this fuller creative involvement), she enjoyed the work and the fifty-three years with the firm.

Olive's reputation in the art world rests mainly on the painting side of her career (her output in Clokey's being credited to the firm, not to the individual). She has been a regular exhibitor in Belfast since 1928, firstly at the Belfast Art Society, then at the Ulster Academy of Arts and subsequently, at the Royal Ulster Academy (of which she is an Academician). In addition, she is a founder member and past President of the Ulster Society of Women Artists. She has also shown at the Royal Hibernian Academy, the Irish Exhibition of Living Art, the Oireachtas and the Watercolour Society of Ireland. Her work includes subject pictures, still-life and landscapes, with boats and gates being among her favourite motifs, because of their shapes. Pattern and shape have always attracted her — which is why she liked stained glass — and are the dominant characteristics of her style. Her paintings, though representational, often seem almost abstract, because of these traits, and frequently contain interesting and exciting images. An exhibition featuring work from her studio was held at the Shambles Art Gallery, Hillsborough, county Down, in 1986.

Her paintings are represented in the Ulster Museum, the B.B.C. (Northern Ireland) and the British Council, London.   EB

Herbert, Gwendolen (1878-1966)

Gwendolen Herbert the sculptor and craftworker, was born at Cahirnane House, Killarney, county Kerry into a junior branch of the Herberts of Muckross (see *Burke's Landed Gentry of Ireland*). By 1898 the family fortunes had moved to a point where the family seat had to be sold, and Gwendolen moved to Dublin with her mother.

She began attending classes at the Metropolitan School of Art in 1899, won a studentship in 1900 and studied modelling. From 1904 she studied enamelling and metalwork under P. Oswold Reeves.

Her modelling talents attracted her to the 'Irish Art Companions', an Irish Revival Industry which was founded in Dublin in 1904. The Companions manufactured plaster from native gypsum and produced Irish Art Products in the form of plaster figures and statues both secular and ecclesiastical. She joined them, along with Joseph Corre and Mervyn Lawrence (other companions were Mr. Hanrahan and Mrs. Vanston). She modelled some charming studies of Irish peasantry — old women, itinerant fiddlers and workmen with their staves — very different in feeling and treatment from the 'bog oak Paddies with pigs' that were then so prevalent.

She moved to London in 1907, supporting herself by teaching and making garden statues, and returned to Killarney in 1929.

She exhibited at the Irish International Exhibition in Dublin 1907, at the Royal Hibernian Academy, the Royal Academy and the Walker Gallery in Liverpool.

An example of her work is in the National Gallery of Ireland.   PL

See cat. no. 51.

Herbert, Mary (1817-1893)

Mary Herbert was born at Whittinghame, East Lothian, Scotland, the second child and second daughter of James Balfour Esq. of Whittinghame and Lady Eleanor Maitland, daughter of the 8th Earl of Lauderdale.

Though the female members of the Balfour family were considered artistic, Mary received little formal training, other than the drawing lessons which formed a part of most young ladies' education at the time.

In 1837 Mary married Henry Arthur Herbert Esq. of Muckross, county Kerry, who was later to be Chief Secretary for Ireland from 1857-1858. From this time on she developed her skills as an artist and more especially as a landscape watercolourist, concentrating, almost exclusively, on Irish landscape. Her increased experience both of her medium and her subject transformed Mary's early rather fussy style into one that was relaxed and confident, enabling her to capture the capricious beauty of the Irish landscape.

Examples of Mary's work are in Muckross House Museum and the National Library of Ireland.   NS

See cat. no. 24.

Heron, Hilary (1923-1976)

Born 1923 in Dublin; she attended the National College of Art, Dublin, and went on to develop her ideas by looking at primitive sculpture as well as that of her English contemporaries. In 1947 she was awarded the Mainie Jellett Travelling Scholarship. In 1948 she studied Romanesque sculpture in France and Italy, then returned to work in Ireland. She died in 1976.

Exhibitions: 1943, Irish Exhibition of Living Art, Dublin; 1945, Royal Hibernian Academy, Dublin; 1950, First one person exhibition, Dublin; 1956, Venice Biennale, with Louis le Brocquy.

Hone, Evie (1894-1955)

A member of the Hone family which has provided Ireland with a number of gifted artists over the centuries, Eva Sydney Hone was born 22 April 1894. Before the first World War she started training at the Byam Shaw School of Art; she also had some training from Walter Sickert, after which she worked with Bernard Meninsky, who advised her to go to Paris. She and her close friend Mainie Jellett followed this advice and became the pupils of André Lhote and then of Albert Gleizes. They spent nearly ten years visiting Gleizes each summer. Evie was devoutly religious and, for a short time in 1925, joined an Anglican religious community in Truro, Cornwall, but soon returned to painting. Later she became a Catholic and this interest in religion was one of the main inspirations of her artistic works. All her life she had to fight against ill-health caused by infantile paralysis, but this she overcame to a certain degree in later life. She was one of the founders of the Irish Exhibition of Living Art, and both by her own works and by her encouragement of other artists, she exercised influence on modern Irish art.

Evie Hone lived in the Dower House, Marlay, Rathfarnham, and the immediate vicinity provided her with another source of inspiration, as in *Snow at Marlay.* Sometimes her early paintings are hard to distinguish from those of Mainie Jellett, but she had a more florid sense of colour, which finally led to her interest in stained glass. Her window designs also differed from those of her contemporaries in that she showed a much greater affinity to medieval glass. What she had gleaned, mainly from Albert Gleizes, about the value of shape and colour in the stimulation of vision resulted in stained glass windows, as well as paintings, which had a seminal influence on the modern movement in Ireland.

Her works are to be seen in churches throughout Ireland and England, and also in the National Gallery of Ireland, the Hugh Lane Municipal Gallery, Dublin, the Crawford Municipal Art Gallery, Cork and the Ulster Museum, Belfast.   NA

See cat. nos. 120-22.

Horgan, Sara (b.1942)

Born 1942; 1981, Honours Degree in Fine Art (Printmaking), National College of Art & Design, Dublin; 1982, founder member and administrator, Black Church Print Studio, Dublin.

Group Exhibitions: 1980, exhibited regularly in Irish Group shows; 1985, Hangzhou & Beijing, Milwaukee Irish Festival; 1986, Miniprint Exhibition, Barcelona; British Print Biennale, Bradford, England (invited, and awarded prize); 1987, exhibited in Finland; exhibited in Cuba; European Print Biennale, Baden Baden, Germany.

One-Woman Show: 1987, Oliver Dowling Gallery, Dublin.

Collections: CIE, Dublin; The Gordon Lambert Collection, Ronald Tallon, Irish Embassy, Riyadh.

Houston, Sally (b.1954)

Born 1954 in Belfast; 1976, graduated from Edinburgh College of Art, Scotland; 1977, moved to Dublin. Awarded Arts Council of Ireland bursary; 1978-82, part-time teacher at secondary level; 1983-84, worked at Scottish Sculpture Workshop, Aberdeenshire.

One-Woman Exhibitions: 1982, Octagon Gallery, Belfast; 1983, Wexford Art Centre, Wexford and the Arts Council Gallery, Belfast.

Group Exhibitions: 1976, Scottish Young Contemporaries, RSA, Edinburgh; 1977, Ulster Young Contemporaries, Octagon Gallery, Belfast; Group Sculpture Show, Project Arts Centre, Dublin; Young Artists, Lad Lane Gallery, Dublin; 1980, Exhibition of Visual Art, Limerick; Independent Artists, Dublin ('80, '81, '82, '83); 1982, Cleveland International Drawing Biennale, England; Sculpture and Drawing Exhibition, Cork.

Hunter, Mary Ann (Mrs. Trotter) (fl. 1765-1777)

Mary Ann Hunter was the daughter of the celebrated eighteenth century portraitist, Robert Hunter, and was presumably trained by him. Mary Ann exhibited from 1765 to 1777 at the Society of Artists in Ireland, chiefly portraits but also some mythological (*Minerva introducing Venus,* 1773) and biblical (*The finding of Moses,* 1768) subjects. She was awarded various prizes for her portraits during the 1760's and 1770's by the Dublin Society.

In 1774 she married John Trotter (d.1792), a successful Dublin portrait painter; they had two daughters, both of whom became painters. The elder, M. Trotter (fl. c.1809-1815), studied in the Royal Academy School in London and the younger, Eliza H. Trotter, is separately noted.   WR

Hutchins, Ellen (1785-1815)

A delicate, white-blossomed cress from the European Alps bears the name *Hutchinsia alpina,* and a moss-like liverwort from the damp glens of Ireland is called *Jungermannia hutchinsiae*; they are but two examples of plants that are memorials to Ellen Hutchins of whom one contemporary wrote '*Nobilis virgo HUTCHINS nuperimme Bontajae in Hibernia defuncta, a ... genere* Hutchinsia *nec non a ...* Jungermannia Hutchinsiae *sempiternae memoriae tradita, bontanices adeoque difficillimae hujus partis cryptogamiae studium ferventi amore coluit.*'

Ellen Hutchins was born at Ballylickey in west county Cork. Her school-days were spent in Dublin where, because of ill-health, she came to know Dr. Whitley Stokes, a physician and naturalist. Under his influence she took up botany, making her special mark by collecting the cryptogams — the mosses, liverworts, lichens and seaweeds — around Bantry Bay. Dr. Stokes introduced Ellen to James Townsend Mackay, the curator of the Botanical Gardens of Trinity College, Dublin, and she later became a friend and correspondent of other eminent naturalists including Dawson Turner.

For a number of years Ellen Hutchins was responsible for looking after her elderly mother and her invalid brother, Emmanuel. After her mother's death, she moved to live with her elder brother, Arthur, and his family at Ardnagashel House on the shores of Bantry Bay. There Ellen gardened, cultivating plants sent to her by Mackay, Turner and others. But she did not long survive her mother and died on 10 February 1815, at the age of thirty. Her name, however, is not forgotten; the alpine cress and a suite of lichens, a moss, the liverwort and several seaweeds were named after her by botanists who recognised the immense value of her pioneering work among the non-flowering plants.

Ellen Hutchins was not just a collector of plants; she also painted in watercolour some of the specimens, especially the seaweeds which will shrivel quickly and lose their form when removed from their natural habitats. Several of her paintings of seaweeds were used to illustrated Dawson Turner's *Historia Fuci.*

Examples of Miss Hutchin's watercolours are preserved in the Royal Botanic Gardens, Kew, and Sheffield City Museum.
ECN

Jacob, Alice (1862-1921)

Alice Jacob was brought up in Dublin in a well-known Quaker family, which had emigrated to New Zealand, where they lived for several years but returned to Ireland and settled at 88 Thomas Street in the Dublin Liberties. She studied art at the Dublin Metropolitan School of Art in the 1880's, where she was awarded a succession of scholarships and prizes. In 1891 she attended the summer course at South Kensington and subsequently taught elementary design in the Dublin and Cork Schools of Art and later at the Rathmines Technical School.

She was a versatile and much praised designer, gaining particular recognition for her lace designs, some of which can be seen in the National Museum of Ireland. Those for floral damasks, crochet, painted silk and embroidery reveal her sensitive botanical observation and training in free-form brushwork in watercolour illustration from nature, exemplified by her orchid studies for the Botanic Garden's Collection at Glasnevin, 1907-20. The Celtic lettering she favoured in some of these is echoed in her embossed design for leather and reflects her membership of the Gaelic League. She also decorated a set of Belleek porcelain for Dr. Perceval Wright, Professor of Botany in Trinity College, Dublin.

She retired from her position at the Dublin School of Art a month before her death.   NGB and ECN

See cat. no. 68.

Jacob, Mrs. E. W. see Fannin, Marianne Edwardine

Jameson, Flora see Mitchell, Flora

Jameson, Harriet see Kirkwood, Harriet

Jellett, Mainie (1897-1944)

Mainie Jellett was born in Dublin, on 20 April 1897, at 36 Fitzwilliam Square. She was the eldest of four daughters of William Morgan Jellett and Margaret McKensie Stokes. She was christened Mary Harriet, but known from childhood as Mainie. She was educated at home, and then with various art teachers, entering the Metropolitan School of Art in 1915. She went to London, to study under Sickert in the Westminster School from 1917 to 1919. In 1920 she won the Taylor Scholarship, and the following year the Prize for Painting. The money from this allowed her to study in Paris.

She became a pupil of André Lhote, there, in 1921, transferring to Albert Gleizes the following year. She remained his pupil (referred to by him as 'disciple') for the next ten years, visiting him during the summers from Dublin. She exhibited abstract art from 1923, and was the victim of prejudiced criticism by George Russell. She found support from such art critics as Thomas McGreevy, however, and became the leader of the modern Movement in Ireland during the period between the two world wars, holding exhibitions regularly, and writing and broadcasting about art. She was also a teacher.

Her art developed greater realism in the thirties, and became more overtly Christian, though without losing its intellectual rigour, or departing from its Cubist-Abstract principles.

She was involved in various art movements in Dublin, and was a leading figure in the setting up of the Irish Exhibition of Living Art in 1943, becoming the committee's chairman.

She became ill with cancer in the autumn of that year, and died the following February at the age of forty-seven. Her works are in all the major Irish collections.   BA

See cat. nos. 116-20.

Johnston, Henrietta see Dering, Henrietta

Eithne Jordan (b.1954)

Born 1954 in Dublin; 1972-76, studied Dun Laoghaire School of Art; founder member of the Visual Arts Centre, a co-operative studio space for artists, funded by the Arts Council and Dublin Corporation. Lectured in painting, National College of Art and Design, Dublin and is at present working in Berlin on a DAAD scholarship.

One-Woman Exhibitions: 1980, Peacock Theatre, Dublin; 1982, Project Arts Centre, Dublin; 1985, Lincoln Gallery, Dublin.

Group Exhibitions: 1979, Wexford Arts Centre, 3 Woman show; Exhibition of Visual Art, (EVA), Limerick; 1980-85, Independent Artists, Dublin; 1981, Seven Women Painters, Galway Arts Festival; Claremorris Art Exhibition; Irish Exhibition of Living Art, Dublin; 1982, Exhibition of Visual Art, Limerick; 1983, New Artists, New Works, Orchard Gallery, Derry; Belltable Arts Centre, Limerick; Ten Irish Artists, Kelleher Gallery, New York; Irish Graphics, Amsterdam; 1984, Irish Exhibition of Living Art, Douglas Hyde Gallery, Dublin; ContemporEire, Exhibition, Dublin; Temple Bar Gallery, Dublin; 1985, Edinburgh-Dublin Exhibition, Edinburgh Festival.

Collections: An Chomhairle Ealaíon/The Arts Council; Contemporary Irish Arts Society; Allied Irish Bank, Dublin; Bank of Ireland, Dublin; Vincent Ferguson, Dublin; Dublin City Libraries.

Kelleher, Julie (b.1952)

Born 1952; 1979, Exhibition Project Art Centre, Dublin; 1981, Degree Show National College of Art and Design, Dublin; 1981, Guinness Peat Aviation Exhibition, county Wicklow; 1981, Independent Artists Exhibition, Hugh Lane Gallery, Dublin; 1982, Three Girls Group Show, Tyrone Guthrie Centre, county Monaghan; 1983, 'Paintings With Faces' — One Woman Show Triskel Arts Centre, Cork; 1985-87, Touring Exhibition organised by Ireland America Arts Exchange Inc., Venues — Boston; New York, Quebec; 1986, Women's Art Festival, Triskel Arts Centre, Cork; 1986, Performance with Danny McCarthy 'How well Old Men can Dance', 'Soundworks', Triskel Arts Centre, Cork.

Kelly, Frances (fl. from 1929)

Frances Kelly studied at the Metropolitan School of Art in Dublin, and in Paris under Léopold Survage. In 1929, she exhibited for the first time at the Royal Hibernian Academy, and in 1931 she contributed a still life and *The Cossack,* as well as two portraits, to the RHA. She continued to exhibit there until the late thirties. During the 1940's she exhibited with the Dublin Painters, and at the Oireachtas Art Exhibition and the Irish Exhibition of Living Art, and she held four one-man shows at the Dawson Gallery, Dublin. She has rarely exhibited since 1950. Portraits include those of her daughter, Eavan Boland, the poet Máire MacEntee, and writer Frank O'Connor. Her paintings are unmistakable for their pale, harmonious pastel tones, for the broad flat treatment in areas

of light and shade, and for their restrained and introspective character.
                                                                    HP

See cat. nos. 131-32.

Kiely, Bernadette (b.1958)

Born 1958 in Clonmel; 1975-77, School of Art, Waterford; 1982-83, School of Art, Waterford.

Exhibitions: 1986, Guinness Peat Aviation Exhibition, Dublin; 1987, 'Drawing the Line' — Touring Exhibition; Women's Week, Waterford.

King, Martha (c.1803-1897)

Miss King was one of a family of three who emigrated from Ireland to New Zealand in 1840. The Kings were members of an heretical protestant sect, the Socinians, and most probably came from county Cork. With her brother, Samuel Popham King, and her sister Maria, Martha arrived in Wellington in December 1840; after losing all their goods in a shipwreck, they settled on land which they had purchased at Wanganui. Mr. King became one of the local postmasters and the two sisters established Wanganui's first Dame School. Martha also served as a governess. The family later moved to New Plymouth where again the Misses King established a school. Martha King lived in New Plymouth for the rest of her life, and on her death in 1897 she left her garden to the New Plymouth Recreation Grounds Board.

From contemporary accounts it is known that, shortly after arriving in New Zealand, Martha King earned a small living from painting miniatures but none of these are recorded in collections. She also did pencil sketches of landscapes; sixteen local views, dated between 1841 and 1859, are in the Alexander Turnbull Museum, Wellington, Miss King was well-known to her contemporaries as an artist — one recorded that she '... draws very well and was engaged by a naturalist to make drawings of the plants he collected'.

Martha King's principal work is a series of forty watercolours of native plants, commissioned by the Wellington Horticultural and Botanical Society in 1842. These paintings were sent to the New Zealand Company, London, where they remained until 1981 when the Alexander Turnbull Library acquired them. Four of the plant portraits were engraved and published in E. J. Wakefield's *Illustrations of adventure in New Zealand* (London 1845).

All known examples of Martha King's work are in the Alexander Turnbull Library, Wellington, New Zealand.   EC

King, Mary see Ward, Mary

Kingston, Diana (b.1959)

Born 1954 in Guyana; 1959, settled in West Cork; 1974-78, studied at Cork Municipal School of Art.

Exhibitions: 1977, Student Show, Project Arts Centre, Dublin; 1978, Irish Exhibition of Living Art, Douglas Hyde Gallery, Dublin; 1979, Irish Exhibition of Living Art, Bank of Ireland, Dublin; 1980, 'Exposure', Dublin; Summer Exhibition, Tom

Caldwell Gallery, Belfast; Irish Exhibition of Living Art, Douglas Hyde Gallery, Dublin; Independent Artists, Municipal Gallery of Modern Art, Dublin; Tom Caldwell Gallery, Dublin; 1981, Tom Caldwell Gallery, Dublin; Irish Exhibition of Living Art, Douglas Hyde Gallery, Dublin; 1982, Royal Hibernian Academy, Dublin; Irish Exhibition of Living Art, Douglas Hyde Gallery, Dublin; 1983, Oireachtas, Dublin, Claremorris.

Kinkead, Alice S. (fl. 1897-1922)

Alice ('Annie') Kinkead, born in Tuam, county Galway, painted portraits and landscapes. In 1897 she sent a portrait in pastel to the Royal Hibernian Academy from Forster House in Galway, and exhibited at the Salon de la Nationale in Paris. In c.1898 she was in London, living around Chelsea and Brompton Road. She exhibited a portrait of a relation Miss Kinkead, of W. B. Yeats (1904), and other portraits at the RHA between 1897-1907. She showed there again in 1920, and at the Paris Salon two years later.

JC

Kirkwood, Harriet (1880-1953)

She was born Grace Harriet Sara Jameson, in 1880, the daughter of the Rt. Hon. Andrew Jameson, of Sutton House, Sutton, county Dublin. She attended the Metropolitan School of Art, Dublin, both the 1908-09 session and the 1919-20 session (where she is given as Kirkwood, née Jameson; in 1910 she had married Major Thomas William Kirkwood, O.B.E., a director of John Jameson & Co.). She was a friend of John Butler Yeats who encouraged her to study in London and Paris. While he never founded a school, Yeats was a great inspiration to the group of young artists who gathered themselves around Mainie Jellett in the early inter-war years. As a result of this influence, she went to Paris in the 1930's to study with André Lhote, who had earlier been the teacher of both Mainie Jellett and Evie Hone.

Her style was considerably influenced by that of Mainie Jellett, and seems to have followed the changes present in the latter's style. The esteem in which she held Evie Hone may be seen by the fact that she and her husband ordered a memorial window to be designed by Evie for St. Naithi's, Dundrum. She was a prolific artist, whose inspiration tended to come directly from the objects around her. Her fellow exhibitors included, at times, Norah McGuinness, Jack P. Hanlon, Evie Hone and Eugene Judge. She was President of the Dublin Painters' Group, based at 7 St. Stephen's Green, whose other members included Letitia Hamilton. In spite of her earlier importance and her plentiful production, she is now relatively unknown.

Examples of her work are to be found in the National Gallery of Ireland.

NA

See cat. no. 127.

Kyle, Georgina Moutray (1865-1950)

Georgina Moutray Kyle, the daughter of a prosperous business family, was born at Craigavad, county Down. She led a very protected childhood, being the youngest of a large family, and was educated at home, as she was considered delicate. Despite her fragile constitution, her artistic ability was encouraged and at the age of eighteen (never having so much as gone into Belfast unaccompanied!), she was sent to study art at Colarossi's Academy, Paris. Regrettably, nothing is known of her student days there but the atmosphere must have been something of a revelation to a young woman with an extremely sheltered upbringing. On her return to Belfast, she joined the Belfast Ramblers' Sketching Club, in 1889, and later, became greatly involved with its successor, the Belfast Art Society. She held various posts within the Society, including those of Secretary of the Ladies' Life Class, membership of the Committee, and the Vice-Presidency, this latter in 1920, 1921, 1927 and 1928. She subsequently became an Academician of the Ulster Academy of Arts. In addition to this participation on the local scene, she exhibited at the Royal Hibernian Academy, the Royal Scottish Academy, the Royal Glasgow Institute of the Fine Arts and the Paris Salon.

Georgina's favourite subjects were market and harbour views, although still-life and flowers also figure in her output. Her work is highly distinctive and easily recognised, because of its linear emphasis and strong use of pattern. Her character appears to have been as distinctive as her painting: an incessant talker and somewhat eccentric, she was strong-willed and articulate, with a great interest in politics and world affairs (she apparently went on propaganda missions to England, in the cause of Ulster Unionism, during the Home Rule crisis). She travelled extensively on the Continent (many of her market scenes were painted in Brittany) and worked for part of each summer at Ardglass, county Down. She seldom, if ever, sold any of her paintings, preferring to give them to family and friends.

Her work, which is of an impressive standard and always interesting, is represented in the Ulster Museum, Armagh Museum, Queen's University, Belfast and Bangor Town Hall, county Down.

EB

See cat. no. 88.

Lamont, Elish (also La Monte) (1816-1870)

Elish Lamont, a native of Belfast, was a miniature painter, author and school mistress. Born into a respectable business family (the Lamonts were stationers and printers). She studied miniature painting in Londin 1837 and began exhibiting in her home town the following year, at the Belfast Association of Artists. She also showed further afield: at the Royal Hibernian Academy during the 1840's and 1850's and in 1870, and at the Royal Academy during the late 1850's. At this latter venue, she spelt her name 'La Monte' — perhaps in the belief that it would create a more artistic impression than Lamont! (La Monte, incidentally, was used on her death certificate). Such was her reputation by mid-century that a number of her miniatures were presented to Queen Victoria, during the royal visit to Dublin of 1853. A further honour bestowed upon her was the inclusion of engravings after her miniatures of Lady Dufferin and the Dowager Duchess of Manchester in the *Court Album,* a series of portraits of the female aristocracy, published annually in London between 1850 and 1857. However, her output was not confined solely to miniatures; in 1845, Lamont published a series of prints after six crayon drawings by her, illustrative of Moore's *Irish Melodies.*

Elish's talents were also of a literary nature. In January 1843, the *Northern Whig* recorded her as having written *The Gladiator* and *The Mission of the Educator,* and praised her most recent publication, *Impressions, Thoughts and Sketches during Two Years in Switzerland.* In addition, she was an able poet, publishing a book of ballads, *Christmas Rhymes,* with her sister France in 1846, and winning second prize in Belfast's Victoria Fete poetry competition of 1850, with a piece entitled *The Island Queen.* As inferred by one of the above book titles, she was an experienced teacher, an ability she put to good use in 1851, when she opened up a select boarding and day school in Belfast — which, however, flourished for only a few years. According to an advertisement for the establishment, she had taught in boarding schools in England, France and Germany, and with high-ranking families in London.

Elish appears to have spent her latter years in Rochester, where she died on 28 July 1870, aged fifty-four. One of her miniatures is in the Ulster Museum.   EB

See cat. no. 22.

Landweer, Sonja (b.1932)

1952, studied Amsterdam School of Industrial Design; 1954, opened own studio; 1956, won travelling scholarships to Spain, France, Denmark and England; 1963, evolved batiked-ceramic technique; 1964, awarded Verzetsprijs for total *oeuvre*; 1964-65, invited for winter months as guest potter to 'Arabia' in Finland; 1965-66, worked for Kilkenny Design Workshops; 1966, Membre Titulaire, International Academy of Ceramics, Geneva; 1974, awarded 'Prix Artistique' at the 4th Biennale Internationale de Ceramique D'Art Vallauris, France; 1981, Member of Aosdana.

One-Man Shows: 1956, Gallery Liernur, The Hague; 1962, Gallery Ina Broerse; 1963, Kapelhuis, Amersfoort; Museum Prisetun, Leewarden; 1964, Gallery Liernur, The Hague; Gallery d'Eendt, Amsterdam; 1965, Gallery Ina Broerse, Amsterdam; Kapelhuis, Amersfoort; 1967-1981, David Hendriks Gallery, Dublin; 1969, Kapelhuis, Amersfoort; 1971, Kapelhuis, Amersfoort; 1972, Gallerie Inar, Amsterdam; Museum of Decorative Arts, Copenhagen; 1973, Hildesheim Stadtisches Museum, Germany; 1981, Kapelhuis, Amersfoort.

Group Shows: 1958, Van Abbe Museum, Eindhoven; 'Contempory Dutch Ceramics'; 'De Beyerd'; 1978, World Craft Council Exhibition, 'The Bowl', Goteborg; 1979; 'The Bowl', Kilkenny Design Workshops, Kilkenny; 1980, Museum Flehite, 'Gedraaide Vormen', Amersfoort; '3 Keramisten' Gallerie Het Kapelhuis, Amersfoort; 1986, Concorso Internazionale delle Ceramica d'Arte, Faenza; 'Minprint Exhibition', David Hendriks Gallery, Dublin; 1987, Miniature Ceramics, Yugoslavia.

Represented in Public Collections: Museum Boymans-van Beuningen, Rotterdam; Stedelyk Museum, Amsterdam; Hetyen Museum, Düsseldorf; Stadtisches Museum, Osnabruck; Centraal Museum, Utrecht; Gemeente Museum, The Hague; Gemeente Museum, Arnhem; The Dutch Arts Council; Ulster Museum, Belfast; Musée Vallauris, Vallauris; Musée Cantini, Marseille.

Lavery, Lady (Hazel) (1887-1935)

Hazel Lavery was a native of Chicago where her family, the Martyns, were involved in a prosperous meat business called Armear & Co. Hazel showed considerable talent for drawing in her early years. Interested in the revolutionary artistic developments in France, she made her first visit to Europe in her late teens. She wanted to be near the artists colonies and, while she did not study there herself, she was in constant demand for portrait sittings on account of her exceptionally good looks. Her Titianesque hair and huge deep blue eyes were encased in a perfect oval face and this, matched with a bright witty personality, made her the centre of admiration in these colonies.

While staying in Brittany, at Beg-Mai, Hazel met John Lavery who was more than twenty years her senior. They became very friendly and Lavery recounts how they stayed discussing art late into the evenings. Hazel was, however, engaged to a New York surgeon, Edward Livingston Trudeau. She returned to America and married him in January 1904. Their marriage was tragically brief as Trudeau died four months later while Hazel was expecting their daughter, Alice. While she was widowed, Hazel returned to Chicago where she enrolled at the Art Institute of Chicago in the Spring of 1908. She took figure painting and drawing classes with artist-teacher Charles Francis Brown. She was a talented student and was awarded an Honorable Mention for her exhibited work. Five years later Lavery and Hazel met again and were married at Brompton Oratory in 1910. Her great beauty and dramatic sense of dress ensured her a place among the foremost leaders of society fashion. She was a superb hostess and put this to great use during the negotiations for the Irish Treaty in 1922. In recognition of her services to the country, the Irish Government in 1927 commissioned a portrait of her from her husband which would be used on the Irish banknotes. Her image is retained today as the official watermark.

Despite being a society hostess, Hazel continued to paint all her life. She was recognised as a skilled draughtsman and, while still a student, exhibited at the Salon. After her marriage, she exhibited her work through such galleries as the Chenil Galleries and the Alpine Club Galleries where her work sold very successfully. She also contributed to the International show at the Grosvenor Gallery where her watercolour of Anna Pavlova was well received.

Her works are in the collections of the National Gallery of Ireland and the Hugh Lane Municipal Gallery, Dublin.   BM

See cat. no. 56.

Lecky, Emilia (c.1788-after 1844)

Emilia Lecky was born in Dublin and lived with her husband William Alexander Lecky first in Derry and later in Dublin. She exhibited almost continuously at the Royal Hibernian Society from

1826 to 1842. Her range of subject matter was extensive and included genre, history and religious themes as well as portraits. Her portraits were largely exhibited without the identity of the sitter being given. However in 1841 she exhibited a portrait of the Hon. William Porter, Attorney-General at the Cape of Good Hope, which suggests that her sitters were drawn from among the more prominent and influential members of society.

There are no known examples of her work.   WR

Leinster, Duchess of (Charlotte Augusta) (1793-1859)

The 3rd Earl of Harrington had three daughters, all of whom were talented artists in pencil and watercolour.

The eldest, Lady Anna Maria Stanhope (1783-1857) married the 7th Duke of Bedford in 1808. Several miniatures by her are in the collection of the National Gallery of Ireland, including a rather sizeable one depicting herself and her two sisters (cat. no. 7329).

The next eldest sister, Lady Caroline Anne Stanhope (d.1853) married, as his second wife, Mr. Edward Ayshford Sanford, FRS, DL, JP, of Somerset in 1841.

The youngest, Lady Charlotte Augusta Stanhope, married the 3rd Duke of Leinster in 1818, and settled at his splendid mansion and estate, Carton, county Kildare. There she entertained many friends of greater or lesser artistic talent. In the shell cottage are two small panels depicting scenes of courtly love; both of these small stained glass windows are signed: *C A Leinster pinxt 1834.* Clearly staying at Carton at that time was her older sister, Lady Caroline Anne, since two further windows in the same shell cottage are signed: *Caroline Stanhope pinx' 1834.* The draughtsmanship in the stained glass is not as good as in the artists' drawings and watercolours: while the two ladies drew the designs of the windows, the execution of them would have been entrusted to a Dublin firm of stained glass manufacturers.   MW

See cat. no. 17.

McAdoo, Annie Florence Violet (fl. c.1925-1965)

Born in Cookstown, county Tyrone, Violet McAdoo studied at the Belfast School of Art and at the Royal College of Art where she took her Associateship in 1927. She exhibited at the Royal Hibernian Academy, Ulster Academy and Royal Ulster Academy, and Society of Watercolour Artists, and was a member of the Watercolour Society of Ireland. She worked in Belfast and is represented in the Ulster Museum, Belfast.   MA

See cat. no. 109.

MacCann, Louisa (fl. 1890's)

Louisa MacCann was born in Belfast. In c. the late 1880's, she went to Paris, and studied at the Académie Julian, under Robert-Fleury and Lefebvre. She was represented at the Paris Salon in 1890 with a watercolour portrait, sent from the Hôtel de Chartres, Rue Brea.   JC

McCarrick, Eilish (b.1958)

Born 1958 in Dublin; 1981, BA Degree in Fine Art, National College of Art & Design, Dublin.

Group Shows: 1978, Grapevine Art Centre; 1979, Project Arts Centre (Photography show concerning demolition in Dublin); 1979, Douglas Hyde Gallery (Teacher & Pupil show); 1979, Independent Artists Exhibition (1980, 1981, 1982); 1980, NCAD Diploma Show; 1980, Living Art Exhibition (1981, 1982); 1981, NCAD Degree Show; 1984, Guinness Peat Aviation Exhibition; 1985, One Woman Exhibition 'Eilish McCarrick', Temple Bar Gallery; 1985, Group Show of Desire, Temple Bar Gallery; 1986, NCAD, Decade Show, Guinness Hop Store.

McCarthy, Clara (fl.1885-1906)

Clara McCarthy, née Christian, studied art at the Royal Hibernian Academy Schools in Dublin. She later lived alternately in Dublin and London, where she exhibited during the period 1885-1906 at various galleries including the Glasgow Institute of the Fine Arts, the Walker Art Gallery, Liverpool, the New English Art Club, the Royal Academy, the Royal Hibernian Academy and the Society of Women Artists.

Her work *Meditations* was among the early acquisitions to the Hugh Lane Municipal Gallery, Dublin, and it was included in its 1908 exhibition catalogue.   WR

McCausland, Elizabeth (fl. 1806-1807)

Unfortunately nothing is known of the life or artistic background of Elizabeth McCausland. Her existence is recorded solely through two miniatures of Charlotte Edgeworth in the National Gallery of Ireland. These miniatures reveal her to have been rather more than an amateur. Her style was fine and delicate and she had a good sense of colour though there is a slight stiffness of pose which perhaps suggests the work of a self taught artist.   WR

See cat. no. 12.

MacCausland, Katherine (d.1930)

Little is known of Katherine MacCausland's background or training. She was painting at Lowestoft in England in 1883, then moved to France. She settled at the artists' colony of Grez-sur-Loing in c.1890, at first staying at the Hôtel Chevillon and later buying a house of her own. She became friends with American painter Frank Chadwick and his Swedish wife. Emma Löwstadt who lived in the Rue Wilson, beside the river Loing. She became a long-term resident at Grez, popularly known as 'Miss Mac'. She painted portraits, studies of elderly villagers in interiors, and children, for example a portrait of Mlle. Froment, a pretty nine-year old girl in the Maison Leve in c.1902. A neighbouring artist would come to give advice and the child was awarded a fifty centime piece for each sitting. Katherine MacCausland exhibited one of her portraits at the Paris Salon.

The number of artists at Grez had dwindled, but the Chadwicks, Arthur Heseltine and his wife, and composer Frederick Delius were all neighbours of hers. (Delius's time at the village, from

1896-1934, corresponded closely with her own). Katherine died in 1930, and was buried at the cemetery at Saint-Germain-en-Laye.

There are paintings in the town halls of Bourron-Marlotte: 'Bateau de Pêche à Larstoft (sic), Suffolk, 1883 (presented by the artist), 'Le Père Boyer' (gift of Mme. Heseltine), and of Grez-sur-Loing: 'La Mère Moreau', 1891, and in private collections in Grez. JC

McGuinness, Norah (1921-1980)

Born in Derry; 1921, studied at the Metropolitan School of Art, Dublin, under Patrick Tuohy and Harry Clarke; 1924, studied for a time at the Chelsea School of Art, London; 1929-31, studied with André Lhote, Paris; 1944, elected President of the newly formed Irish Exhibition of Living Art; 1957, elected HRHA; 1973, she was given an honorary degree D.Litt. by Trinity College, Dublin; 1980, died.

Exhibited: 1933, Wertheim Gallery, London; 1934, Zwemmer Gallery, London; 1936, The Gallery, Dublin; 1937, Sullivan Gallery, New York; 1938-1949, Victor Waddington Gallery, Dublin; 1939, Paul Reinhart Gallery, New York; Contemporary Pictures Gallery, Dublin; 1941, The Gallery, Dublin; 1947, Leicester Gallery, London; 1950, XXV Biennale di Venezia; Exhibition of Contemporary Irish Painting, USA; 1951, Leicester Gallery, London; 1957, Leicester Gallery, London; 1962, Exhibition of Contemporary Irish Painting, Monaco; 1963, Leicester Gallery, London; Twelve Irish Painters, Art Centre, New York; 1964-1977, Dawson Gallery, Dublin; 1967, Mercury Gallery, London; 1968, Retrospective Exhibition, Trinity College, Dublin; 1976, Keys Gallery, Derry; 1979, Taylor Galleries, Dublin.

Collections: Hugh Lane Municipal Gallery, Dublin; Ulster Museum, Belfast; Arts Council of Ireland; Trinity College, Dublin; Herbert Art Gallery, Coventry; Joseph H. Hirschhorn Collection, New York; Insurance Corporation of Ireland, Dublin; Central Bank of Ireland; Bank of Ireland, Dublin.

McKenna, Theresa (b.1952)

Born 1952; studied at the National College of Art & Design, Dublin and Edinburgh College of Art, Scotland. Graduated with a BA Degree in 1979.

One-Woman Exhibitions: 1979, Aberdeen Arts Centre, Scotland; 1983, Project Arts Centre, Dublin.

Group Exhibitions: 1978, Society of Scottish Artists, Edinburgh; 1979, Scottish Tapestry Artists Group, Edinburgh and London; 1980, Small Tapestries, Scottish Arts Council Touring Exhibition, Australia and New Zealand; 1981, Independent Artists, Dublin; EVA, Limerick; 1984, Three Woman Show, Wexford Arts Centre, GPA Awards Exhibition, Dublin; 1986, NCAD Decade Show, Guinness Hop Store. ·

Collections: An Chomhairle Ealaíon/The Arts Council; Dublin Corporation.

McKeogh, Aileen (b.1952)

Born 1952; 1976, graduated from the National College of Art & Design, Dublin; 1981, MA in Fine Art, Southern Illinois University, USA.

One-Woman Exhibitions: 1981, Fanor Museum, South Illinois University; 1982, Project Arts Centre, Dublin; Irish Arts Centre, New York; 1986, Hendriks Gallery, Dublin.

Group Exhibitions: 1975, Irish Exhibition of Living Art, Dublin; 1976, National Gallery, Edinburgh; 1978, Irish Exhibition of Living Art, Dublin; 1980, A Sense of Ireland, London; 1981, GPA Exhibition, Dublin; 1982, Irish Exhibition of Living Art, Dublin; 1985, New Irish Art, selected by Lucy Lippard, touring USA; 1986, Irish Women Artists, London; EVA, Limerick; NCAD, Decade Show, Guinness Hop Store.

Collections: Ulster Museum, Belfast; An Chomhairle Ealaíon/The Arts Council; Contemporary Irish Arts Society, Dublin.

Mackie, Kathleen Isobel (b.1899)

Born in Belfast and educated at Alexandra College, Dublin, Kathleen Metcalfe studied at the Belfast School of Art and won a scholarship to the Royal Academy Schools where she studied under Gerald Kelly, William Orpen and George Clausen in the early 1920's. In 1926 she married her cousin Jack Mackie and returned to Northern Ireland. Though she exhibited at the Royal Hibernian Academy, Royal Academy and Paris Salon in the 1920's, she hardly exhibited at all after her marriage. She continued to paint, however, and carefully preserved all her work. It was not until the age of eighty-six that she had a retrospective exhibition. 'Kim' (as she has always been known) still lives at Ringdufferin, county Down.

Her painting, Market Scene, is in the collection of the Royal Ulster Academy. MA

See cat. no. 77.

McWeeney, Leslie (b.1936)

Born 1936 in Dublin; studied at the National College of Art, Dublin, under Professors Keating, McGonigal and Herkner; awarded scholarship to the École des Beaux Arts, Paris, and studied under Professor Souverbis.

Group Exhibitions: 1954, Irish Exhibition of Living Art, and subsequent years; 1957, Royal Hibernian Academy, and subsequent years; 1959, Paris Biennale; 1960, Lugano, Switzerland; 1961, Paris Biennale; Long Beach, California.

One-Woman Shows: 1957, One woman show, Clog Gallery, Dublin; 1961, Ankrum Gallery, Los Angeles, USA; The Dawson Gallery, Dublin.

Collections: An Chomhairle Ealaíon/The Arts Council; Trinity College, Dublin; The Haverty Trust; Santa Barbara Museum of Art, California.

Madden, Anne (b.1932)

Born 1932 in London; 1950-52, Chelsea School of Art, London; 1958, married Irish artist, Louis le Brocquy, and settled in France.

One Woman Exhibitions: 1959, Leicester Galleries, London; 1960-74, Dawson Gallery, Dublin; 1961, Leicester Galleries, London; 1964, Dawson Gallery, Dublin; 1967, Leicester Galleries,

Dublin; Oxford Gallery, Oxford; Gimpel Weitzenhoffer, New York; New Art Centre, London; 1971, Richard de Marco Gallery, Edinburgh; 1972, New Art Centre, London; New Art Centre, London; Ulster Museum, Belfast; 1976, Galerie Darthea Speyer, Paris; 1978, New Art Centre, London; 1979, Galerie Darthea Speyer, Paris; Taylor Galleries, Dublin; The Arts Council of Northern Ireland, Belfast; 1980, Galerie Le Dessin, Paris; 1982, Taylor Galleries, Dublin; 1983, Fondation Maeght, Saint-Paul de Vence, France; 1984, The Bank of Ireland, Dublin; Wexford Arts Centre, Ireland; 1985, Galeria Maeght, Barcelona; Galerie Joachim Becker, Cannes; 1986, Armstrong Gallery, New York.

Group Exhibitions: 1952, Royal Hibernian Academy, Dublin; 1965, Municipal Gallery of Modern Art, Dublin; Art 65, American Express Pavilion, New York; Worlds Fair; IVth Paris Biennale; Open Painting Exhibition, Arts Council, Ulster Museum, Belfast and Municipal Gallery of Modern Art, Dublin; 1967, First Edinburgh Open 100; 1969, Modern Irish Painting, Helsinki, Gothenburg, Norrkoping, Stockholm; 1970, Manufacturing Art, Camden Arts Centre, London; Oireachtas, Dublin; The Irish, Oxford Gallery Oxford; 1971, ROSC, The Irish Imagination, Municipal Gallery of Modern Art, Dublin; 1972, IXme Biennale Internationale de Menton; International Biennal Exhibition of Prints, Tokyo; 1974, Irish Directions of the 70s, Ulster Museum, Belfast, Municipal Gallery of Modern Art, Dublin and American venues; 1977, Fondation Rothschild, sponsored by Ministère des Affairs culturels, Paris; 1984, ROSC '84, Guinness Hop Store, Dublin.

Collections: Contemporary Art Society, London; Financial Times, London; Gulbenkian Foundation, England; An Chomhairle Ealaíon/The Arts Council; Trinity College, Dublin; Bank of Ireland, Dublin; P. J. Carroll Collection; Municipal Gallery of Modern Art, Dublin; Ulster Museum, Belfast; J. H. Hirshhorn Foundation, Washington DC; Fondation Maeght, St. Paul, France; Musée d'Art Moderne de la Ville de Paris; Centre National d'Art Contemporain Georges Pompidou, Beaubourg, Paris.

Madden, Bernadette (b.1948)

Bernadette Madden was born in Dublin in 1948. She studied at the NCAD in Dublin and in 1972 was awarded first prize in the Royal Dublin Society's craft competition. She specializes in the batik medium.

She has exhibited frequently in group exhibitions and has had several one-person shows: at the Davis Gallery in 1971 and subsequently in the Peacock Theatre, the Barrenhill Gallery, Dublin and in Sydney, Australia.

Her works are included in the collections of Aer Lingus, Coras Tráchtála and in many important collections both in Ireland and abroad.

Magee, Margaret E. (b.1958)

Born 1958; 1982, BA Degree in Fine Art, National College of Art & Design, Dublin; 1985, MA Degree in Fine Art (Video), The School of the Art Institute of Chicago, Chicago, Illinois.
Exhibitions/Screenings: 1984, Douglas Hyde Gallery, Dublin,

Irish Exhibition of Living Art; Olympia Media Exchange, Olympia Wa, part of video collection; Art and Media Studies, Syracuse University, New York; The School of the Museum of Fine Art Boston, Boston, Ma.; California Institute for the Arts, Valencia, Cal.; Franklin Furnace Gallery, New York, Live Art from Ireland; The Joe and Emily Lowe Gallery, Syracuse, New York; Temple Bar Studio, Dublin, New Video from Chicago; Project Arts Centre, Dublin, Irish Exhibition of Living Art; 1985, Museum of Sound and Image, Sao Paolo, Brazil, Chicago Video; Museum of Art of Rio Grand do Sol, Porto Allegre, Brazil; Scan Gallery, Sapporo, Hokkaido Island, Japan, Recent Recordings; International Student Exhibition, SAIC Gallery, Chicago; Medium West Art Gallery, Minneapolis, 3 Video Works; 1986, Institute of Science and Technology; Chinese Artists Association, Shanghai, China; Battersea Art Centre, London, Eye to Eye; Guinness Hopstore, Dublin, NCAD Decade Show; International Art Expo, Navy Pier, Chicago, TV or Not TV; The Center for New TV, Chicago, Tales from Chicago-Visual Narrative.

Maguire, Helena (1860-1909)

Helena Maguire was born in London, the daughter of Thomas Herbert Maguire (1821-1895). She was a watercolourist and concentrated largely on subjects which included children and animals. Although permanently resident in London, she did have some links with Ireland and, besides exhibiting at the Royal Academy and the Institute of Painters in Watercolours, of which she was a member, she also sent works for exhibition to the Royal Hibernian Academy in 1886 and 1888. Her sisters, Adelaide Agnes Maguire (1852-1875) and Bertha Maguire (fl. 1881-after 1913) were also painters, though they do not appear to have exhibited in Ireland. WR

See cat. no. 26.

Maher, Alice (b.1956)

Born 1956. 1974-78, National Institute for Higher Education, Limerick, BA (European Studies); 1981-85, Crawford Municipal College of Art, Cork, Diploma in Fine Art; 1985-86, University of Ulster, Belfast, MA in Fine Art; 1987, San Francisco Art Institute, post graduate in painting, Fulbright Scholarship.

Exhibitions: 1984, Irish Exhibition of Living Art, Douglas Hyde Gallery, Dublin; 1985, Listowel International Print Biennale; 1985, CAN '85, Major Survey of Contemporary Cork Artists; 1986, 'Eight Artists from Ireland', Oxford, England; 1986, Graduate Print Exchange, University of Peking, China; 1986, Royal Ulster Academy Exhibition, Belfast; 1987, 'On the Wall' Gallery, Belfast; Recent Work — Alice Maher & Paul Wilson; 1987, Six Artists 'On the go . . .' Touring Exhibition, Derry, Dublin, Cork; 1987, Selected Group Exhibition; Diego Rivera Gallery, San Francisco.

Manning, May (d.1930)

She studied in Paris, perhaps a contemporary of Sarah Purser there, and also became a friend of Louise Breslau. She visited John Hughes on a later visit to Paris, and also encouraged her pupil Mary Swanzy to study there. She is mentioned in the *Sarah Purser correspondence,* in the National Library of Ireland, in a letter dated 15 November 1887. An example of her work is in the National Gallery of Ireland.

JC

Markievicz, Countess (Constance) (1868-1927)

Were she working today, Constance Markievicz must have been a performance artist, vigorously attacking social and political ills. At an Irish Women's Franchise League benefit in 1914, she organised a tableau, with herself in silvered cardboard as 'Joan of Arc in full armour, appearing to a suffragist prisoner in her cell'. This costume was exchanged for the uniform of staff lieutenant in the Irish Republican Army in 1916, where she was an inspiration to many during the short-lived Easter Rising. She was sentenced to death, the sentence commuted to life imprisonment; and after she was released she became the first woman cabinet minister in Western Europe in the original Dáil Éireann in April 1919.

While she is chiefly remembered for her political role, Constance Markievicz first made her name as a painter, in Dublin in the early years of this century. She was the daughter of Sir Henry Gore-Booth, explorer and philanthropist, of Lissadell, in Sligo, and elder sister of Eva Gore-Booth, poet and social reformer. In 1892, she had her first lessons in London, from the Swedish artist, Anna Nordgren. The following year she entered the Slade, to work with Alphonse Legros. In 1897, she went to Julian's in Paris, to study under Jean-Paul Laurens, and here met the Polish count, Casimir Markievicz, whom she later married. They went to live in Dublin, in 1903, where they painted, acted, and were increasingly drawn away from high society into developing political events. From 1904 to 1909, she exhibited with AE (George Russell), Dermod O'Brien, W. J. Leech and others at the Leinster Hall, and in the Sinn Féin Aonach. She was also a co-founder of the United Arts Club. Her paintings of moonlight and misty gardens had much in common with those of AE, echoing his visionary romanticism, but lacked his personal subtlety. In 1908, she designed the title page of *Bean na hÉireann,* the woman's paper advocating 'militancy, separatism and feminism'. In latter years she painted little, but was an ardent member of Fianna Fáil. She is represented in the Hugh Lane Municipal Gallery, Dublin.

HP

See cat. no. 57.

Marsh, Clare (1874-1923)

She was born Emily Cecil Clare Marsh, in county Meath. According to Mary Swanzy, she was 'one of a devoted family of brothers and sisters of great good looks and charm, with a background of impecuniosity'. She attended the Metropolitan School of Art, taking night classes in sculpture with John Hughes and Oliver Sheppard, and studied under John Butler Yeats at Miss Manning's studio, about 1898, when she first met Mary Swanzy. She and Yeats developed a life-long friendship. He urged her to sketch, and to make her portraits from sketches; years later, he criticised her portrait of his daughter, Lily, for the way she

exaggerated defects. Norman Garstin, with whom she worked in Penzance, was another early influence. From 1900 to 1921, she exhibited at the Royal Hibernian Academy, portraits, landscapes, genre scenes and flower paintings, gradually leaning towards French Post-Impressionism, but never wholly abandoning the academic mould. In 1912, she paid a visit of six months to New York, to stay with J. B. Yeats. On her return she became interested in the suffrage movement. She was sharing a studio with Mary Swanzy in autumn 1920, and they held a joint exhibition of their work. Writing about the posthumous exhibition, held in the Stephen's Green Gallery in June 1923, the *Irish Times* reviewer commented, 'Miss Marsh was an avid student of modernism in painting, but adopted its methods only so far as they matched with her own conceptions of the scope and purpose of her art.'

Examples of her work are in the Hugh Lane Municipal Gallery, Dublin, and in private collections.

HP

See cat. no. 89.

Martyn, Hazel see Lavery, Hazel

May, Elizabeth (fl.1810)

Elizabeth May, born Elizabeth Sinclair, whose date of birth is unknown, was the eldest daughter of a wealthy merchant, William Sinclair of Fort William, county Antrim and Donegall Place, Belfast. Co-heiress to her father's fortune, in 1809, Elizabeth married the Rev. Edward Sylvester May, whose brother, Sir Stephen May, was M.P. for Belfast and whose sister was married to the Marquess of Donegall. Born in 1783, Edward May had matriculated at the age of seventeen at St. Mary's Hall, Oxford and in the same year as his marriage to Elizabeth Sinclair, was installed as rector of St. Anne's, Belfast.

It is interesting to note that the Rev. Edward May appears with the Marquess of Donegall and other members of the May and Sinclair families in Thomas Robinson's painting *The Review of the Belfast Yeomanry by the Lord Lieutenant in 1804.*

Due to her comfortable circumstances, Elizabeth May was not obliged to sell her paintings and if she exhibited at all, one would expect the pictures to have been shown anonymously or under a pseudonym. 'By a lady' or 'a young lady' were usual catalogue entries at this date, and would explain the delay in the rediscovery of her work until now.

COC

See cat. no. 13.

Metcalfe, Kathleen Isobel see Mackie, Kathleen Isobel

Millard, Caroline (d.1894)

Caroline Millard was born in Dublin, the daughter of Benjamin Clayton II (1786-1862) an engraver. She married in 1841, Thomas Millard, a cabinet-maker and builder. In 1844 she was awarded a prize by the Irish Art Union for her title-page for the *Spirit of the Nation* after Frederick William Burton.

Caroline studied with her father and became a successful wood engraver. WR

Flora Mitchell (1890-1973)

Flora Mitchell was born in America and came to live in Ireland following her marriage. She studied in Dublin at the Metropolitan School of Art. She specialized in painting views of Dublin in watercolour. She is best remembered today for her book *Vanishing Dublin*, published in 1966, which contained views of well-known Dublin streets and buildings many of which have since been demolished.

The National Gallery of Ireland holds a substantial collection of her work with over three hundred watercolours and drawings including many of those illustrated in *Vanishing Dublin*.

Mitchell, Grace see Henry, Grace

Monsell, Diana (1813-1851)

Unfortunately very little is known about this accomplished lady flower artist who produced a beautifully mounted album of sixty-eight flower and foliage watercolour drawings, evidently studied from nature. Diana, the only daughter of Thomas Bewley Monsell, Archdeacon of Derry, was born on the 26th June 1813 and in 1842 married her first cousin, Conyngham Ellis, in Dunloe church. She was a cultured but apparently retiring and modest person whose studies of flora have a painstaking accuracy of detail and striking realism. She painted mainly the more common flowers of the fields and hedgerows. Many other women of the period also produced similar albums as it was considered a suitable pastime for ladies to draw or paint such subjects.

Though we do not know where she received her training, if any, her work was highly thought of. Sir Frederick William Burton, a Director of the National Gallery, London and an artist himself, noted on seeing her drawings that they were 'beautiful little pictorial hymns to Flora. . . I have not for a long time seen anything that gave me so much pleasure to dwell on . . . they make my own work appear so rude and false that I am more than ever alive to my defects.' (National Gallery of Ireland file no. 6339). Burton also appears to have made a portrait of Diana in 1846, five years before she died (National Gallery of Ireland cat. no. 6339).

An album of Diana Monsell's work is in the National Gallery of Ireland. KMM

Moore, Lady (Phylis) (d.1974)

Phylis Moore is still well-remembered throughout Ireland, Britain and the United States of America as a gardener, a magnificent plantswoman who knew the best and finest garden plants and cultivated them with consummate skill. Her husband, Sir Frederick Moore, was for over forty years Keeper of the Royal (now National) Botanic Gardens at Glasnevin and after his retirement in 1922, the couple lived at Willbrook in Rathfarnham where they formed a garden unrivalled for the variety of plants grown. Both Moores served on the council of the Royal Horticultural Society of Ireland, and they were together honorary directors of the American Rock Garden Society which was founded in 1934 — Lady Moore being described at the inaugural meeting as 'the true godmother of the ARGS'! Several plants bear her name including a beautiful double-blossomed quince, *Chaenomeles* 'Phylis Moore', and a now-extinct bulb, *Lachenalia* 'Phylis Paul', a garden hybrid raised at the Botanic Gardens by her future husband.

Phylis Moore was one of the daughters of William Paul; she married Frederick Moore in 1903.

Lady Moore painted in oils, and also drew in ink. At least two oil paintings by her survive in private collections. Several of her pen and ink drawings of plants are preserved in the National Botanic Gardens, Glasnevin, including two which were published in the 1930's in *Gardening Illustrated*. ECN

Morgan, Jane (1831-1899)

Jane Morgan, painter and sculptor, was one of five children of Anthony Morgan of Prospect Hill (now called Ardnalee), Carrigrohane, county Cork. She received her early training at the Cork School of Design and later studied modelling in Dublin with the sculptor J. R. Kirk, winning a prize for sculpture in the Taylor competition of 1860. In 1864 and 1865, she exhibited busts at the Royal Hibernian Academy. In the latter year (1865), she went to Rome with her sister Maria and there became one of a colony of women artists which included the American sculptors Harriet Hosmer and Emma Stebbins. Though there is little information available on her life at this time, one can imagine that it must have been an exciting experience to mix with a group of like-minded women, who had left the confines of home and family, to work as artists and lead independent lives. She remained in Rome for a few years, then studied in Copenhagen, Düsseldorf and Munich, where she spent fifteen years. In 1884, she accepted an invitation from her sister Maria, to decorate her new home in New York.

Jane lived with Maria (the first female journalist to be employed by the *New York Times*) for the rest of her days, devoting five years to the marquetry decorations in the main living area of the house, which was also furnished with many of her paintings and copies after the Old Masters. After completing the commission, she resumed her painting career and continued to work almost until the end of her life. She died on 4 April 1899. After her death, her paintings and marquetry were left to a nephew, who sold them to a relation, Col. A. H. Morgan. In 1903-04, Col. Morgan recreated the sisters' living room, with Jane's marquetry, in his new home, Hollybrook House, Skibbereen, county Cork. The room is there still, an impressive testimony to Jane's artistry and skill. Jane's paintings eventually passed to Col. Morgan's nephew, who sold a number of them in 1961. These are now in private collections in Ireland and elsewhere.

Although Jane Morgan has faded into oblivion, her known works show her to have been highly competent, skilled at depicting the human figure and capable of working on a large scale. One of her oil paintings is in the Ulster Museum. EB

See cat. no. 30.

Murray, Eileen (1885-?)

Eileen Francis Jane Bunbury Chester was born in Templemore, Cork on 21 December 1885. Her father was Col. W. L. Chester R.A.M.C. She was educated privately and studied painting with Stanhope Forbes at Newlyn, Cornwall. After marrying Major F.S.J. Murray she spent some years in India, where she painted and exhibited in Simla, Bombay and Calcutta, winning numerous awards. She exhibited twenty-four paintings in all at the Royal Hibernian Academy of Indian and Irish subjects, portraits and figure subjects, in 1908, 1923, 1925, 1926 and 1929. In her latter years she lived at Mosstown House, county Longford.   EB

See cat. no. 86.

Murray, Julie (b.1961)

Born 1961; 1984, BA Degree in Fine Art, National College of Art & Design, Dublin; 1987, Fulbright Award to Academy of Art College, San Francisco. Part scholarship to attend California Institute of the Arts.

Exhibitions and Film Shows: The Academy of Art College, San Francisco; Artists Television Access, San Francisco; The 16th Note, San Francisco; Media, San Francisco; The One Act Theatre, San Francisco; Telegraph Cinema, Berkley; NCAD Decade Show, Guinness Hop Store.

Nairn, Anna Langley (fl. 1844-1848)

She was the daughter of George Nairn and Cecilia Margaret Nairn, both well known painters, and granddaughter of John Henry Campbell. With her artistic background it is not surprising that she became interested in painting early in life. She began exhibiting landscapes at the age of eighteen at the Royal Hibernian Academy.

Her landscapes included views of well known beauty spots in Wicklow and Kerry executed in oils and watercolour. After her marriage to Robert William Armstrong in 1848, she concentrated on designing decorations for the Belleek Pottery factory of which her husband was a director.

There are no known examples of her landscape painting.

Nairn, Cecilia Margaret (1791-1857)

Cecilia Margaret Nairn, daughter of landscape painter John Henry Campbell, studied under her father and began exhibiting in Dublin in 1809. She continued to contribute to various exhibitions in the city until 1821, and thereafter occasionally showed at the Royal Hibernian Academy, from 1826 until 1847. Many of her landscapes were painted around Wicklow and Killarney. In 1826, she married the artist George Nairn. There is little information on the latter years of her life. She died of bronchitis in Oak House, Battersea, on 4 June 1857, aged sixty-five.

Not surprisingly, Cecilia's watercolours (which are better known than her oils) tend to be close, in style and technique, to those of her father. Her work is represented in the Ulster Museum.   EB

See cat. no. 15.

O'Brien, Brigid see Ganly, Brigid

O'Connell, Deirdre (b.1956)

Born 1956 in London; 1974-75, Hertfordshire College of Art and Design, St. Albans; 1975-78, BA Honours Fine Art: Sculpture, North Staffordshire Polytechnic, Stoke-on-Trent, Staffordshire; 1979-80, MA Fine Art: Sculpture, Ulster Polytechnic, Belfast.

One-Person Exhibitions: 1986, Sentinel, Crescent Arts Centre, Belfast; Newry and Mourne Arts Centre, Newry, county Down.

Installation: 1982, The Palatine's Daughter, Art and Research Exchange, Belfast; 1986, Here For the Duration, City Artists Association, Hackney, London.

Selected Exhibitions: 1978, New Contemporaries, I.C.A., London; Making the Grade, Arnolfini, Bristol; 1980, New Contemporaries, I.C.A., London; Crossing, Forebank Gallery, Dundee; 1981, Artists Inc., St Paul's Gallery, Leeds; Aspects of Drawing, Maysfield Leisure Centre, Belfast; 1982, SADE Sculpture and Drawing Exhibition, Crawford Municipal Gallery, Cork; 1984, Collected Images, Queen Street Studios, Belfast; 1985, Claremorris Open; EVA, Limerick; Irish Exhibition of Living Art, Guinness Hopstore, Dublin; Artists Collective Postcard Exhibition, touring various venues 1985/86; 1986, Collective Images, Harmony Hill Arts Centre, Lisburn (touring); Artists at Work, Queen Street Studios, Belfast; Sculptors' Drawings, Harmony Hill Arts Centre, Lisburn; 1987, Irish Exhibition of Living Art, Guinness Hopstore, Dublin; Artists from Queen Street Studios, Plassey Arts Week, NIHE, Limerick.

O'Connell, Eilis (b.1953)

Born 1953 in Ireland; 1970-74, studied at the Crawford School of Art, Cork; 1974-75, BFA Course in Sculpture, Massachusetts College of Art, Boston, USA; 1975-77, Diploma of Fine Art (Sculpture), Crawford School of Art, Cork.

One-Person Shows: 1978, Exhibition of Sculpture and Painting, Cork; 1981, Exhibition of Sculpture and Drawing; David Hendriks Gallery, Dublin; 1983, Exhibition of Sculpture and Wall-Pieces, David Hendriks Gallery, Dublin; 1986, Exhibition of Sculpture and Wall-Pieces, the Douglas Hyde Gallery, Dublin; Exhibition of Recent Work, Hendriks Gallery, Dublin; 1987, Octagon Gallery, Belfast.

Selected Group Shows: 1974, Contemporary Irish Sculpture Exhibition, Dublin; 1975, 'OASIS' Outdoor Sculpture Exhibition, Merrion Square, Dublin; 1977, '77 Exhibition', Limerick; 1978, Living Art Exhibition, Dublin (1979, 1980, 1981); Independent Artists Exhibition, Dublin (1979, 1980, 1982); Claremorris Art Exhibition; 1980, 'Works on Paper', The Angela Flowers Gallery, London; Group Show, Triskel Arts Centre, Cork; 1981, The Guinness Peat Aviation Exhibition; 1982, Kenmare Art Exhibition; SADE, Cork; EVA, Limerick; Paris Biennale; 1983, Women in Art, The Wexford Arts Centre; 1984, 10 Artists, Accademia Britannicia, Rome. Quattro Boriste Straneri, Spoleto, Italy; Hendriks Gallery, Dublin; ROSC, The Guinness Hop Store, Dublin; 1985, 'Irish Exhibition', The Armstrong Gallery, New York; CAN (Cork Art), Crawford Municipal Gallery, Cork, travelling to Amsterdam; EVA, Limerick; 'Four Artists from Ireland', Sao Paolo Biennial, Brazil, touring to Rio De Janeiro, Porto Allegre.

O'Dowd, Gwen (b.1957)
Born 1957 in Dublin; 1980, graduated, the National College of Art & Design, Dublin.

One Woman Exhibition: 1984, Project Arts Centre, Dublin.

Selected Group Exhibitions: 1978-85, Independent Artists; 1979, Staff and Student Show, NCAD, Douglas Hyde Gallery, Dublin; Irish Exhibition of Living Art, Douglas Hyde Gallery, Dublin; 1982, Exhibition of Visual Art, Limerick; 1983, Kilkenny Arts Week, Kilkenny; Claremorris Open; 1984, Two-Person Show, Wexford Arts Centre; Guinness Peat Aviation Exhibition, Dublin; Arnotts Landscape Show, Dublin; October Exhibition, Temple Bar, Dublin; Irish Exhibition of Living Art, Douglas Hyde Gallery, Dublin; 1985, Listowel International Print Biennale; Edinburgh/Dublin Exchange Exhibition; Claremorris Open; Milwaukee Irish American Festival, USA; 1986, Exhibition of Visual Art, Limerikck; Mid-Wales Open, Aberystwyth, Wales; The Barn Arts Centre, Aberystwyth; NCAD Decade Show, Guinness Hop Store, Dublin; 1987, Irish Exhibition of Living Art, Guinness Hop Store, Dublin.

Collections: An Chomhairle Ealaíon/The Arts Council, Dublin; Vincent Ferguson, Dublin; The Gibney Collection; The Board of Works, Dublin; National Institute for Higher Education, Dublin; Educational Building Society.

O'Hara, Helen (1881-1919)
Though now practically unknown, Helen O'Hara was a watercolourist of some talent. A monogrammed and dated watercolour of 1882, brought into the Ulster Museum by an enquirer in 1986, showed an Irish boreen or country lane very much in the style of Mildred Anne Butler. She was active in Portstewart, county Londonderry, Belfast and Lismore, county Waterford. She exhibited at the Royal Hibernian Academy, the Royal Institute of Painters in Watercolours and the Society of Women Artists between 1881 and 1908. She was a corresponding member of the Belfast Art Society in 1891, her address given as the Castle, Portstewart. Her address in 1897 was 1 Glandore Park, Antrim Road, Belfast, but in 1898 it had changed to the Mall House, Lismore, county Waterford, where she lived until 1919. In 1896 she was elected a vice president of the Belfast Art Society and in June 1904 was elected an honorary member along with Mildred Butler, John Lavery and Frank Spenlove. She did not exhibit with the BAS after 1910 but remained an honorary member until 1919.

She is represented in the Ulster Museum, Belfast.   MA

See cat. no. 53.

O'Kelly, Alanna (b.1955)
Born 1955; studied at the Regional Technical College, Galway; the National College of Art & Design, Dublin, graduating in 1978;

1986-87, studying for an MA degree in Fine Art, at the Slade School of Art, London.

One-Woman Exhibitions, Installations, Performances: 1981, Barriers, One Woman Show, Dublin; 1985-86, Chant down Greenham, Performance USA and Canada.

Group Exhibitions, Installations, Performances: 1980, Without the Walls, ICA, London; 1980-82, Hibernian Inscape, Douglas Hyde Gallery, Dublin, Belfast and UK; 1983, Independent Artists, Marlay Park, Dublin; 1984, Seen Apart, A Woman's Festival; 1986, Eye to Eye, London; Still beyond the Pale, Dublin; GPA Awards for Emerging Artists; NCAD Decade Show, Guinness Hop Store.

Olverson, Vicki (b.1956)
Born 1956 in Liverpool; studied at Southport Art College and at Cardiff College of Art, Wales; 1980, moved to Ireland; 1983, awarded Arts Council Bursary.

Group Exhibitions: 1981, Ceramic Show, Tulfarris Gallery, county Wicklow; Galway Arts Festival; Royal Dublin Society; 1982, Royal Dublin Society; Christmas Art, Design and Crafts Show, Mansion House, Dublin; 1983, Independent Artists, Douglas Hyde Gallery, Dublin, Kilkenny, Limerick; GPA Emerging Artists, Douglas Hyde Gallery, Dublin; Dunlavin Arts Festival; Figurative Image, Dublin; 1984, Dunlavin Arts Festival.

O'Regan, Ann (b.1959)
Born 1959 in Waterford; 1978-83, Waterford School of Art, NCEA Dip. Fine Art; 1983-84, Crawford School of Art, Cork, post-graduate studies; 1986-87, Visual Arts Organiser, Garter Lane Arts Centre, Waterford.

O'Reilly, Geraldine (b. 1957)
1983, BA Degree in Fine Art, National College of Art & Design, Dublin; awarded Arts Council Travel Bursary, and again in 1986; 1981-84, 13 Murals for the Arts Council 'Paint on the Wall' Project; 1984, assisted Susan Ortega City Arts Workshop, New York; 1985, One-Woman Show, Lincoln Gallery, Dublin.

Group Exhibitions: 1984, Independent Artists Exhibition, Dublin; 1985, Eight Artists, Crawford Art Gallery, Cork and City Art Gallery, Limerick; EVA, Limerick; Arnotts Portrait Award Exhibition, Dublin; 1986, The School Show, Arts Council Touring Exhibition; NCAD Decade Show, Guinness Hop Store.

Orpen, Bea (1913-1980)
Born 1913 in Carrickmines, Dublin; 1932-35, trained at the Dublin Metropolitan School of Art and at the Life Schools of the Royal Hibernian Academy, where she was a prize-winning student; 1935-39, studied at the Slade School of Fine Art, London, where she was awarded 1st Prize in decorative composition in 1936, and the Diploma in Design in 1939; also studied at the School of Typography in Fleet Street, and attended courses in the LCC Central School of Arts and Crafts; 1934-80, exhibited every year at the Royal Hibernian Academy; 1936-80, exhibited every year

but one at the Watercolour Society of Ireland; 1944-80, exhibited regularly in the Oireachtas. Died 1980.

One-Person Shows: 1939, 1947, 1954, 1977, in Dublin.

Osborne, Edith see Blake Lady (Edith)

Osborne, Grace see St. Albans, Duchess of (Grace)

Osborne O'Hagan, Harriet (1830-1921)

Harriet Osborne was born in Dublin. She became a pupil of George Sharp, and first exhibited at the Royal Hibernian Academy in 1849, aged only nineteen, with a lithograph portrait of Mrs. Hone. In 1851 she sent four portraits from 195 Great Brunswick Street to the RHA: one in watercolour and one in chalk. She may have moved to London c.1854, when she sent a portrait to the Royal Academy from 193 Stanhope Street.

George Sharp encouraged her to continue her studies in Paris. She went to Paris in c.1866 and between 1866-78 studied with Cogniet, Robert-Fleury and Realist painter Thomas Couture, probably attending his summer schools in the 1870's: 'one of many mature artists who went to Couture to revitalize their techniques.'

She became a teacher herself, and it is said, opened the first academy for women artists in Paris. She visited Normandy in 1880. She was primarily a portraitist, and also represented landscapes and interiors. She worked in both oil and charcoal. Her charcoal portraits of her sisters Eugenie and Marguerite dated 1869 are particularly sensitive. Her daughter Marguerite Lemercier O'Hagan and grandson Eugene Emmanuel Lemercier were also artists. She remained in France, and died in Paris in 1921. 'Madame O'Hagan Osborne had always an artist's love of her native country and died regretting she was unable to return to it.'

Four of her drawings and two of her oils are in the collection of the National Gallery of Ireland.   JC
See cat. nos. 27-28.

O'Sullivan, Anna (b.1958)

Born 1958 in Dublin; 1978-82, BA Degree in Fine Art, National College of Art & Design, Dublin; 1980, Exchange Program, University of Massachusetts, Amherst, for Spring Term; 1984-85, Whitney Museum of American Art Independent Study Program, New York. Currently Performance Co-ordinator, Franklin Furnace, New York.

Exhibitions/Performances: 1981, Irish Exhibition of Living Art, Dublin, and 1983, 1985; 1982, 7th Paris Biennale; Guinness Peat Aviation Awards for Emerging Arts, Douglas Hyde Gallery, Dublin; 1983, 'They call it puppy fat', Franklin Furnace Inc., New York; 1984, 'The Life Stone', Whitney Museum of American Art Open Studio, New York; 1986, 'Eye to Eye', Irish Women Artists, London; 1986, Performance, Sarah Lawrence College, New York; 'Divisions, Crossroads, Turns of Mind — Some New Irish Art', selected by Lucy Lippard, Toronto, Alberta, New York, Williamstown; NCAD Decade Show, Guinness Hop Store; 1987, Dixon Place, New York City.

Oulton, Eileen see Reid, Eileen

Parsons, Lady Alicia (1815-1885)

Lady Alicia Parsons, a daughter of the 2nd Earl of Rosse, was born at Birr Castle, county Offaly (then the King's County), the family seat of the Parsons family in Ireland. From an early age she filled sketch books with spirited cartoons of the goings on between the officers of the militia garrisoned in the town and the local ladies. Some include witty captions and are a unique record of the period.

In 1837 she eloped to Gretna Green with Sir Edward Conroy's son, John, disguised in her sister's clothes, her elder brother Lord Oxmantown in hot pursuit from London. Prophesies as to the doomed nature of the union were soon justified and she returned to Birr.

Later conventional watercolour paintings by her in the collection at Birr would suggest a formal training e.g. a bucolic Italianate landscape, with peasants and a Dutch-influenced pastoral snow scene, both heavily painted and revealing none of the fresh spontaneity of a series of town and seascapes, also at Birr. NGB

See cat. no. 25.

Paul, Phylis see Moore, Lady (Phylis)

de Pearsall, Elizabeth see Harrington, Countess of (Elizabeth)

Perrott, Freda (fl. 1899-1940)

Freda Perrott exhibited her work over a period of forty years at the Royal Hibernian Academy. Her subject matter was flowers.

She is represented in the Hugh Lane Municipal Gallery, Dublin.
                    WR

Perry, Lilla (1888-1974)

Lilla Perry was the youngest daughter of Richard Bagwell of Marlfield House, county Tipperary. Lilla grew up at Marlfield House and in 1915 married Captain John Perry of Birdhill, a neighbouring estate.

Nothing is known of Lilla's training and it is likely that she was self taught. It appears, from a collection of illustrated books which belonged to Lilla and are now in the possession of her family, that she knew, and possibly studied, the work of some of the eighteenth and nineteenth century British watercolourists. However there is little evidence of their direct influence on her style. Lilla signed and dated nearly all of her paintings and so it is possible to see a clear development in her work from a preference for detail and slightly muted colours at the onset of her career in the 1920's to a considerable brightening of the palette and a loosening of the brushwork in her later period.

Although she continued to paint throughout her long life her most active stage was during the 1920's and 1930's. This is illustrated by her existing dated works as well as by her exhibiting career; she exhibited at the Watercolour Society of Ireland almost continuously from 1920, at the London Salon and at the Royal Hibernian Academy from 1927 to 1930.

Her subject matter, which changed little over the years, was drawn extensively from Marlfield, Birdhill and the area around Clonmel. Her main interest was in views of rivers, trees and gardens.

Examples of her work are in private collections.   WR

WR and KOG

Plunket, Katherine (1820-1932)

The Hon. Katherine Plunket painted flowers and landscapes during her long life — she died just thirty-nine days short of her one hundredth and twelfth birthday. During the early 1880's Miss Plunket exhibited landscapes in London and in 1903 presented a bound album of botanical watercolours to the Museum of Science and Art in Dublin; this album is now in the National Botanic Gardens, Dublin.

According to the inscription which she herself supplied, the album of wild flowers contains the work of both Katherine Plunket and her younger sister Frederica. Unfortunately the individual watercolours are not signed by the sisters and thus it is impossible to tell which works belong to Frederica. Some of the paintings are dated, and most of the dates indicated that they were painted by Katherine Plunket after her sister's death in 1886.

Twelve hundred different plants are depicted in the album, each one on a separate, tinted card-paper rectangle about the size of a post-card, and each one with its botanical name written beneath. The plants were gathered in Ireland, Britain and continental Europe. The quality of this vast collection varies from very poor to very good, and in general the plants are portrayed without any sense that they were three-dimensional objects. None of the paintings was published during the lifetime of the Hon. Katherine Plunket.

Katherine and Frederica Plunket were respectively the eldest and the fourth daughters of the Right Rev. Thomas Plunket, Bishop of Tuam, Killala and Achonry, 3rd Baron Plunket.

ECN

Plunkett, Grace see Gifford, Grace

Powers, Mary Farl (b.1948)

Born 1948 in Minnesota, USA; 1951, came to live in Ireland; 1978, awarded major Arts Council grant; 1980-81, received Fellowship as Printmaker in Residence at the Northern Ireland Arts Council's print workshop; 1981, became member of Aosdana; is currently a director of Graphic Studio, Dublin.

One-Woman Exhibitions: 1972, Peacock Theatre Gallery, Dublin; 1977, Godolphin Gallery, Dublin; 1979, St. John's University, Minnesota, USA; St. Catherine's College, Minnesota, USA; 1981, Tom Caldwell Gallery, Belfast; Taylor Galleries, Dublin; 1984, Taylor Galleries, Dublin; Gordon Gallery, Derry; 1987, Fenderesky Gallery, Belfast.

Group Exhibitions: 1973, International Print Biennale, Ljubljana, Yugoslavia; 1974, International Print Biennale, Segovia, Spain; International Print Biennale, Frechen, Germany; 1976, Retrospective Exhibition, Graphic Studio, Dublin; International Print Biennale, Frechen, Germany; 1976, Retrospective Exhibition,

Graphic Studio, Dublin; International Print Biennale, Frechen, Germany; 1975-84, Listowel Graphics Exhibition, Ireland; 1978, Triennial Exhibition of the Lalit Kala Akedemi, New Delhi, India; 1979, International Print Biennale, Heidelberg, Germany; 1980, Delighted Eye, Sense of Ireland, London; 1982, British Council/Arts Council of Northern Ireland Travelling exhibition, West Germany; International Print Biennale, Fredrikstad, Norway; 1984, International Print Biennale, Bradford, England; Museo Francisco Goitia, Zacatecas, Mexico; Galeria Tierra Adentro, Mexico City; 1985, Octagon Gallery, Belfast, Contemporary Northern Irish Prints, travelling to Southern Germany.

Collections: An Chomhairle Ealaíon/The Arts Council; Ulster Museum, Belfast; Municipal Gallery of Modern Art, Dublin; University College, Dublin; Contemporary Arts Society, Dublin; Northern Ireland Arts Council; Listowel Graphics Permanent Collection; Lalit Kala Akedemi, New Delhi; St. Catherine's College, St. Paul, Minnesota, USA; Collection of Modern British Prints, Fylde Arts, Blackpool, England.

Praeger, S. Rosamond (1867-1954)

Sophia Rosamond Praeger was born in Holywood, county Down. In 1879 she went to the Sullivan School with her brother Robert Lloyd Praeger, who was to become the Director of the National Library and Ireland's foremost botanist in the early part of this century. After leaving school, she spent four years at the Slade, where she studied under Legros; there she won prizes for clay modelling and drawing and a scholarship in her final year. She also studied in Paris before returning to work in Ireland, first in a studio in Belfast, then in Holywood. She first exhibited in 1891 and at the Royal Hibernian Academy in 1899; she also showed at the Royal Academy. Her reputation was established in 1913 by her hugely popular *Philosopher,* a delightful statuette of a seated small boy, cast first in plaster, then carved in marble. In 1914 she built herself a studio and successfully practised as a sculptress and book illustrator.

She particularly enjoyed depicting children and fairies, but also did portraits, narrative groups and whimsical subjects with quizzical titles. She also modelled Irish mythological subjects. She usually worked in plaster in the round on a small scale, or in bas-relief, but also in terra cotta, marble and sometimes stone (e.g. her monument to Sir H. Harty in Hillsborough Church graveyard and circular medallions and relief sculpture for Belfast Maternity Hospital). Her larger scale portrait heads were usually cast in bronze; she also made lead insets for headstones in the 1930's.

She was a member of the Guild of Irish Art Workers and exhibited with the Arts and Crafts Society of Ireland. In 1920 Lavery nominated her as a member of the Belfast Art Society and in 1927 she was elected an HRHA; she exhibited 53 pieces with the RHA between 1899-44. She was also the President of the Royal Ulster Academy, having been elected one of its first twelve academicians in 1930. In 1938 Queen's University awarded her an Hon. MA and in 1939 she received an MBE.

Her love of children is reflected in the many enchanting

children's books she illustrated and, in most cases, wrote, between 1896-1919. She also provided about two hundred line illustrations for three of Lloyd Praeger's books, c.1895-1905, many of which are now in the collection of the National Botanic Gardens, Glasnevin. When she was eighty, she published her last book, *Old Fashioned Verses and Sketches.*

Her sculpture is to be found in the National Gallery of Ireland, the Ulster Museum and Ulster Folk Museum as well as other public and private collections in Ireland. She was honoured by an exhibition in Holywood in 1975, International Women's Year.

NGB

See cat. nos. 104-05.

Prendergast, Kathy (b.1958)

Born 1958 in Dublin; 1977-83, studied at the National College of Art & Design, Dublin; 1980-81, trained and worked as video cameraman, RTE Studios, Dublin; 1981-82, worked on Commission for Irish Arts Council and on work for Paris Biennale 1982; 1983-86, presently studying for MA Degree in Sculpture, Royal College of Art, London.

Group Shows: 1980, Irish Exhibition of Living Art (1982); Douglas Hyde Gallery, Dublin; 1981, Guinness Peat Aviation Exhibition, Dublin; Environmental Show, Blessington, Co. Wicklow; 1982, Independent Artists Exhibition, Dublin; Paris Biennale; 1982-83, Biennale Travelling Show; 1983, Guinness Peat Aviation Exhibition; 1984, Hendriks Gallery, Dublin; 'The Rattle Bag' — Hendriks Gallery, Dublin; 1985, Hendriks Gallery, Dublin; 1986, Arts Council Bursary Exhibition; NCAD Decade Show, Guinness Hop Store.

Collections: Municipal Art Gallery, Dublin; Guinness Peat Aviation Ltd., Shannon Ireland; Fitzwilton Ltd., Dublin, Ireland.

Proctor, Jane (b.1957)

Born 1957; 1983, BA Degree in Fine Art, National College of Art & Design, Dublin.

Exhibitions: 1982, Five Years of Print, Bank of Ireland, Dublin; 1984, May to May, New Art Studios, Dublin; Twenty-one Years of Design, Kilkenny Design, Dublin; 1985, Four for May, New Art Studios, Dublin; 1986, Four Views Touring Exhibition; EVA Limerick; Eigse '86; NCAD Decade Show, Guinness Hop Store.

Purser, Sarah Henrietta (1848-1943)

The artist's parents were Benjamin Purser and Anne Mallet, whose families were established in Dublin's brewing and engineering industries. She was related through the Mallets to the painters Frederick Burton, and William and Walter Osborne. At school in Switzerland she already painted, and began exhibiting at the Royal Hibernian Academy in 1872. At its 1879 exhibition she earned favourable press comments with a *plein air* urchin picture sent home from Paris, where she briefly attended the Académie Julian and adopted a realist style, robust technique, and subjects reflecting fashionable Parisian taste. Sharing accommodation with the Swiss painter Louise Breslau and the Italian singer Maria Feller, and frequently revisiting them, Purser had a niche in a milieu

recorded with envy in Marie Bashkirtseff's famous diary. Degas was an acquaintance, Forain a friend. The flavour of this Parisian circle is caught in Purser's *Petit Déjeuner* (National Gallery of Ireland cat. no. 1424) for which Feller posed in 1881 or 1882.

Bashkirtseff regarded Purser as 'peintre et philosophe'. Contemporary Irish critics quickly noted this combination of art and intellect in Purser, repeatedly hailing her technical prowess and analytic powers, and relishing her 'modernity'. She ranged successfully through every genre, but with her livelihood at stake began building a portrait practice. Stephen Gwynn recognised that 'mordant intellectual power which made of Miss Sarah Purser a painter born to divine and portray character.' Already in 1883 one reviewer claimed that she had 'by common consent the portrait of the year' at the Royal Hibernian Academy. She gain the cachet of London successes with portraits shown at the Royal Academy in 1885 and 1886, soon had Viceregal patronage and the largest clientele in Ireland, and was elected H.R.H.A. in 1890.

Professional success gave her status, which she put to use in promoting fellow artists and the visual arts. With generosity, public spirit, and of course acumen, she organised exhibitions; founded, financed and managed a stained-glass co-operative; supported Hugh Lane's Modern Gallery plans; helped govern the National Gallery of Ireland for three trying decades; formed Friends of the National Collections of Ireland, and endowed university art history scholarships.

First, however, she was a painter; and a solo exhibition in 1923 and election as an Academician in 1924 crowned her artistic career. Examples of her work are in the National Gallery of Ireland and Hugh Lane Municipal Gallery.

JOG

See cat. nos. 36-40.

Pym, Kathleen see Fox, Kathleen

Quigly, Kathleen (1888-1981)

Her family travelled between South Africa, Sicily and London before coming to live in Dublin in 1906. She went to school in London between 1893 and 1901. She exhibited enamels and leatherwork under Alice Jacob at the 1910 Arts and Crafts Society of Ireland Exhibition. The following year her work was singled out in *The Studio* magazine. She became a member of the Guild of Irish Art Workers and worked with both Harry Clarke and An Túr Gloine before setting up her own studio in the mid 1920's at 14 Westmoreland Street, where she advertised herself as illuminating on vellum and painting miniatures. Her charter and certificate for the Irish Theosophical Society date from 1921. In 1925 she exhibited a poster for poultry food as well as enamels and stained glass. She exhibited work in a variety of media at the Royal Hibernian Academy in 1917, 1921, 1925, 1930, 1931, 1933 and 1934; at the Arts and Crafts Exhibitions of 1921 and 1925 and at the Aonach Tailteann Exhibition of 1932.

She emigrated to South Africa in 1934.

NGB

See cat. no. 82.

Redmond, Mary (fl. 1880-1890)

Surprisingly little is known of the life and work of Mary Redmond in view of the fact that she was chosen presumably from among a number of other sculptors to execute the statue of Father Matthew for O'Connell Street in 1890. She had a studio in Mountjoy Square and she exhibited at the Royal Hibernian Academy from 1880 to 1886.

WR and JS

Reid, Eileen (1894-1981)

Eileen Reid was born Eileen Oulton in 1894 at the house which was to become her life long home, 19 Upper Mount Street. Her father, George Nugent Oulton, was a barrister. Initial education was at the German school in Wellington Place, but her artistic nature and love of music saw her going on to the Royal Hibernian Academy of Music, where she carried off the Coulson Prize. This ability in turn led to teaching music, and she was in fact earning as much as £80 per annum at the outbreak of the Great War. Eileen Oulton's love of painting ran parallel to her interest in music: in about 1919 she set off for London, and enrolled in the Royal Academy Schools. Here her progress was as rapid and successful as it had been in music. Her ability received praise from several of the foremost artists of the day — and in particular, from Sir William Orpen, whose influence on her style and handling can be seen.

In 1923 Eileen Oulton married Hugh C. Reid of Sloane Square, London. Hugh Reid was in the Colonial Service, stationed in Nigeria; he returned to his job, with his bride booked to follow on afterwards. As she was preparing for the long journey, the news arrived that he had died of black water fever, on 14 February 1924. He was aged thirty.

The shock of this tragedy cannot but have altered Eileen Reid's whole spirit and direction in life. Over the following years oil painting gave way to watercolours, which, in turn, gave way to her becoming Secretary of the Watercolour Society of Ireland — a post she held for over thirty years. Her early promise and success, her student work and her short ten years exhibiting career, gave way to an art related position basically administrative. She showed works at the Society from about 1933 until 1942, usually two or four watercolours every year.

Her works are in various private collections.

COC

See cat. no. 87.

Reid, Nano (1905-1981)

Born 1905 in Drogheda, county Louth; c.1920, won a scholarship to the Metropolitan School of Art, Dublin, where she studied under Patrick Tuohy, Leo Whelan, John Keating and Harry Clarke; she also studied in London at the Central School of Art and Chelsea School of Art, returning to Dublin in 1930; 1972, awarded the Douglas Hyde Gold Medal, and the Arts Council award; 1981, died.

Exhibitions: 1934, The Gallery, Dublin; 1936, Daniel Egan's Gallery, Dublin; 1939, The Gallery, Dublin; 1941, The Gallery,

Dublin; 1942-45, The Dublin Painters' Gallery, Dublin; 1947-76, The Dawson Gallery, Dublin; 1950, Victor Waddington Galleries, Dublin; St. Georges Galleries, London; 1952, Hanover Gallery, London; 1964, The Arts Council Gallery, Belfast; 1974, Retrospective Exhibition, Municipal Gallery of Modern Art, Dublin; 1975, Retrospective Exhibition, Ulster Museum, Belfast.

Collections: Municipal Gallery of Modern Art, Dublin; Ulster Museum, Belfast; Trinity College, Dublin; Santa Barbara Museum and Art Gallery, California; An Chomhairle Ealaíon/The Arts Council; The National University, Dublin; The Arts Council of Northern Ireland; New York Irish Institute; Contemporary Irish Art Society; Bank of Ireland.

Rhind, Ethel Mary (c.1878-1952)

Ethel Rhind was born in Bengal, where her father was an engineer. She attended Derry High School and was living in Belfast before she was awarded a scholarship to study mosaic at the Dublin Metropolitan School of Art in 1902. She held this for three years, exhibiting a mosaic *Head of Juno* in 1904 and three stained glass panels in 1907, the year she joined Sarah Purser's stained glass and *opus sectile* Cooperative, An Túr Gloine (The Tower of Glass). Her designs for *opus sectile* are superior to those for glass and she became Ireland's foremost artist in this medium (see her Stations of the Cross at Spiddal Catholic Church (1918-28), at Loughrea Cathedral (1929-33) and the Friary, Athlone (1934-6)). In 1912 she designed a tapestry for the Dun Emer Guild (National Museum of Ireland) and in 1913 was depicted as Salome by Harry Clarke. She was strongly influenced by Wilhelmina Geddes, with whom she sometimes collaborated. She exhibited regularly with the Arts and Crafts Society of Ireland and was a member of the Guild of Irish Art Workers, but only exhibited once with the Royal Hibernian Academy, in 1913.

NGB

See cat. no. 83.

Ritchie, Anna (b.1937)

She was born in Australia in 1937, received her art education in Melbourne, at the National Gallery School of Art. Afterwards she travelled widely in Europe, settling for a number of years in Northern Ireland. She exhibited regularly during the fifties with the Irish Exhibition of Living Art and had a one-person exhibition at the Ritchie Hendriks Gallery in 1961. Subsequently she returned to Australia.

Rivers, Elizabeth (1903-1964)

Born 1903 in England; she studied first at Goldsmith's College, and then won a scholarship to the Royal Academy, where she studied for five years; 1931, she studied in Paris under Lhote and Severini, and also at the École de Fresque; 1934, she returned to London, and visited Aran where she went to live the following year. She lived on Inis Mor until 1941, exhibiting during these years in Manchester, London and Dublin, including the RHA in 1936. During the war years she worked in London as a fire warden, but returned to Aran, publishing *Stranger in Aran* with the Cuala Press in 1946; 1946-55, she painted in Dublin, and assisted Evie Hone in her stained glass studio. She contributed regularly to the Irish Exhibition of Living Art; 1956-57, she published *Out of Bedlam* and *Out of Bondage, Israel*; 1960, One-Woman show, Dawson Gallery, Dublin; 1966, memorial exhibition was held in Dublin; 1964, died.

Roberts, Hilda (1901-1982)

Hilda Roberts was born in Dublin into a Quaker family. She drew and painted from an early age and was educated at Nightingale Hall. In 1919 she entered the Metropolitan School of Art for two years where she was taught by Tuohy and completed twenty-four illustrations for a volume of *Persian Tales* published by Macmillan. She then spent two years studying drawing, anatomy and painting at the London Polytechnic. On her return to Dublin, she studied sculpture under Oliver Sheppard, winning three awards for modelling in 1924 and 1925 which enabled her to go to France. This broadened her conception of painting and her sense of colour. Back in Ireland in 1929, she decided to abandon sculpture for portraiture and set off for the West of Ireland, where she mostly painted children. This, and several portrait commissions, as well as watercolour and oil landscapes, drawings and illustrations, led to her first two exhibitions in 1930 and 1931 at the St. Stephen's Green Gallery which received critical acclaim. At this time she was heralded as holding 'the premier place for fine, free work as a draftsman' and as exhibiting the 'only really modern picture' in the Royal Hibernian Academy, to which she contributed fairly regularly from 1922 until 1979. She was a member of the Dublin Painters' Society, an H.R.H.A. and a prizewinner at the Aonach Tailteann Exhibition of 1932 but exhibited less after her marriage to the pioneering headmaster, Arnold Marsh, of Newtown School, Waterford. She continued to paint and draw and also made excursions into needlework and stained glass, exhibiting the latter in the first Irish Exhibition of Living Art. The Taylor Galleries in Dublin gave her a retrospective show in 1979. She is represented in the Hugh Lane Municipal Gallery, Dublin, the Ulster Museum and Waterford Municipal Collection, among others.   NGB

See cat. nos. 128-30.

Roberts, Mrs. A. see Fannin, Marianne Edwardine

Robertson, Barbara (20th century)

A landscape and portrait painter, Barbara Robertson exhibited five works at the Royal Hibernian Academy from 1935 to 1937. Her style is characterised by broad brush strokes and the occasional use of impasto which is reminiscent of post impressionism though her colouring is generally more subtle. An example of her work is in the Hugh Lane Municipal Gallery, Dublin.   WR

Robertson, Clementina (1795-c.1853)

Clementina Robertson was born in Dublin where she is recorded as having been trained by her father, Charles Robertson. This was doubtless the case as her style closely resembles that of her father. Both specialised in miniature portraits. They portrayed their sitters in a precise and unsentimental manner, though Clementina's approach is often more sensitive, particularly in male portraits.

Clementina continued to paint after her marriage in 1830 to John Siree, a medical student whose portrait by her is in the National Gallery. Her perseverance in her profession as miniature painter and teacher of drawing, a relatively unusual occupation for a woman in the first half of the nineteenth century, may have been in part due to the influence of her father. Charles Robertson, apart from having an active career, exhibiting frequently both in Dublin and London, was Secretary and later Vice-President of the Hibernian Society of Artists. Clementina herself exhibited in 1926, 1928 and 1931 in the newly founded Royal Hibernian Academy.

Examples of her work are in the National Gallery of Ireland.
                                                                    WR

See cat. no. 21.

Robertson, Joanna (b.1960)

Born 1960; 1984, B.A. Degree in Fine Art, National College of Art & Design, Dublin; awarded Taylor Bequest RDS; Maurice McGonigal Memorial Award.

Exhibitions: 1983, Artists with Promise, Solomon Gallery, Dublin; 1984, Young Irish Artists, Mansion House, Dublin; Three person Show, Kilkenny Arts Week, Kilkenny; Oireachtas Art Exhibition, Dublin; EVA, Limerick; Graduate Show, Temple Bar Gallery, Dublin; 1986, Royal Hibernian Academy Annual Exhibition, Dublin; Oireachtas Art Exhibition, Dublin; Three person Show, Kilkenny Arts Week, Kilkenny; NCAD Decade Show, Guinness Hop Store; 1987, Five person Show, Tom Caldwell Gallery, Dublin.

Robinson, Anne Marjorie (1858-1924)

Marjorie Robinson, miniature painter, was born in Belfast. Her artistic inclinations became evident during her school days, when she used to spend hours drawing decorative borders around the pages of her exercise books. Realising she was gifted, her teacher introduced her to educationalist Vere Foster, who in turn recommended her to illuminator John Vinycomb, head of the Art Department of Marcus Ward's publishing firm. She studied drawing and illumination under Vinycomb and later attended the Belfast Government School of Art. On completing her studies, she worked as an illuminator, with considerable success. In the early 1890's, she began exhibiting at the Belfast Art Society, showing mostly portraits and landscapes; also miniatures, from 1900 and occasionally sculpture, from 1911. In 1907, deciding to specialise in miniature painting, she went to London, to work under Alyn Williams and subsequently, in 1912, was elected to Associate membership of the Royal Society of Miniature Painters. While in London, she also studied modelling. She returned to her native city on the outbreak of World War I.

Apart from these seven years in London, Marjorie spent all her life in Belfast, showing regularly at the Belfast Art Society, and occasionally at the Royal Academy, the Royal Hibernian Academy and Society of Women Artists (of which she was elected an Associate in 1917). The high point of her career came in 1922, when she was invited by Princess Marie Louise to contribute to a portfolio of drawings for Queen Mary's Doll's House, at Windsor Castle. Majorie's tiny painting of an Irish colleen (measuring only 3.8 × 2.5 cm) is stored in one of the drawers in the Library of the House, and consequently cannot be seen. The model itself, however, is on display to the public. The aim of the Doll's House (the brainchild of the Princess), was to show future generations how an English King and Queen lived in the twentieth century. With this in mind, leading authors and artists of the day were asked to contribute books and paintings (in miniature!) to the House, for its Library and walls. To be included was a signal honour for Marjorie and says much for her reputation.

Examples of her miniatures can be found in the National Gallery of Ireland and the Ulster Museum (which also owns sculpture and a self portrait, in oils).   EB

See cat. no. 62.

Roche, Vivienne (b.1953)

Born 1953 in Cork; 1970-74, Crawford Municipal School of Art, Cork; 1974-75, School of the Museum of Fine Arts, Boston, USA. Lives in Garrettstown, county Cork.

One-Man Exhibitions: 1978, Cork Arts Society Gallery; 1980, David Hendriks Gallery, Dublin; 1983, David Hendriks Gallery, Dublin; 1984, Cork Arts Society Gallery; 1986, Allied Irish Banks, Cork; 1987, The Hendriks Gallery, Dublin; 'The Wind Bower', Bank of Ireland, Baggot St., Dublin.

Recent Group Exhibitions: 1980, 'Works on Paper', Angela Flowers Gallery, London; Independent Artists (1982); EVA, Limerick (1982); 1981, Guinness Peat Aviation' Emerging Artists', Triskel Arts Centre, Cork; 1982, Oasis, River Liffey. SADE, Contemporary Irish Drawing; University of Vermont; 1983, Cibeal '83, Kenmare; 1984, 2nd Biennale Européene Sculpture de Normandie, France; 1985, CAN, 'Living with Art', Douglas Hyde Gallery; Open Air Sculpture, Marlay Park; Sculpture at East Link; 'Insight' Triskel touring show; 1986, Festival Interceltique de l'Orient, France; Women Artists in Cork, Triskel Arts Centre; AIB Collection, Douglas Hyde Gallery; Sculpture in Context, Fernhill, Dublin; Claremorris Arts Festival; 1987, Cork Artists, University College, Cork.

Public Collections: University College, Dublin; Regional Technical College, Cork; The Arts Council of Ireland; Allied Irish Banks; The Hugh Lane Municipal Gallery, Dublin; Contemporary Irish Art Society, Dublin; Office of Public Works; Insurance Corp. of Ireland.

de Ros, the Honourable Frances Charlotte Fitzgerald (d.1851)

Little is known about this lady; the date of her birth is unrecorded, but she was a daughter of William, 23rd Baron de Ros, of Oldcourt, Strangford, county Down. Her grandmother, Baroness de Ros, in her own right, married Lord Henry FitzGerald, 4th son of the 1st Duke of Leinster. The Hon. Frances Charlotte FitzGerald de Ros was a visitor to Carton, county Kildare, in the time of the 3rd Duke and Duchess of Leinster. She died in her twenties on 21 February 1851.   MW

See cat. no. 18.

de Ros, Olivia Cecilia (d.1869)

Probably born in Ireland, the daughter of Charlotte, Baroness de Ros, she married on 22 October 1833, Henry, Earl Cowley. Olivia, though clearly an amateur painter, shows great skill in her watercolour of her children dressing for a party, presumably in the late 1830's. She is also known as a landscape painter. The name de Ros is sometimes spelt de Roos.   AOC and KOG

Ross, Florence (1870-1949)

As a child, Florence Ross came to Dublin with her mother and two brothers to live with their grandmother, Mrs. Traill, in Orwell Park near the Dodder. In 1872 another daughter of Mrs. Traill, newly widowed, came with her five children to live next door. Florence Ross and her cousin, the writer John Millington Synge, were the youngest children and spent much time pursuing their love of nature in the grounds of Rathfarnham Castle nearby, drawing animals, plants and birds. In 1882 they collaborated on a detailed Nature Diary. Every summer from 1874 to 1891 the Rosses and Traills spent in a large house Mrs. Synge took at Greystones. In 1891, on her mother's death, Florence Ross went to live with the Synges, now in Kingstown. The following summer, they spent the first of many years at Castle Kevin at Annamoe, where Florence Ross spent much time exploring and sketching. In 1895, she went out to Tonga in the Friendly Islands to help her brother, a doctor, with his family. She spent eleven years abroad, visiting New Zealand, Australia, the Argentine, Santa Fe. On her return, she devoted herself to watercolour painting, travelling all over Ireland in the summer, but being particularly fond of county Wicklow. She loved the Blasket Islands and went by curragh to the (still inhabited) Great Blasket with her cousin, where, among other things, they sketched the 'King's House' in which J. M. Synge had stayed.

She wintered near Dublin, belonged to various painting societies, exhibited regularly (e.g. at the Aonach Tailteann Exhibition of Irish Art in 1932) and held solo shows in the Hall at 35 Molesworth Street.   NGB

See cat. no. 90.

Ross, Margaret Murray see Sherlock, Margaret Murray

St. Albans, Duchess of, (Grace) (1848-1926)

Grace was probably born at Newtown Anner, daughter of Ralph Bernal and his wife Catherine Osborne, heiress of Sir Thomas

Osborne of Newtown Anner, county Tipperary. On 3 January 1874 she married, as his second wife, William, Duke of St. Albans. Her mother, Mrs. Osborne, must have been interested in the arts as the Swiss landscape painter, Alexandre Calame, stayed in the house and may have given some lessons to her daughters Grace and Edith, later Lady Blake. Thomas Shotter Boys was also a visitor probably in 1865 or 1866 when he exhibited a work painted at Newtown Anner. As a girl, with her sister and friend Fanny Currey, Grace decorated envelopes as a pastime, showing a real feeling for genre scenes of local people at work. Later watercolours, done when an adult, show her to have been a most competent painter, and it is a pity that her social position undoubtedly prevented her exhibiting or developing her art.   AOC and KOG

See cat. no. 16.

Scally, Caroline (20th century)
Born Dublin 1894. Studied at Metropolitan School of Art, Dublin under William Orpen and in Paris and Italy. Regularly exhibited in Dublin and Cork. An example of her work is in the National Gallery of Ireland.

Shackleton, Lydia (1828-1914)
Of Quaker stock, Lydia Shackleton may be regarded as the principal botanical artist working in Ireland during the latter part of the nineteenth century. She was commissioned by Frederick Moore, Keeper of the Botanic Gardens, Glasnevin, to record faithfully the numerous orchids, pitcher-plants, peonies and other plants, that flourished in the Gardens under his direction. In the National Botanic Gardens today, approximately fifteen hundred watercolours by Miss Shackleton are preserved.

Lydia was the third child in a family of thirteen. She was born at Ballitore, the Quaker village in county Kildare, and had a sound education; indeed being one of the eldest she had to teach her younger brothers and sisters. In 1850, Lydia was studying art at the School of Art in Dublin and a few of her classwork sketches survive in a private collection; at the time she wrote that she disliked copying other artists' paintings.

In the latter part of her life she lived in Lucan where she had a small school, but it seems her preferred occupations were reading, painting, and gardening, and she also wrote poetry. Lydia Shackleton made two prolonged visits to the United States in the 1880's, and some of her paintings of North American wild plants and of landscapes in Ohio survive in a set of sketch-books.

The watercolours of the plants grown at Glasnevin are a remarkable archive, depicting the species and cultivated varieties that Frederick Moore garnered so avidly. At the time Glasnevin was one of the finest gardens in the world, with a collection of orchids, in particular, that was unrivalled and Miss Shackleton's portraits of those flowers proclaim that richness. The paintings of *Lachenalia* and *Sarracenia* hybrids record hybrids raised at Glasnevin which are no longer known in cultivation; these paintings have true historic significance.

Lydia Shackleton was fifty-six years of age when she began working at Glasnevin for Frederick Moore, and she painted there for twenty-three years until her failing eyesight forced her to give up the work to Alice Jacob.

As far as can be traced, none of Miss Shackleton's paintings was published during her lifetime, although an unsigned and unacknowledged portrait of several *Sarracenia* hybrids printed in the *Garden* was most probably by her. Apart from some paintings scattered in private (mostly family) collections, all her work is preserved in the National Botanic Gardens, Glasnevin.   EC

See cat. no. 29.

Sherlock, Margaret Murray (1886-1966)
Margaret Murray Ross was brought up at Summerfield, Dalkey, partly educated in London and when she was eighteen, illustrated a series of doorways for the Irish Georgian Society. In 1905 she was admitted to the Dublin Metropolitan School of Art, where she studied under Orpen and won various prizes. In 1910, the year her work was selected for the School's decade show in the Hall, 35 Dawson Street, she married Captain Charles Sherlock from the Army Medical Corps and went out to India. She returned to Ireland on leave in 1914 with her young daughters but rejoined her husband when war was declared. Although he was killed in Mesopotamia in 1917, she could not get back until 1919. Once back in Ireland, although she drew regularly, supplied anatomy illustrations and exhibited occasionally, she was never moved to paint as she had been in the Orient. She returned to India in 1933 and 1936 and went on painting holidays in Italy, but the spontaneous magic was gone.   NGB

See cat. no. 67.

Simonds-Gooding, Maria (b.1939)
Born 1939 in Quetta, India; 1947, moved with family to county Kerry; c.1960, studied briefly at the National College of Art & Design, Dublin and subsequently in Brussels and England.

She first exhibited at the Royal Hibernian Academy in 1967 and periodically there afterwards. She is also a regular contributor to the Oireachtas exhibition. She won a Carroll Award at the Irish Exhibition of Living Art in 1970. Her paintings and graphics have been exhibited in numerous group shows in Ireland, London and New York.

Beginning in 1965, a series of one woman shows were held in The Gallery, Brown Thomas. She also exhibited singly in Dublin at the Project Arts Centre, the Lad Lane Gallery and the Taylor Galleries as well as at the Betty Parsons Gallery in New York. A retrospective exhibition of her work was held in Cork in 1985.

Collections: Hirshhorn Museum, Washington DC; An Chomhairle Ealaíon/The Arts Council, Dublin; The National Gallery of Modern Art, New Delhi; P. J. Carroll & Co. Ltd., Dublin; Commission of the European Communities, Brussels.

Sinclair, Frances see Beckett, Frances

Siree, Clementina see Robertson, Clementina

Smith, Joan (b.1946)
Born 1946; 1971, graduated, ATC, National College of Art and Design, Dublin; 1972-82, many commissions throughout Ireland, and between 1978-79 in Spain; 1982, moved to live in Australia.

Group Exhibitions: 1974, Northern Ireland Arts Council Gallery, Belfast; Architectural Projects, Churchill House, Belfast; 1976, Municipal Art Gallery, Waterford; 1979, Casino Puerta Banus, Spain; 1981, Tulfarris Environmental Show, Blessington; Art in Sport, Tulfarris Art Gallery.

One-Woman Exhibitions: 1978, 'Flying Free', El Pinar Gallery, Marbella, Spain; 1980, 'Fragments of a Woman', Heineken Gallery, Amsterdam, Netherlands; Central Beheer Gallery, Apeldoorn, Netherlands.

Solomons, Estella F. (1882-1968)
Estella Frances Solomons was born in Dublin, the elder daughter of Maurice Solomons J.P., an optician originally from Yorkshire. She went to finishing school in Germany, and then returned to Dublin to attend the Royal Hibernian Academy schools under Osborne, and the Metropolitan School of Art. In 1903, she visited Paris, with the Elvery sisters and Cissie Beckett, taking classes at Colarossi's. She went to London to continue her studies under Orpen, and painted the streets of Chelsea. An influential event was the visit to Amsterdam in 1906, to see the Rembrandt tercentenary exhibition, after which she turned from the subdued impressionist manner of her early landscapes to *chiaroscuro* in portraits, and a quality of introspection which she retained even after her portrait style lightened to become colourful and expressive. The visit may also have prompted her interest in etching. She worked at least ninety-two copperplates, many of old Dublin, which she used to illustrate D. Kelleher's *The Glamour of Dublin* (1918 and 1928).

She first exhibited with the Young Irish Artists in 1903, and at the RHA in 1905, and was elected ARHA in 1925. In her latter years she became an HRHA. During the revolutionary period, she joined Cumann na mBan, and was active behind the scenes during the Rising. During the Troubles, her studio became a hiding place for those on the run. After her marriage with Seumas O'Sullivan (James Starkey), the poet, she went to live in Rathfarnham for some years, painting landscape there, and visiting Donegal and Cornwall. In 1938, she moved back to Dublin to Morehampton Road, where she painted some of her most impressionist views, of the grove behind their house and the adjoining road. Though her portraits of personalities prominent in the building of a new Ireland have always attracted attention, in recent years there has been a new interest in her landscapes, and a comprehensive exhibition of her career as a painter of landscape was mounted in the Crawford Municipal Art Gallery in Cork in May 1986. Her work is represented in Sligo Museum, Trinity College, Dublin, the National Gallery of Ireland, and in the Hugh Lane Municipal Gallery, Dublin.   HP

See cat. nos. 75-76.

Somerville, Edith Œnone (1858-1949)
Born in Corfu, Edith Somerville spent her childhood and most of her life at Drishane, Castletownshend, county Cork. She drew from an early age and in 1877 spent a term in London at the South Kensington School of Art. Her parents were reluctant to let her travel abroad but because her cousin, Egerton Coghill, had a studio in Düsseldorf she was allowed to spend two terms there in 1881 and 1882, working under Gabriel Nicolet and Carl John. Between 1884 and 1887 she spent each spring in Paris, first at Colarossi's atelier for young ladies and later at his studio in the Rue de la Grande Chaumière. In the 1890's she spent two further terms at Delacluse's. The accounts in her diaries and her later reminiscences of life as a female art student are rich and lively. In 1885 *Cassel's Magazine of Art* published her article on Paris studios. The accompanying drawings and caricatures of her fellow students have the same distinctly humorous bent which characterises much of her later work as an illustrator.

In 1886 she met her cousin Violet Martin (Martin Ross, 1862-1915) for the first time, and shortly afterwards they began their now famed literary collaboration. Their first novel *An Irish Cousin* was published in 1889 and thereafter they produced many works together, the most acclaimed being *The Real Charlotte* (1894) and *Some Experiences of an Irish R.M.* (1899). The numerous books provided Edith Somerville with a huge outlet for her illustrations and it is as a black and white artist that she is now best known. However, she painted in oils, mostly landscapes, all her life and exhibited frequently during the 1920's in London, and in New York in 1929. The degree of D.Litt. was conferred on her by Trinity College, Dublin in 1932 and in 1943 she took part in the Irish Exhibition of Living Art.

There is a portrait of *Violet Martin, 1886* in the National Portrait Gallery, London, *An old widow woman* in the Hugh Lane Municipal Gallery, Dublin and *The Goose Girl* (1878) is in the Crawford Municipal Gallery, Cork. Her diaries and numerous illustrations are in the Library in the Queen's University, Belfast and there are a number of sketches of Louis Pasteur, drawn from life, in the Library in Trinity College, Dublin.   FG

See cat. nos. 41-43.

Souter, Camille (b.1929)
Born 1929 in Northampton, of English parents; 1930, came to Ireland and was educated here; 1948, studied nursing at Guy's Hospital, London. During this period she became ill with tuberculosis, and whilst recuperating began painting again. It was this illness which led her to be called Camille. She gave up nursing for painting; 1951, she married Gordon Souter. During the 1950's she travelled through Italy and continued to paint. She came back to Dublin but returned intermittently to Italy.

She began to exhibit in Dublin in the late 1950's, and since then her work has appeared in numerous group exhibitions: the Irish Exhibition of Living Art, Oireachtas, and occasionally the RHA. She has had very few one woman shows.

In 1960 she married again and settled in Calary Bog in 1962.

Her husband died in 1971. She now lives and works in Dublin, but spends much of her time on Achill Island.

Selected Exhibitions: 1957, Irish Exhibition of Living Art (and subsequently in 1958, 1960-67, 1973); 1960, Independent Artists, Dublin (and subsequently in 1961-64, 1967, 1971-2, 1979); 1961, One Man's Meat, Municipal Gallery of Modern Art, Dublin; 1963, Twelve Irish Painters, New York; 1965, Two Painters from the Collection of Sir Basil Goulding, bt., Ulster Museum, Belfast; Paintings and Sculpture (1945-65) from Private Collections in Ireland, Municipal Gallery of Modern Art, Dublin; 1966, Royal Hibernian Academy; 1970, Oireachtas (and subsequently 1971, 1973, 1977, 1978); 1971, The Irish Imagination 1959-71, Rosc, Municipal Gallery of Modern Art, Dublin; 1973, Royal Hibernian Academy; 1976, Elements of Landscape, Municipal Gallery of Modern Art, Dublin; 1977, Some Irish Fish, Dawson Gallery, Dublin; Festival International de la peinture, Haut de Cagnes, France; Grand Prix International d'art contemporain de Monte Carlo, Monaco; 1978, Claremorris National Art Competition; 1979, Women's Show, Project Art Centre, Dublin; 1980, The Delighted Eye — Irish Painting and Sculpture of the Seventies, 'A Sense of Ireland', London and Dublin; Retrospective Exhibition, The Douglas Hyde Gallery, Trinity College, Dublin; 1982, Six Artists from Ireland, European Touring Exhibition; 1984, EVA, Limerick; 1986, Taylor Galleries, Dublin.

Collections: Hugh Lane Municipal Gallery of Modern Art, Dublin; Ulster Museum, Belfast; Crawford Municipal Gallery, Cork; An Chomhairle Ealaíon/The Arts Council, Dublin.

Spilsbury, Maria see Taylor, Maria

Stanhope, Lady (Charlotte Augusta) see Leinster, Duchess of (Charlotte Augusta)

Steyn, Stella (20th century)

Stella Steyn studied at the Metropolitan School of Art, Dublin. She exhibited landscapes and figure subjects at the Royal Hibernian Academy between 1927 and 1930. Her style is fresh and direct and she was skilled in a number of media including watercolour and pen and ink. Her work was exhibited at the Manchester City Art Gallery and at the New English Art Club. She is represented by two works in the Hugh Lane Municipal Gallery, Dublin.

WR

Stokes, Margaret McNair (1832-1900)

Born in Dublin, she was the eldest daughter of William Stokes, a noted Dublin doctor and his Scottish wife Mary Black. Miss Stokes had no formal training, but from childhood was familiar with her father's friends who included all the most notable figures in Irish archaeology of his day, including George Petrie and Lord Dunraven. Petrie was also a watercolourist of note but on stylistic grounds it seems that Petrie's protegé, Frederick William Burton, whose watercolours show the influence of the Pre-Raphaelites, was the most influential on Margaret Stokes' style as a painter.

However Petrie and Dunraven were her mentors as an art historian. Her best remembered paintings are illustrations to Sir Samuel Ferguson's poem Cromlech on Howth, published in 1861. She also illuminated the text with decorations based on early Irish manuscripts such as the Book of Kells.

Apart from editing Dunraven's Notes on Irish Architecture, left unfinished at his death, she published numerous other articles and books including her Early Christian Architecture in Ireland (1878) and her illustrated limited edition of the Cross of Cong, where the lithographs are based on her own magnificent drawings.

She was always interested in comparative art history, travelling from time to time and corresponding with English and continental notabilities, including Viollet-le-Duc, in connection with her research. But it was only after her father's death in 1879 that she had the freedom to travel for prolonged periods. Her two books, Six months in the Appennines ... (1892), and Three months in the Forests of France ... (1895) were both accounts of pilgrimages made 'in search of vestiges of the Irish saints'. Both include as illustrations beautiful landscape drawings, made by herself.

She appears to have exhibited only once in 1895 in the Royal Hibernian Academy. A number of her drawings are in the National Gallery of Ireland.

AOC

See cat. no. 23.

Stuart, Imogen (b. 1927)

Born in Berlin. Came to Ireland in 1950. Studied for five years with expressionist sculptor Otto Hitzberger, and attended the Academy of Fine Arts in Munich. She works mainly in wood, stone, bronze, steel, clay, plaster and terracotta. ARHA in 1982. Elected member of Aosdana.

Represented in churches and public places throughout Ireland, as well as England and Rome. Religious commissions include works at Galway, Armagh and Longford Cathedrals; President Childers's grave site; the official commemorative medal and stamp for the canonisation of St. Oliver Plunkett; Liam McCormick churches in Donegal; Ballintubber Abbey; chapel at UCC; Arts Block UCD, Belfield; monument for the John Paul II Library, Maynooth College.

Exhibitions include RHA from 1950 onwards; Living Art (1955-65); Salzburg Biennale; retrospective in conjunction with Oireachtas; Trinity College Library; Expo, New York.

Stuart, Louisa Ann see Waterford, Marchioness of, (Louisa)

Swanzy, Mary (1882-1978)

Mary Swanzy was born in Dublin on 15 April 1882, second daughter of surgeon Sir Henry Rosborough Swanzy, resident in 23 Merrion Square. She studied art at May Manning's studio, (meeting John B. Yeats there), and modelling with John Hughes. In 1905 she first exhibited a portrait at the Royal Hibernian Academy and continued to show portraits there for the next ten years. Encouraged by Miss Manning she went to Paris in c.1906, and studied under Delacluse, and in c.1907 at La Grande

Chaumière and Colarossi's. She may also have studied briefly at Matisse's atelier. At Gertrude Stein's house she saw paintings by Cézanne, Gauguin, Matisse and Picasso. Being in Paris at this crucial period, when Cubism was evolving, had a lasting influence upon her work. However, she was also an admirer of William Orpen, and at first followed a conventional career in Dublin, working as an illustrator and portraitist. In 1913 and 1919 she held one-person shows in Dublin and in 1914 first exhibited at the Salon des Independants.

After the First World War she did relief work in Czechoslovakia, and painted Balkan peasants in traditional costume and cheerful mountain landscapes. She became a committee member of the Salon des Independants in 1920. In Dublin she showed with Jack B. Yeats, Paul Henry and others. In c.1923-24 she visited Honolulu and Samoa, painting colourful canvases of native women in tropical landscapes. She exhibited these in Santa Barbara in California and at the Galerie Bernheim Jeune in Paris in 1932. Exhibitions were held in London in 1934 and in Dublin in 1943. During the War she returned to Dublin for three years. She was represented in a group show in London (with Braque, Chagall, Henry Moore and others) in 1946, and on her own in 1947. Her later years were spent in seclusion in London but a large retrospective of her work was held at the Hugh Lane Municipal Gallery, Dublin in 1968. This gave her renewed encouragement and she continued painting up to her final year. She died in London in 1978, aged ninety-six.

She is one of the most individual of twentieth century Irish artists, but her work is highly eclectic: from the early portraits, to impressionist and 'fauve' landscapes, Cubist studies of nature, and figurative and allegorical War paintings, and finally personal poetic subjects, reminiscent of early Picasso, Chagall and the School of Paris. Examples of her work are found in the National Gallery of Ireland, the Hugh Lane Municipal Gallery, and in Cork, Waterford and Limerick.   JC

See cat. nos. 133-37.

Sykes, Angela see Antrim, Countess of (Angela)

Taylor, Maria (1777-c.1823)
Maria was born in London, the daughter of John Spilsbury, an eighteenth century English engraver. Before marrying and settling in Ireland in 1813, Maria made a reputation for herself as a genre and portrait painter in London where she exhibited at the Royal Academy from 1792 to 1808 and at the British Institution from 1806 to 1813. In Ireland, Maria exhibited first at the Hibernian Society in 1814 and 1815 and afterwards at the Dublin Society's house in Hawkins Street. Her work was much admired in Ireland and several of her genre pictures were engraved.

An example of her portraiture is in the National Gallery of Ireland.   WR

See cat. no. 14.

Thompson, Elizabeth see Butler, Lady (Elizabeth)

Thompson, Sydney Mary (Madame Christen) (1847-1923)
Sydney Mary Thompson was born at Whitehouse, county Antrim, into an upper middle class family. Although information on her early life is regrettably scanty, her parents appear to have had liberal ideas concerning her education, for she grew up with a wide range of interests, including art, natural history and literature. Her formal art training appears to have begun in 1870, at the Belfast Government School of Art. There, she quickly established herself as one of its most gifted students and won numerous prizes in the School's own competitions and in national competitions organised by the Department of Science and Art, South Kensington. From 1886, she was a frequent exhibitor on the local scene, firstly at the Belfast Ramblers' Sketching Club and later, at the Belfast Art Society (which the Club became in 1890). It was through the Society that she met her future husband, Swiss artist Rodolphe Christen, who came to give lessons to the group in 1893. Despite a sizeable age gap — Sydney Mary was Christen's senior by twelve years — the couple were married in 1900 and eventually, in 1902, made their home at Ballater, in the Scottish Highlands. Sadly, their marriage was to be of short duration, as Christen died in 1906.

Little is known of Sydney Mary's life, after her marriage. She stopped exhibiting at the Belfast Art Society in 1901 and seems not to have shown anywhere else. That she continued to paint, one can only assume. She obviously maintained her interest in art, since she became a patron of the Society many years later, in 1921. In 1910, she wrote and published a touching tribute to her husband, *Rodolphe Christen The Story of an Artist's Life.* Though the book is a biography of Christen, the author's character and spirited vigorous views (particularly in support of the higher education of her sex), shine through. Her chief interest besides art was geology (she was well known in Irish geological circles) and it appears to have claimed much of her attention during her later years, her last expedition being to see the volcanoes at Auvergne, at the age of seventy-five.

Paintings by Sydney Mary are scarce, though her output was quite prolific, judging by exhibition catalogues. Her work, mostly landscapes in watercolour, is of a high standard. An oil portrait is in the Ulster Museum.   EB

Tighe, Caroline see Hamilton, Caroline

Timoney, Anne (b.1962)
Born 1962; 1985, B.A. Degree in Fine Art, National College of Art & Design, Dublin; 1986, awarded post-graduate scholarship to the Netherlands.

One Woman Exhibition: 1986, Thomastown, county Kilkenny.

Group Exhibition: 1985, College of Architecture, University College, Dublin; Graduate Show, Temple Bar Gallery, Dublin; Postcard Exhibition, Artists Collective, Belfast; EVA, Limerick; Reflections, Temple Bar Gallery, Dublin.

Tisdall, E. M. (fl. 1888-1900)

Miss Tisdall's artistic competence is known from a series of plant portraits reproduced in one of the major Victorian horticultural periodicals, the weekly journal, *The Garden,* which was founded by the Irish-born horticulturist, William Robinson.

All of the plants which Miss Tisdall painted were grown in William Edward Gumbleton's renowned garden at Belgrove, east of Cobh in county Cork. Undoubtedly it was W. E. Gumbleton who commissioned E. M. Tisdall to prepare the original watercolours which were the templates for the lithographs reproduced in *The Garden.* His garden included many rare, tender plant species and innumerable new cultivated varieties, and these were the subjects chosen for Miss Tisdall to paint. Gumbleton had earlier (between 1880 and 1890) commissioned a Miss Travers about whom nothing else is known, to do similar work.

Tisdall exhibited her work at the Dublin Sketching Club in 1888, 1892 and 1893.

None of her original watercolours are known to be extant.

ECN

Townshend, Harriet Hockley (1877-1941)

Born in Ireland, Harriet Hockley Weldon was the daughter of Major General Walter Weldon by his second marriage on 3 June 1876 to Annie Homan Molloy. We do not know where Harriet obtained her initial training but she started to exhibit portraits at the Royal Hibernian Academy in 1903. She may have gone to an English or continental school. However, in 1909 she followed a course in the Metropolitan School of Art for one year before she married Thomas Loftus Uniacke Townshend on 8 June 1910. After that date she exhibited under her married name, exhibiting in all at the RHA from 1903-1935. She worked in oil and in pastel. Two of her pastels are on loan to the Castletown Foundation.

AOC

See cat. no. 61.

Trevor, Helen Mabel (1831-1900)

Helen Mabel Trevor was born at Lisnageaol House, Loughbrickland, county Down on 20 December 1831, eldest daughter of Edward Hill Trevor. Helen began drawing as a child, and worked at home for many years, painting studies of dogs and kittens, and on one occasion the *Hounds of the Newry Hunt* (1856). She first exhibited at the Royal Hibernian Academy in 1854 and again in 1856, 1859 and 1865. After her father died, she decided to study art seriously, attending the Royal Academy in London for four years in the late 1870's. She went on to Paris c.1880, and studied with Henner, Merson and Carolus-Duran.

She first visited Brittany c.1880-81, and sent a canvas *Breton Boys en Retenue* to the Royal Academy in 1881. In August she and her sister Rose travelled in Normandy and Brittany, visited Douarnenez, and stayed at the artists' colony of Pont-Aven c.1882 where Helen attended life classes at the Hotel des Voyageurs. In 1883 she sent two pictures to the RHA from Concarneau. In August she visited Italy. Helen 'studied the great old masters and

saw such marvellous works of art there she could not leave Italy for six years', and painted landscapes and figure studies at Florence, Venice, Perugia and Capri.

The Trevors returned to Paris in 1889, and Helen re-entered Carolus-Duran's studio, working with students of all nationalities. From her high-up flat she made sketches of St. Germaine, Les Invalides and the newly constructed Eiffel Tower. In the early 1890's, she and Rose re-visited Brittany and spent the winter of 1895-96 at Concarneau. Her earlier Breton and Italian subjects, of school-children and flower girls had been sentimental. She was now a keen advocate of painting from nature and her studies of elderly Breton women and interiors, have increasing realism. She was interested in the lives and traditions of the Bretons and other Celtic peoples.

She was a regular exhibitor in Dublin, London and Paris, showing portraits, Breton and Italian subjects at the RHA in 1883 and 1887-97, the RA 1894-95, and the Paris Salon, 1889-99. She had various addresses in Paris in the 1890's: the Rue Sufflot, 1 Rue Cervantes, 159 Boulevarde Saint-Germain, and 55 Rue du Cherche-Midi. It was at this latter address, her Montparnasse studio, that she died suddenly of heart disease in 1900.

Examples of Trevor's work are in the National Gallery of Ireland, the Ulster Museum, and in private collections in Ireland.   JC

See cat. nos. 32-34.

Trinseach, Sadhbh (1891-1918)

Francesca Chenevix-Trench was born in Kent into a clerical, liberal Anglo-Irish family (her grandfather had been Archbishop of Dublin). She was educated in England, studied painting in Paris but also came over to Ireland where she studied Gaelic, hence the Irish version of her name by which she became known. She even pursued Celtic studies at the Sorbonne. She and her sister Margot came to live in Ireland, where she drew posters and Christmas cards for the Gaelic League and published a number of articles, often illustrated. She met Diarmuid Coffey, a cousin of Constance Markievicz and son of George Coffey, Keeper of Antiquities at the National Museum, when he was working for Horace Plunkett's Irish Agricultural Organisation Society and planning for a New Ireland. They were married in 1917, when George Russell (Æ) painted a superb portrait of her; another pastel depicts her in Celtic dress. She worked in a variety of media, experimenting with colour, scale and a variety of subjects — portraits, gardens, lively sketches, using a bright palette, of rural scenes, imaginative studies. She was just starting to develop as an artist when she was killed by the virulent flu epidemic which hit Dublin in the autumn of 1918. Ten of her drawings are in the National Gallery of Ireland.   NGB

See cat. nos. 65-66.

Trotter, Eliza H. (fl. 1800-1814)

Eliza was the daughter of the portrait painters Mary Ann Hunter and John Trotter.

She exhibited portraits, genre and history paintings with numerous institutions in Ireland and England including the Dublin Society, the Royal Academy and the British Institution. In Dublin she decorated the walls of the Harp Society's House at Glasnevin and painted a portrait of Patrick Quinn, harper to the Society, an engraving of which is in the National Gallery of Ireland.

WR

Trotter, Mary Ann see Hunter, Mary Ann

Vanston, Dairine (Doreen) (b.1903)

Born 1903 in Dublin; educated at Alexandra College; c.1920, studied at Goldsmith's College, London, and then at the Académie Ranson, Paris; 1926, while in Paris, married a Costa Rican law student and took the name Vanston de Padilla. They settled in San Jose, Costa Rica; 1932-33, on the break up of her marriage, she returned to Paris and studied briefly with André Lhote; 1940, escaped from France to London and thence to Dublin where she settled permanently except for a brief visit to Costa Rica during 1947-48; 1941, joined the White Stag Group and exhibited with them regularly throughout the war years; 1943, exhibited at the first Irish Exhibition of Living Art; exhibited annually thereafter in IELA and the Oireachtas Exhibitions; founder member of Independent Artists; member of the Graphic Studio.

Van Stockum, Hilda (b.1908)

Born 1908 in Rotterdam, of a Dutch father and half-Irish mother; she studied at the Metropolitan School of Art in Dublin under Sean Keating and Patrick Tuohy, and at the Academy of Fine Art in Amsterdam under Richard Roland Holst and Hendrick Wolter. Her paintings have been exhibited in the Dublin Painters Gallery; de Kuyl Gallery, Bilthoven; Corcoran Gallery, Washington; Montreal Museum of Art; the Royal Academy, London; the Royal Hibernian Academy, Dublin. A one-woman show was held at the Tom Caldwell Gallery, Dublin in 1986.

Her work can be seen in the National Gallery of Ireland.

Walker, Una (b.1955)

Born 1955 in Belfast; 1973-77, B.A. Degree in Fine Art, College of Art & Design, Belfast; 1977-78, lived and worked in Anglesey, North Wales; 1979, moved to Strangford, county Down.

One-Woman Exhibitions: 1978, Drawing Exhibition, Theatyr Gwynedd, North Wales; 1982, Finite and Bounded, Art & Research Exchange, Belfast; 1985, At the Back of the North Wind, Fenderesky Gallery, Belfast; Crannog, Peacock Gallery, Craigavon, N. Ireland and Crescent Arts Centre, Belfast; Old Wives Tales, Women's Festival, Olympia Community Centre, Belfast; 1986, Installation and Drawings, Wexford Arts Centre, Wexford.

Group Exhibitions: 1981, Aspects of Drawing, Maysfield Leisure Centre, Belfast; 1982, Irish Exhibition of Living Art, Dublin; 1983, Silent Memory, Riverside Theatre, Coleraine; 1984, Contemporary Artists, Enniskillen; 1985, Postcard Exhibition, Artists Collective of Northern Ireland, touring UK; Irish Exhibition of Living Art, Guinness Hop Store, Dublin; 1986, Collective Images II, Artists Collective of Northern Ireland, touring; Irish Art Now, Contemporary Irish Art, Antichi Chiostri, Turin, Italy; Critic's Choice, Alliance Francaise, Dublin and Lorient, Brittany; Women on Women, Fenderesky Gallery, Belfast.

Wall, Lorraine (b.1955)

Born 1955 in Ennis; graduate of Limerick College of Art & Design.

Selected Exhibitions: 1977, EVA, Limerick (1978, 1980, 1984); Interaction, Project Arts Centre, Dublin; 1978, AIB Limerick; Stone Art Gallery, Spiddal; Triskel Arts Centre; 1979-80, Claremorris Open Exhibition; 1981, Group Exhibition, Belltable, Limerick; Oireachtas Exhibition (1982, 1983, 1984); 1982, 'Belltable Foursight', Arts Council Touring Exhibition; SADE, Cork; 1983, Beltaine, Limerick and Brittany; 1985, One-Woman Exhibition, Belltable, Limerick; 1986, Douglas Hyde Gold Medal, Oireachtas Exhibition; Grafton Gallery, Dublin; Grattan Gallery, Tralee.

Wallace, Patricia see Griffith, Patricia

Walsh, Louise (b.1962)

Born 1962 in county Cork; 1981-85, Crawford Municipal College of Art, Cork. Graduated with a Diploma in Fine Art, with distinction; 1985-86, University of Ulster, Belfast, M.A. in Fine Art (Sculpture).

Group Exhibitions: 1986, Royal Ulster Academy, Belfast; Nicholas Treadwell Gallery, Canterbury, England; 'Self Direct', Smyths Gallery, Covent Garden London; 'Six Artists', Foyle Centre, Dublin; 1987, 'Six on the Go', Temple Bar Gallery, Dublin; Recent Work, Crawford Art Gallery, Cork; Otter Gallery, Belfast; Nicholas Treadwell Gallery, Canterbury, England.

Ward, the Hon. Mrs. Henry (Mary) (1827-1869)

Mary King was a native of Ferbane in county Offaly; her parents the Rev. Henry King and Henriette Lloyd, lived in Ballylin, a spacious country house set in parkland between Tullamore and Birr. Henriette King's sister was the wife of the second Earl of Rosse, whose son William became the 3rd earl and was the brilliant astronomer. Mary King frequently visited Birr Castle, the seat of the Earls of Rosse, during the time when her cousin was erecting his 'Leviathan' telescope, and she shared with him the passion for astronomy.

In 1854 Mary married Henry Ward of Castle Ward in county Down; the couple had six children, the youngest of whom became the 6th Viscount Bangor. Mary Ward was killed when she fell from a steam-driver carriage that her cousin, the Earl of Rosse had built; the tragedy occurred in The Mall leading to the main gates of Birr Castle. One obituarist wrote that the Hon. Mrs. Ward was '. . . distinguished alike by her talents and energy, her scientific acquirements, her genial and affectionate disposition and her many virtues.'

Mary's scientific interest were extraordinarily broad. Her parents encouraged her, and she made microscopy and entomology her particular fields of research. In 1856, with her sister Lady Mahon as co-author, Mary Ward published *Entomology in sport,* and in the following year at Parsonstown (Birr), Mary alone published *Sketches with the microscope.* In 1858, her finest work was printed: *The world of wonders as revealed by the microscope* was illustrated with a series of plates she herself had drawn. This book was revised and expanded several times — the last edition, under the title *Microscope teachings,* appearing in 1864.

Apart from her excellent illustrations of the microscopic details of insects, bird feathers and fish scales, Mary Ward painted animals including the natterjack toad (this was printed in the *Intellectual Observer* early in 1864), and drew the telescopes of her cousin Lord Rosse, and of Sir Isaac Newton for Sir David Brewster's biography of Newton. Also for Sir David Brewster, Mary Ward studied under the microscope and drew fragments of glass excavated at Nineveh during 1849; the drawings illustrated a paper Brewster published in 1861. ECN

Warren, Barbara (b.1925)

Born 1925 in Dublin; studied National College of Art, Dublin; Regent Street Polytechnic, London; 1951, studied with André Lhôte in Paris; 1955, Purser Griffith Scholarship. Travelled in Spain and worked in the studio of Luis Maria Saumel. 10 years Lecturer in NCAD Numerous one-woman shows in Dublin: Dublin Painters' Gallery; Dawson Gallery/Taylor Gallery.

Exhibited in 'Seven Irish Painters', Germany; Irish and Dutch Painters; Living Art; Oireachtas; RHA; Figurative Image; United Arts Club.

Collections: Arts Council and many private collections in Ireland, America, England, Switzerland. Returns each year to paint in the West of Ireland.

Waterford, Marchioness of, (Louisa) (1818-1891)

Louisa Ann was born and spent her childhood in Paris, where her father, Lord Stuart de Rothesay was Ambassador. On 8 June 1842 she married the 3rd Marquess of Waterford. Her married life was largely spent at Curraghmore, county Waterford, and at Ford Castle, Northumberland, where she lived after her husband's death in 1859. She was a pupil of Ruskin and a friend of Watts and Burne-Jones. The influence of Ruskin is obvious in her watercolours and she was described by a critic as 'reviving the glories of the Venetian School'. Her drawing is occasionally weak but she had a fine sense of colour and composition. She exhibited her watercolours at the Grosvenor and Dudley Galleries in London during her life and in 1910 a large exhibition of her work was shown at 8 Carlton House Terrace in London.

At Ford Louisa Ann was a model chatelaine and among her improvements was the building of a new village school which she decorated with watercolour murals of biblical childhood scenes. At Curraghmore she provided stained glass for the six side windows in a small church on the estate. The figures in these are of a quality and strength comparable to the best Dublin

workshops of the period. The glass is still in position in this building known as Clonegam Church.

Her watercolours can be seen in the British Museum, the Victoria and Albert Museum, the Richmond Library and the National Gallery of Scotland. FG

Watson, Caroline (c.1760-1814)

Caroline Watson was the daughter of the Irish mezzotint engraver James Watson (d.1790). Like her father, Caroline became one of the leading London engravers. She specialised in stipple engraving and was particularly noted for her works after Reynolds, Romney and Hoppner. In 1785 she was appointed engraver to Queen Caroline.

There are several examples of her work in the National Gallery of Ireland. WR

Watson, Mrs. (fl. 1767-1771)

Mrs. Watson was the wife of a portrait painter, William Watson (d.1765). Little is known of Mrs. Watson other than that she exhibited fruit and flower subjects at the Society of Artists in Ireland from 1768 to 1772. She began exhibiting after the death of her husband which may indicate that she was painting in a professional capacity in order to support herself. Apart from her work in watercolour and pastel she was also praised for her influential role as an embroidress.

Unfortunately none of her works have been traced. WR

Webb, Josephine (1853-1924)

Josephine Webb was born in Dublin, one of the younger children of a large family. Her father traded under the name of Thos. Webb and Fisher, Boot and Shoe Manufactory, Tailoring and Gentlemen's General Outfitting Warehouse, at 35 and 36 Sackville Street Upper. Two of the older daughters ran a specialist wool shop next door to their father. The family were prominent members of the Quaker community.

Josephine was educated at Alexandra College and at the Queen's Institute where she won two Silver Medals in 1875 for her drawing. Almost all the family were keen amateur artists, but only Josephine became a full-time painter. She had a studio in St. Stephen's Green North, and in 1899 removed to.20 Lr. Pembroke Street.

In 1877-78 Miss Webb went to Paris where she studied at the Académie Julian (Sarah Purser was a student there that spring). The Professor of Drawing at that time was M. Robert Fleury, who came to criticise the student's work every Saturday. Josephine's mother, Mary Webb, preserved excerpts from her daughter's letters home; they describe the studio — which she said reminded her of the Turkish Baths in Lincoln Place — and the very cosmopolitan group of women students.

Miss Webb probably went to Holland in the summer of 1888, as her pictures exhibited in the watercolour exhibition the following March were of Dutch landscapes. She also painted flowers and portraits.

Josephine Webb moved in the lively circle of artists and writers of that time. There is a charming sketch of her by John Yeats and her own of Dora Sigerson, (National Gallery of Ireland cat. no. 6026) is of the same informal type. Miss Webb held a one-man exhibition in Dublin in 1913. She signed her pictures in monogram and exhibited at the Watercolour Society of Ireland in 1889, 1892 and 1893, the Dublin Arts Club (1892), the British Artists, Suffolk Street (1892) and the Royal Hibernian Academy from 1881.

SAD

See cat. no. 63.

Webb, Maria D. (fl. 1873-1886)

Maria Webb was living at Shanganagh, county Dublin in the early 1870's, then Palmerstown Park, and later Killiney. She exhibited at the Royal Hibernian Academy in 1873, from 1876-79, and 1881-86. It is possible, although not certain, that like her contemporary Sarah Purser, she studied briefly in Paris. She painted river scenes, along the Liffey and Dargle, and landscapes in Wicklow, Antrim and Wales. She visited Brittany in c.1883, and painted a number of Breton scenes; of a wet market day, of Breton peasants and fishing people. Two of these she exhibited at the RHA 1883-84, and two at the Paris Salon in 1884. She also exhibited during the 1880's at the Watercolour Society of Ireland, the Dublin Sketching Club and the Arts Club. The young Mary Swanzy attended her art classes in the 1890's.

JC

Wejchert, Alexandra (b.1920)

Born 1920 in Krakow, Poland; c.1950, studied at the Faculty of Architecture, Warsaw University; 1956, graduated from the Academy of Fine Arts, Warsaw; 1957-59, studied art and architecture in Italy, then practised as an architect and artist in Warsaw; 1963, took up painting full-time; 1965, came to live in Ireland, where she continued to paint but gradually concentrated on sculpture; 1981, became a member of Aosdana.

She has exhibited in major exhibitions of Irish Art in Ireland and abroad over the past twenty years. One woman and group exhibitions include Ireland, Europe and the USA.

Collections: Museo Comune di Roma, Galleria dell'Arte Moderna, Rome; An Chomhairle Ealaíon/The Arts Council, Dublin; University College, Dublin; P. J. Carroll & Co. Ltd., Dundalk; Coras Tráchtála, Dublin; Gordon Lambert Collection, Dublin; Dr. J. B. Kearney Collection, Cork; Galway University; Municipal Gallery of Modern Art, Dublin; Peter Stuyvesant Collection, Amsterdam; Bank of Ireland, Dublin; Allied Irish Bank, Dublin; Irish Life Assurance Company, Dublin; Jefferson Smurfit Group, Dublin; Lombard & Ulster Banking, Dublin; Barclays Bank (Ireland) Ltd.; Stokes Kennedy Crowley Collection, Dublin; National Selfportrait Gallery, NIHE, Limerick.

Weldon, Harriet Hockley see Townshend, Harriet Hockley

Wheeler-Cuffe, Lady (Charlotte) (1867-1967)

In 1897 Charlotte Williams, grand-daughter of the Rev. Sir Hercules Langrishe of Knocktopher, married F. L. Wheeler-Cuffe who was the heir to another Kilkenny baronetcy. Otway Wheeler-Cuffe was a civil engineer attached to the Public Works Department in the Indian sub-continent. For most of the twenty-five years from her marriage until 1922, Charlotte Cuffe lived in Burma where she developed a great interest in the native flora. She sometimes accompanied her husband on his travels to inspect engineering projects, and during these trips, Charlotte collected and painted flowers. In 1911, with Mrs. Winifred McNabb, she ascended Mount Victoria, the highest peak in western Burma, and there, in addition to collecting plants, she sketched the scenery and the flowers of the mountain.

Lady Cuffe's numerous watercolours include landscapes and plant portraits, some of which she exhibited at the Watercolour Society of Ireland during the 1920's. She also painted animals but these are rather solid and less lifelike than her botanical sketches. While not pedantic in their botanical details, her flower paintings are most pleasing, oriental in style because of the open and sparse technique that she used. A collection of sixty-six watercolours of Burmese and Indian orchids, painted between 1897 and 1922, was presented by Lady Cuffe to the National Botanic Gardens, Glasnevin, but only one of these (in badly damaged condition) can now be traced.

Apart from two damaged watercolours in the National Botanic Gardens, Dublin, there are no paintings by Lady Cuffe in public collections; her sketch-books remain in private collections.

ECN

Williams, Charlotte see Wheeler-Cuffe, Lady (Charlotte)

Williams, Lily (1874-1940)

Born in Dublin, she was the daughter of a wholesale druggist. She was taught first by May Manning, who was a formative influence on many young women artists around the turn of the century, and then attended the Metropolitan School of Art. In 1903, she exhibited with the Young Irish Artists, and she probably went to Paris about this time. In early years she painted landscape and portraits of her family; but a coolness arose with the family because of her republican sympathies at the time of the Rising. From 1915, she taught for about ten years at her studio in Pembroke Street, after which she concentrated on portrait painting. She was elected an ARHA in 1929, and continued to exhibit at the Royal Hibernian Academy until the year before her death. She was one of the contributors to *The Book of St. Ultan,* a collection of contemporary work by Irish writers and artists, compiled by Katherine McCormack in 1920. In 1923, she designed the Cross of Cong stamp for one of the first definitive series of stamps in the newly created Irish Free State. Her oil portrait of Arthur Griffith is in the Hugh Lane Municipal Gallery, Dublin.

HP

See cat. no. 91.

Wilmot, Martha (1775-1873)

Martha Wilmot was born in Ireland, the daughter of Captain Edward Wilmot and Martha Moore. After leaving the army her father became a Port Surveyor of the Revenue Board, first at Drogheda and later in Cork where they lived near Glanmire. She does not appear to have studied drawing and remained a prolific amateur throughout her life.

Following the death of a beloved brother in 1802, it was suggested that Martha should travel and through the introduction of a friend, she went in 1803 for five years to stay with Princess Daschkov in her country retirement near Moscow. There she made many fascinating sketches. She returned to Cork in 1808 and after travelling in Ireland in 1812, she met and married in England the Rev. William Bradford. They lived in Sussex though Martha continued travelling, visiting her sister in Paris in 1817 and 1818. Between 1819 and 1829 she lived in Vienna where her husband was Chaplain in the British Embassy. In 1840 she published *Memoirs of the Princess Daschkov.* On the death of her husband in 1857 she returned to Dublin to live with her daughter Catherine and son-in-law William Brooke, Master in the Irish Court of Chancery. She died in Taney Hill House, Dublin in 1873.

AOC and KOG

Wise, Kate see Dobbin, Lady (Kate)

Workman, Jane Service (1873-1943)

Jane Service Workman was the daughter of Thomas and Margaret Hill Workman of Craigdarragh, Helen's Bay, county Down. She took painting classes with Miss Douglas in Belfast, who specialised in *chiaroscuro* watercolour studies and was an active member of the Belfast Arts Club. She and her sister, Ellen, first visited the Low Countries when she was only sixteen. She also studied in Paris, where Ellen worked in Whistler's studio and painted her portrait in oils. 1896 saw the publication of the intricately coloured drawings she and another sister, Margaret had done for their father's two volumed *Malaysian Spiders,* on which he was the authority. She exhibited, mainly watercolours, at the Royal Academy and at the Ulster Academy and often painted, especially in Donegal, with John Workman, the grandfather of Tom Carr. In 1901 she married James Yeames, a marine engineer, the nephew of the painter W. F. Yeames R.A. who painted the well-known *And When Did You Last See Your Father?*; he encouraged her career. She continued to paint but exhibited mainly in Belfast. NGB

See cat. no. 52.

Wynne, Gladys (1878-1968)

Gladys Wynne, the youngest daughter of the Archdeacon of Aghadoe, was brought up at Woodlawn, Killarney, from which she exhibited two flower studies at the Royal Hibernian Academy, in 1889. She went to Florence and Rome for her artistic education, and later Somerset and Scotland. She would often paint with a friend, Constance Rochford, or her aunt in Delgany, Edith Wynne. Her sister Maud also painted but died young. In later years she was a friend of Mildred Butler and Mainie Jellett. In 1907 she moved to Lake Cottage at Glendalough, near other artistic Wynne cousins at Avoca, and lived there for the rest of her life. Many of her watercolours depict views of Glendalough. She began exhibiting c.1910 and was a member of the Dublin Sketching Club and Irish Watercolour Society. NGB

See cat. no. 54.

Wynne-Jones, Nancy (b. 1922)

Born Dolgellau, Wales, December 16th, 1922, studied at Heatherleys; Chelsea; St. Peter's Loft; St. Ives.

One-Person Exhibitions: 1962, New Vision Centre, London; 1963, Galleria Numero, Florence; 1964, Dolgellau, Wales; 1965, New Vision Centre, London; 1970, Project Arts Centre, Dublin; 1975, Emmet Gallery, Dublin; 1977, Emmet Gallery, Dublin; 1978, Lad Lane Gallery, Dublin; 1982, Lincoln Gallery, Dublin; 1984, Lincoln Gallery, Dublin.

Principal Group Exhibitions: 1957-66, Newlyn Society of Artists; 1959, 11 British Artists, Jefferson Place Gallery, Washington D.C. (with Lanyon, Hilton, Frost, Wynter, Heron, Wells, Blow etc.); 1960, Twenty Cornish Painters, Falmouth. (Lanyon, Hilton, Frost etc.); 1962, The Arts Council as Patron, London and Touring (Irvin, Weight); Europe '62 N.V.C. London, (Hartung, Hayter, Fontana, Tapies, Ayres, Atlan, Baz etc.); 1963, Nostra Internazionale D'Arte D'Avantguardia, Livorno; Gallery Artists, NVC London; Red, White and Blue, London Galleries, Leeds; Midland Twenty-One, Nottingham; Commonwealth Biennale of Abstract Art, London; 1964, Gallerie Wirth, Berlin; 1965, Artists in Cornwall, Leicester, (Hepworth, Hilton, Lanyon, etc.).

Collections: Arts Council of Ireland; Arts Council of Great Britain; Welsh Arts Council; Bank of Ireland; Allied Irish Investment Bank; Trustee Savings Bank; Provincial Insurance; Manchester Education Authority.

Yeames, Jane Service see Workman, Jane Service

Yeats, Anne (b.1919)

Born 1919 in Dublin; 1933-36, studied at the Royal Hibernian Academy schools; 1936-40, worked as assistant stage designer and then as chief stage designer at the Abbey Theatre; 1940-46, did free lance stage designing in Ireland, and began painting in 1941; 1947, joined the Irish Exhibition of Living Art as a committee member.

One-Person Shows: 1946, 1948, 1963, in Dublin; exhibited in group exhibitions in America, Holland, Germany, Scotland and Monaco.

Collections: The Arts Council of Ireland; Hugh Lane Municipal Gallery, Dublin; Ulster Museum, Belfast; Sligo County Museum; Trinity College, Dublin.

194

Yeats, Elizabeth Corbet (1868-1940)

Born in London, she was the younger daughter of John Butler Yeats, the artist. She taught at a Froebel school in Bedford Park, where she developed a brushwork technique later published in two manuals, in 1895 and 1898. After she moved to Ireland, she continued to teach painting in watercolour, without preparatory drawing, influencing her niece Anne Yeats, and others. On the advice of Emery Walker, she took a month's course at the Women's Printing Society in London, before joining the Dun Emer Industries, founded by Evelyn Gleeson, and establishing the Dun Emer Press in autumn 1902. 'Unlike other private presses of the period, which concentrated on beautiful reprints, Elizabeth Yeats's aim was to produce the new literature of Ireland in worthy editions' (L. Miller, 'The Dun Emer and the Cuala Press', in *Essays in Perspective* (1965)). She enlisted the advice and editing of W. B. Yeats in her first productions. Dun Emer and the Cuala Press, which she founded with her sister in 1908, published his current work, as well as the poetry of Frank O'Connor, Lyle Donaghy and Louis MacNeice. For seven years, until 1915, the Press published *A Broadside* each month, a collection of ballads and new poems illustrated by Jack B. Yeats and coloured by hand.

Elizabeth Yeats designed the Women's National Health Association of Ireland Christmas stamp in 1909, with a shamrock and 'Sláinte'. She also designed Cuala cards, illustrating poems by An Craobhín, W. M. Letts, Stephen Gwynn and Susan Mitchell. Her pen and ink style is vigorous, and pictorial, sometimes influenced by her brother's work in that medium, but occasionally more decorative and stylised. Her work in watercolour is represented in the Sligo Museum. HP

Young, Mabel (c.1890-1974)

Mabel Young was the youngest of seven born on the Isle of Wight, where her father ran all the horse transport. Motorisation brought financial disaster so she was sent away to be a seamstress. She hated that, so came to Dublin to work as an assistant to her sister, who was the manageress of the Shelbourne Hotel. In 1924 she met Paul Henry while holidaying in Enniskerry, county Wicklow (they were both keen and energetic naturalists) and became completely involved with him until his death in 1958. They went to live in a cottage, Carrigoona in the Rocky Valley in county Wicklow, where he built a studio and painted and taught her to paint. She particularly loved painting trees and the landscape of county Wicklow, although when they went off to Clifden to paint in the West, she was enchanted by the light. When Paul Henry had a stroke, they moved down to a house in Bray, from which they both exhibited their work. She also exhibited with the Royal Hibernian Academy from 1928-61 and at the 1932 Aonach Tailteann Exhibition of Irish Art. They were finally married on Grace Henry's death in 1953.

She is represented in the Hugh Lane Municipal Gallery, Dublin, and, her friend, the artist Flora Mitchell, had a particularly good collection of her work. NGB

See cat. no. 106.

Select Bibliography

GENERAL WORKS

Barrett, Cyril, *Irish Art 1943-1973,* Crawford Gallery, Cork, Rosc exhibition catalogue (1980).

Barrett, Cyril, *Irish Art in the 19th Century,* Crawford Municipal School of Art, Cork Rosc exhibition catalogue, (1971) here abbreviated as *Irish Art in the 19th century.*

Campbell, Julian, *The Irish Impressionists. Irish Artists in France and Belgium, 1850-1914,* National Gallery of Ireland exhibition catalogue, (1984) here abbreviated as *The Irish Impressionists.*

Catto, Mike, *Art in Ulster: 2* (1977).

Coxhead, Elizabeth, *Daughters of Erin,* (1965).

Crookshank, Anne and The Knight of Glin, *The Painters of Ireland c.1660-1920* (1978) here abbreviated as *The Painters of Ireland.*

Gordon Bowe, Nicola, *The Dublin Arts and Crafts Movement 1885-1930,* Edinburgh School of Art exhibition catalogue (1986).

Hewitt, John and Snoddy, Theo, *Art in Ulster: 1* (1977) here abbreviated as *Art in Ulster: 1.*

Knowles, Roderick, *Contemporary Irish Art,* (1982).

Le Harivel, Adrian and Wynne, Michael, *Acquisitions 1982-83,* National Gallery of Ireland exhibition catalogue, (1984) here abbreviated as *N.G.I. Acquisitions 1982-83.*

Le Harivel, Adrian and Wynne, Michael, *Acquisitions 1984-86,* National Gallery of Ireland exhibition catalogue (1986) here abbreviated as *N.G.I. Acquisitions 1984-86.*

O'Doherty, Brian, *The Irish Imagination 1959-1971,* Hugh Lane Municipal Gallery, Dublin, Rosc exhibition catalogue, (1971).

Pasquin, Anthony (i.e. John Williams), *An Authentic History of the Professors of Painting, Sculpture and Architecture who have practised in Ireland,* (1796), reprinted (1970), here abbreviated as *Pasquin.*

Potterton, Homan and Wynne, Michael, *Acquisitions 1981-82,* National Gallery of Ireland exhibition catalogue, (1982) here abbreviated as *N.G.I. Acquisitions 1981-82.*

Pyle, Hilary, *Irish Art 1900-1950,* Crawford Municipal Art Gallery, Rosc exhibition catalogue. (1975) here abbreviated as *Irish Art 1900-1950.*

Stephen, Leslie and Lee, Sidney (eds.), *The Dictionary of National Biography,* 66 vols., London, (1885-1901 and later editions), here abbreviated as *D.N.B.*

Stewart, Ann, *The Royal Hibernian Academy of Arts, Index of Exhibitors 1826-1979, Vol 1, A-G, Vol 2, G-M,* (1986).

Strickland, Walter G., *A Dictionary of Irish Artists,* 2 vols, (1913) here abbreviated as *Strickland.*

Wynne, Michael, *Recent Acquisitions 1980-1981,* National Gallery of Ireland exhibition catalogue (1981) here abbreviated as *N.G.I. Acquisitions 1980-81.*

Wynne, Michael, *Stained Glass in Ireland, Principally Irish Stained Glass 1760-1963,* Ph.D. thesis, Trinity College Dublin, (1975), here abbreviated as *Stained Glass in Ireland.*

INDIVIDUAL ARTISTS (TO 1943)

Alment, Mary Martha (1834-1908) *Strickland.*

Annesley, Mabel (1881-1959) *Art in Ulster:1.*

Ball, Anne Elizabeth (1808-1872) G.E. Hutchinson, 'The harp that once...,' *Irish Naturalists Journal,* (1982), vol.20, pp.457-66.

Barry, Moyra A. (1886-1960) *N.G.I. Acquisitions 1982-83.*

Barton, Mary Georgina (fl. late 19c.-early 20c.) S. Armstrong-Duffy, *Late Nineteenth century sketching Clubs in Ireland,* B.A. thesis, T.C.D. (1984).

Barton, Rose (1856-1929) *Irish Art 1900-1950. The Irish Impressionists. The Painters of Ireland. Rose Barton,* Crawford Municipal Art Gallery, Cork, exhibition catalogue, (1987).

Beckett, Frances (1880-1951) *Irish Art 1900-1950.*

Benson, Charlotte (1846-1893) *Strickland.*

Benson, Mary Kate (d.1921) *The Irish Impressionists. Strickland.*

Blackham, Dorothy (1896-1919) Elizabeth L. Fitzpatrick, *Dorothy Blackham,* Neptune Gallery, Dublin, exhibition catalogue, (1977).

Blake, Lady (Edith) (1845-1926) *D.N.B.* P. Gilbert, *Butterflies,* (forthcoming).

Brett, Rosa (1829-1882) Pamela Gerrish Nunn, 'Rosa Brett, Pre-Raphaelite', *Burlington Magazine,* (October 1984), p.630.

Brooks, Sarah Theresa (1850-1928) R. Oldham, *The Brooks family of Israelite Bay and Balbinia Station,* (1974). *Early Days,* vol.7, no.VI, pp.35-48.

Bushe, Letitia (fl.1731-1757) *Strickland.*

Butler, Lady (Elizabeth) (1846-1933) Ellen C. Clayton, *English Female Artists,* 2 vols., London (1876). Wilfrid Meynell, 'The Life and Work of Lady Butler', *The Art Annual,* (1898). Charlotte Yeldham, *Women Artists in the 19th Century France and England,* 2 vols., New York and London, (1984). *Lady Butler: battle artist,* National Army Museum, London, exhibition catalogue (1987).

Butler, Mildred Anne (1858-1941) *N.G.I. Acquisitions 1981-82. The Painters of Ireland.* Anne Crookshank and the Knight of Glin, *Mildred Anne Butler,* Dublin and Kilkenny exhibition catalogue, 1981.

Caulfield, Mrs. (fl.1774-1778) *Strickland.*

Clarke, Margaret (1888-1961) *N.G.I. Acquisitions 1981-82. N.G.I. Acquisitions 1982-83. Irish Art 1900-1950.*

Clayton, Eleanor Creathorne (1834-1900) *Strickland.*

Corr, Fanny (1807-1883) *Strickland.*

Cox, Kathleen (1904-1972) *The Dublin Arts and Crafts Movement 1885-1930.*

Curran, Amelia (1775-1847) *Strickland.*

Davidson, Lilian Lucy (d.1954) *Irish Art 1900-1950.*

Delaney, Mary (1700-1788) *The Painters of Ireland.* Lady Llanover (ed.), *Autobiography and correspondence of Mary Granville, Mrs. Delany,* 6 vols., (1861). C. E. Vulliany, *Aspasia: The Life and Letters of Mrs. Delany* (1937) R. Hayden, *Mrs. Delany: her life and her flowers,* (1980). R. Hayden, 'Mrs. Delany: A talented lady of the eighteenth century', *Irish Georgian Society Bulletin,* vol. 26, (1983). H. Pyle, 'Artist or Artistic? The Drawings of Mary Delany', *Irish Arts Review,* vol.4 no.1 (Spring 1987), pp.29-31.

Dering, Henrietta (fl.1694-1728/29) *The Painters of Ireland.*

D'Olier, Helen Campbell (1829-1887) *Strickland.*

Drury, Susanna (1733-1770) *Strickland. The Painters of Ireland.* M. Anglesea and J. Preston, 'A Philosophical Landscape' Susanna Drury and the Giant's Causeway', *Art History,* vol.3, no.3, (September, 1980), p.252.

Duncan, Mary (1885-1960) *Irish Art 1900-1950.*

Fannin, Marianne Edwardine (1845-1938) Mary Gunn and L.E. Codd, *Botanical exploration of Southern Africa,* (1981), pp.152-53.

Forster, Miss (fl.1780) *Pasquin. Strickland.*

Fox, Kathleen (1880-1963) *Irish Art 1900-1950. The Irish Impressionists.*

Geddes, Wilhelmina Margaret (1887-1955) *Irish Art 1900-1950.* Stephen Gwynne, 'The Art of Miss W.M. Geddes', *The Studio,* (October 1922). Nicola Gordon Bowe, 'Wilhelmina Geddes', *Stained Glass* (Journal of the Stained Glass Association of North America), vol.76, no.1, (1981). Nicola Gordon Bowe, '20th Century Stained Glass' in *Recent Irish Art Series,* the Arts Council, Dublin (1983). Peter Cormack, *Women Stained Glass Artists of the Arts and Crafts Movement,* William Morris Gallery, Walthamstow, exhibition catalogue, (1986).

Gifford, Grace (1888-1955) *Irish Art 1900-1950.*

Gleeson, Evelyn (1855-1944) *The Dublin Arts and Crafts Movement 1885-1930.* Sheila Pim, 'Dun Emer — An Unrecorded Chapter in the Life of Augustine Henry', *Moorea,* vol.3, (1984).

Glenavy, Lady (Beatrice) (1883-1968) *Irish Art 1900-1950. The Dublin Arts and Crafts Movement 1885-1930. The Painters of Ireland. Stained Glass in Ireland.* Beatrice, Lady Glenavy, *'Today we will only Gossip',* (1964). Alan Denson, *John Hughes,* (1969), pp. 438-40.

Gonne, Anne (1816-c.1876) *Strickland.*

Greatorex, Eliza (1820-1879) George C. Groce and David H. Wallace, *Dictionary of Artists in America 1564-1860,* (1957).

Gubbins, Beatrice (1878-1944) Francis Russell, *Beatrice Gubbins,* Crawford Municipal Art Gallery, Cork, exhibition catalogue, (1986).

Guinness, May (1863-1955) *Irish Art 1900-1950. The Irish Impressionists.*

Hamilton, Caroline (1771-1861) Miss Eva Bell, *The Hamwood Papers,* London, (1930). Marianne C. Hamilton, 'A Short History of the Hamiltons of Hamwood and their Antecedents, (1851).

Hamilton, Eva (1876-1960) *Irish Art 1900-1950. The Irish Impressionists. The Painters of Ireland.*

Hamilton, Letitia (1878-1964) *Irish Art 1900-1950. The Painters of Ireland.*

Harrison, Sarah Cecilia (1863-1941) *Irish Art 1900-1950. The Irish Impressionists. The Painters of Ireland.*

Hartland, Gertrude (1865-1954). Megan Morris, 'Irradiating the present; restoring the past — the Hartlands of Cork', *Moorea,* vol.4, (1985), pp.27-41.

Henry, Grace (1868-1953) *Art in Ulster:1. Irish Art 1900-1950. The Irish Impressionists.*

Henry, Olive (b.1902) *Art in Ulster:1.*

Herbert, Gwendolen (1878-1966) *N.G.I. Acquisitions 1984-86.*

Hone, Evie (1894-1955) *Art in Ulster:1. Irish Art 1900-1950. The Painters of Ireland. Stained Glass in Ireland.* Stella Frost, *A Tribute to Evie Hone and Mainie Jellett,* (1957). *Evie Hone,* Trinity College Dublin, exhibition catalogue, (1958).

Hunter, Mary Ann (fl.1765-1777) *Strickland.*

Hutchins, Ellen (1785-1815). E.C. Nelson, 'Orchid painting at Glasnevin', *Orchid Review,* (1981), pp.373-77.

Jacob, Alice (1862-1921) *The Dublin Arts and Crafts Movement 1885-1930.*

Jellett, Mainie (1897-1944) *Art in Ulster:1. Irish Art 1900-1950, N.G.I. Acquisitions 1980-1981. Irish Art 1900-1950. The Painters of Ireland.* Stella Frost, *A Tribute to Evie Hone and Mainie Jellett,* (1957) Eileen MacCarvill, *Mainie Jellett, the artists vision,* (1958). *Mainie Jellett, A Retrospective exhibition of Paintings and Drawings,* Hugh Lane Municipal Gallery, Dublin, exhibition catalogue, (1962). Neptune Gallery, exhibition catalogue, (1974). Neptune Gallery, Dublin, exhibition catalogue, (1976).

Kelly, Frances (from 1929) *Irish Art 1900-1950.*

King, Martha (c.1803-1897) Moira Long,'Martha King, botanical artist'. *The Summer Book,* vol.2, (1983), pp.56-65.

Kinkead, Alice S. (fl.1897-1922) *The Irish Impressionists.*

Kirkwood, Harriet (1880-1953) *N.G.I. Acquisitions 1982-83. The Irish Impressionists.*

Kyle, Georgina Moutray (1865-1950) *Art in Ulster:1.*

Lecky, Emilia (c.1788-after 1844) *Strickland.*

Lamont, Elish (1816-1870) *Art in Ulster:1. Strickland.* Eileen Black, 'Of Art and Artists', in J.C. Beckett *(et al),* Belfast. *The Making of the City,* (1983), p.90.

McAdoo, Annie Florence (fl.c.1925-1965) *Art in Ulster:1.*

MacCann, Louisa (fl.1890's) *The Irish Impressionists.*

MacCausland, Katherine (d.1930) *The Irish Impressionists.*

Mackie, Kathleen Isobel (b.1899) *A Retrospective Exhibition of Kathleen Mackie,* Castle Espie Gallery, county Down, exhibition catalogue, (1985).

Maguire, Helena (1860-1909) *Strickland.*

Manning, May (d.1930) *The Irish Impressionists.*

Markievicz, Constance (1868-1927) *Irish Art 1900-1950.*

Marsh, Clare (1874-1923) *Irish Art 1900-1950.*

Millard, Caroline (d.1894) *Strickland.*

Morgan, Jane (1831-1899) *Strickland.* Eileen Black, 'Jane Morgan: A Forgotten Irish Artist', *Irish Arts Review,* vol.3, no.4, (Winter 1986), pp.21-23.

Nairn, Anna Langley (fl.1844-1848) *Strickland.*

Nairn, Cecilia Margaret (1791-1857) *Strickland. The Painters of Ireland.*

Osborne O'Hagan, Harriet (1830-1921) *The Irish Impressionists.* Albert Boime, *Thomas Couture and the Eclectic Vision,* (1980).

Plunket, Katherine (1820-1932) M.J.P. Scannell and C.I. Houston, 'Wild Flowers from Nature painted by Katherine Plunket (1820-1932) and Frederica Plunket, (d.1886) at the National Botanic Gardens, Glasnevin', *National Botanic Gardens, Glasnevin, Occasional Papers, 2,* (1985).

Praeger, Rosamond (1867-1954) *Art in Ulster:1. Irish Art 1900-1950.*

Purser, Sarah Henrietta (1848-1943) *Irish Art in the 19th Century. Irish Art 1900-1950. The Dublin Arts and Crafts Movement 1885-1930. The Irish Impressionists. The Painters of Ireland. Stained Glass in Ireland.* James White and Michael Wynne, *Irish Stained Glass,* (1963). Alan Denson, *John Hughes,* (1969). John O'Grady, *Sarah Henrietta Purser,* Ph.D. thesis, National University of Ireland (1974). John O'Grady, 'Sarah Purser', *Capuchin Annual,* (1977), pp.89-104.

Quigly, Kathleen (1888-1981) *The Dublin Arts and Crafts Movement 1885-1930.*

Reid, Eileen (1894-1981) *The Studio of Eileen Reid 1894-1981,* Cynthia O'Connor Gallery, Dublin, exhibition catalogue, (1984).

Rhind, Ethel Mary (c.1878-1952) *The Dublin Arts and Crafts Movement 1885-1930.* James White and Michael Wynne, *Irish Stained Glass,* (1963).

Roberts, Hilda (1901-1982) *Irish Art 1900-1950.*

Robertson, Clementina (1795-c.1853) *Strickland.*

Robinson, Anne Marjorie (1858-1924) *Art in Ulster:1.* Princess Marie Louise, *My Memories of Six Reigns,* (1956).

Shackleton, Lydia (1828-1914) B. Morley, 'Lydia Shackleton's paintings in the National Botanic Gardens, Glasnevin', *Glasra* vol.2, (1979), pp.25-26. E.C. Nelson & G.M. McCracken, *The Brightest Jewel; a history of the National Botanic Gardens, Glasnevin,* (1987), pp.184, 187.

Solomons, Estella F. (1882-1968) *Irish Art 1900-1950. The Irish Impressionists. N.G.I. Acquisitions 1981-1982. The Painters of Ireland.* Hilary Pyle, *Portraits of Patriots,* (1966). Alan Denson, *John Hughes,* (1969), p.498. L. Millar, *Retrospect, the work of Seumas O'Sullivan and Estella F. Solomons,* (1973). Hilary Pyle,

Estella Solomons, Crawford Municipal Art Gallery, Cork, exhibition catalogue (1986).

Somerville, Edith OEnone (1858-1949) *Irish Art 1900-1950. The Irish Impressionists. The Painters of Ireland. Edith OEnone Somerville,* Neptune Gallery, Dublin, exhibition catalogue, (1968). Frances Gillespie, *Edith OE Somerville 1858-1949,* Castletownshend, exhibition catalogue, (1984).

Stokes, Margaret McNair (1832-1900) *Margaret Stokes: an exhibition of oil paintings, watercolours and woodcuts,* Robinson Gallery, Dublin, exhibition catalogue, (1980).

Swanzy, Mary (1882-1978) *Irish Art 1900-1950. The Irish Impressionists. The Painters of Ireland. Mary Swanzy Retrospective Exhibition,* Municipal Gallery of Modern Art exhibition catalogue, (1968). Julian Campbell, *Irish Artists in France and Belgium, 1850-1914,* (Ph.D. thesis, T.C.D.), (1980). Julian Campbell, *Mary Swanzy,* Pyms Gallery exhibition catalogue, (1986).

Taylor, Maria (1777-1823) *Strickland. The Painters of Ireland.*

Thompson, Sydney Mary (1847-1923) Sydney Mary Christen, *Rodolphe Christen. The Story of an Artist's Life,* (1910).

Trevor, Helen Mabel (1831-1900) *Strickland. The Irish Impressionists. The Painters of Ireland.* Helen Mabel Trevor, *Ramblings of an Artist,* London, (1901). James Thompson, *The Peasant in French nineteeth century art,* Douglas Hyde Gallery, Dublin, exhibition catalogue, (1980).

Trinseach, Sadhbh (1891-1918) *Irish Art 1900-1950.*

Trotter, Eliza H. (fl.1800-1814) *Strickland.*

Ward, Mary (1827-1869) O.G. Harry, 'The Hon. Mrs. Ward (1827-1869), artist...', *Irish Naturalists Journal,* vol.21, (1984), pp.193-200.

Waterford, Louisa Ann, Marchioness of (1818-1891) *Stained glass in Ireland.* H.L. Mallalieu, *Dictionary of British Watercolour Painters up to 1920,* (1976).

Watson, Caroline (c.1760-1814) *Strickland.*

Watson, Mrs. (fl.1767-1771) *Pasquin. Strickland.*

Webb, Maria D. (fl.1873-1886) *The Irish Impressionists.*

Williams, Charlotte Isabel (1867-1967) E.C. Nelson, 'The Lady of the Rhododendrons — Charlotte Wheeler Cuffe', *Rhododendrons,* (1982), pp.33-41.

Williams, Lily (1874-1940) *Irish Art 1900-1950.*

Yeats, Elizabeth Corbet (1868-1940) *The Dublin Arts and Crafts Movement 1885-1930.*

Souter, Camille (b.1929) Cyril Barrett and Anne Crookshank, *Camille Souter,* Retrospective exhibition, The Douglas Hyde Gallery, Dublin, (1980).

McGuinness, Norah (1903-1980) Anne Crookshank, *Norah McGuinness,* Retrospective exhibition, Trinity College, Dublin, (1968).

Reid, Nano (1905-1981) Sean O'Faolain and Jeanne Sheehy, *Nano Reid,* Retrospective exhibition, The Arts Council in Ireland, (1974).

Wilmot, Martha (1775-1873) Martha Wilmot and Catherine Wilmot, *The Russian Journals of Martha and Catherine Wilmot* (1934).

Index of Lenders

and catalogue numbers

Index

Featured artists appear in bold type